KING'S X
THE ORAL HISTORY
GREG PRATO

A Jawbone book
First edition 2019
Published in the UK and the USA by
Jawbone Press
Office G1
141–157 Acre Lane
London SW2 5UA
England
www.jawbonepress.com

JACKET DESIGN Paul Palmer-Edwards, www.paulpalmer-edwards.com

Printed in China

ISBN 978-1-911036-43-2   2 3 4 5 22 21 20 19 18

CONTENTS

fo **FOREWORD**
A CONVERSATION WITH
SCOTT IAN ABOUT KING'S X
PAGE 04

in **INTRODUCTION**
BY GREG PRATO
PAGE 06

ca **CAST OF
CHARACTERS**
PAGE 08

01 **BEGINNINGS**
PAGE 10

02 **CROSSING
PATHS**
PAGE 18

03 **THE EDGE/
SNEAK PREVIEW**
PAGE 22

04 **HOUSTON—SAM
TAYLOR—KING'S X**
PAGE 33

05 **MEGAFORCE**
PAGE 41

06 **OUT OF THE
SILENT PLANET**
PAGE 48

07 **GRETCHEN GOES
TO NEBRASKA**
PAGE 71

08 HITTING THE ROAD, HARD–PART 1
PAGE 84

09 FAITH HOPE LOVE
PAGE 92

10 HITTING THE ROAD, HARD–PART 2
PAGE 107

11 KING'S X
PAGE 118

12 DOGMAN
PAGE 136

13 THE TIMES THEY ARE A-CHANGIN'
PAGE 151

14 EAR CANDY
PAGE 169

15 BEST OF KING'S X
PAGE 183

16 TAPE HEAD
PAGE 188

17 PLEASE COME HOME ... MR. BULBOUS
PAGE 197

18 MANIC MOONLIGHT
PAGE 204

19 BLACK LIKE SUNDAY
& LIVE ALL OVER THE PLACE
PAGE 212

20 IN CONCERT
PAGE 221

21 OGRE TONES
PAGE 225

22 XV
& LIVE LOVE IN LONDON
PAGE 234

23 MOLKEN MUSIC
PAGE 246

24 THE THREE KINGS
PAGE 249

25 ON THEIR OWN
PAGE 276

26 TODAY
PAGE 297

27 LEGACY
PAGE 303

fo FOREWORD
A CONVERSATION WITH SCOTT IAN
ABOUT KING'S X

Anthrax was on Island Records, but we were all involved with Jonny Z and Megaforce. I remember when they signed King's X, I heard the demo and thought it was great. And then I heard *Out Of The Silent Planet*, and it definitely struck a chord with me, because it didn't sound like anything else at the time. They sounded completely original. Some people categorize them as a metal band, some people categorize them as a hard rock band. There was no way for me to categorize it. If anything, it's almost like they had more in common with a band like U2 or The Beatles than they did with anything else. But I just connected with it. It was really moving and heavy and dark and uplifting—it was *everything*. It was everything I wanted out of a band, and it was just these three dudes. It was really incredible.

Anthrax took King's X out with us in Europe in '89. We were lucky enough to be in a position to take out bands that we loved—whether or not it made sense on paper, as far as a 'metal bill' goes. It didn't really matter to us—we loved King's X so much, we wanted to get to see them every night. So, what better way than to take them out on tour with us? And they ended up going over really well. They're just one of those undeniable things—I don't think it really matters who they're playing with. If you put that band onstage, they are going to connect to an audience. They did tours with AC/DC. You want to talk about a tough audience to make a connection with, because everyone is just there to see AC/DC—they don't really give a crap about anyone else that's playing. And King's X was even able to connect with an audience *while opening for AC/DC*. There's something deeply touching about their music. You can't deny it.

The scene that I was a part of was thrash metal. And they were nothing like the scene that we were a part of—at all. But every band that was a part of our scene loves King's X. *Everyone*. It's kind of across the board. You could talk to anyone, and they were, like, everybody's favorite band. I think just because they were so original. There was nothing that sounded like them—whether you were a part of the thrash metal scene, or there was the more poppy/LA kind of scene, bands like Mötley Crüe and Ratt and bands like that, that were really big at that time. And there was a hardcore scene and a punk rock scene. They didn't fit into any of these things. Because they were so original, it made it hard for a lot of really dumb people to figure out what 'shelf' they belonged on. They couldn't just format them. You couldn't just say, 'This fits under *this* format.'

It's a shame it wasn't the 70s—when formats were much looser, and you could take a band like King's X and play them on the same radio station that would have been playing AC/DC, Rush, Aerosmith, or any number of bands that got played on the radio. But this was the late 80s, and radio was already starting to change, and labels were being run by the accountants. Everything was becoming more corporate, and King's X didn't fit into a nice, neat little package. Which I think that is the best thing in the world for a band, because that means you're doing something you've never done before. That's the best compliment you can pay to a band—that you're an original. But at the same time, for them, I think it made it hard for people who don't really want to do any work to know how to market that band.

They were on Megaforce and Atlantic at the time—if you put me behind one of those desks, and I've got *Out Of The Silent Planet* and *Gretchen Goes To Nebraska*, I'm saying, 'This band is the next U2. That's how big this band should be. This record is *The Joshua Tree*—that's where we need to go with this.' But, sadly, I wasn't working at Atlantic in 1988. But I feel like everybody needs to hear them, and anything we can ever do to spread the word about what a great band they are, we always try our best.

I love these guys so much. I've known them forever. They've been such a huge part of my life. They've literally lifted my soul and made me a happier person, by writing the songs that they've written. And I'm so proud of them and glad that they've stuck it out for so long. Constantly having to climb uphill. Constantly fighting the battle. And constantly making great records and being an amazing live band. That's not an easy thing to do. They love what they do, and that's all that matters. I'd like to thank them from the deepest parts of my soul, because their records make me so happy.

in INTRODUCTION

'WHY AREN'T KING'S X MORE POPULAR AND SUCCESSFUL?' That's a common question I've heard from just about every fan of the band I have crossed paths with over the years. And, once upon a time, I too agonized over trying to solve this puzzling problem—why wasn't this ridiculously great, talented, and original band selling millions of albums and packing out stadiums throughout the world? And then I realized—King's X *are* popular and successful. Let me explain …

First off, they continue to go strong, and they still attract large groups of fans to their shows—who sing along to most every song they choose to play. (I even have a chum who once saw the trio back in the early 90s, and remarked that, to this day, he is still taken aback by how 'vocal' the audience was.) Also, there are countless rock and metal bands that scored legitimate radio and MTV hits in the late 80s/early 90s, and a gold or platinum album … but can they attract as many people to a show as King's X do this far into their career? Will the entire audience sing along to what seems like every song? Will a large portion of the audience remain at the venue after the show to meet the band, and express their gratitude for all the music? The answer is simple. *No.*

As I type this, it is the morning after what must have been close to the twentieth time I attended a King's X concert, and I can honestly say that they sounded as great as they did the first time I ever saw them (on June 14, 1991, at the Ritz in New York City, to be precise).

One of the definite pluses of doing what I do for a living is that I am able to write about subjects that I am a fan of and/or feel strongly about. And, since late 1989, I have been a major fan of King's X. Certain albums and songs of theirs

also have the uncanny ability of serving as a 'musical time machine,' instantly transporting me back to specific times of my life, as well as when I think about particular King's X shows that I attended.

Over the years, I have introduced countless friends to the music of King's X. And, unlike some bands whose music has not aged well over the years, the music of King's X sounds as great today as it did when it first hit. King's X are also one of the select few rock bands that never 'jumped the shark'—every single one of their albums contains at least several tracks that hold up splendidly.

Since becoming a King's X fan, I have read as many articles and interviews with the band over the years as I could come across—and I've been lucky to interview Doug, Ty, and Jerry over the years for a variety of magazines and websites, and become friendly with each of them. But I always wanted to read the band's complete story—from prior to their inception through to the present day. In the midst of witnessing a truly amazing/inspiring show by the band in the summer of 2015 (at Stage 48 in NYC), it became clear as day—I needed to write a book, and put it all into perspective for myself, the band, and, of course, King's X fans throughout the world. Three years later, *King's X: The Oral History* was completed.

Music, music, I hear music,
GREG PRATO

PS QUESTIONS? COMMENTS? FEEL FREE TO EMAIL ME: GREGPRATO@YAHOO.COM.

ca CAST OF CHARACTERS

JERRY GASKILL	King's X singer, drummer; solo artist
DOUG PINNICK	King's X singer, bassist; solo artist
TY TABOR	King's X singer, guitarist; solo artist
JEFF AMENT	Mother Love Bone, Temple Of The Dog, Pearl Jam, Tres Mts. bassist
CHARLIE BENANTE	Anthrax drummer
NUNO BETTENCOURT	Extreme guitarist
REX BROWN	Pantera bassist
BUMBLEFOOT	Sons Of Apollo, Art Of Anarchy, ex Guns N' Roses guitarist; solo artist
RICHARD CHRISTY	Death, Iced Earth, Charred Walls Of The Damned drummer; *Howard Stern Show* writer
JOHN CORABI	Ex Mötley Crüe singer
BILLY CORGAN	Smashing Pumpkins singer, guitarist
ROBERT DELEO	Stone Temple Pilots bassist
WALLY FARKAS	Ex Galactic Cowboys guitarist; lead vocalist on 'Walter Bela Farkas (Live Peace In New York)'; contributor to various King's X–related projects; head of Molken Music
MARIA FERRERO	Megaforce Records former director of publicity and A&R
ALEXANDER FORD	King's X management and merchandising
GUNTER FORD	King's X manager, 2007–present
MARTY FRIEDMAN	ex Megadeth, Cacophony guitarist; solo artist
JULIE GASKILL	Jerry Gaskill's wife
RITA HANEY	Dimebag Darrell's longtime partner

ALAIN JOHANNES	Eleven singer, guitarist; guitarist on Doug Pinnick's *Strum Sum Up*
JOHNNY KELLY	Type O Negative drummer
BOB KULICK	Meat Loaf guitarist; Kiss session guitarist; solo artist; producer
SHANNON LARKIN	Godsmack drummer; also appears on Doug Pinnick's *Massive Grooves*
RAY LUZIER	KXM, Korn drummer
GEORGE LYNCH	KXM, Lynch Mob, Dokken guitarist
MICK MARS	Mötley Crüe guitarist
ROD MORGENSTEIN	Dixie Dregs, Winger, Platypus, Jelly Jam drummer
KEVIN MOURNING	King's X tour manager, sound engineer
JOHN MYUNG	Dream Theater, Platypus, Jelly Jam bassist
CHRISTIAN NESMITH	video director
JAY PHEBUS	King's X tour manager, sound engineer
MATT PINFIELD	DJ; VJ; MTV *120 Minutes* host
LEA PISACANE	Atlantic Records former director of rock promotion
MIKE PORTNOY	Winery Dogs, Sons Of Apollo, ex Dream Theater drummer
BILLY SHEEHAN	Mr. Big, Winery Dogs, Sons Of Apollo, David Lee Roth, Talas bassist
BRIAN SLAGEL	Metal Blade Records founder
ANDY SUMMERS	The Police guitarist
KIM THAYIL	Soundgarden guitarist
MICHELLE THOMAS	Ty Tabor's long-time significant other
DEVIN TOWNSEND	The Devin Townsend Band, Strapping Young Lad, Steve Vai singer, guitarist
EDDIE TRUNK	radio, TV host; Megaforce Records former vice president
DOUG VAN PELT	*Heaven's Metal* magazine founder
MICHAEL WAGENER	*Ogre Tones*, *XV* producer
KIP WINGER	Winger singer, bassist
JON ZAZULA	Megaforce Records co-founder; Marsha Zazula's husband
MARSHA ZAZULA	Megaforce Records co-founder; Jon Zazula's wife

01 BEGINNINGS

WHO ARE KING'S X? EXPLORING THE BACKGROUNDS
OF DOUGLAS THEODORE PINNICK, JERRY
WAYNE GASKILL, AND TY RYAN TABOR.

DOUG PINNICK [King's X singer, bassist; solo artist] I'm from the Chicago area—Braidwood, Illinois. I was born in Joliet, Illinois, on September 3, 1950—there was no hospital in Braidwood. I lived in Braidwood for fourteen years, and then I moved to Joliet to live with my mom and my six younger siblings. I went to high school there, and lived there until I was about twenty-nine. And then I left and moved to Missouri, and that's when I met up with Ty and Jerry.

When I was about three, my mom had to go away, and I thought she had left me. So, my great grandmother raised me and led me to believe that my mother didn't care about me. I didn't have any answers other than I didn't have a dad, and she also said to me that my mom did not want to be bothered with me. When I was about sixty years old, my mother told me that my great grandmother kicked her out and wouldn't let her have me. But no one ever told me. That was just the way my great grandmother said things. And I don't know if she meant it, but at three years old, that was a knife in my heart. And I've never gotten over it. I love my mom.

I had this obsession with music, and I kind of put myself into that. Even my mom said I was singing melodies before I could talk. But my mom had to go, so I immersed myself into music and art, and found ways to entertain myself. There was nothing else to do but stay in my room and deal with that, and to become a temperamental, highly emotional, insecure, controlling person. And it's been that way ever since. I've been singing all my life. Every time I'd sing when I was a kid, I would see people cry or react, or have some kind of thing to say about it. And I never could understand it. But I kind of was obsessed with it, and I kept doing it. My music teacher would take me aside and play things on the piano and have me sing things, and I learned a lot of things. She would periodically put me in different sections in choir class. I learned to play sax also, but quit a year later.

My art teacher was the same way—I could draw and paint, so my art teacher took me aside, and she was kind of my buddy, too. In that way, I had these people that guided me into my obsession of being an artist. I wasn't interested in anything else. I flunked everything in school—from first grade up. That's how I was the whole time growing up. Absolutely no concentration on anything but music and drawing. I was the only black kid in my grade school, so I was embarrassed that I couldn't pass even one class.

The first time I ever noticed the bass, I was six or seven years old, maybe younger—whenever Frankie Lymon & The Teenagers put out the single 'Why Do Fools Fall In Love?' [1956] I remember I was sitting on the couch in my cousin's house, she was playing that song on the record player, and I heard the bass line. I was so mesmerized by this bass line that I memorized it in my head and I never forgot it.

From that day on, I was obsessed with bass—I wanted to hear it, and wanted to turn the bass on the stereo up, and, if I saw a band play, I'd be standing in front of the bass player. That's all that mattered. And when I listened to music, I didn't realize there was anything else going on. I really was *so* focused on bass … it was really stupid! And I stayed that way until after meeting Ty and Jerry. After that song, I remember James Jamerson with Motown was the one that really caught my ear, and Donald 'Duck' Dunn with Booker T & The MG's—they were the house band for Stax. Those two bass players were all I listened to. And in soul music, the bass was a dominant thing, anyway. So those two bass players ruled in my head. And then I wanted to play bass. I can't remember when I decided I wanted to play bass, but I always used to run around the house with a broom—left-handed—pretending I was playing bass.

I finally got a bass when I was twenty-three. It didn't take me long to play it, because it was exactly what I wanted to do. I was a bass player in my head all my life—I just had to get my fingers to go to the places that they needed to go. So, I never remember really learning how to play bass—I just remember it was so much fun figuring out how to do it, I never thought about it myself or thought it was hard. I was so happy to play two notes. Literally, if I played one note, I got goose bumps. [*Laughs*] Then, after that, I heard a song called 'Roundabout,' by Yes. And Chris Squire playing the bass line on that was something that I had never heard before—because I was used to soul music and everybody doing that kind of style. Even in rock music, most bass players back in the 70s sounded like soul players—from Led Zeppelin on down, they all played like that. But when Chris Squire came out, he had a whole unique approach to bass, and I fell in love with that. And I went back and found his tone, figured out how he did it, and learned everything he did. I play a lot like him—people probably don't realize that. But if you listen to Yes and then listen to my bass lines, I ripped him off.

Like I said before, I was singing all the time, but back in the late 60s and early 70s, I guess I was singing in rock bands—but it was a blur at that time. Because soul music and rock music … everybody was playing it together. There would be an R&B band playing and a rock band playing, and it seemed like everybody was trying to be each other. So, I was always asked to sing in bands. And if it was a funky band or a rock band, I was singing in it. The first band I was in, we did Sly & The Family Stone stuff, and then Chicago Transit Authority. I just sang then. There was a lot of brass kind of music that I sang— rock bands with brass. But I always say it kind of blurred, because it seems like in the late 60s and early 70s, *everybody* wanted to sound like they were in a soul band—no matter what color they were. And me being black and loving rock music, it felt completely natural. To me, it wasn't something outside of what I had been hearing all my life.

JERRY GASKILL [King's X singer, drummer; solo artist] I was born in a little town in southern New Jersey, called Bridgeton, on December 27, 1957. Music seems to have been something that has always been in my life. I can't recall a time when music wasn't a part of my life. I was four years old when I got my very first real drum. And even before that, I had a toy set. So, it's hard for me to decide that moment when I decided I was going to do music. I do remember when The Beatles came to America and I saw them on *Ed Sullivan*, and that pretty much sealed the deal for everything. From that moment on—like many, many other musicians—there was nothing to do but to do what The Beatles did.

When I was seven years old, because my dad knew how much I wanted to play, we started a band with my dad on rhythm guitar, my brother on lead guitar, and me on drums. We called ourselves Jerry & The Knights. We were a completely instrumental band, no vocals at all. We did anything from a waltz to a polka to a 40s classic to a Beatles song. We did weddings, lodges, house parties, wherever people would have us. We even played on a float in the local Thanksgiving Day parade one year! I continued in that band until I was about fifteen years old.

But I think my first real gig happened when I was seven years old—even before we called ourselves Jerry & The Knights. We didn't have a name, so we called ourselves The Question Marks. My dad drew this big question mark and put it on the front head of my kick drum. The gig was playing a party for a contestant in the *Miss New Jersey* pageant, who happened to be a good friend of ours. I got two dollars for that gig. I remember thinking, *I can do this and even get paid? Wow!* Then, after we played, she came up to me and kissed me right on the lips, and said, 'This is for your dad.'

When I was eight years old, in 1966, a band was put together to audition for a Kool Aid commercial. It consisted of me on drums, my brother Herb on guitar, Jackie Neff on bass, and Robbie Neff on vocals. We all went to New York City, headed for the big time. I remember being in someone's apartment and performing for them with no instruments. We were just standing there, going through the motions. And, later, we ended up in a studio actually performing. I don't remember what we were playing, but at one point, the guy in the control room asked if we could play something that featured the drummer. So, we did 'Wipe Out' by The Safaris. I think we all thought we were gonna be stars … but nothing ever came of it. Then, many years later, my mom told me that they were only interested in me. She said the parents felt bad and didn't want to hurt anyone's feelings, so they just let the whole deal go. Sometimes I wonder, what if I did get that gig? I'd be in the 'whatever happened to that Kool Aid kid?' file.

When I was about twelve years old, I would go see this band called Frog Ocean Road—at this local pool party that happened maybe every Saturday or so. They were all older than me, and to me, they were like gods. The drummer— whose name is Ed Supernavage—was a great inspiration and influence on me as a drummer. I remember talking to him between sets one time, and I felt like I was talking to one of the guys in Led Zeppelin or something. Then, when I was around fourteen years old, they asked me to join the band. It was like a dream come true. I felt like I had made it.

Here's a funny story—that wasn't so funny at the time. When I was about thirteen years old, I was asked to do this gig. And of course, I was always excited to play. At that stage in my life, I always wore these jeans with holes and patches all over them. That was my *look*. My dad insisted that I change those pants before I could do this gig. I was thinking, *I can't do that. This is my look. I have to be who I am.* He continued to insist as he sat at the kitchen table drinking his coffee. And I continued to think, *I can't.* So, at one point, I thought of the worst thing I could possibly say, and I blurted out the word *FUCK!* That completely threw him over the edge and he slammed his cup on the table. Coffee flew everywhere, even reaching the ceiling. He proceeded to chase me up the stairs, kicking me in the ass, screaming, 'I'm gonna kill you!' I could tell he wouldn't really do that because he was kicking me very softly—I think just to get his point across. I remember my brother—who is about three years older than me—was saying, 'Dad, don't kill him!' So, finally, I changed my pants, and we went to the gig—only to discover that they had found another drummer in the meantime.

From The Beatles, I'd say a lot of the late-60s/early-70s/mid-70s stuff— Grand Funk was a big influence in my life. Don Brewer was a favorite drummer of mine. John Bonham is probably my biggest influence of all the influences. Buddy Rich, too! I got to see him when I was thirteen years old. He did things that seemed absolutely *impossible* to do. To me, if you could meld John Bonham and Buddy Rich into one drummer, then that would be perfect drumming! Led Zeppelin, I got to see them twice—in 1970 and 1972. In 1972, around when the fourth record, *Led Zeppelin IV*, came out, I had ninth row seats on the floor at the Spectrum in Philadelphia—to this day, probably the most amazing thing I've ever seen onstage. *Absolutely incredible.* Led Zeppelin at the absolute height of their glory. And Cactus—Carmine Appice was a big influence. And Carl Palmer from ELP was somebody that I enjoyed as a drummer. And, of course, Ringo.

But basically, it was whatever music I listened to that caught my ear and my eye is what influenced me—like I'm sure everybody. I was in Jersey, finished high school, and didn't have any real thoughts of what I was going to do from there. My girlfriend—who became my wife, later—was going to go to school in Springfield, Missouri, and we decided to go together. That's how I got to Springfield. And always in the back of my mind, I knew that the reason I'm leaving to go to another place was to meet other musicians. I mean, that's the only reason I thought anything was going to happen in my life. And that's exactly what happened—I ended up meeting Phil Keaggy, and, ultimately, Ty and Doug.

TY TABOR [King's X singer, guitarist; solo artist] I grew up in Pearl, Mississippi. I was born in Jackson, Mississippi, on September 17, 1961, and grew up in a little town that was a suburb of Jackson—it actually wasn't incorporated until I was twelve years old, and then it became the town of Pearl, Mississippi. My mom and dad are both very musical—they sing. My dad plays a lot of instruments and he always encouraged me. He was the first one to teach me to sing harmony with him—early in the morning, before he went to go to work, or when he came home from work. He would play his acoustic guitar, and I was always enthralled. So, I watched his fingers and learned my first few chords watching my dad, and learned about harmonies from my dad.

Then, exactly at the same time, my parents were in a bowling league, and were going bowling a couple of times a week, so we had a neighbor who would come over to babysit, who happened to be one of the best guitar players—still, to this day—that I've ever heard in my life. A guy named Mickey Pogue. Mickey had a brief moment of touring with Black Oak Arkansas and The Ruby Starr Band. He had a moment of being noticed, but not really was known worldwide for how good he was. Because he's a Jeff Beck type of guitar player—on *that* scale. And every time I heard him play, it did something to me that I couldn't explain. It was just different. It ripped my whole soul out. He could play one note and it meant more to me than anything anybody I knew playing guitar around was doing. And, lucky for me, he was my babysitter for years as a kid growing up. I got to watch him playing guitar, he gave me an SG when I was about fourteen, just to borrow and play, because he had just bought a new Les Paul.

And it was Mickey who would always bring Beatles records over. I was a huge Beatles fan, because my earliest musical memory was going to a friend's birthday party when I was a small child—barely over two years old, and I still remember this, and my parents confirmed that it's true—my friend had just turned three, and he got a small turntable. I have this fragmented memory of this little turntable, and us having towels on our heads, and jumping around—singing and dancing—in his room. And it was to the song 'I Want To Hold Your Hand' by The Beatles. I remember freaking out, and from then on, I wanted a

Beatles record for my birthday, Christmas, whatever—I just wanted *Beatles*. And then, during that same time, I was playing music with my dad and my brother—we were playing bluegrass music. And we actually toured around doing festivals and shows here and there as a bluegrass band.

I first started out just playing around with bluegrass stuff, and we were doing big shows in front of big crowds—festivals, opening for people like Minnie Pearl, Grandpa Jones, Bill Monroe, and Lester Flatt. The absolute legends of bluegrass—we were doing shows with those people. I was playing in front of thousands of people when I was very young. I had some neighbors that played music and I would occasionally go down to a friend of mine named Eddie Moore's house—he was a drummer and he had some gear set up in a garage. And I would jam with him until the neighbors would complain or the police would show up, and make us stop. Because it was outdoors and very loud. But that's how I started out doing rock'n'roll—playing at my neighbor's house, goofing off.

I had a best friend named Marty Warren, and we learned to play electric guitar together at the same time. And every day, we were both at his house or my house, trying to push each other to learn something new—or who could figure out this lead or that lead, or how to make a string have vibrato. We were paying attention to those kinds of things super early on—mainly because of my neighbor, Mickey Pogue. He was the one that got us to say, 'We've got to figure out how to play leads. It's the coolest thing in the world!' And we realized what he was doing was different than anything we heard anybody else doing.

Marty and I eventually formed a band, and we started doing little rock gigs here and there. Didn't really amount to much. So, all the way through high school, for the most part, I was doing a little rock thing here or there, but nothing that mattered, other than a brief stint with a band called CJB. I was mainly doing bluegrass stuff that was in front of reasonable crowds. And then, toward the end of high school, I started getting a little more into playing out with rock bands and guest playing. But I wasn't really in a band myself. What happened was, one of my best friends joined a band called Matthew—which happened to be one of my favorite bands in the South. And they played about a three or four state area, and were somewhat known in Mississippi.

One of the guys in the band was my best friend at the time, named Kirk Henderson, who was one of the earliest members of King's X, actually, before we were called King's X. Eventually, there was an opening in that band where a guitar player left, and I had been hanging out with them in the studio some, and they were doing some song with a really tricky guitar part. So, Kirk is doing a really killer guitar part on a song called 'Sunshine,' which had this really cool, Phil Keaggy–type riff. I'm sitting out in the front area of the studio, just tinkering around on an acoustic, and I figure out the guitar part and I start playing it along with him. Before I know it, the producer and engineer comes walking into the room and says, 'Did you just figure that out right now?' I say, 'Yep.' And he says, 'Do you want a job?' I say, 'Sure!'

Then, Matthew had one of their guitar players leave, and they asked me to join, and I finally joined a really good band—the band I wanted to be in. And the day I graduated high school, I left on tour with them across the south—on my very first real tour. And it was literally the day after I graduated. We started the tour that day, so I could graduate and then leave. That's how I got started touring and playing for real. Did that with those guys for a while, and left that band about eight or nine months later, and decided to go to college. So I moved up to Springfield to go to school, and I decided, 'Well, I did my little tour thing. It was great, I starved to death, it was hard like I thought it would be, and we got nowhere like most bands. Now, I'll go get some school.' So I go up to school and decide to do a journalism major, and I am completely miserable in school, because I didn't want to be doing anything that any of the majors are. I realized, *I just want to play music.* But during college I put my guitar in the closet. I was done with playing. So this is just a fluke that I met Doug and Jerry.

02 CROSSING PATHS

HOW DOUG, TY, AND JERRY FIRST MET AND
BEGAN PLAYING MUSIC TOGETHER.

DOUG PINNICK I played in several bands in the 70s, and every band I was in I thought was going to be the greatest band in the world. I don't know, we probably sucked really bad. But I kept playing music with bands, until one day I was in a Christian band, and we were going to this church. We were playing music, but we weren't getting anywhere—Christian rock bands back in the 70s were a no-no in the Christian world. They really felt it was wrong, and it was 'of the devil.' And regular rock music didn't want to hear about Jesus. But we had a mission—we thought we were supposed to do that.

Eventually, the guys in the band got married and they all started having kids, and all of a sudden they said, 'We can only practice twice a week, and maybe do one gig every two months.' And I said, 'OK. You guys go with your families, I'm out of here.' I actually even said, 'Lord, if you open the door, I'm going through it,' and probably a week later, Greg Volz from Petra called me, and said, 'Do you want to play bass in the band?' And I said, 'Hell yeah!'

Jerry had joined the band the same way I did. Greg called Jerry and said, 'Do you want to be the drummer?' Because they needed a rhythm section. Jerry agreed, so I went to Springfield, Missouri, to meet Jerry and Greg. But when we got to town, there was no band—the band broke up. After that, Jerry and I stuck it out, and we played with Phil Keaggy for a while.

JERRY GASKILL I remember the very first time I met Phil Keaggy—it was at the very same church that I would later meet Ty. Phil was coming and was going to play I guess that night, and Greg Volz was the guy who introduced us all, and asked me if I wanted to come and play as well. I said, 'Well, of course I do!' And I remember seeing Phil Keaggy getting out of the van, and it was absolutely incredible to see Phil Keaggy right there in front of me. It was like seeing one of the Beatles getting out of the van—that's how much it affected me. And I played, and it was fun and great, but later, I was asked to join his band. So, I did.

I went up there—Doug and I, both … well, actually, what happened was, the whole Petra thing fell apart. And I think Greg felt bad, because Doug had moved down there, so my understanding is he talked to Phil, and said, 'Hey, I've got these guys.' So, we went up there and rehearsed a little bit, and ended up being in *his* band. And that was incredible. Then we went on the road. It was a true honor. It was an encouragement for me to think, *Hey, I can play with Phil Keaggy. I must be OK.* I never recorded with Phil in the studio—they recorded some of the live shows—although Phil played on my latest solo record [*Love & Scars*, 2015].

DOUG PINNICK Playing with Phil Keaggy was one of the greatest things I ever did, as a learning experience. He is still probably one of the greatest guitar players I've ever seen. And, every night, I got to sit there and listen to him—even when he would do his half-hour acoustic sets, I'd sit in the audience and watch it. He is amazing. So, Jerry and I, we were rookies. We didn't know what we were doing. We had never played in front of people who were doing anything major. So, for us, we were very overwhelmed. But we did have fun. Phil is such a unique guitar player that you'd have to play in the box that he plays in, and I'm not good at it. He's a really jazzy kind of player, lots of notes and things going on.

And I could never remember some of the riffs that he made. He'd say, 'Hey, do this riff,' and he'd play this four-measure riff, and I'm going, 'Wait a minute …' [*Laughs*] I'd have to sit there and go over it like, a hundred times, and I would never nail it. So, I always felt like I was never good enough. But he never complained. He just played and had his guitar. But we only stayed with him for like a year-and-a-half or something like that. He said we were the *rocking-est* band he ever played with. He used to tell us to lay back a little bit, because he had nowhere to go. Jerry and I have always played hard.

JERRY GASKILL The first time I ever met Ty, he was in a band opening for the Phil Keaggy Band, that Doug and I were in. He came up to me and asked if he could use my drums. And I came to find out later that their drummer had left, and he said, 'Well, *I* can play drums,' so he did it that one night. And he asked me to play my drums in a very thick Southern accent. I didn't think anything of it—I said, 'Yeah, you can play my drums!' And then, later, I was doing some demo work for this other person named Tracy Zinn, and Ty was the guitar player on that project. I remember him sitting in the corner of this church building—which was where we were rehearsing—and he was playing these licks. And I was going, 'My goodness … this guy can play the guitar!' That was my first real impression of Ty.

DOUG PINNICK I used to go to the college that Ty went to—Evangel College, in Springfield, Missouri—and hang out. I was new in town and didn't know anybody. Phil Keaggy was in Kansas City, but I was basically in Springfield and didn't know anyone. I found myself gravitating toward the Christian college and started hanging out with some people there. I can't remember how I met these folks, but I started hanging out with one of the guys at the dorm, and he invited me to a Spring Fling show—the college was having a thing where all the musicians would get up and pick songs and do songs. I was in the gym, watching these bands play, and it was OK. Nothing was impressing me. And then, all of a sudden, they were doing a song, and this kid does this lead, and it was like, 'Are you kidding me? Who is that?' And nobody knew. So, my buddy started asking questions, and he found out: 'His name is Ty Tabor.'

TY TABOR So, there's this show at the college—which is a talent show, that happens right after this Keaggy show. The talent show is a big deal—it's called Spring Fling. Everybody goes. It's hugely attended in a massive auditorium. Thousands of people. This girl that was singing at the thing heard that I had a guitar in the closet, and she came up to me and said, 'Can you play lead, by any chance?' And I said, 'Yeah.' And she says, 'Can you play something like this Rita Coolidge song?' And I said, 'Yeah, no problem.' 'Will you do this with me at Spring Fling in a couple of days?' 'Sure!' So I go do this thing with her—I don't even know who she is, really. I play the song, leave the stage, and think nothing of it.

Doug happened to be in the audience, and he went over to see Jerry and his wife to eat supper, and was telling them about this guy he just heard play a lead on this song, and, 'We've got to find out who he is, because we've got to call him and get him to jam with us.' So, they figure out who I was, and Jerry's wife at the time looked me up in the school directory, dialed the number, handed it to Doug, and said, 'Here … *this is him*!' Doug wasn't even planning on calling me, and he didn't know what to say. Doug's like, 'Uh … Ty, my name is Doug. You don't know me, I play in the Phil Keaggy Band.' I say, 'Heck yeah! I know who you are—I saw you play the other day, it was fantastic.'

He came over with a friend named Dave Gouty—another really key, instrumental person in the forming of King's X, who was a friend of all of ours. So, Dave, Doug, and I jammed together some in my dorm room. We got to know each other and started jamming together, and then, at the same time, The Tracy Zinn Band—who I had played drums in—asked me to play guitar, after they heard me play guitar. They said, 'We don't have a drummer, but we have a demo we're doing next week, and Greg Volz is going to produce it, and he's going to bring a drummer in.' So, I show up at the studio, and the drummer he brings in is … Jerry!

So, I'm in a band with Jerry, Jerry's in a band with Doug, I'm jamming with Doug separately, and playing in another band with Greg Volz. This whole circle of all these people, we all hang together. And then Doug makes a call, and says, 'Why don't you play with me, Jerry, and Dan McCollam?' And I say, 'Sure.' I went over there and started playing with them.

The very first time that all four of us played together was at Doug's house in the kitchen, and we made recordings of stuff called *The Kitchen Tapes*, from early on. It was instant that we all knew this was what we'd been looking for. I remember that I was afraid to talk too much about it, and none of us did, but we all were like, 'Holy crap … this is magic when we play together.' So, right then and there—before we had anybody caring about us at all, before we had any demos, before we had done anything—I think we decided this was the band that we were going to make happen. At that point, we were committed. Period. No matter what.

JERRY GASKILL Once we got together—the three of us—we realized immediately that this is the band we want to be in.

03 THE EDGE/ SNEAK PREVIEW

BEFORE THERE WAS KING'S X, THERE
WAS ... THE EDGE AND SNEAK PREVIEW.

DOUG PINNICK I said, 'Hey, let's start a band. I've got this great name—*The Edge.*' And they said, 'Sure!' So, during Christmas vacation, I had a four-track and wrote several songs. I played everything frightfully, horribly—no joke, *really* bad. Even the drums ... and I had never played drums. But somehow, I got the songs to a point where they at least knew what was going on. Then we made *The Kitchen Tapes*. And we actually described our music, because we actually had a focus—we used to call it 'heavy melody.' We thought the name was stupid, but we always wanted to play really heavy, but with a lot of melody. We never talked about it after we originally agreed on it. But everything we do is heavy and has a melody.

JERRY GASKILL The Edge formed in, I think, November of 1980. Dan McCollam was the other guitar player, and then at one point, he left—the next year, maybe. And then we got another guitar player—a friend of Ty's—named Kirk Henderson, until, I think, '83. Then he left the band, and we became Sneak Preview. Just the three of us.

TY TABOR The first manager we had was just a friend of mine from college who offered to manage us. We didn't even know what a manager did—we just knew we could probably use one. So, he became our manager, and his name was Steve Yake.

JERRY GASKILL The Edge was a band that was a vision of Doug's ... and a vision of mine, too, ultimately. But we realized when we were at the height of the Phil Keaggy thing, the height of the Christian world, I think we both realized, *This is not where we belong. We need to have a band—our own band—and do the music we want to do, and say the things that we want to say.* And that's sort of how The Edge formed. It was the music that we felt we wanted to make, and I don't think we had any rules and we weren't trying to fit into any certain category—we were trying to make music that we wanted to make. We wanted it to rock, we wanted it to be hard, we wanted it to be heavy, we wanted it to be melodic. So, we did that.

TY TABOR In the early days, when we were trying to make a living, Doug was renting a two-bedroom house. And I lived there with him … along with seven other people. Roadies, friends, whatever, and other band members at one time, because when Kirk moved up, he lived there, too. So we're laying all over the floor, we're sleeping in shifts—there's all kinds of stuff going on. Our soundman lived with us. But Jerry was with his wife and kids at a small apartment—a campus apartment, I think. And we all lived in that place where we all didn't have a legitimate place to sleep. And because we all sometimes only made $25 for a show, we were starving to death. But we were legitimately working as much as we could, any jobs we could do—digging ditches, shoveling snow, or anything. We were in Springfield, Missouri, and it's not exactly a job mecca. There's not a lot to do there. So, at one point, every one of us was on food stamps, and we would pile our food stamps together and give them to Doug, and Doug was our cook, and would cook huge, massive things of spaghetti and stuff like that, so that we had food.

We went through about a year of starving—living on food stamps, getting $25 for a gig, playing in pinball houses or wherever. Anywhere anybody would let us play. We traveled to other places, and we started eventually getting paid a little bit, then, over a five-year period, we were getting paid well and all over the place—everywhere from Colorado to North Carolina. We were a cover band … that did a whole lot of originals. That's kind of what we were known for. And we were also known for only playing covers that were old rock'n'roll—that nobody else in the whole country that we were aware of was doing this at the time. There was no such thing as 'classic rock' because it was just barely passed, and we were into the 80s. We're talking about 70s music, so nobody was playing 70s music—it was, 'You don't do that. You play the new 80s hits.' So we were the band that played 70s rock and said,

'Screw it.' And we became known as the very first classic rock band in clubs in the Midwest.

KEVIN MOURNING [King's X tour manager, sound engineer] I was a technician with friends of mine that were in high school—they were in a band called The Extremes. And I worked with them as a tech or sound guy—a lot of times just hauling their equipment around and setting it up. So, The Extremes would sometimes open up for The Edge. That's how we got to know each other. I happened to be at the right place at the right time when they fired one of their lighting technicians/roadies, and Doug looked at me and said, 'Do you want a job?' I said, 'Yeah!' He goes, 'Pack your bags—*we're leaving tomorrow*.'

We were gone for a couple of months. I just packed it up and went. I was nineteen. They were kind of like father figures to me as I went along. Just basically helped shape me into manhood. They were super-religious, and some of the greatest people you'll ever meet—honestly.

One of the funniest things that sticks in my mind—and kind of jolted me, my first week on the road—was that they were like, 'You're rooming with Doug.' Well, Doug used to have these night terrors—he'd scream at night, that were unlike anything I'd ever experienced. And I remember the first night after he had one of those night dreams—I was thinking, *What in the heck did I get myself into?* It was *really* bad. I mean, screaming and moaning. It was horrible. So, I roomed with Doug most of the time, and he actually tried to bleach his hair blonde, and it didn't work—it was like, bright orange. They called it the 'clown afro'! He didn't know what do—he was like, 'I've got to go onstage, but my hair is a mess.' He dealt with that for a few days before he could get it to go the other way. But it was bright orange—like a clown wig.

TY TABOR There is this place we used to play, called the Wine Cellar, in Little Rock, Arkansas. It was our best-paying gig, but we had to play five sets a night—whether anybody was there or not—six nights a week, playing until almost five in the morning. It was miserable, because a lot of the times, there would be nobody there—or maybe three people. But the owner always wanted us to play—just in case somebody came in.

We stayed in a really horrible, horrible hotel, called the Mark 4000. At any moment, at any time, you could count multiple roaches on the walls. It was *swarming* in roaches. The very bottom of the barrel of the very lowest-living kind of hotels you could possibly find—and it's in Arkansas. It's a doozy. But the one thing about the Mark 4000 that we liked about staying there was somebody who worked at the phone company told us about a trick you could do with their phone system, where you could dial a code before you made your call, and the call was free. This is back in the day, way before cell phones. There was no such thing as having the convenience of grabbing your cell phone and calling whoever you wanted.

One night—during the five sets a night—there were only about three people there, and it was four in the morning or so. It was way into the morning. They came in, and we were like, 'Good grief.' As we're playing, we realize that they've got their backs turned to us and were talking to each other really loud. We realized they're not even paying attention to us. So, we had this digital delay that had an infinite repeat on it. I looked at Kevin, our soundman, gave him the signal, and went to the mic and made a farting noise into the mic. He put it on infinite repeat, so every two seconds, it was going [*makes fart noise*]. And then he slowed it down, so it would be a lower pitch and go longer. And the whole time that this is going off, every time that it made the sound, I turned my butt to these three people at their table, and squatted almost every time it made the noise … and they never even noticed the large fart noise coming through the PA, nor that I was doing it right at them!

There was one night when there were a handful of people in there, and we decided to go into an improv jam for the entire set—the forty-five-minute set—where we had no idea what we were going to play. And at the end, they clapped—they thought it was something we had worked out! Another night, there were two guys and two girls at a table—early hours of the morning, again—and all of a sudden, they break into a fistfight, where they are grabbing pitchers of beer, smashing each other's faces. I mean, whole faces being cut open. Blood everywhere. This is in the middle of our set. That's what life was like at the Wine Cellar in Little Rock, Arkansas.

Then other places we'd play, we would do something called 'Stump The Band.' People started showing up at the shows just for that—at the end of the night, because we would have periods of time during the last set when people would call out whatever they wanted, and we would try it. Even if we never played it before, we would give it our best. And, a lot of times, we would have people get up onstage and sing with us—and do it with us. One time, we had a girl come up and do Pat Benatar with us, and she floored the whole crowd, because she sounded just like her. The place went nuts.

Another time we were doing it, we were in this little tiny hole in the wall, in a town called Muldrow, Oklahoma, and I have two vivid memories of that place. We would play there every once in a while—in the middle of nowhere. In a tiny little club. Some dude wanted us to do some Lynyrd Skynyrd, and got up onstage with us. And the dude even looked the part—long hair, beard, same kind of clothes. We went into something like 'Sweet Home Alabama'—this was after the crash—and this dude, I swear, was like a ghost of Ronnie Van Zant onstage. *It gave us all chills*. The whole crowd went nuts. The dude sounded just like him. It was eerie, eerie, eerie. It was one of those amazing things that happened in this little town. He never came to another show and never did Stump The Band with us again. But it was totally amazing.

And there were low points, too, like in Austin, Texas, at Cardi's. This dude shows up for Stump The Band, and he looks like a mix between Rod Stewart and Mick Jagger. He has all white leather on, hair sticking straight up—looks like a rock star. He comes up, and goes, 'I want to do some Stones with you!' We go into 'Jumpin' Jack Flash,' and the dude starts strutting across the stage like Jagger. The crowd starts cheering, and we're thinking, *This dude is pretty badass!* Then he starts *whistling* into the mic, because he can't even sing at all. The whole place starts booing, and I had to turn around toward my amps, because I'm laughing uncontrollably, and Doug is looking at me with his mouth gaping open. Night after night after night, we had countless stories of adventures on the road.

In the very early days, out of absolute boredom, we used to do whatever to amuse ourselves. Jerry and I used to sometimes race each other across a parking lot. Something else that Jerry and I used to do all the time—it would start out by one of us walking up to the other and kind of tapping him on the chin. And then I would do the same thing back a little harder. And then he would do it a little harder. We would keep doing it, until both of us were knocking the crap out of each other! And we used to be dying laughing about it. But I'm not kidding—we were hitting each other *hard*.

I remember one time, we were playing in Joplin, we just finished breaking down the gear, and we started doing that, and some female friends of ours were there, and they literally started crying, because they wanted us to stop. They couldn't stand to see us do that. But the way it ended was, one night I think we were in Little Rock, and it was late at night in a hotel. Nobody else was around, and we started doing that to each other, and we both hit each other harder than we ever had—to where we both were, like, *blacking out*. So, at that time, we kind of looked at each other, and said, 'OK. I think we probably ought to stop this!'

DOUG PINNICK There was a lot of new-wave stuff happening, as well as Judas Priest and AC/DC was going on. But we were still rocking out like Led Zeppelin and The Beatles. I guess it never left us. Even though we tried, and did music like The Police—I was obsessed with The Police. And U2—I discovered them after I named the band The Edge—and we got into stuff like The Producers. We loved The Producers—they were like The Beatles *on steroids*. I didn't know there was much metal going on until I left Missouri. Metal wasn't cool in Springfield colleges.

JERRY GASKILL There's one band that was an influence on all three of us—The Producers. All three of us have very different musical taste and direction a lot of the time. But that was one band that all three of us loved. When we first started The Edge, it was just to do all our own music. And then we quickly realized we couldn't get any gigs doing that. Nobody wanted to hear all original music. So we started doing cover tunes, but we would pick cover tunes that nobody had ever heard of—we'd pick obscure things like The Producers, and people didn't know the originals, anyway! We wound up doing some classic rock and hits of the day—you had to do that to get a gig.

DOUG PINNICK The Edge had a really good following. To me, it wasn't *that* big. But I also never thought we have a lot of people who like *King's X*, so I see things a lot differently when it comes to that. But to me it seemed like, 'Well, we're in Springfield, and we can pack out a club.' But we would go to Oklahoma or places where there would be ten people, and that wasn't fun. I remember the places that people showed up more than the times that we had sparse crowds. But we had some good shows. We opened for some people, like Three Dog Night to a thousand people, and got a standing ovation. And nobody even knew who we were—we did cover songs. Every time we played out with anybody, people's jaws dropped. And we never could understand. But back in the 80s, there was some pretty crappy stuff. [*Laughs*]

TY TABOR We met this guy that owned a sound-and-light company, John Gott, and John offered to manage us at that point. John took over when we had been a band for a couple of years, and he was our manager all the way to '85. We also had a light show and huge PA, and we really did it up 'major' as best we could and as best we could afford, and built up a reputation of being this rock band with a show.

Dan McCollam eventually decided to get married and get real with his life—because it was a hard life we were living. So I called my friend Kirk Henderson from Matthew, in Mississippi, and said, 'Hey, we just had a guitarist leave. Would you like to join our band?' He said, 'Yeah! What the heck—I'll see what it's like to live in Missouri.' So he packed his bag and headed to join us. Kirk was the fourth member for a while, and we were called The Edge still during this time. We started getting a real good reputation and started opening for some big bands—we opened for Mountain and Uriah Heep, who back then were still playing theaters and doing good. And we opened for Three Dog Night when they reunited with original members.

Kirk stayed with us for about a year, but it became evident during that time that he seemed not to fit in like the three of us did. We three were on the same page—always—and Kirk had to kind of be corralled to be on the same page. We thought, *Without Kirk, we're just not the same, so we might as well change the name of the band.*

JERRY GASKILL We had a pretty good following as The Edge, and then we decided to become a three-piece and call ourselves Sneak Preview. We made this big announcement at one of our shows, like, 'Here's our new name'—the big drum roll and everything—'Sneak Preview!' And the place went completely silent, like, 'What the hell does that mean? What kind of a name is that?' It felt like everything that we had built up to that point had just kind of dwindled away, and we had nothing—like we were starting all over again. But we did start to build, and as time went on, I think we built back our following—like we had as The Edge. But I remember after we announced that Sneak Preview thing, we went down into the crowd, and some of our faithful followers were there. And this one girl comes up to me, and says, 'I really feel for you guys.'

DOUG PINNICK It was, like, forty-five minutes of throwing names at each other and hating all of them. And then we got to Sneak Preview, we got tired and said, 'OK … *Sneak Preview*,' and we just let it be. And it was the most stupid name. They will tell you—that was the worst name we ever could have come up with.

TY TABOR At that time, U2 was starting to be heard of and known, and they had somebody in the band named The Edge. Of course, we had that before then, but we had never heard of him, because nobody had heard of them back when we formed. Around that same time—'83 or so—it was like, 'We might as well try to do some different music and change the name of the band.' So we learned a whole bunch of stuff we could do as a three-piece, changed the name of the band, and went back out to play this big place called the Hangar—that we normally packed out.

We walk out onstage as a three-piece, and told everybody the new name of the band and started playing the new stuff … and we almost empty out the building. Even our fans that were diehards, we went to sit down at the tables afterward, and they were shaking their heads, like, 'We're sorry guys … *this is the end.*' [*Laughs*] It was like a punch in the gut—everything we had built up, all of a sudden, we were a laughing stock. I mean, we changed our look and everything—we took a big chance when we did this. And it flopped.

But, we kept it up, because we had already learned all these songs, and we had these other gigs. By the time we got into five or six gigs, people started packing it out again, because they got used to the idea, and they realized we were taking the same intensity and jamming—just into a little bit different style of music. And it took so much paying dues that I skipped over—a couple of years of playing to nobody, traveling over icy roads three hundred miles to get to some Iowa gig and load our massive lights and PA up totally iced over metal stairs, risking our lives to do a gig. Literally—I mean, somebody risking a PA falling down two flights of stairs on them and killing them. We were doing that stuff to get stuff into gigs to play for three people. And we did that for eight years before things got OK.

KEVIN MOURNING I remember the transition when they went from The Edge to Sneak Preview. That transition was, 'We are going to play our original music—

damn everybody and damn what they think.' And I remember getting fired from certain clubs, because we were like, 'We are going to play our original music.' And they were like, 'No. We want to hear Lynyrd Skynyrd!'

That transition was the hardest thing for the band. The crowd would always yell, 'SKYNYRD!' And they would also yell out for them to do 'Cocaine' by Eric Clapton. And Doug changed the lyrics—to make fun of the crowd—instead of singing 'Cocaine,' he'd sing, 'Coffee.' And no one ever caught on to that …

JERRY GASKILL We got to the point where we bought this truck—this big box truck. We called it the Chuck Wagon, because on the side, it had the name of some kind of business by this guy, Chuck. We put all the equipment in the back, and we built bunks behind the driver's seat, so we could all sleep. We took turns driving, and that's how we lived.

DOUG PINNICK My God, I'm so glad we're still here. We would do, like, five or six sets in Arkansas, and then tear it all down, put it in the Chuck Wagon, and drive four hours through the mountains, to get back to Springfield, and get home by sunlight—in snow blizzards and stuff. I don't know how, but we did it. We survived. I remember driving down the road, and you can't keep your eyes open, so you pull over and say, 'Somebody, *wake up*!'

TY TABOR I remember one time, being in the Chuck Wagon, and we were a hundred feet from the continental divide in Colorado, going uphill. Once you get to that spot, it's all downhill from there—up to the next town, fifteen to twenty miles on the road we were on. Our truck died in view of the crest of the hill and it was about eight degrees outside—and getting colder. We had to survive at night in bitter dead cold, with wind blowing. Just a few feet from being able to roll down to the next town, and we just couldn't do it. We were all huddled together in blankets. Then, when we finally did get some help getting pushed over the hill, we still couldn't crank the engine, and we had to roll in the dark down the mountain behind a car, using their lights, to see.

KEVIN MOURNING Chuck's truck! It was an emergency road service truck, and I remember there were a couple times where … because it said 'emergency road service' on it, we actually were able to get through some barricades. I believe we were in Mobile, Alabama, and the roads were closed because they had a light dusting of snow. And for us in Missouri, that's nothing. So, we would move barricades to get back on the interstate, because there was a barricade closing the interstate. And we would pass highway patrolmen and police—we never got stopped! I remember Jerry asking me if he could take the truck to McDonald's. And here I am, nineteen years old, and they're all older, and they're asking *me*. I'm like, 'Yeah, but you better be careful—don't go through the drive-thru.' He ends up trying to go through the drive-thru … and the top of the truck rams into the overhang.

JAY PHEBUS [King's X tour manager, sound engineer] I started working with them in Springfield, Missouri, just after they changed from being The Edge to Sneak Preview. Ty and I were best friends back in high school—he lived two blocks away from me, and his wife at the time was my next-door neighbor. It's probably '83, I'm thinking, when Ty came home for Christmas break, and Jerry had just been in a car accident—the guy he was with got killed. Jerry had busted ribs and a hurt back, so they needed help. The one guy that was doing everything, was Kevin Mourning—he was their sound engineer and lighting guy, and they basically did all their own setting up the PA and lights—the band and Kevin. Jerry being out because he was hurt, they needed somebody to take up his part of the workload. So, I basically came in as an apprentice and learned everything that Kevin was doing.

Then, subsequently, Kevin's wife became pregnant and wanted him to come off touring. This was about nine months later, and I had been in college and was going to be a pilot in the air force, and I got to one last thing, then I had allergies that knocked me out of the flight program. They said I could do everything except fly, and I said, 'That's *the only thing* I want to do.' So, I was in kind of a tailspin during that Christmas break that Ty came home, and he was like, 'Hey, can you come help us out?' And I was like, 'Well, I was planning on taking a break this semester anyway, so yeah, I'll go help.' So that's how I got started and involved. From then on, I took over and put in twenty-five years with them.

KEVIN MOURNING They've been really close friends to me. Like a family. Even back when I was still working for them and I was having babies with my wife, they would cancel shows so we could all be home when we needed to be. It's a really tight, close family of incredible people. They helped shape my life as a man when I was nineteen years old and forward. Amazing people.

JERRY GASKILL We pressed an album and made like a thousand copies of it, and we ended up giving them away. That was a different kind of period. That was the new-wave time—I think we were thinking more in that direction of new-wave music, and we filtered that through what we were doing. That was a really different kind of time for us—we had just become a three-piece band, changed the name, changed the direction a little bit. But we were still true to ourselves. We've always just done what we do.

DOUG PINNICK I remember we went in to do the record, and we did all the songs live—except I don't think I did the vocals. Ty played all his guitar parts clean, so that we had a scratch track, and then you'd later go over and do the overdub of the distorted parts. Little did we know that after the record was recorded, the manager produced, mixed, mastered, and printed up albums, and the cover was done without us knowing. So, we put the record on … and he had mixed the distorted guitar on the left, and the clean guitar on the right. *For the whole record.* And it was already pressed and ready to sell.

JERRY GASKILL I think any time you're on your way to a place and you have a dream and you have visions and you have hopes, it's not going to be happening, sometimes. So, there's definitely some discouragement along the way. But I think we were young enough and we believed enough that we kept going. And finally, somehow, something just happened. I mean, discouragement is part of life.

04 HOUSTON–SAM TAYLOR–KING'S X

THE BAND RELOCATE TO HOUSTON, WHERE THEY
HOOK UP WITH MANAGER/PRODUCER/SONGWRITER
SAM TAYLOR AND ARE RECHRISTENED THE MYSTERIOUS
NAME THAT WE NOW ALL KNOW AND LOVE.

JERRY GASKILL There was a record company down there in Houston, Star Song Records, who believed in what we were doing, and they wanted to help us get a real record deal. They asked us to move to Houston and be the band for one of the artists on their label, Morgan Cryar—which we did.

DOUG PINNICK Star Song was a Christian label, and this guy had heard about us through the grapevine—through the Christian world, because some people were talking about these Christian bands we used to play with, like Phil Keaggy. You know how the buzz goes in all circles. They had this young guy, Morgan Cryar, who was this pretty boy, and they wanted to push him in the Christian world. They needed a band, and we were starving—doing cover music. Like I said, we did well in Springfield, but once we left town, we were playing to nobody—for fifty bucks a weekend. And we said, 'We're ready to go.' So, we all moved down to Texas. The record company paid for the trip and brought us down, and we were Morgan's band for a year. We got fired because all the churches said, 'Don't bring that band back—*they rock too hard.*' [*Laughs*]

TY TABOR There was a group of guys from a record company called Star Song— which used to be the biggest record company in the Christian rock scene. And they've got a group of guys filling up arenas and doing very well at the moment when they see us. *But we are not a Christian band.* But they knew we were singing about a lot of spiritual stuff that seems Christian. So, they come to talk to us, and they say, 'You want a record deal?' And we say, 'No.' [*Laughs*] We say, 'We really don't want anything to do with that or that industry. That's just not us.'

Then they came back to us a little later with a different offer, and said,

'We've got this artist, Morgan Cryar, and he's got one album out and he's kind of catching on. People really like him, he's really talented—he's a great singer, a great writer. What would you think if you guys moved to Houston for one year; we'll pay off the rest of your PA and your lights, so you don't have that debt; we'll give you a weekly salary, we'll set you up in apartments, and all you've got to do is gig with Morgan as his band, and write music with him to record an album?' And we said, 'That's not really our deal. That's not what we really want to do.' But we thought about it. And then they came back and said, 'OK. And if you do all that, we'll put you in the studio with some producers and shop you for a regular record deal.' We said, 'We're in. We'll do it. It's only one year of our lives, we'll get out of debt, we'll get paid, it's something we have to do.' So we did it.

We moved down to Houston, left Springfield at the very height of things happening for us, and thought, *Oh my God. This is so crazy that we're doing this ... but these guys are going to help us get a record deal. What the heck, let's do it*. We put in actually more than a year with them, because they kept stringing it on, stringing it on, until we finally had to put our foot down and end it after a year and a quarter. But we did make an album with this guy [*Fuel On The Fire*, 1986], I wrote a whole bunch of music with him that had hits on the album, that ended up being good money, and a very big album for this artist.

But after I was done, I went to the guys and said, 'I will *never* write a formulaic song again for the rest of my life.' Because I felt like a whore. I hated what I was writing. Even if it was successful, it was not from the heart. Meanwhile, they did actually get us together with one producer—a guy named Jimmy Hotz—and we did a demo with him. And it was pretty lame. It was trying to form us into a sound that Jimmy Hotz does, rather than bringing the best out of us and finding out what that was. So it ended up being a waste of time.

JERRY GASKILL We toured with Morgan Cryar, but I never played on any of the records. Actually, I was going to play on one record, and the producer didn't like me. He didn't think I was good enough, I guess, so he canned me, and I didn't play on the record. But then, after he had heard some of the demos we had done, he called me and apologized to me, and he was begging me to forgive him, and he wishes I would play on the record. I said, 'Whatever, man.' But it was through the label that we met Sam Taylor. And then, the Sam Taylor era began.

TY TABOR We ended up leaving that place without a record deal, and without anything. But Star Song had recently met Sam Taylor from ZZ Top—he was head of their video production stuff. So, they had met him and told him about us, and they said, 'Look. We have this band that we made promises to, that the truth is we don't know what to do with them. They are one of the best bands we have ever heard in our lives, but they don't fit any category or anything that we can do, and they don't really want to be a part of our industry, so we can't help them. See what you think of these guys.'

So we went and played all our music for Sam, and, truthfully, I wasn't happy with the music we were doing—*at all*. But Sam was very impressed with us as a band. He thought, *This might be one of the best bands I've ever seen, as far as people that play together. I really get something from these guys that's special ... but the songs aren't there.* And I agreed. I felt like we were writing stuff that was trying to be trendy with whatever was out on radio—instead of being our own thing. And it was driving me nuts.

So, during the time that we were writing all this commercial crap, I started writing music on my own, and not playing it for Doug and Jerry. Just trying to make myself happy. And I told you about Marty Warren—my best friend that I learned to play leads with back in the old days. Well, Marty moved up to Houston and moved in with me, because I told him, 'Look, man—I've got a paycheck, I'm just sitting around occasionally doing a gig, so I have time to write.' And Marty was one of my favorite people on earth to write music with. I said, 'Let's write music and come up with something new, something different, something of our own.' We started writing music together and getting really fired up about all this stuff that we're coming up with. And I started tuning down to drop-D for everything I was writing—to get these heavier riffs.

We started writing like that together, and then we called another best friend of ours, Dale Richardson, and said, 'Dale, come up here and join us. You've got to be a part of this! Bring your bass and let's write music!' Dale ended up moving up there, so, for most of the year, it was me, Marty, and Dale, writing other music, besides the stuff I was hired to write for Morgan and the stuff I was writing for King's X. And we came up with thirty or forty songs of crazy, different stuff that was so different from anything I'd ever heard of before. And 'Pleiades' was one of the songs.

All of a sudden, one day, we get this phone call from Morgan Cryar, and he says, 'Hey guys, we've got this one last gig. It's a big deal—they're saying it will be broadcast to about two and a half million people worldwide. And it's going to be at Heritage Village, for some New Year's worldwide broadcast, with some of the biggest Christian artists in the industry.' And because we had this album just come out that was mega and a big hit, they wanted us to come play. So we go to Heritage Village … which was one of the most disgustingly horrible experiences of my entire life. I was completely disgusted by the waste of money and decadence I saw at that place while they begged poor grannies to send their last $10 in. I left that place saying, 'You guys can all go to hell. You ain't got nothing to do with anything in scripture I've ever seen.'

DOUG PINNICK That's the day that I woke up and realized that Jesus was for sale, and people were making a lot of fucking money doing it. *Wow*. I don't know what to say. It scared me. I understood … not *understood*, but I got a glimpse of how Jesus must have felt when he went into the temple to do his sacrifice, and there were all these people out there selling shit. To me, religion wasn't something for sale. I hate hypocrisy, and through that, it opened my eyes up to the hypocrisy to a lot of aspects of the Christian community.

TY TABOR I said to everybody, 'The time is over for this thing with Morgan. I'm done. *It's over*.' But on the flight, there was the one thing that changed the course of the history of this band. On the flight there, we had these Walkmans, and we had these adapters where we could listen to stuff together, with more than one input. We all sat in this row close together, and Doug said, 'Hey, I've got some music that I don't think you guys are going to like, but I'm going to play it for you guys, to see what you think.'

So he played some stuff for us. And I think it might have even been the initial riff—without it being worked into a song—of 'Over My Head.' And he was thinking it was a throwaway idea. But we were both like, 'We have to make a song out of that! We have to finish that up.' And he was like, 'Really?' He started playing us some more weird stuff. And we were like, 'Man, we like this the best. *This* is what we should be doing—different stuff.' And I said, 'OK guys. I've got something for you. This is the same thing—I didn't tell y'all about this, it's just something I've been doing on the side with Marty and Dale. It's really bizarre, but I love it. So here, give it a listen.' And I played the original demo of 'Pleiades' for them. And they absolutely freaked out and said, 'This is who this band is. We can do this. *This is what we need to be doing.*'

DOUG PINNICK I'll never forget that day. He said, 'Listen to this song. I don't know if it's any good or not.' Both Jerry and I said, 'We like it!' We learned it, and it was drop-D tuned. I had never heard anything in drop-D tuning like that. We knew a few bands that had a few drop-D songs, but nobody had done, like, *a whole record* of it—or really made it a *genre*.

I went home and turned my E string down to D, and wrote half the first record, and he wrote the other half basically—in drop-D. I think he realized there was something different. I couldn't compare it to anything, so I thought no one would like it. *I* liked it—but I didn't think anybody else was going to like it. But I was driven to do it, because drop-D-tuned guitar parts are so easy to make and come up with for me. It opened up a whole flood of ideas in my head.

TY TABOR We were *so* inspired. I started playing them a bunch of other stuff I had been writing, and they loved it. In fact, a whole lot of stuff on the first album is stuff that came from me, Marty, and Dale—from those original writing sessions. That's what formed the whole directional basis of what happened. And then Doug started writing in drop-D, and he came up with 'Power Of Love' immediately.

We started writing in drop-D together as a band, and we came up with 'Wonder' together. All of a sudden, magic started happening, and we had a direction. We found home. It was like, '*This* is home. *This* is what we're meant to do. *This* is what we do naturally—without trying to be anybody else.' And it was such a relief. That was the beginning of truly being King's X.

DOUG PINNICK Sam came around right when we left Morgan. We were still with Star Song Records, and they said, 'We don't know what to do with you guys no more.' They were giving us a salary, and they were going to cut us off. They said, 'We're going to have to let you guys go. We don't know what else to do with you. But we've got this guy, Sam Taylor, who used to work with ZZ Top.' So, they sent Sam over to a rehearsal, and Sam said to us, 'You guys are pretty good.' He seemed not too impressed, but he was willing to work with us, and then he went home. His ex-wife later told me he thought he had found the greatest thing in the world—that he might have found 'the next Beatles' and they were going to get rich. [*Laughs*] But he didn't tell *us* that.

JERRY GASKILL Apparently, Sam came from the ZZ Top camp. From what I understand, he was, like, second in command. He was pretty big in that organization. He came to hear us play, he liked it, and I guess he had a vision for us—like we had a vision for ourselves. And we decided to pursue something together. So we did.

The first demo we made was with Andy Johns, which was really exciting. That was a trip in itself—Andy was a trip, man. [*Laughs*] It was sad to see him go, but we all have to go at some point, right? [Johns passed away in 2013, at the age of sixty-two.] That was quite an experience, but nothing really happened with that demo—nothing happened to it. I think 'Wonder' was on there, and I can't remember the other songs. There were three other songs. 'Wonder' was the only song that made it onto one of our records.

TY TABOR We then showed Sam some of that music, and he gravitated instantly toward that a lot more than any of the other stuff we had done. What Sam did is, he started getting us to be professional, by having a rehearsal hall—for one thing—that we rented downtown in Houston. It was a whole top floor of a building that was eventually going to be built into a bunch of rehearsal rooms. But at the time, we had the whole place. And it was massive. So we went up there and lived in there—with Sam. Day after day, we were doing long, long days. We would break to go have lunch, go back in and work more. We were taking all these songs we brought in, and playing them over and over, and really thinking about, *Well, what if on the third chorus when it goes to this one note, what if he we change this one thing?* All this 'polishing' and really thinking about the songs and working on vocals together. We did vocal rehearsals together—practicing scales and singing and harmonies. Just to get strong.

JERRY GASKILL I enjoyed working with Sam. In many ways, he brought out some of the best in us—probably things that we couldn't have brought out ourselves. He worked us really, really, really hard. And, for some reason, we allowed him to work us really hard. [*Laughs*] Which seems to be against our nature. But we did. He's a very talented guy, very creative in his own right. I think his influence helped those four records become what they were. He's a great talent—he's a great piano player and played a little bit of guitar. It became something other than just a great relationship.

I think it was 1985—I think we had just met Sam Taylor, and we had just moved to Houston from Springfield—I remember I woke up one day, I was lying in bed, and I put my arms behind me to stretch a little bit, I looked down, and under my left armpit, I saw this lump. As if somebody had stuck a golf ball under my arm. So, I went to the doctor to have it checked out. And as soon as he saw it, he goes, 'I don't know what the hell that is, but you need to get to the emergency room. *Right now.*' Here I am, driving to the emergency room, going, 'OK … I'm going to die.' Then they did all the tests, and did a biopsy, and it ended up being Hodgkin's disease—in the very earliest stages. Which, ultimately, was good. But the whole procedure after that was quite grueling and quite dehumanizing, and a lot to go through. And I must say that Sam was there with me and for me through that whole thing. I remember one time, sitting in a waiting room together at the hospital before I even knew what was going on yet, and he was reading the zodiac thing in the paper, and he looks at me and says, 'Look, Cancer … *that's you.*' It was actually funny at the time.

They had to do a surgery to make sure it hadn't spread—which I really didn't want to do. I was very leery about that. I had to go away from home—I visited my mom, halfway across the country. I had to get away and think about it. I was thinking, *I don't want to do this. I don't want to cut myself open. I don't want that to happen.* I remember lying in bed one night at my mom's house, and this thing came over me, like, *What if you don't do it, and it has spread? And then all of a sudden, you're in this immense pain and there's nothing you can do about it, and you're going to die?* At that point, I thought, *OK. I'm going to have to get the surgery.* So, I did. I went through six weeks of radiation—five days a week. And that was that. And now I'm OK, although I've had heart attacks! [*Laughs*] I go *big* when I do things.

DOUG PINNICK When we found out that they thought he had cancer, at that point, I didn't know what to think, because he was so young. They put him in the hospital and they tore his body in half and pulled out all his lymph nodes. Oh my God, that must have been one of the hardest times of his life. But he healed up, and we played. Jerry has had more physical problems than any of us have.

And to watch him recuperate and not complain or act like anything's wrong is amazing to me. The boy's got so much stamina, it's really something.

JERRY GASKILL We still didn't have a name. We were throwing out different ideas, and I think at one point, Sam had mentioned *King's X*. I think maybe his brother was in a band called King's X ... I don't really even know. Somehow, King's X was thrown into the pile. I remember thinking, *Well, it doesn't really have any certain meaning. It might be cool*. At one point, I think Sam said, 'So ... are we King's X or what?' And I got up and said, 'OK. *We're King's X.*'

TY TABOR It had a whole different bunch of meanings when it was presented to us originally. It was Sam Taylor who suggested it, because we had a whole bunch of names that we didn't like—including King's X, to be honest. King's X didn't really strike us as a great name, but Sam said, 'Look. My brother used to be in a band called King's X that split up years ago. They wouldn't mind us having the name if we wanted.' But King's X is the name of a game in Texas from the old times, that's like tag. And a 'King's X' is a safety, where you get a break. And we thought, *Well, that's a pretty cool connotation for a name*. And he said, 'Other people will look at it as Martin Luther King and Malcolm X, and Christians will look at it as King and the cross.'

DOUG PINNICK I never liked the name—ever, ever, ever. But that's our name, and people are used to it.

TY TABOR That's around the time we made a four-song demo with Sam in the studio, and we all worked together. That's why it always said, 'Produced by Sam Taylor and King's X'—because we were all hands on. I know that I used to go in and get the music where I liked it, and then Sam would work on mainly vocals. We would all contribute. We would all complain about this or that, and 'I want this to be this way' or whatever. But we did it until we were all looking at it, going, 'This is a good representation of us, and we're all pretty well happy with it.' So, we made these four songs and we sent it out to every label we knew. And got nowhere—got rejections from everybody. And then, Doug sends a tape out to Amy Grant's drummer at the time ...

05 MEGAFORCE

IN 1987, MEGAFORCE RECORDS HAD PROVED
ITSELF TO BE THE WISEST LABEL OUT
THERE–BY SIGNING KING'S X!

JERRY GASKILL We made another demo, and we sent it to every record company imaginable, and nobody wanted it and nobody seemed to care. And there was one label, Megaforce … I think what happened was, we were told not to give the demos out to anybody. But I think Doug did anyway, because, that's what Doug does. [*Laughs*] And it got into the hands of somebody, and they sent it to Megaforce, and it had Sam Taylor's name on it.

DOUG PINNICK Sam had gotten to the point where he was really super-controlling of everything we did. And we had done this demo, and Sam had made me promise not to play or give it to anybody—because I've been giving demos out to friends for almost as long as I've been writing music. He was trying to stop me from doing that—he didn't want anything leaked out. I did promise that I wouldn't give it out … but I did. The drummer from Amy Grant [Greg Morrow] heard the demo, asked me what was going on, and I said, 'Well, the truth is we sent our demo out to every major record label we knew of, and we got a rejection letter from everyone.' And he said, 'Well, there is a label in New Jersey called Megaforce Records. Why don't you send them a cassette?' So, I had to go back and tell Sam that I fucked up … but we might get a record deal. [*Laughs*]

MARSHA ZAZULA [Megaforce Records co-founder; wife of Jon Zazula] I knew nothing of King's X. I had worked with a group in the South called Fire Choir. There was a fellow in that band called Steve Taylor, and he had other bands, like DeGarmo & Key, if you remember them. Anyway, Fire Choir sort of came and went, and we couldn't get them off the ground. We remained friendly, time went by—I'd say about a year—and I got an envelope in the mail, and the return address was 'S. Taylor,' and it was from Texas. My memory got jarred, and I thought, *Oh my God ... it's Steve from Fire Choir! I wonder what he's doing? Maybe DeGarmo & Key finally did something*. I grabbed the cassette—because I was in my car when I picked up the mail—and thought, *Let me hear what this is all about*. I stuck it in my tape deck.

Well, it turns out it was not DeGarmo & Key, but what I heard was instantly incredible music. I had to be on the road that day and I wasn't with Jon, and I kept playing it over and over. Finally, when I stopped somewhere, I pulled out the letter, and I found out it was from this fellow, Sam Taylor, who introduced himself as having this great band, called King's X. So, I kept it to myself, and I spent a week—every time I was in my car—listening to it, going, 'Am I crazy, or is this the greatest thing since sliced bread?' Finally, after being convinced that it *was* the greatest thing since sliced bread, I took it to Jon. I said, 'Jonny, I found our newest signing. You've got to listen to this. I'm not crazy. I'm cheering for this to be on Megaforce.'

JON ZAZULA [Megaforce Records co-founder; husband of Marsha Zazula] I did not want to sign King's X. We had family fights over King's X! She was so adamant. There was a moment I said no, and she made me listen to it again. And for some reason, it finally clicked—with 'Shot Of Love.' It was like, 'Listen to that bass sound, man. *Oh my God*!'

EDDIE TRUNK [radio, TV host; Megaforce Records former vice president] My recollection of that whole time is pretty vivid, because we were at a point with the label where we were looking to evolve beyond just the thrash and speed metal that we had been known for. It was one of the things that I really wanted to do with the label when I came on board—and I had talked about Jonny and Marsha about doing, and they were supportive of it. So, me bringing in Ace Frehley was the first step in that direction of sort of getting a 'radio band.' We were trying to figure out, 'Where do we go from here? What would be cool? What would work and maybe appeal to a wider range of people?'

So, Jonny had gotten the demo for King's X. And what I remember very clearly about it was the timeframe we are talking about, it was not a cassette or anything like that. It was actually a VHS videotape that came in as the demo. And that was kind of unique at the time—for a band to service their demo as a video, as opposed to just a tape. Jonny had watched it, and then he brought it in to me, and I remember very clearly him walking into my office, and he said, 'I need you to check this out.' We put it in the VCR, and it was King's X, and they were playing on what looked like a construction site. I think they were even wearing hardhats!

There were two or three songs that they played. I tend to remember one of the songs being 'King,' but I just had a conversation recently with those guys about this, and they said it wasn't 'King'—it was a different song on the demo. It was a video demo, and we watched it, and Jonny said to me, 'What do you think?' And I said, 'I think they're really unique and cool. I think they could be really great. They're a great band. But I don't know if they're going to connect. I don't know if they'll sell records. And I don't know if we're the right label that could sell their records.' And he said to me, 'I agree with you. But I think they're amazing. I think we need to sign them.'

CHARLIE BENANTE [Anthrax drummer] The first time I heard them, I was with our then-managers, Jonny and Marsha Zazula. And Marsha had a demo tape. She would usually let me listen to things and get my thoughts on it—the same with Jonny. I remember immediately digging King's X. Visually, I had no idea, but musically, I thought it was a very heavy, Beatles-ish sound that I was listening to. And the singer almost had a bit of a Phil Lynott meets Sly Stone approach—so I was intrigued.

TY TABOR Marsha played it for Jonny Zazula, and he was like, 'OK. We're booking them for New York right now. We'll book a showcase gig for them and see what these guys are like live.' They booked us at the Cat Club, for an album release party for Ace Frehley. So, we played for the album release party. And there were a whole lot of famous people there—famous bands, people from Atlantic Records, people from all kinds of different major labels, people from the biggest booking agents in the world, like ICM … all these mega-players from the rock'n'roll world were there. Joey Ramone was five feet in front of me with his arms crossed, staring, and not moving—the whole show!

DOUG PINNICK I never talked to Joey about what he thought of the show, but every time he came through town, I always went, got backstage, hung out with him, and drank a beer. There would be a lot of people talking to him, so we never did have any real conversations. But he always knew who I was. And the thing with him though was he had that crooked eye, so no matter which way he was looking … sometimes, he would say something, and I wouldn't know he was saying something to me, because the eye was going the other way. And he would get really frustrated! I wish he was alive today—it would be great to talk to him again, because there are some things I'd like to say to him. But I was kind of nervous, because he was like a rock god to me.

TY TABOR So we got to play our show … and we feel it was a train wreck. We didn't really feel like we got it together—the monitors were horrible. Doug at one point got pissed and kicked the monitors over, because they were ruining the show for him, and he decided to sing without them. It went *bad.*

DOUG PINNICK I remember I walked up to the mic, and the mic kept shocking me. Finally, I got pissed and said, '*Somebody fix this fucking mic*!' And, from that point on, I was pissed. And when I got pissed, Jerry and Ty got pissed. All three of us had the same kind of emotions, and we stepped it up. All of a sudden, the energy level went up. And at that point, we were giving it, because we were like, 'Fuck this shit!'

TY TABOR We finish, get offstage, go back to the dressing room, and we're looking at each other like, 'Well … we thoroughly blew that, didn't we?' We're depressed. A few minutes pass, our manager comes in with this look on his face. We say, 'Yeah, we know.' He goes, 'It wasn't your best. But I've got some people outside here that want to meet you.' So, the first thing, he sends in Jeff Rowland, who has the #1 booking agency in the world, ICM. And he goes, 'I want to be your booking agent.' We're like, 'OK!' We shake hands, and we're like, 'Holy crap! How did that happen?'

Bill McGathy comes in next—he's the #1 radio promo guy in the world—and says, 'I want to work with you. I want to be a part of this.' We're like, 'You've got to be kidding. OK!' Jonny Zazula comes in next, before anyone else from labels can come in—because there are people from Atlantic and other labels—and says, 'You're not leaving town until you sign papers with me.' We were like, 'YES!' We just got a record deal! It was high times for us.

ROD MORGENSTEIN [Dixie Dregs, Winger, Platypus, Jelly Jam drummer] Winger had just signed with Atlantic Records, and somewhere in 1987, I forget if it was Kip Winger or someone else in the band said, 'Do you want to go down to the Cat Club tonight? Atlantic Records people are going to be there'—that was the record company Winger had recently signed with—'and King's X are playing.' I didn't know who King's X was. I was just going down there to be part of the Atlantic Records hang, and introduce myself to the label. Then … I got to experience King's X for the first time. They're a great live band—each one of them individually are amazing on their instruments. And plus, the fact that they have such great vocals.

Just as a funny aside, I remember feeling cool, like, 'Hey, I just signed to Atlantic Records,' and I would notice someone who was pointed out to me at the party, like, 'That is so-and-so from Atlantic,' so I would go over to them, and go, 'Hi, my name is Rod, and I play drums in Winger.' And they'd go, '*Who? Never heard of you.*' And they'd give me the cold shoulder and walk away! I might have tried it with one or two other people, but nobody seemed to have even heard of us, and we were one of the recent signings for them—it was sort of an 'air let out of the balloon' experience. But King's X was really fantastic … but anybody who sees them live comes off feeling that way.

EDDIE TRUNK And then, we flew them from Houston to New Jersey—to Jonny's house. It was in the summer. We had a barbeque, spent a couple of days with them … and signed them to a record deal. It was very much like that. Megaforce was a very sort of 'mom and pop' record label by some fans working out of a house in Old Bridge. We weren't going to misrepresent what we were to the band—we were fans, and we would do the best we could for them. But it wasn't going to be some lavish thing. We had a barbeque and a pool party, they signed the contracts, and away they went.

MARSHA ZAZULA They came to Jersey, and we had a big barbeque at my home, and we introduced them to all the people in the office. By that point, everybody in the office was on board with the signing. I believe they brought some album cover art with them at that point, and some additional music. It all was like a kismet—we all clicked in together. I was very fond of Doug Pinnick—I had a very nice relationship with him. Also with the other guys, but I had an especially fond relationship with Doug. We signed them to the label, and went with our best foot forward. Atlantic was very much into the project and got behind it with radio. [Megaforce was distributed by Atlantic at the time.]

MARIA FERRERO [Megaforce Records former director of publicity and A&R] Megaforce Records was—at the time—probably the most important, successful, and busiest independent record label that handled hard rock or heavy metal. There were other labels, like Metal Blade and Roadrunner, but honestly, I think because of Metallica's success and Anthrax's success with Megaforce, they weren't as mainstream. There was no mainstream crossover— they were still a little bit underground. And Roadrunner were European, so it wasn't really as developed yet here in the States. But Megaforce was the most important at the time. Megaforce had signed Metallica, Anthrax, Mercyful Fate, Ace Frehley, Testament, and a bunch of other artists, and launched some great careers with some amazing bands that are still around, and still extremely important and influential. And another thing that set Megaforce apart—we had major distribution. Atlantic Records was our distributor, where Metal Blade was kind of indie—a little bit not as mainstream, because they didn't have a major label behind them, pushing it. The same thing with Roadrunner. So we had a lot of the backing. Atlantic Records did support Megaforce financially, but we had our own staff.

EDDIE TRUNK I do remember we had a fifth-anniversary party for Megaforce at the Ritz. And I know King's X were included in that. It was a little bit of a strange thing for King's X, because they were ... even Ace obviously had a hard rock following and a hard rock pedigree, and a huge influence on all these hard rock bands that we had signed or were a part of. So it was an easy thing for Ace to fold into that world. I think for King's X, they weren't sure what they were walking into there, because they're coming into a label, and they were just going to this party, and it was Testament, Overkill, Anthrax ... and here's King's X.

Although King's X is certainly a hard-rocking band—don't get me wrong— they're cut from a different cloth. And the irony is that all of those bands loved King's X. But they were definitely a different band. For Megaforce to even present a band that looked and sounded like that, it was going to be a little while before they were going to sink in and people were going to get what they were doing. But I'm very happy to say that the critics and the bands themselves got it really quickly, and became their biggest, earliest supporters.

King's X also had a manager at the time, and his role in the story is enormous—Sam Taylor. And Sam was essentially the fourth member of King's X. He produced the records, and the reason why that material came in as a video is because Sam had done videos and was a video guy for ZZ Top's organization. Sam looms huge in their story. Nothing happened without Sam signing off on it. Sam was involved in every aspect of the band. He produced the records, and would say *yay* or *nay* if there were things that we wanted to do that we felt would help broaden them out or help bring them to a bigger audience. But those were 'his guys,' and he was very controlling about it—for better or worse.

MARSHA ZAZULA I think Sam had a good sense of what you needed to do, but he didn't have all of the tools to do it. He was a mild-mannered person, and he was very behind the band. I respected that he was doing it all with smoke and mirrors, because they didn't have any money, and he was trying to promote it the best he could. And, of course, coming to Megaforce was sort of a long shot for him, because up until then, we were pretty much only heavy metal. I had no problems dealing with him, particularly. They believed in Sam Taylor implicitly. Sam got very involved in the songwriting, which—not that it was bad, but it didn't come from the band. It didn't have the same impact for the band.

JERRY GASKILL I was very excited to be on a label—they believed in us and wanted to give us some money to make a record and promote it. And they were distributed through Atlantic, so it all seemed great. But I've always felt that King's X was pigeonholed into the wrong places—whether it be the Christian world or the metal world. And, with Megaforce, their 'force' or stronghold was metal. And I didn't really feel like we were a metal band. But they had Ace Frehley— that was cool. So, I felt like we always seemed to be in that place that we really weren't … if that makes any sense. But I was very thankful that we had a deal.

DOUG PINNICK For me, I sat there, and I kind of had this feeling of, *Oh no. Now we're the little fish in the big sea. Now we've really got to step up to the plate. Now everybody is going to hear us. Oh no, oh no, oh no.* It wasn't like, 'Oh my God, we've got a record deal!' It was, 'Oh shit. It's really happening!'

06 OUT OF THE SILENT PLANET

THE STORY BEHIND THE DEBUT STUDIO ALBUM
BY KING'S X, RELEASED ON MARCH 28, 1988.

JERRY GASKILL We decided that we were going to share everything equally in this band. So, if somebody writes a song completely, we still all put our names on there. But once a song becomes a King's X song, we all three have put ourselves into it. And it can only be that song because of the three of us. Therefore, in a sense, we all are making this music together—whether we actually write the song or it's a total collaboration, that's just the way we do it. We share everything equally as King's X.

We did the first four records with Steve Ames at Rampart Studios in Houston—it was his studio and he was the engineer. I have really good memories of all that stuff. It feels—now that I think about it—like all good experiences. We were in the studio *a lot*. We were there—it seemed like—eighteen hours a day. We would take naps there and we were always in the studio. And there were times I was like, 'I've got to go home! I've got to see my kids!' Because we were always at the studio, playing games and throwing balls around, and every once in a while, recording.

TY TABOR So, now, we have to record the album with Sam. We go back to Houston, and we decide that we're going to record it in the same place we did the four songs that got us the record deal, because it's the only place where we've done a demo out of all the different times we tried to do demos, where we felt like something special happened. So, we go in, and we decide we're going to keep doing what we were doing on this—just take more time to do it better.

We spent about three to four grueling months of *outrageous* hours—mostly seven days a week, taking no time off, going home at midnight, getting up early the next morning to get there, and starting out already burnt. It was drudgery as far as physical abuse. [*Laughs*] We killed ourselves doing that record, is what I remember. But, at the same time, I loved a lot of it. Just because it was getting to be in the studio and getting to be free to try things.

So, on one hand, it was like nirvana. On the other hand, it was like one of the hardest things I've ever done. And trying to really be 'pro' on that level, and really being critical, would emotionally drain you. You become a zombie by the time you're done with it. You feel like there's nothing else you can give. That was the biggest surprise, I think, of doing that album—that's how it felt. It felt like I lost two or three years of my life in that short amount of time—just by how much was put into it. Emotionally, the stress, fighting with our manager—which happened all the time—just how much of a toll it was. But when we were done, we sat back and listened to it in sequence, and all of us were stunned, like, 'Wow. It really is a piece as a whole that has a beginning and an end, and goes somewhere.' And none of us saw it coming. It was almost like hearing something from another band—even though we knew we did it.

DOUG PINNICK I remember it was something brand new for me. I'd never been in the studio doing music that I had done in a professional fashion. We'd been in studios in the past—little rinky-dink studios—and not known what we were doing. But it was a big deal, and I realized that they were spending a lot of money, and there was a lot of pressure. Making the record, I don't remember a whole lot, because I was too busy trying to do my part and make sure I was right, so I didn't have to go back and keep doing it over again. I think a lot of it for me was to do my part and hope everybody liked it. *Gretchen* was also a long, tedious process, but the first record took us a month to do. After a month, I burn out and I lose interest. So, by the time we got to the end of the record, I had lost interest. Some of the things I didn't like about the record, I didn't fight for. We didn't know any better back then, so we kind of went along with the program and trusted people.

JERRY GASKILL I remember being very excited that we were making a record. I can remember driving around in my car, hearing some early mixes, and going, 'Wow. This sounds really great. This sounds like *a real record*.' That was exciting to me. And we believed in it. We worked hard all these years to make this record, and we're making it and we believed in it. It was very exciting. And I thought we had a pretty cool cover.

THE SONGS

'IN THE NEW AGE'

TY TABOR I wrote that with my friend Marty Warren—that was one of those songs of the zillions of songs we wrote in the apartment, while we were getting paid to write music for Morgan Cryer. It was completely written by Marty and me, and [the band] basically learned it and added our own flair to it. But it's pretty much a demo. Lyrically, the song is about the bombardment of all kinds of three-steps of spiritual ideas, and the bombardment of all the different types of new-age-movement stuff that was going on at the time. Just basically stuff that was being called 'new,' and it was nothing new at all. That is what the song is saying—there is nothing really anything new about it at all. It's called 'ancient wisdom,' and it has been around forever. It's religion, really.

'GOLDILOX'

TY TABOR I was at a club in Houston, with my friends Marty and Dale. We were going out to a place called Cardi's in Houston, which is where we actually used to see Pantera play all the time, when they were in spandex, playing Loverboy! It was this really big club—a lot of great bands came through all the time, so it was a great place to see killer musicians. We would go and check out pretty much anybody that came through town. And, one night, there was this beautiful girl with long, curly, gold hair, a couple of tables in front of me. But I was too chicken to bother her. I went home, and I had this music in my head, and I couldn't get it out of my head. I didn't even really have anything to write about, so I took that incident and turned it into this whole big deal, which to be honest with you, *wasn't* as big as the song makes it seem. But that was the inspiration for it. It was a real person that I never met.

JERRY GASKILL That is a very popular song with the fans. Every show, we do it, and they sing it. We don't even have to sing it anymore. It's very, very nice.

DOUG PINNICK People love that song. I'm glad people say it's one of the greatest ballads ever written. And I'm glad Ty wrote it. I don't like the way I sang it. I had a hard time singing it, because it was such a tender song, and when

Ty sings the song, he has a way of singing it from his heart. And I can't interpret that, because I'm a totally different singer. So, when I went in to do it, I tried to do it my way, and he didn't like it. I tried to do it his way the best I could, and everyone seemed to be happy with it. But I've never been able to stomach it, because I don't feel like I did a good job on it. I felt like I was just doing what I was told, and didn't get a chance to *own it.*

As far as I'm concerned, I can't stand listening to myself singing. But I heard someone else sing it one time, and I almost cried—it was so beautiful. I heard a girl sing it—a friend of mine [the late Janet Rains, aka Jane Train]. She recorded it, and when I heard it, I thought, *I get it now.* When I hear somebody do a King's X song and somebody else sings it, I go, 'OK. I can see this can be a hit song.' I always feel like there's something about my voice that people just can't deal with, so that's why we don't sell as much as we could.

TY TABOR It seemed to be a crowd favorite because of the harmonies. We would notice that people were singing it with us—after a couple of years of doing it live. I think it was probably over in Europe, I would guess, that it happened first—in England. Probably London. Because over there, people would sing along with every word, as loud as they could. So, I'm sure we dropped out and let them do it in England somewhere. After that, it just became a thing.

'POWER OF LOVE'

DOUG PINNICK When Ty wrote 'Pleaides' and it was drop-D tuned, I remember going home and taking my guitar and drop-D tuning it. It was a whole new ballgame for me. And that was one of the first songs I wrote in drop-D. I had been listening to Metallica and Sepultura, and I was going for that 'metal chunk' thing. Lyrically, I was trying to get that whole sing-along gospel cadence thing, where the singer sings and then the choir sings behind him. That was what I was going for—that gospel kind of vibe over a brutal, bluesy groove. And, lyrically, I like to sing about love and unity, because I feel like there's not enough of it. And it's on my mind a lot—caring and loving and understanding people. Not trying to push myself away from them or hate people. It's tolerance and understanding people, and realizing that love covers all the shit. That was my mindset a lot back then.

'WONDER'

JERRY GASKILL 'Wonder' is the first song that we all got together and wrote together from scratch. I had these lyrics laying around that ended up being the chorus. '*There's a wall between us / A partition of sorts*'—that part.

TY TABOR 'Wonder' we all wrote together. And it came together very quick. I was trying a different guitar tuning that I'd never tried before, that I think was based on a Jimmy Page tuning. Possibly. And I came up with the opening riff … I actually came up with most of the musical ideas, but we did all write it together. In other words, whatever words were being thrown out, everyone was saying whether they liked this or that, and we pieced it together in one day, during one rehearsal. And it was the only song on the album that was completely collaborative—from the first note to the end—that was created with everybody there from the start. Lyrically, it's about life. About all the questions and confusion of life, and all the road signs that we see that turn out to be just commercials and not truth, and how much that can cloud you of real life.

'SOMETIMES'

TY TABOR I wrote 'Sometimes' with Marty Warren. He actually came up with the initial intro guitar riff, and then I wrote the rest of the music to the song, I believe. And then I took it to the band as one of those many that had come about during that time of massive writing with Marty and Dale. And they didn't like the lyrics, so we all sort of pitched in on lyrics—but mostly probably Doug and Sam on the lyrics, changing them up. That's another one of those songs that kind of tried to promote hope and belief, in that if you just hang on, it will get better.

JERRY GASKILL I remember really liking this song, but something about the lyrics didn't seem right to me. So I wrote the lyrics for the chorus, and I think Doug wrote the lyrics to the verses. Originally, I had, '*I stand here crying / The world is laughing / I stand surrounded yet I see the lies.*' Then I said, '*I sit here waiting for New Jerusalem / I know it's greater than the world outside.*' And somebody said, 'Why are you *sitting* for that? I think we should be standing for that, too.' But in my mind, to sit and wait for the best thing—while everything else surrounded us—was a bit more powerful. So, we changed it to 'stand,' which is OK. It's always been the case that if someone is not happy with something, we don't do it.

'KING'

DOUG PINNICK I was into Bow Wow Wow for a second. They had this jungle beat with a funky slap-bass player. So my demo sounded like them—but a bad rip off. Jerry's then-wife heard us playing it and said it was a stupid song. So, when we were making *Out Of The Silent Planet*, I said, 'Let's scrap the jungle thing, and let's just jam it out.'

Back in the day, I was a believer—I think we all were. And I was trying to subtly write things about my faith, without being blatant or turning it into an evangelical type of song. I just wanted to rock out and have fun. When I sang, '*King is coming*,' it's sort of like saying, 'Whoever is going to come and fix everything, they're on their way. Your big brother, your lover, your God, Jesus—whatever.' It's sort of a victory song. A song of hope, of, 'Hey man, these people have been fucking us over for a long time, but your time is coming—someone is going to come fix this.'

'WHAT IS THIS?'

DOUG PINNICK Another drop-D tune—same type of riff from learning this new tuning, same type of chords. That was about believing in God, but questioning everything that I believed. It was like a prayer, saying, 'Are you real?'—in my own way.

'FAR, FAR AWAY'

TY TABOR This was sort of a musical experiment for me. I was experimenting with things that were not usual. And the way I came up with this song was, I had a drum machine that I put a bunch of random beats in, that had a few hiccups here and there—where things turned around or got backward. And I wrote to the drum machine. I did that on purpose, to make myself come up with this thing that was disjointed and wrong in places. And I believe Marty … he helped sing on the original demo, but I don't think he helped write that one. I think that one was all me.

I wrote it about the earth. Looking back on it now—I didn't think anything about it at the time—it was like the first thing I had written that was the kind of message that is usually attributed to someone who is outspoken about certain things, and that is not normally me. It was like my view that we've already gone too far to save the earth, and people are too stupid to wake up to see it. That's what the song is about, really, and it was a long time ago that I wrote it, and then kind of moved on from that thought. And then found myself in my adult life almost being consumed by that thought and writing about that a lot these days. But that was the beginning of it, I guess.

'SHOT OF LOVE'

TY TABOR That one is totally Doug's, and I believe it's pretty close to the way he wrote it. We did work on it together—like we do all songs—and I'm sure there were a few little 'touches' put on it. Well, obviously there were—there are little stops and changes in the vocals. We took the initial idea and put a couple of shiny things on it. But that one's Doug's.

DOUG PINNICK I remember my demo sounded like Jon Anderson singing it, and the music had so much echo that you couldn't tell what was going on. They turned that mess into a song! Especially the vocal parts, I love it when Jerry sings a line like my favorite band, Sly & The Family Stone. Another prayer—saying, 'Look, we want some love down here, so send us some love, because this world is falling apart and it's all fucked up.' Like I said, that was my mindset back then, and I was like, '*Come on everybody.*' I had this naïve thing that love could save the world. I come from the hippie generation, and we thought, *All we have to do is just love each other, and then everybody will be happy.* I still had that mentality at that time.

TY TABOR My favorite vocal line of Jerry's—as far as how his voice sounds, how cool it sounds—is a line in the chorus, '*Across the mountains to the sea.*' I thought his voice sounded cool on that.

'VISIONS'

TY TABOR 'Visions,' I think we all kind of wrote that one together, based on some basic idea that Doug had. But it's written about Jerry. It's Doug singing about Jerry's crazy head, because, especially back then, we were young and getting to know Jerry—we thought he was crazy! He was very different than anyone I had ever met before—he *still* is. We all know and get him deeply now, but he was definitely coming from a different world from where I was coming from. It took us a while to learn how to communicate. But that song is about him. The way he would word things. The way he would explain things and see things—it would be a perspective that would be unusual, and yet wise, most of the time. Not always, but most of the time.

He's uniquely different in ways that are hard to explain, unless you know someone. It would be like: how do you explain to someone how Truman Capote is different? I'm not saying Jerry is *that* different, I'm just saying if you ask a room of 150 people one question, and you get 149 same answers, Jerry will be the one that is uniquely different. I remember the song's instrumental section being the kind of thing where we decided, *Look, let's go off to eleven here, and get nuts with it.* It felt like the song was this big dirge, but was building to something that needed to happen. I remember laughing about it at times, because we would play it as fast as we possibly could when we were first trying to do it, and it would have nothing to do with the original beat of the rest of the song.

OUT OF THE SILENT PLANET PEAKED AT #144 ON THE *BILLBOARD* 200, AND QUICKLY WON THE BAND MANY ADMIRERS.

EDDIE TRUNK We didn't have any problem with reviews; we didn't have problems with people who saw the band live loved them. But we could not get it to cross over. We could not get it to sell. We could not get people to actually *buy* the record. I used to always say, 'If we could get it to be like if giving records away and promos counted as sales, King's X would have had a gold record.' But we couldn't get it to that point.

Songs like 'King,' 'The Power Of Love,' 'Visions' was super-heavy, 'Shot Of Love,' and one of my favorite songs they ever did was 'Goldilox.' I mean, that was all stuff that we all felt should have been really, really big. It really should have crossed over and really should have gotten on the radio. We had Atlantic Records behind us at that point, and we tried everything. But it didn't translate to records actually being sold. And that was really, really frustrating for everybody.

GEORGE LYNCH [KXM, Lynch Mob, Dokken guitarist] I was sitting on a beach in the north shore of Hawaii when I heard *Out Of The Silent Planet*. I could not stop listening. To me, it sort of encompassed everything that I felt should be incorporated into a rock band. It had all the elements of Beatles harmonies, and had great, dark guitar riffs, and the sexiness of it—all the grooves. And of course, Doug—gospel and blues, and what he does with his vocals. And the production was phenomenal.

I lived with that record, and also the subsequent record, *Gretchen*. It really was the main thing that I was spinning and living off of for a couple of years there. And was a huge influence in the creation of the first Lynch Mob album, *Wicked Sensation*. Although it might not be super-obvious or evident, listening to it, it really was an inspiration for the writing process for that record.

Then there was actually a night that the singer [Oni Logan] and I went out—after rehearsal or something—and we ended up partying a little bit. In my wisdom, I decided to take some acid with him. [*Laughs*] At my age, I had no business doing anything like that, but whatever—just hanging with the guys. And we ended up driving through the desert—it was out in Arizona—at night, listening to either *Out Of The Silent Planet* or *Gretchen*, in the car, under the stars, driving through the desert. It was magical!

RAY LUZIER [KXM, Korn drummer] I grew up in Pittsburgh for eighteen years, on this giant, secluded farm. I was kind of sheltered from a lot of things, because I didn't even have a neighbor for a mile. The only music I was exposed to was what my sister—who was five years older—listened to. And my mom playing The Beatles, Chuck Berry, and Elvis. My sister is the one who got me into the heavier stuff, like Ozzy, Sabbath, Rush, Kiss, and all that stuff. But I didn't really discover King's X until I moved to LA. When I was eighteen, I moved to Hollywood to go to a music school, and one of my locker-mates used to share these labs, and he would always play this music. And I was like, 'This sounds so great.' Because I was always a fan of heavy riffs but beautiful melodies. Like Beatles kind of harmonies. I remember he was playing the *Out Of The Silent Planet* album a lot, and I was like, 'God. This band is amazing. Who is this?'

JOHNNY KELLY [Type O Negative drummer] When I was a teenager—right around the time I finished high school—I used to work at this rehearsal studio in Brooklyn. And there was a small space in the studio that a local music paper rented out, and they did their paper, and he had boxes of advance cassettes. They were *all* cassettes back then! When I was working, I'd go through them, to check out new music while I was working. I ran across *Out Of The Silent Planet*, and I immediately fell in love with it. So, that was before the record came out, since it was an advance cassette—I still have it, it's in my garage! And I've been a fan since the first record.

SHANNON LARKIN [Godsmack drummer] My band at the time was called Wrathchild America, and we were on Atlantic. I had heard of King's X when Wrathchild America first had gone to Texas. And, around the same time we got signed to Atlantic, King's X got signed to Atlantic. So, *Out Of The Silent Planet* was sent to me by Atlantic, and, of course, I fell in love with that record.

REX BROWN [Pantera bassist] We first heard King's X when we were at a signing at a music store in Dallas. This must have been '87 or '88—we were promoting our new record, *Power Metal*. And there were these dudes that were sitting over in the corner and had their own booth. They were playing their music over there. They had the outfits on—The Beatles thing. I was like, 'What the fuck is this?' But we were hearing what was going on, and go, 'Who's playing?' We started digging it. Instantly, we said, 'This is cool shit.' And then we went over and met the guys. This is the start of a relationship that still goes today. We got one of their CDs and took it home, but I didn't really think about it.

Dime called me, and said, 'Dude, have you heard this? Have you checked out King's X?' We went on a long road trip, and we must have listened to that first record I don't know how many times. And then we couldn't stop. I was such a fan-boy—and I hadn't done this since I was thirteen or fourteen—where I wrote the lyrics of the songs down! I don't think the lyrics were included with the first album. I remember writing down 'King.' This was the sound that Dime and I were always looking for. It still had that blues/soul kind of deal—I think that's why we really took a shine to it. And the bass sound was so unique. The production of it was so insanely good for what they were doing. During that first year, we met Doug, and he used to come see us at this place called Backstage in Houston—between '88 and '89.

RITA HANEY [Dimebag Darrell's longtime partner] Doug came to a show that Pantera was playing, and brought Darrell a cassette tape, and it was *Out Of The Silent Planet*. He brought it home, and we jammed it all the time—in his truck, and we would go on late-night bike rides after the clubs we were out at or that the guys would be playing. Darrell had a Walkman taped to the front of his bike, with little tiny speakers, and we would jam *Out Of The Silent Planet*. I got to see them before Darrell did—Pantera were on the road. King's X was playing a club in Dallas, called Dallas City Limits, and it was *amazing*.

BRIAN SLAGEL [Metal Blade Records founder] I first heard them when the first album came out. I got an advance copy of it. I believe, at that time, I was still getting cassette advance copies. But I heard the first record and thought it was phenomenal. Like, *Where did these guys come from?* After listening to the first record, I became a huge fan.

BUMBLEFOOT [Sons Of Apollo, Art Of Anarchy, ex Guns N' Roses guitarist; solo artist] I first heard King's X when *Out Of The Silent Planet* had just come out. All my friends were talking about this new band with this cool sound. And the first time I heard it, I was instantly blown away—like someone turned a light on in my head, in a spot where it was dark the whole time. I know others have said this—and I don't think that the guys in the band feel this way—but, to me, they were the pioneers of grunge. They were the start of music that went deep, and wasn't afraid to not go to … not dark places, but more complex/less shallow places. It had *depth*.

They had everything that I was craving in music and not getting from what we were being served. People used to tell me, 'Oh no, you need a lead singer that is going to wear spandex and kick in the air. You can't be a *singing musician*. That's not in style.' And a few years later, there you have it. But King's X were the first ones to deliver that with such conviction and integrity, and make kickass music. They have it all. They have The Beatles harmonies that you love, they have groove, they have soul—they've got *everything*. And I fell in love instantly—the first time I heard 'What Is This?' into 'King' into the whole album, top to bottom.

JOHN CORABI [Ex Mötley Crüe singer] I think the first song I heard from those guys was 'King.' I do remember hearing it on the radio. I can't remember where I was—I don't know if I was back east or if I was in LA already. But I remember hearing that song, going, 'This is pretty cool.' I loved the voices and the harmonies they were doing.

BILLY SHEEHAN [Mr. Big, Winery Dogs, Sons Of Apollo, David Lee Roth, Talas bassist] I think I heard them on a cassette in Paul Gilbert's car, and I instantly was like, 'Who is this?' I went nuts for them. I thought it was the perfect band. I thought, *These guys must be bigger than U2. They've got to be at some point.* That's how great they were. I thought musically, emotionally, soulfully, songwriting, vocals, guitar tone, drumming, bass tone … forget about it. It was so great and it all came together in this perfect cohesion of awesomeness.

KIP WINGER [Winger singer, bassist] I was fresh out of Alice Cooper, and I was working with Reb [Beach]—we had a small studio in New York and we were working on our demos for the first Winger album. And a guy who was working in the office played the *Out Of The Silent Planet* album from top to bottom, and our jaws dropped—because the sound was unique, and it was so different from what was going on. It was very inspired music. It wasn't contrived in any way— it was this whole new element, coming out of nowhere. It was very inspiring to us at the time, because we were in the throes of writing our first album.

WALLY FARKAS [Galactic Cowboys guitarist; session player; head of Molken Music] I just heard that a Houston band got signed, which at the time, down here, was a really big deal, because other than ZZ Top, we didn't really have a cache of rock bands that came out of here around then. This is going to sound terrible, but *Out Of The Silent Planet* came out, and I got it, came home, and I played it like, one time … and didn't get it. [*Laughs*] I didn't get it because it was *so* different. I don't know if it was more of reading too much hype ahead of time, prejudging how I would receive it. But all I remember is, 'Man, every song is in D.' I'd heard some drop-D stuff before—like Queen's 'Fat Bottomed Girls,' and a handful of other songs. But not *a whole album* like that. I didn't realize the uniqueness of their style at first. I even thought some of the production was a little dated. I hate to sound critical or negative, but that was how it hit me, and I didn't give it a chance. I kind of filed it away. Fast-forward a year later, *Gretchen* comes out, I go get it … and my mind is just blown. Of course, I then pulled *Out Of The Silent Planet* back out, and I fell in love with that album as well. But *Gretchen* seemed like years ahead to me—whether it was or not, I had an instant reaction. From that point, I saw them two or three times in support of that album.

CHARLIE BENANTE There's a song, 'Visions,' which is the last song, which I thought was extremely melodic—but seriously heavy, too. Of course, 'King,' 'What Is This?'—which was one of my favorites off that record. There's 'Wonder,' 'Shot Of Love'—that was one of the videos they did, where they incorporated a sitar. There's your Beatles influence.

DOUG VAN PELT [*Heaven's Metal* magazine founder] I was the publisher, owner, and editor of a magazine called *Heaven's Metal*, which started in 1985. The magazine shortened its name to *HM* in '95, and it's still in publication today—but it's online only now. It was in print all the way up to the end of 2011. So, the magazine was started to cover a sub-genre of a sub-genre. Everybody hates the term 'Christian metal,' or 'Christian rock,' because it's so limiting and confining, and it doesn't really do it justice—especially to an artist like King's X. But I first heard about King's X through a friend of mine from San Francisco—a guy named Jimmy Arceneaux. He was the singer for a band called Soldier. And he was like, 'Dude, have you heard of King's X yet? The name of their album is *Out Of The Silent Planet*, and, judging by the lyrics, there's something going on here.'

I went out and bought the CD at a Sound Warehouse, and it came in a cardboard long box. I kept the cardboard long box of *Out Of The Silent Planet* for many years—I may even still have it. And I checked out the lyrics, and, sure enough, I was convinced that there was kind of a Christian worldview that was informative in the song lyrics.

So I just dialed information in Houston, asked for Doug Pinnick, and got his phone number that way, and quickly struck up a conversation—that turned into a friendship. And I did an interview with each of the three band members. I asked them about their music, album, and faith. When I got to talk to them the first time and talk about their faith, they were guarded—they articulated their faith without using completely telling or forthright labels or descriptions. Like, I remember Jerry Gaskill said something about, 'There are a lot of pathways to God, but there is only one door. And I've walked through that door.' They were kind of referencing Christ or the Christian faith through veiled references like that, that a thinking person could understand, but it wouldn't allow them to be tagged as evangelical or Christian rock, or something that might limit them. Because faith in the United States is not always portrayed fairly in the media, and they were keenly aware of that, and they wanted to avoid that, I think—which is pretty smart of them. They weren't really part of that scene. They probably experienced the confining parts of it, and maybe some of the unfortunate sides of that industry, and the flaws of it. I can't speak for them, but I'm assuming they probably didn't want to have anything to do with that.

MIKE PORTNOY [Winery Dogs, Sons Of Apollo, ex Dream Theater drummer] I heard them as soon as the first album came out. I remember seeing the video for 'King' on *Headbangers Ball*. In 1988, I was a few years into the early days of Dream Theater, and always on the lookout for new bands and new music. I was really impressed with the harmonies. The three-part harmonies really clicked with the Beatles fan in me. I'm a Beatles fanatic. So, as soon as I heard those guys, it was such a unique sound and blend of vocals. It was mixing the power-trio musical approach with the three-part harmony approach of The Beatles. It immediately clicked with me.

LEA PISACANE [Atlantic Records former director of rock promotion] I started working at Atlantic in 1988, and the first song of theirs I heard was 'King.' And I was like, 'It sounds like Grand Funk! I love the vocal!'

DOUG PINNICK I remember, for the 'King' video, we went way out into the middle of Texas, out in the mountains. I mean *miles*—it took half a day to get out there, way in the middle of nowhere. Scorpions, rattlesnakes, mountains, and weeds. It was very exciting! Sam believed in spending a lot of money on videos, and record companies wanted to throw a lot of money at you. So it was pretty extravagant. We had a helicopter flying around, shooting us, and we're on the side of a mountain. It was pretty cool. And we did some acting in town. My nephew was in it, Jerry's son was in it—we hired these kids to sort of play 'King's X's kids.' My mother and sister were in it—in the restaurant, my mom was a waitress and my sister is sitting on the bus, talking to this guy.

JERRY GASKILL The 'King' video had my son in it—he was playing the young 'me,' which was very exciting. It was a new and great experience for me, to be a part of this thing that felt like it was for real. It was like, 'We're making a real record, and now, we're making a real video—with a crew and the whole thing.'

TY TABOR I remember the 'King' video was pretty wild. We went out way to the desert of West Texas—Big Bend. We were driven way out to a little remote area of the desert. Just dropped in the desert—with a boom box, a bunch of batteries, and some guitars and the basics of a drum kit. Then they left, and we were just sitting out there for a while, and we were instructed, 'The helicopter is going to come flying by every once in a while. So just start playing the song whenever you see us start coming back. We're going to refuel, then come back and do a few laps around you—just play the song.'

That's what we did, but we were out there for a long time, to get the shot. We were finding scorpions at our feet and stomping around, trying to scare them off. We were in the wild desert. They came back out and got us, and then took us back to camp, and I remember going four-wheeling for a long way to a remote cabin, way out in the middle of the desert. And that's where we shot the inside stuff with the kids—inside the cabin and on the porch of the cabin. It's some cabin from the 1800s, I believe—out in the middle of the desert of Texas. It has been kept there as a historical site or something. We had to get permission to do what we did.

We also filmed 'King' in downtown Houston—in an area called the Fifth Ward, which is a very lower-income area, right next to downtown Houston. Just to walk around in the Fifth Ward—with the city right there in your face—it kind of gives you perspective. We used to go down there to eat at the place where we shot the video. We'd go down there because they had real good home-cooked meals. This black dude who owned the place would cook total backwoods food, and it was fantastic. It was like home cooking from Mississippi. We would go down there and eat once in a while, and we decided, 'Let's shoot the video down here.' They let us into the restaurant to shoot there, and Doug invited his family down. Some of the people in the restaurant in the video are his family.

JERRY GASKILL There was also a video for 'Shot Of Love.' I thought I looked pretty good in that video … I remember liking the way I looked!

DOUG PINNICK For the 'Shot Of Love' video, I remember Sam had this big idea—this 'stage idea.' And it took them too long to build the stage—it wasn't going to get done by the time of the video shoot. So, he said, 'Let's shoot the video while they're making the stage.' And that's how that happened. I think at the end of the video, you do see the full stage. [*Laughs*]

TY TABOR I used to *hate* doing videos. I just hated doing videos. One thing that I always felt was that I didn't sign on to do videos—I'm not an actor. I felt really uncomfortable faking it in front of a camera. I still do, to this day. Despise it, hate it. For me, the only thing that I think about is, we did them, and I couldn't wait to get done and be out of there. That's really the only way I think about those videos—I couldn't wait to be finished and out of there.

> WITH ITS SOULFUL, PROG-Y, BEATLES-ESQUE SOUNDS, *OUT OF THE SILENT PLANET* CERTAINLY STOOD OUT FROM MOST OTHER HEAVY METAL/HARD ROCK RECORDINGS OF THE TIME, WHICH SEEMED TO FALL UNDER EITHER THE THRASH OR HAIR METAL CATEGORIES.

WALLY FARKAS I'm not knocking the records—because they're classics—but production-wise, you've got to remember too what was going on back then. The hair metal stuff with big drums, gated reverb on everything. I hear a lot of the over-the-top digital reverb sounds on the drums, and I can't recall, but I'm pretty sure I remember—it may have been the first album—when Jerry tracked his drums, he wasn't even allowed to play any of the cymbals. Crash cymbal, ride cymbal, hi-hat. So, he would have to track the songs by just playing the actual drums, and then go back and overdub the cymbals and hi-hats. I don't know if

I'm remembering that correctly, but I swore I heard something like that! I guess because Sam wanted everything really clean and isolated, but sometimes the ambience you get from doing all that together has got the vibe that glues things together. I'm not knocking the production, I'm just saying it was symptomatic of the production of what was going on at the time. But it never seemed like a representation of them.

JERRY GASKILL Hmmm … you know, I do remember that being somewhat the case. I can't remember if I played not using the cymbals, but I do remember we did put cymbals in later, as well. Whether I played during the recording or not, I'm not exactly sure. I do remember going back in and adding cymbals after the recording. It might have been the first record, because there are absolutely no cymbals on the first record. And that's always bothered me—I've never understood why we couldn't have cymbals on the record. But they are not there. Maybe that is why we tried to overdub them, and it just didn't work. I don't know. But they're not there—I know that.

DOUG PINNICK We went down to this place in Galveston, where they sold a lot of military jackets and band jackets. That was kind of our *look*. Sam Taylor talked us into it. He said, 'You guys have to look like *something*. Let's go here and check this out.' Because he knew I was into Jimi Hendrix, so he said, 'Well, let's find some band jackets, and see if we can make something *hybrid* out of it.'

TY TABOR We just liked the look of military formal jackets and stuff like that. At the time, it was kind of somewhat 'in'—we certainly weren't the only people wearing that kind of stuff. But the jackets I was wearing in a lot of those pictures were military jackets that belonged to my dad. And one of the white jackets that Jerry was most famous for wearing is also one of my dad's military jackets.

DOUG PINNICK I was watching MTV one time—back in in probably 1986, 1987—and Jean Beauvoir was on there, doing his solo thing, and he had a white Mohawk. He and I look a lot alike, and I saw that white Mohawk, and I went, 'That is exactly what I want.' I decided to shave the sides of my head, and I got some black hair dye and dyed my hair black. I didn't want it to be white, like his—I could have never gotten my hair that white.

JERRY GASKILL Touring behind the first album was really rough. The conditions weren't the best, and we opened for some bands that made things difficult. But there was some good stuff, too. Your first tour, no one knows who you are. You go out there, and you're traveling in a mini-Winny—it's not even a Winnebago. The situations aren't great, but you're on fire, you're young, you're excited, you have a record out, and you're believing in what you're doing. So, you just keep moving forward. We played with Hurricane, and that was a rough one. It was like, 'Who are they?' And we're opening for *them*.

DOUG PINNICK We didn't really get to see Hurricane that much or talk to them. It was more like road crews and stage setup, and not having enough room to set up in front of them. Just the typical opening for a band, and how a lot of crappy shit happens. The funny thing is, we always had a bad attitude about that tour looking back, but I have been hanging out with these guys—because I've been living out in LA—and they have no clue! [*Laughs*] All they talk about is, 'Man, we did our first tour together.' And we talk about it and laugh about it. I thought, *Well, I'm just not going to mention how we felt, and go along with it*. In fact, I've jammed with the guitar player a couple of times—we did a couple of songs at the Ultimate Jam up here in LA.

TY TABOR One of the first tours that meant anything that was great was with Blue Öyster Cult. They were super-nice to us. We got to see them play every night for a while, and it was very exciting. In the very early days like that, we were lucky to get a lot of cool shows. We also did some co-headline stuff that wasn't fun at all—with other up-and-coming bands that had big egos and made touring absolutely miserable. So, we quit doing that. We said, 'Look, either we headline or we play with somebody where it's obvious who the opening band is, so there is no crap about it. We know our place.'

All of a sudden, within the first couple of years of being out there touring, we were already getting offers to tour with Cheap Trick; we opened for Robert Plant up in DC—a lot of those types of things. And, at one point, people were pretty surprised we were getting the gigs we were getting. But we did get lucky with opening acts.

JERRY GASKILL We did some shows with Blue Öyster Cult, and that was really cool. And since then, I've played with this guy, Jon Rogers, who was in Blue Öyster Cult at that time. He always tells me how we were doing a soundcheck; he heard it, went back to the guys, and said, 'You've got to hear this band—these guys are great!' And we did some shows with Cheap Trick, too, which was pretty awesome. So there were good times as well as bad times.

DOUG PINNICK Cheap Trick is one of my favorite bands—I watched them every night and got to hang out with them a little bit. I talked to Tom Petersson at times. It was really cool. I remember that I was standing right at the side of the stage, and Tom was standing next to me with his twelve-string bass in his hand, and he was getting ready to go on. The lights had gone off, their intro music had started, and I said, 'Dude, I want to get one of these things.' And he goes, 'Check it out!' He took it off, put it on me, and had me play it. I'm left-handed, so it was upside down and backward, but the way it felt and sounded was so amazing. I said, 'I've got to get one of these,' and he said, 'Call Hamer and get one, dude!'

Right around that time, Hamer Guitars approached Ty and said, 'Can we make guitars for you?' And I remember walking up, saying, 'What about *me*?' And they said, 'Sure!' So, they made me some twelve-strings and some four-strings. That was my first bass guitar endorsement. Before that, I had been playing two Fender Precision basses—an old vintage one from 1963, and a newer model from about 1980.

TY TABOR There was a cover story about us in *Kerrang!*—they couldn't have talked bigger and better about us, and couldn't have hyped us any more. [On February 20, 1988, the magazine put the band on the cover alongside the headline 'Monarchy In The US: Houston Heavies King's X Usher In A New Age Of Metal.'] The next several years, *Kerrang!* kept being behind us and supported us. *Majorly.* We were very grateful to them. I remember being stunned that we go over to England, and we're on the cover of the magazine that really matters. We were coming from playing in front of three or four people in Houston, where nobody even knows who we are.

When we found out we were on the cover of *Kerrang!*, it was hard to put in words. And then the kind of article it was, it didn't put pressure on me, it made me feel like, *Let's go to Europe! Let's roll. They want us. Let's go.* We were gung-ho—we didn't have any doubts or pressure or worry. We could not wait to get over there. Because somebody over there got us. We were like, 'Let's play for these people—this is going to be incredible!' And it absolutely was. It was astonishing.

JERRY GASKILL We went over to England for the first time in our lives, and it was exciting to think, *Oh man ... we're in the land of the Beatles*. And we played the Marquee.

DOUG PINNICK I remember when we got there, I was nervous as hell, because it was our first show in England. And, up to that point, it seemed like every show that we did on our own, there were three or four people sometimes ... or forty or fifty. So we're playing London, and I'm thinking, *We're going to be playing the Marquee—the place where everybody played*. It was a big deal for me. And I thought, *We're going to go out there, and there is going to be nobody in the audience, and it's going to suck.*

I was so nervous about it—because *Kerrang!* had made such a big deal about us—that I couldn't eat all day. And I remember I was shaking, because I was so hungry, and we had about an hour-and-a-half before we had to play, and somebody asked me if I needed some food, and I said, 'Please, get me some food!' And they went and got me some fish and chips. English fish and chips. Oh my God ... *pure grease*. I took one bite and couldn't eat it. They brought it in rolled in newspaper—with grease dripping off of it. I didn't know that's what fish and chips were! So, I couldn't eat it.

I remember the tech came in and said, 'It's time to play,' and they usher us out onto the stage, and the place is dark and the stage is dark. And I'm thinking, *Nobody's going to be here*. I get my amp ready, turn around, Jerry clicks off, and we start 'King.' And I remember the lights come up, I look out ... and it's sold out and they're all jumping in time to the beat! I went, *Wow*, and it was on at that point. We had a great time. I think it was the first time we ever had a real, live King's X crowd that knew all the songs and knew everything about us, and was ready to go. It was very overwhelming for us.

TY TABOR We played four separate encores, to where we were doing cover tunes at the end, because we had nothing left to play—we actually played a song by The Isley Brothers ['Climbing Up The Ladder']! But it was absolute mass pandemonium when we got to England and played that show. We couldn't believe it, because we were coming from America, where we would play to three or four people in Houston, and nobody cared. Like, *What the heck is this music?* Because we moved down from Springfield, nobody knew who we were. We had no fans in Houston. *At all.* It was horrible. We went from that to sold-out mass pandemonium in England.

EDDIE TRUNK You've got to remember what was going on musically—it was the height of big choruses and melodic hard rock and pretty boys on MTV. And King's X were none of that. They weren't—with all due respect to those guys—pinups. They weren't pretty boys that were going to be plastered on people's walls. They didn't have a look that was going to get them loved by MTV and looking like Bon Jovi or whatever. It was none of that, obviously. But that's what was what made them unique. And their music was not commercial. It certainly had hooks and certainly had so many great qualities to it. But it wasn't that big gang chorus/commercial thing that so many of those bands were doing at that time. It was a mix of blues, R&B, hard rock, and the harmonies were what jumped out at everybody immediately. The fact that all three of them could sing lead vocals made for incredible harmonies. So, they had all these elements that really not a lot of bands had at the time. Ty was a great guitar player, they were all great at their instruments individually, and they were a unique package—something very different than what was happening in music at that time.

CHARLIE BENANTE I think King's X really knew their sound, and they really knew how to write songs and they knew how to really go for those hooks. I've always said that the song 'Goldilox' is the song that people just missed out on, because that to me was one of the greatest songs that I had ever heard. Still, to this day, I hold that song up pretty high.

MARSHA ZAZULA Atlantic wanted a radio-friendly song. And that's why 'King' and 'Shot Of Love' became the tracks we led with. They felt that would be what radio would take to, versus 'Goldilox.'

JERRY GASKILL Nobody ever heard 'Goldilox.' The only people that heard it were King's X fans. Just like most of our music, it was never given to the mainstream of people.

DOUG PINNICK I was told that Sam Taylor said that he wouldn't allow it to happen, because he didn't want our career to go too fast. He thought that 'Goldilox' would be such a big hit that we wouldn't be able to control it. So he took matters into his own hands, and said, 'Don't put it out yet.' Which was a big mistake. I think it was probably one of his biggest mistakes that he ever made.

JERRY GASKILL For some reason, we seemed not to do the most obvious things to propel us. I don't know why we didn't do that. I really don't know why. Maybe because we did not want to be known for a ballad? I don't know. But it was one of our songs—who cares? I don't know why—it just didn't happen. But it probably *should* have happened.

BILLY SHEEHAN 'Goldilox,' I actually did a bass version of that on a bass tour I did—just the bass playing the parts. There's a lot of classic songs that everybody plays—'The Shadow Of Your Smile' or 'Fly Me To The Moon.' Great classic songs that have lived on for decades. And I go, 'We currently have songs that are destined to be classics. And here's one of them: "Goldilox."' And it's a bass version of it. You can take any great song and do it in a number of different ways and it still works, and it's the proof that it's a great song. You can play a country version, a heavy metal version, this version, that version, on a ukulele or a piano, and you still go, 'Ah, that's the song. I recognize that song!'

As soon as you play 'Yesterday' by The Beatles—on any instrument, in any format—people will instantly recognize it. To me, 'Goldilox' is a song like that. No matter what, anywhere, you hear those opening notes, and, instantly, it's 'Goldilox.' So, playing it alone on bass—bass, drums and guitar, no vocals—it was an intense thing. And I wanted to do right by it, because I love Doug—a dear, dear friend of mine.

BUMBLEFOOT Every once in a while, I may bust a King's X song out and play it at a soundcheck—or even during a show. 'Goldilox' is definitely a favorite. And 'Sometimes.' The first album may still be my favorite, because if I'm just going to bust out something, it's almost always something off the first album. I might have to go with that one as a favorite.

JERRY GASKILL The album did what it did, and I'm thankful for what it did. I always wished everything was more popular—I wished every record sold hundreds of millions of copies … and then we'd probably not be talking right now, as I'd be off and nobody would even know where I was!

DOUG PINNICK I didn't think anybody would buy it, and I was shocked that people coined it as such a great record at the same time. It didn't sell a whole lot, and the record company sort of said, 'Well, that's what happens when you put your first record out. We'll put your second one out and keep pushing.' So we went back to the drawing board and started on the second one—hopefully to make a better one than the first one.

TY TABOR The first album didn't sell very well, at all. I mean, according to today's sales, it would be a successful album. It would be a *hugely* successful album compared to today's sales. But back then, in the first year in America, I think it only sold around thirty thousand or so, which was dismal back then. Thirty thousand now in America is a high-charting album. There was promotion, and there was definitely some money spent on videos and on trying to get them played on MTV. And they *were* played on MTV—but they didn't really catch on. Because the album wasn't selling, they didn't keep playing it.

The album just came out, did its thing, and then went away, but it was critically acclaimed—off the absolute charts. I mean, it got attention worldwide—*massively*. And we were on the covers of magazines in other parts of the world. And people were heralding us as the next big thing: 'This is going to be the band of the 90s, so get on board!' That kind of stuff. We were all over the press at this time. So even though it didn't sell, the critical acclaim was building up to the second album—majorly—the whole time. Something was really starting to happen.

07 GRETCHEN GOES TO NEBRASKA

THE STORY BEHIND THE BAND'S SOPHOMORE
STUDIO ALBUM, RELEASED ON JUNE 27, 1989.

TY TABOR We kind of knew that the next album was going to do a lot more, because the setup for it ahead of time was a lot more—with all that had happened. There was some pressure: 'We're going to have to really deliver. This has got to be the work of our lives. This has got to be another step.' So we spent quite a bit more time in pre-production for that album. We worked hard on every single utterance and note of every song—plus songs that didn't make it on the record. It was grueling work. And at the same time, it was more creative than the first album. We were trying all kinds of different creative things. They were time-consuming, just to try to get one sound.

I can remember us wasting so much time on putting water in a fire bell, and hitting it and tilting it just right, to try and get the right tone for this one spot in a song. And it was going to be something not really even noticed, but you would feel it—that kind of a thing. And there is so much of that on the album. We were taking a whole lot of time on little bitty things. One time, we had mics all over the room, and we were throwing cymbals across the studio into the wall, to get the right kind of crash. I remember hammering on mic stands and stuff, to get a 'clank' on one note of something—just the right place for the right note—and dampening it with sand bags. It was ridiculous. Every day was something. And cutting tape into pieces—this was before the digital world, so we were taking tape off machines and running it backward and doing all this stuff physically.

We spent four months in the studio doing that album. And for me, I felt like I lost one or two years of my life. But for Doug, in particular, that album took its toll—he was just done with ever working that hard on an album ever again. He was miserable with how long things took, and all the little things we were doing for the finesse of the album. It was hard for him, but I know that when we were done, we were extremely happy with it. And when we listened to it in context, all together, for the first time in the studio, we knew we had something again. We knew, *OK, this is even different than the first one, and it really is unique. And we like it. We did our job—hopefully others will like it, too.* And I also remember filming a lot of it—nobody's ever seen it. I carried a camera around, recording us while we were doing *Gretchen*—including Doug doing the vocals for 'Over My Head.' It's so old, I hope it could still play.

DOUG PINNICK It was real tedious, because Sam wanted us to make a record that you could put on a hundred years from now and hear something that you never heard before. He wanted it to be as classic as a Beatles record. And as timeless. He really, really meticulously worked at it—for us to get that. It was a lot of things that we had to do, that I got tired of. You know, making noises, throwing things on the floor, and recording them. He had us recording crazy stuff. And, after a while, I didn't see the vision anymore—I just wanted to go home. After three-and-a-half weeks of making this record, I was done. But we did it, and we stuck it out. As a result, it's what the record is—I love it *and* I hate it. I think because everyone says it's a great record, I won't disagree with them. But for me personally, I don't feel I was very good on that record. I felt like, when I sang the songs, I was singing to make a good record—not singing from my heart and what I felt. So, when I heard it back, I don't get it when other people do, because anything that I do is going to be real, anyway. But it's what's going on in my head when I'm doing it, and how it affects me when I listen to it when I hear it back.

JERRY GASKILL *Gretchen Goes To Nebraska* isn't a concept album by any means. What happened was, back in the early days—before anybody knew who we were, and we were traveling around in the Chuck Wagon—we were trying to come up with album titles, if we ever were to make a record. And Kevin Mourning just threw out that title.

KEVIN MOURNING I remember the reason why I came up with that was because we actually were driving from Lincoln, Nebraska, to, I believe, Denver, Colorado. The drive was so mundane through the plains. There was nothing to see, and we were like, 'Oh my gosh. This is the worst drive *ever*.' *Gretchen*

Goes To Nebraska just came to mind. I have a random sense of humor.

JERRY GASKILL It hit all three of us, and we were like, 'Oh man! Someday, if we make a record, we're going to call it *that*!' And then, I started writing this story, and I didn't have *Gretchen* in mind at all when I started writing the story. I just started writing. But as I went on with it, it became apparent to me that, hey, Gretchen is going to be our heroine—she's going to be the star of this story. I kind of incorporated Gretchen and Nebraska into it, and made Nebraska whatever Nebraska became. And that's how that came about. [Jerry's hard-to-decipher story was included inside the album.]

THE SONGS
'OUT OF THE SILENT PLANET'

JERRY GASKILL That's a song that I felt somewhat 'commissioned'—in a sense—to write the lyrics. Because Ty wrote the song and had no lyrics, he said, 'Hey, just come up with *something*.' He gave me an idea of what he was thinking, and the vision he had in his head, then I came up with the lyrics.

'OVER MY HEAD'

JERRY GASKILL That's a song that Doug wrote, and he always tells a story of that being a song that he didn't want to play for us. He never wanted us to hear it—he thought it was a throwaway tune that nobody would care about. And finally, he did, and we said, 'It's a great tune, Doug. We've got to record that!' So we did record it. I also remember standing in the vocal room all together, and doing that breakdown part, where there is just vocals and handclaps, and we were adlibbing some parts—whatever came into our mind.

TY TABOR It wasn't a full song—what Doug had was just the first riff. That was one of the things he played for us that Jerry and I said, 'We will make that into a song.' So we took that idea and worked it into a song—as a band.

DOUG PINNICK I wrote that a long, long time ago—back in '82 or '83. I wrote it with a little drum machine—it was a Mattel drum machine. It had four pads on it, and it had a snare, a kick, and a hi-hat, and you had to hit all of them to stay in beat … which I didn't. Then I had a two-track cassette recorder, and I borrowed another two-track cassette recorder from a friend, and basically played it on two tracks, then played it in the room with the other two-track next to it—recording it as I played the other parts. It was the worst recording you've ever heard! All the parts were there—with the church ending.

When we were talking about making *Gretchen*, we got all our demos together and started listening to music. And when we got to 'Over My Head,' I stopped it and moved it forward, and said, 'It's just a crappy song. We don't need to listen to it.' And Sam and Ty said, 'No, no, no. We need to listen to it.' And when they listened to it, Ty said to me, 'Promise me you'll play me *everything* that you write.' [*Laughs*]

It's like a negro spiritual. It was an old thing—'*Over my head, I hear music in the air / There must be a God somewhere.*' It's an old gospel thing that I grew up listening to all my life. And when I wrote the song, all I could hear was, '*Over my head, I hear music in the air.*' And I went, '*Oh, Lord, music over my head.*' But I kind of figured, well, I'm not going to say, 'There must be a God somewhere.' Also, I remember that Lenny Kravitz had written 'Let Love Rule,' and when he got to the chorus, the chorus went down instead of up. Usually, a chorus is supposed to lift the song. But 'Let Love Rule' brought it down—it was the opposite effect. And I thought it was genius. So, I figured I would try it on 'Over My Head,' and that's why I wasn't screaming or yelling on the chorus. It was inspired by those two things.

I think I was also somehow trying to portray a church service in that song. Because one of my biggest influences growing up in a gospel church was listening to these people sing every day, and the preacher preach, and all the emotion that went on. It had nothing to do with religion to me—it was this pure entertainment, and learning from these great singers, how they could get up and sing and command a church, and get people to jump up and down and scream, yell, and cry. I'm going, *Wow!* It was something that fascinated me, and as a result of that, I've actually been able to do it. So, I'm happy about it.

My great grandmother raised me, and late at night, I would hear some noises—it would sound like somebody was talking in her bedroom in the middle of the night. *A lot.* I would wake up and hear it, so I figured she was praying. I don't know what was going on—she could have been having a nightmare, for all I know. But my interpretation was she was praying. So that's why I wrote the lyrics, '*Grandma used to sing every night when she was praying.*' It was kind of a fictional story, taken from a few incidences, I guess.

'SUMMERLAND'

TY TABOR I wrote that one. My friend Marty sang it on the original demo. It's a song about Jackson, Mississippi, and it was written during that time when I had my friends from Mississippi living with me, and we were coming up with our own ideas. 'Summerland' was one of those freeform songs, that didn't do all the standards of a verse/chorus/verse/chorus/bridge/chorus/out kind of thing. We sort of rearranged it to be a little bit closer to that kind of a thing from its original idea.

'EVERYBODY KNOWS A LITTLE BIT OF SOMETHING'

DOUG PINNICK I always loved the slap/pluck technique on bass, so I was trying my stab at it—funk metal with harmonies. I just listen to everybody tell me this and that, and everybody contradicts each other. And, at the end of the day, I thought, everybody knows a little bit of *something*—they just don't know everything. None of us do. So, that's kind of what it was about. But it related to my faith again, too, because I was questioning what I had grown up to believe.

'THE DIFFERENCE (IN THE GARDEN OF ST. ANNE'S-ON-THE-HILL)'

TY TABOR That was another one I wrote. It was inspired by a particular chapter in a book called *That Hideous Strength* by C.S. Lewis. It's a moment in a story where a person has an epiphany, and suddenly sees things differently, and it happens instantly—without warning and without understanding. That is what the song is about—whenever we experience that kind of a thing.

'I'LL NEVER BE THE SAME'

DOUG PINNICK I wrote the lyrics. Ty and I can't remember who wrote the song. I remember we talked about that one day—I thought I wrote it, but there's a part in it that I know that I didn't come up with, so he had to do that. I think it was a jam or something, and Ty had some guitar parts, and we jammed it out.

'MISSION'

TY TABOR It's a Doug song. I came up with the riffs and we all—mainly Doug—sat around coming up with lyrics. And there is a preacher that you can barely hear in the middle section of the song, where there is a voice in the background—it's a real preacher from a real service that I stole and put in there. Because what he was saying was so ridiculous that it fit the song. The song is basically saying, just because someone claims to be a preacher or a priest or a teacher or a whatever, it doesn't mean that they know anything. And it's asking the question, 'What's the mission of the preacher man?'

And it sort of points to all of them—the ones who do it from a good heart and help people, and the vast sea of ignorant people who do it for whatever reason. It's a song about that, because it was just coming out of that time period of turning my back on everything organized Christian at the moment—because of that visit to where Jim and Tammy Bakker lived. I felt very negatively, coming out of that. We knew a lot of Christians were starting to think we were a Christian band, and this was one of those songs that basically throws a wrench in it, and shows: 'No. We're *questioners* of all that. And want you to question it, too.'

DOUG PINNICK We wrote that sort of together. I remember Ty had to go to the doctor or do something, and Sam had to take him, so they were going to be late to rehearsal. So, me and Jerry were at rehearsal, hanging out, and I said, 'Hey, let's start jamming on something.' We started coming up with the verse I think it was—we came up with a couple parts for that song, and then Ty showed up. He picked his guitar up and he came in and put his part on there, and he helped rearrange it a little bit. And, by the time we got done with it, we had a song. Jerry wrote the verses and I wrote the chorus.

JERRY GASKILL I remember saying to Doug that I had this idea for a song. I sang it to him, he figured it out on the bass, and I think he came up with some other parts. And then, when Ty and Sam came back, we played it for them, and Ty said, 'It kinda sounds like Three Dog Night.' So we completely changed it, and it became the song that it is today. I wrote the lyrics to the verses, and I believe Doug wrote the lyrics to the chorus.

'FALL ON ME'

DOUG PINNICK I remember I was thinking about Robin Trower. I wrote the riffs in my head, then went to the music store and had a guy program the drum machine for the song. I hummed the riffs and he made up a crappy drumbeat for it to separate the parts. It was enough for King's X to build a song out of it. It was, again, singing about love, and feeling my childhood. I look around the world and see all the lonely and sad people, and how people don't care about each other. That song was about that—'*Love fall on me.*'

'PLEIADES'

TY TABOR I was thinking about how there is so much out there that it makes no sense to me, that we are the only thing in the universe. So, the song, where it gets 'Pleiades' from, believe it or not, is from a Bible verse, that says, '*Who can restrain Pleiades / Or know the laws of Heavenly's.*' It's basically saying, 'Who among you can claim to know anything that is so vast?' I was contemplating those kinds of things—contemplating the first person who said the world was round, who got burned at the stake for it. Contemplating ignorance, and how much we don't know while looking up at the stars.

'DON'T BELIEVE IT (IT'S EASIER SAID THAN DONE)'

TY TABOR 'Don't Believe It,' I believe, was a Doug song, originally. And then we all collaborated on making it into a song—all the vocal parts and all the harmonies. We worked together on that one pretty hard—coming up with vocal lines and harmonies. That one was much more difficult to play and do than it sounds—which is why we don't do it live. We have actually done it live, but it was in the early days—before everyone had cellphones and could record stuff to capture it. But it was so difficult that it was dropped pretty early. Another one of those hopeful songs of, *Don't be beat down by everything that is coming at you, because it is just a lie, anyway.*

'SEND A MESSAGE'

DOUG PINNICK That was another four-track demo, and we modified the original chorus, and wrote the lead break together. I remember it was the last demo I wrote before Sam joined us. And I vividly remember us playing it for him, because I had gotten stoned for the first time the night before, and I had not smoked weed in almost ten years. It's me questioning my faith, questioning God, and questioning if there is so much horrible stuff going on, send a message to whoever can bring us some kind of peace. In my mind, it was saying, 'Send a message to Jesus and to God.'

Everything I wrote was not pro-Christian—it was me searching, and I was kind of being sacrilegious. Like, *Send a message to him, and tell him to fix this shit. Two thousand years! Give me a break! All the pain and suffering I've seen in this world, and it's only a fraction of what's really actually happening, and you can't stop this?* That's what I was saying. *You're up there and everybody tells me that you love me and you're coming back and you're going to save the world? Well ... what the fuck?*

That was my idea about it. That's why I said, '*I am who I am and I don't doubt it / You are who you are is what I know.*'

'THE BURNING DOWN'

TY TABOR That one was written at a time when I was tired of even caring about being in a relationship. I was just kind of singing and writing, 'If you're out there, we'll meet one day,' or whatever the sentiment was—it was a song to the fictitious, 'whoever you are going to be' person.

GRETCHEN GOES TO NEBRASKA PEAKED AT #123 ON THE *BILLBOARD* 200 AND BROUGHT THE BAND SOME MAJOR KUDOS FROM BOTH THE MUSIC PRESS AND FELLOW ROCKERS.

CHARLIE BENANTE I was waiting to hear something at this point, and I got an advance of *Gretchen*. I remember I was flying to Europe, I believe. And, from start to finish, that record was flawless. The tone of the record completely grabbed me. Ty's guitar tone—to this day—is one of my favorite guitar tones on a record. And his style of playing, I think that those guys completely got it, and *Gretchen* was like, *Wow*. I was completely blown away by it. I loved that record. To this day, I can't listen to it in pieces—I have to listen to the whole thing. But songs like 'The Difference,' 'Mission,' 'Fall On Me' … all these songs were amazing. 'Summerland.' It was like, 'These guys made a record of songs that have such depth and such a variety, plus they all sing. This is something that I think people should really listen to.'

JOHN MYUNG [Dream Theater, Platypus, Jelly Jam bassist] I remember the buzz was that King's X was going to be the next biggest band. It was a tremendous amount of respect, and everybody in the industry was talking about them. And, even while Dream Theater was discussing our first record deal, at the time, the people we were talking with were talking about them. They had a video on MTV, and I remember getting an advance cassette of *Gretchen Goes To Nebraska* and being floored—completely floored. Like, *This is the best album ever*. It really resonated with me. They just have a really great way of blending their influences and making them present—making it be King's X music. Very Beatles-influenced.

KIP WINGER It wasn't like a sophomore jinx—the second record was *incredible*. The talent in the band was so astounding, and the sound was so original. It had some elements of so many other cool records put together in a very unique way. We were all kind of like, 'Game over. This is going to be massive.'

DOUG PINNICK The 'Over My Head' video was a fun time. We did it at Rockefellers—a really cool club with a balcony. And it's really small, too. We invited people to come in for free, just to be a part of it. We filled this little club up, and we videoed the song in this cool rock club. It's a cool-looking video. And then Sam did a couple of stage props, and we did some acting. It seemed like MTV loved it, too, so I have no problem with that video at all.

JERRY GASKILL My middle son, Joey, who is a very talented drummer/singer/songwriter himself—he makes some of my favorite music, actually, and I don't think it's because he's my son, it's because it's really great music—was in that video. He's the little boy dancing with the black grandmother. That's my son.

I remember him being really excited about doing it—he was, like, five years old. He got all excited, and then when it came time for him to do it … he froze. [*Laughs*] But finally, he did it, and I think it's really cool.

DOUG PINNICK I don't remember much about the 'Summerland' video, but I did like it. But I thought I looked real gay in it—made me look all made up to look cute, which I am not. I think the blue screen stuff looks cheap—it just could have been a better concept, I think. I remember Sam had us walk into a blue screen, and he told us what would happen at the end of the video [when the band and the *Gretchen* album cover become one]. Because most of the stuff was done with blue screen, we didn't know what Sam was going to do. We just kind of did what he told us.

JERRY GASKILL I remember thinking that it wasn't my favorite look—the way I looked in that video. The video is really cool, but it wasn't my favorite look for me. [*Laughs*] I'm sure if I saw it now, I'd go, 'Oh, it's not as bad as I thought.' But we always judge ourselves harsher than anybody else, I think.

JON ZAZULA 'Over My Head,' MTV really loved it. We did get one of the videos to #2 in the nation on MTV. It could have been 'Over My Head'—I'm not sure.

MARSHA ZAZULA I know it was that one, because my youngest daughter was about two years old, and she ran down singing, '*Music, music, I hear music / Over my head.*' Because MTV was always on, it would come on and she would be dancing to it.

EDDIE TRUNK The closest we ever came to a hit was 'Over My Head.' That got some good video airplay, people really liked that song—it was a big chorus that popped up on that *Dial MTV* countdown show. We started to get some traction there, and we started to get a little radio play. It was a great record for the record they had to make at that time—for a follow-up, I thought it was a great step forward. But it didn't do what people think it did. That's the thing about King's X that I think to this day amazes people when I bring this up to them—the band never had a gold record.

RICHARD CHRISTY [Death, Iced Earth, Charred Walls Of The Damned drummer;
Howard Stern Show writer] I first heard King's X when I saw 'Over My Head'
on *Headbangers Ball*. It must have been 1989, and my first impression was
that I loved them. I loved that the vocals were melodic and amazing. The thing
that immediately made me a huge King's X fan is that bass sound. Doug's bass
sound is maybe the best bass sound *ever*. It always kind of stuck out. And I love
trios, too—I'm a big Rush fan. The mix of Doug's bass and vocals was perfect,
and I was a fan of the other guys, as well.

Something else that stuck out for me was the vocal harmonies—they had
such beautiful harmonies. And I loved too that the drummer, Jerry, was a singer.
Because I am a drummer, and I thought, *Apart from the band Triumph, you don't*
see too many drummers singing that much. I loved that. And then, later on, when
I read an interview with them, I found out that they had lived in Springfield,
Missouri, which, when I was growing up in Kansas, was only three hours away.
So, I was blown away that this amazing band that I heard on *Headbangers*
Ball—and bought their album—lived fairly close to us, where I grew up.

MICK MARS [Mötley Crüe guitarist] I thought they were an amazing band. I
heard them and said, 'This stuff is cool.' They had soul, they had feeling. All the
stuff that was lacking in this music, they had. Heaviness, soulfulness, phrasing
with their music—all that stuff—they had it all. It was amazing.

ALAIN JOHANNES [Eleven singer, guitarist] I remember it must have been
something off of *Gretchen*—whatever one of their earliest MTV videos was.
Doug had this crazy hair. I remember Natasha [Shneider, Johannes's longtime
musical partner] and I being super-stoked. I remember 'Over My Head' on
Headbangers Ball, too. Their voices were incredible—Doug has one of those
incredible voices. And, also, the chemistry of the three of them, the power of the
groove, and the power-trio thing—which obviously, in Eleven, I always loved,
even though Natasha did it with the keys instead of bass.

I remember we were really blown away. We became fans, buying the
records. And I forgot how it came about, but, suddenly, I interviewed Doug
for one of the magazines. We spoke on the phone, and we immediately had a
long conversation. It turns out that he and the other two dudes were there in
'85, when What Is This? [a band comprised of Alain plus Hillel Slovak and

Jack Irons, both of whom would also play in the Red Hot Chili Peppers] played Houston. There were, like, four people in the audience, and I think three of them were the cats in King's X! So, we had a good laugh about that. And, after that, we got to hang out here and there.

JEFF AMENT [Mother Love Bone, Temple Of The Dog, Pearl Jam, Tres Mts. bassist] I think I first heard King's X on the *Gretchen* record. I read a review of it somewhere and went and picked it up. 'Summerland' is on that record—that was the song that really made me a fan. And that still is probably *the* record—I think it's that thing when you first fall in love with something, it sort of ends up being your favorite, no matter what, although they made great records after that—*Faith Hope Love*, the self-titled one, *Dogman*.

The obvious thing to me was the blending of harmonies and heaviness. They were probably the first band for me that combined those elements. Especially in a less punk rock way and more of a prog-y sort of way. Because, at that time, I was really into trying to play lots of notes and trying to be involved with writing songs that had more clever arrangements. And they sort of hit all those spots to me. You could say that Nirvana had those same things—they had that Beatles element to their music, and then they also had a Metallica element to their music. I think King's X had those same things, but they were completely different.

DEVIN TOWNSEND [The Devin Townsend Band, Strapping Young Lad, Steve Vai singer, guitarist] The first I knew of King's X was that ad that came out in all those magazines. [The ad contained quotes from such musicians and admirers as Vernon Reid, Charlie Benante, and Kip Winger, as well as publications like *Kerrang!*, which said, 'In five years there won't be venues big enough to hold them,' and another from *Metal Hammer*, which stated, 'At times they write melodies even The Beatles would be proud of. Perfection!'] I thought, *Well shit—I'd better get on board!* At that time, I had never heard of them. I had thought they were called 'King's Cross.' It was that iconic ad, and I think it really did a lot for them—where it had a picture of the *Gretchen* album cover, and then all the quotes from musicians that I did listen to at the time, basically saying they were the best of the best of the best, and the fact that they were unknown was a crime, and this, that, and the other thing.

So, my friends and I—I was probably about seventeen or so—kept an eye out for the album. But it wasn't available commercially in the same ways that a lot of the other records were. And I actually ended up going down to the States—as we did to find records, at the time—and I came across the *Gretchen* album. I bought it based on that ad alone. And I remember when I put it on, my first thought was it was much different than I was expecting. It was not immediate. It's not that I disliked it at all, but it just wasn't something that my ears were familiar with. So I kept listening to it—because at the time, an investment of a cassette was a big deal.

And then there was one night in particular—maybe I had the tape for three or four days, maybe five days—and I was up late, and I got to the end of the record, and then 'The Burning Down' came on ... and it totally was a paradigm shift. I don't even know what it was about the song or the experience, but from there, the next morning, I woke up and I remember feeling like I wasn't the same person the next day. And *Gretchen* ended up becoming an album that, when I got my first car, I listened to that record *incessantly*—that and *Nothing's Shocking* by Jane's Addiction. Those were the two albums that I played more than anything. And everything about the sound and Doug's voice and the bass and the harmonies and everything, it was this really intimate sort of quirky but very profound album for me.

It's interesting, too, because I was always into the sound of Ty's voice, because it also reminds me of the other 'secondary singers' in the bands that I used to love—like when Trevor Rabin sang in Yes, or when David Gilmour sang in Pink Floyd. All three of those guys have a really mellower and reedier sort of quality to their voice that I really like. In fact, it's funny that as we're talking about this, I never sort of connected the dots that that was Ty singing. But it wasn't about who sang. It was the *intention* behind that song. It seemed to resonate with that era of my life—when I was moving out of my parents' home, girlfriends, and all this sort of stuff. There was just something about that song that seemed so resigned that totally ticked the boxes for me.

08 HITTING THE ROAD, HARD–PART 1

WITH NEITHER RADIO NOR MTV GOING GAGA OVER
KING'S X, THE BAND SPREAD THE WORD THE OLD
FASHIONED WAY–BY NONSTOP TOURING.

CHARLIE BENANTE I remember talking to Jonny and Marsha, and saying, 'We need to have these guys come on tour with us.' And we did.

TY TABOR When we were leaving to get on the plane to go back to England, to meet up with Anthrax, I remember our manager looking at us and saying, 'All right, guys … *it all starts now.* Hold on to your pants.' And he was absolutely right. That was the beginning of at least the amount of whirlwind that we were to experience in the next two to three years as King's X.

CHARLIE BENANTE Eighty-nine was when we took them on tour in Europe. And every night, I would sit behind Jerry and watch, and sometimes play cowbell. I was in awe of three guys creating such beautiful music.

TY TABOR By the time we went back to Europe with Anthrax, we were playing in front of huge crowds that are jumping up and down in unison to the songs and singing—like they're there to see us, too. It was huge. Mind-boggling. Beyond words for how it was compared to the world we were coming from.

WALLY FARKAS The first time I saw them, *Gretchen* had just come out. It was in Houston, at a now-gone rock club called Backstage. Masters Of Reality were opening up for them, supporting their first album, which was out on Def American. King's X came out, and it was mind-blowing, because they sounded even better than the first two records. There was so much power and fullness, and heft. It was astonishing that all this was coming from three guys live—with no tapes secretly piping in the background vocals. It was all right there. I don't know how else to describe it … it was *electrifying*. The place was packed. The crowd was way into it. But I had never seen anything like that. I didn't get to see The Beatles and Zeppelin and Hendrix. And it was like, all wrapped up in one. I might have been twenty years old at the time, but still, to this day, I haven't seen many concerts on that level.

JERRY GASKILL I felt as though everywhere we were going, crowds were getting better. People were recognizing us—we were being shown on MTV on a regular basis. It did feel like something was happening with that record.

TY TABOR And then we did a bunch of headlining tours—going to Canada and doing some headlining. And the headlining gigs were getting better for us. Around this time, we were selling out the Ritz in New York City, and Studio One in New Jersey. Selling out these big two-to-three-to-four-thousand-seat places.

At that time, when *Gretchen* came out and 'Over My Head' started getting some MTV play, it was taking off for us. And that album was selling a bit more than the first one—even though it wasn't selling as much as everyone was hoping for. Definitely, things were taking off. Everything was ramping up to bigger and better stuff. We also did a tour that was us, Blue Murder, and Billy Squier for most of the tour. And we hung out with Blue Murder for most of the time. It was awesome. That's when we got to know Carmine Appice really well. That was a really fun tour, and Billy was super-cool to us, too. That was also at the beginning, when *Gretchen* was taking off—so that was good exposure for us.

JERRY GASKILL We did the Billy Squier thing, which was very interesting. I love Billy Squier. I've seen him many years later, and he's said that he asked for us to be on that tour himself. I remember one time, walking past his dressing room, and he was just standing there, and he says, 'Hey! I'd really like to write some songs with you guys.' And I was like, 'Oh, OK! That would be nice.' Of course, it never happened.

DOUG PINNICK That was a good tour. It was great exposure for us—we only had like a half-hour slot. We went on, and it was, *wham, bam, thank you ma'am*. Hopefully, it gave us some more clout. But we thought it was fun. Opening for a full crowd of people when we had just begun was really exciting. Because we knew these people hardly knew who we were, and we had the opportunity to be in front of them and give them everything we had. It was a lot of fun. We loved hanging out with the guys in Blue Murder—Carmine Appice was one of my favorite drummers. Jerry and I loved Cactus, so we were like little kids around this rock star. We've become friends now, and it's all cool, but we were starstruck when we first met him.

JERRY GASKILL We did one show with Winger, at the Santa Monica Civic Center. We played with Winger and Mr. Big. I remember going into the catering room, and as I was going in, Kip Winger was going out. And he stopped in his tracks, looked at me, and goes, 'You're a God!' [*Laughs*]

I mentioned it to him many years later—we were at Michael Wagener's studio, having some picnic thing outside. I said, 'You know, the first time I ever met you, you said to me, You're a God!' And he said, 'Well … *you are*!' [*Laughs*]

KIP WINGER I pulled them into that show. I specifically requested them. I used to go out of my way to mention them in interviews—I felt that they weren't getting anywhere near the attention they should be getting. I was the one that made the call to get them on that show. I would have liked to have had them on a lot more shows. Although I felt kind of like, *You guys should be headlining*.

BILLY SHEEHAN Santa Monica Civic Center—famous for Van Halen playing there. I have photos of all the bands playing there together. Winger were huge King's X fans, too—who wasn't? *Everybody* loved that band.

DOUG PINNICK I remember playing that show, and everybody seemed to be there—from Zakk Wylde to Blackie Lawless. I mean, it was like, *crazy*. And there was a party afterward. But after we were done playing, we walked in this big dressing room, where all the bands were hanging out. And all the guys in Mr. Big started playing 'Goldilox.' They played the whole song, note for note—harmonies and everything! We didn't know what to do. It was so cool. But that's when I met Kip Winger and all those guys—we've been friends ever since.

JERRY GASKILL I know that I met [Kiss drummer] Eric Carr backstage at that show. I remember having a conversation with him about cancer, because he had cancer around that time—which eventually took his life. [Carr died on November 24, 1991, at the age of forty-one.]

MIKE PORTNOY The first time I saw them live was on the *Gretchen* tour, which was around '89. I saw them at Toad's Place in New Haven, Connecticut. It was myself and my friend Chuck Lenihan, who was in the band the Crumbsuckers at the time. And we were both huge fans of the *Gretchen* album. I don't remember why we went to Connecticut, as opposed to a New York show, but somewhere I even have a picture of me and Chuck with Doug, Ty, and Jerry. I was blown away that they could pull off those vocals live. And I loved the contrast of Doug's soulful, Paul McCartney vocals to Ty's more psychedelic, John Lennon vocals. They were an amazing live band—as well as a studio band.

JOHN MYUNG The first time I saw them live was probably at a club out on Long Island called Sundance. They were a band with a great presence—they came out, they sounded awesome. This was right around the time that Dream Theater's first album [*When Dream And Day Unite*, 1989] was happening as well. I remember them being a really great live act, and sounding great. I remember Doug knowing about Dream Theater's first album, and talking to Doug about it after the show.

BUMBLEFOOT The first time I saw them was in Brooklyn, at the famous club L'Amour. I was stunned at how incredible their harmonies sounded, and how tight they were. I've seen them plenty after that, as well, over the years. But at that L'Amour show, from beginning to end, I was mesmerized. They were flawless. And when I say flawless, I don't mean they were technically perfect— which they were—but I mean that they left you feeling exactly the way you hoped you would feel … but even more. They were inspirational. You'd hear them, and you'd feel like you were on ecstasy! It feels like you're in love with being alive for that moment that they're making music.

SHANNON LARKIN The first time I saw them was on the *Gretchen* tour in '89. I saw them at the Bayou, in Washington, D.C.—which was around where I grew up. I waited in line after the show, and they came out and did a meet-and-greet with the fans. I waited in line, walked up, and I was around twenty-one, but I felt like I was thirteen, meeting Kiss or something! I was so blown away by Doug's presence, and my drumming was so influenced by Jerry Gaskill—to the point that after I saw that show, I reconfigured my whole drum kit, and took away my double bass drums.

BRIAN SLAGEL I missed them on the first tour, but when they came out touring for the second album, that's when I saw them. And that pushed them even further over the top for me—just what an unbelievable live band they are. I think they opened for somebody. Then, shortly after that, they did a headline tour, and I saw them at a club in Anaheim, California. I can't remember the name of the club, because it does not exist anymore. It was kind of a small club, but it was completely packed. By that point, they had a pretty good buzz going on. *They completely destroyed me.*

JEFF AMENT They played Seattle in 1989. There were two or three shows in a row—I remember at the Central, seeing Flaming Lips, and then I saw Faith No More, and then I saw King's X. All within a month or something … at least that's my memory of it. And I remember I didn't have a car then, so I rode my bike down, and I brought a Mother Love Bone shirt. I saw Doug, gave him a shirt, and I think he cut the sleeves off of it and wore it at the show! Which was pretty exciting stuff for me—somebody that you met for two minutes and had a little exchange with. I'm pretty sure at least one or two of the guys from Soundgarden were there, and I know some of the Alice in Chains guys were at that show. Our manager, Kelly Curtis, shared a management office with Susan Silver [who managed both Alice in Chains and Soundgarden at the time], which was two doors down from the Central. The OK Hotel was right around the corner. It was kind of a little scene in that area—Pioneer Square.

I was a big Cheap Trick fan and I was a big fan of twelve-string bass. I think we made *Apple* right around the same time they played at the Central. And I had rented a twelve-string bass that I had played on 'Stardog Champion,' and I think I played it on the 'Holy Roller' breakdown. And I had been in contact with a guy at Hamer about building me a twelve-string bass. And then to see King's X—I don't think I knew that he was playing twelve-string on those records—and to see the full power of a twelve-string bass live. At that point, I was like, 'OK, that is going to be a part of my future arsenal,' because it was such a unique sound.

The Melvins and Soundgarden—that was the first time that we had seen people tuning down. So, Green River, there are songs that are drop-D, and in Mother Love Bone there are certainly plenty of songs that are in drop-D. I think that came more from the Melvins and Soundgarden. I mean, King's X were tuning down to C-sharp and C, I think, at that point. And we were drop-D, and I think Alice tuned down further than that, too. But there was definitely something about the Alice sound that sort of changed around that time. They were sort of coming from a little different scene, and when they moved to Seattle, I think they probably absorbed some of the elements of things that were going on in Seattle at the time. I'm not sure [if Andy Wood ever heard them]. He for sure heard about King's X through me—at the very least—because I was a huge fan at that point.

BUMBLEFOOT I'm trying to think of who else at the time—in the late 80s—that was really doing drop-D. I mean, most bands, they were either just in E-flat—like a lot of the hair bands … or Kiss or Van Halen. But as far as them taking it down to D, I think they may have been the only one.

MIKE PORTNOY I still think that *Gretchen Goes To Nebraska* stands as their masterpiece. *Out Of The Silent Planet* was kind of laying down the groundwork of what the band was about. But *Gretchen* was the album where they really nailed it and knocked it out of the park. It was the songs, honestly. Every song from 'Summerland' and 'Over My Head' to 'Everybody Knows A Little Bit Of Something'—all those tunes were great sing-along songs. And the production was great. If I'm being honest, though, my favorite album is probably *Faith Hope Love*. But *Gretchen* was the undeniable fan favorite, and the one that is still the quintessential King's X album.

RAY LUZIER The typical thing to say is *Gretchen* [is the best King's X album]. And there are a lot of great songs on there, and they still hold true today.

JEFF AMENT Those first two records, it's almost like hit after hit. That whole *Gretchen* record—'Pleiades' and all those songs—are *so* great. And 'I'll Never Be The Same.' The last time I saw them four or five years ago, the whole crowd sang 'Over My Head,' too.

KIP WINGER For me, [the first two King's X albums] were like two concept albums. I never focused on a track. I wouldn't actually want to pick out one song, because for me, the band was a band that was still an album band. The point of the band was, you don't just play one song—you have to listen to the whole record to immerse yourself in the experience of King's X. And the other part of this equation is that live, they are *fucking amazing*. So here comes this band that completely turns the heads of all the musician community—I can't speak from a non-musician point of view. But when you went to see them live, they were every bit as riveting. That's rare, man. Usually, nobody can pull this shit off live.

DEVIN TOWNSEND I know that they went through some serious problems with their producer, which is really unfortunate. And it's unfortunate more so because a lot of it was the production that was so unique. I ended up going back and getting *Out Of The Silent Planet*, as well, and it was those two records. I mean, I also had *Faith Hope Love* and *Dogman* and a bunch of things, but it was *Out Of The Silent Planet* and *Gretchen* that were the two albums for me. *Gretchen* specifically. And a lot of it was the production, because it was so different. It was so idiosyncratic. And the guitar sounds were really unique, and the bass was really big, and Doug has a really expressive voice—in ways that a lot of other bands didn't sound like that. The whole package almost underlined what I look for in music—and that is something that fits in while being completely different. They were almost the archetype of that.

REX BROWN They would play once a month in Houston, so we saw them a good ten times. And this was when Pantera was really starting to find our niche of what we wanted to do with Philip [Anselmo] in the band. He had been in the band for about a year when we met Doug, so we were gigging a lot—playing the scene in Texas. We got passed by twenty-eight labels—the whole story. But we started showcasing. This is around the time everything with the hair metal shit went away. After King's X, it was Soundgarden next, you know? And then [Nirvana's] *Bleach*, and then the Red Hot Chili Peppers. We put it all on a mix tape. And King's X was definitely on that mix tape that we'd drive to gigs three or four hours in a car. Texas is big—five hours, sometimes. So, we'd have tape upon tape—depending on what our mood was for the day.

And then, when *Gretchen* hit … it takes me back to these memories of great, great times. We were still young and even though we had been around the clubs for five years, it was still that we were out there on a national level, anyway. When all that was being heard, you had Jane's Addiction. So, the whole landscape was changing. The one thing about King's X was the chemistry and the songs. That band had been together for quite a while before. Doug was forty when I met him—you knew that he made the rounds.

DEVIN TOWNSEND I was *so* into the band, I remember when we were first looking for management for my little local band in Vancouver, I wrote up my contract—naïvely—that I gave to these people that were interested in managing me, and one of my stipulations was that if King's X came to town, we had to get the gig! And I remember them very politely telling me that that was out of their hands.

MARSHA ZAZULA All through the relationship, we were always—as a label—really behind the guys. We really believed it. Even though it wasn't really shooting fireworks the way other people would have wanted. But you know what kind of a band it was? *Musicians* loved the band. They were intrigued with the fact that they did all that down-tuning, and that they had these messages—even though they weren't a Christian band, they wrote from their hearts. From their souls. And more than a fan-base band, they were a musician's band. And I think to this day, any number of musicians out there will tell you they looked up to them for their innovativeness.

JON ZAZULA They're all very interesting people. There are three brilliant people in that group. I had wonderful times with them. They were like family to me. I don't know what Marsha or I was like to them, but they were like family to us, and to everybody at Megaforce.

DOUG PINNICK Again, *Gretchen* was critically acclaimed. *CD Magazine* named it the #1 Sounding Record, because *CD Magazine* was all about sonics and how things sounded. So, they gave us the #1 slot for best-sounding record of that year, which blew my mind. And there were all these great things said about it. But at the end of the day, it didn't sell much, either. So, at that point, I'm going, *OK. We've got two records out, and everybody is telling me all this stuff that's going to happen and what we're going to be ... but it seems like it's not.*

09 FAITH HOPE LOVE

THE STORY BEHIND THE BAND'S THIRD STUDIO
ALBUM—AND THEIR LAST FOR MEGAFORCE—
RELEASED ON OCTOBER 23, 1990.

TY TABOR We only saw things as getting bigger during all that time. And things *were* getting bigger—everything we believed was starting to happen. It was easy to believe, and we just went with it. We were young—I was in my twenties back then, and it was all exciting and what I expected my life to be from early on. I had no doubts as a child what I was going to do, and I was going to do it. And I think we all had that stubborn ignorant belief or whatever—because it doesn't work out for everybody. I looked at *Faith Hope Love* as another step upward, and I couldn't wait to see what we came up with musically. It was all exciting.

JERRY GASKILL *Gretchen* was good, and people were liking that. I remember thinking, *Now, we're going to make another record, and it's not going to be another Gretchen record, because there's still so much more left in us to do. We have other directions to go.* I even had a song on that record that I wrote, 'Six Broken Soldiers,' which is very different than most other things King's X does. All of my stuff is different than what King's X usually does. I remember telling people, 'There are many other things left for us to do.' I kind of went into that record thinking that way … maybe not going *into* the record, but later, when people started asking questions about the record.

DOUG PINNICK I don't remember recording it a whole lot. I think at that point, I was tired of the tedious things that I had to deal with to make a record. I was tired of being in that same studio, I was tired of listening to the crappy mixes before the record was done—I was listening to other things that sounded so much better than how our records sounded, and I didn't know what to do about it. And I didn't have much say-so back then, because Sam pretty much tried to control everything with the band. So, for me, I just went through the motions and did the record. I was happy with a lot of the songs—not quite happy with how they sonically turned out, and I don't care for the record, myself.

TY TABOR I think, with *Faith Hope Love*, we kind of fell more into a groove. And we gave ourselves a time limit for the first time ever—where we promised Atlantic, 'We will give you the record on *this date*.' And we did. And in order to do it, we were recording right up to the last second. Even going into the last day or two before we needed to be finished, and recording the song 'Faith Hope Love'—adding that long, epic thing to the album at the last second.

I'm not sure why we did that—why we gave ourselves a time limit. I philosophically felt that made it impossible to do the very best album we could, but I could be wrong with that. There is that forever battle between never being finished and doing too much. I remember feeling we got lucky, and feeling that I didn't like the whole new way of doing things. It didn't leave us artistically free to create—that's the point of this. So that was the very first negative experience of recording. But we got lucky, and we did pull it off.

DOUG PINNICK I think it was just as tedious as *Gretchen*. But I don't think that we were trying to make a record that was going to be timeless. That was *Gretchen*. This one, we were going for something else, I guess. Trying to step it up.

THE SONGS
'WE ARE FINDING WHO WE ARE'

TY TABOR That was an 'all of us' song. I can't remember who had the initial riff, but the initial riff got completely destroyed, and we totally rewrote the song as a band. And that included Sam—all four of us worked that one really hard, and kept changing things and changing things. We even put it aside for a little while—more than once—and gave up on it, because it was too much work and it wasn't right. It wasn't coming together. And then I remember, one day, we spent all day on it, and gave it one last try, and some ideas started coming and flowing. We started getting excited about it, and, finally, it came together and we finished it. But that one was like pulling teeth for a long time—until it decided to happen. Lyrically, we were all pitching in. I remember it mainly being Doug and Jerry, and probably Sam pitching in, too.

DOUG PINNICK I remember my demo of this was nothing like the final product. I think maybe I had some of the words and the chorus melody; the rest of the song, we wrote together. It was about believing that we are going to live forever and that life goes on. I was always trying to write about encouraging things— that there's a light at the end of the tunnel. Everybody seemed to be writing about they hate themselves and everything is bad and wrong. I didn't want to focus on that, so I was trying to be happy again.

'IT'S LOVE'

TY TABOR That one was probably one of the easiest songs that came to me in my life. And what inspired it, to be honest, was, I was listening to some Dokken. I was listening to George Lynch, in particular—some of his voicings on guitar on a couple of songs. And I was playing around with some of those voicings on my guitar, and tried to use them in a different way and come up with something different—but with those types of voicings. He did a lot of interesting two- and three-note voicings in Dokken—they were key to the songs being cool, in my opinion. So that's what got it going. I started messing around with the riff, which ended up being the verse. Just using those two-note and three-note voicings that were similar to what he would do sometimes, and that was how I came up with the song. And then, all of a sudden, it kind of took on its own vibe and started heading in a different direction, and became a heavier, kind of Beatles-ish groove. But I don't know how it happened. It's almost like somebody came down from heaven and handed it to me in my lap, because it just happened. I didn't even have to work for it.

And even the little [four-note hook] came naturally. What I was thinking of—believe it or not—was the riff on 'Earache My Eye' from Cheech & Chong. That came to my mind at the end of the phrase, as far as the guitar. And then, vocally, it was something that came to me naturally, because I love Beatles harmonies and melodies—it fell into my lap. Lyrically, I think it was yet again me delving into those things that bother me most these days—growing up and seeing the irresponsibility of human beings.

In the video, we tried to make it obvious, because there is one line that says, '*There's a ship on the ocean / And I can't decide if I like it.*' My brother one time—laughingly—asked me what the hell that meant, because it seemed like nonsense to him. And my point was, man's progress is wonderful and everything, but when the ship turns over and poisons all the fish, that's *not* so wonderful. So, it was me contemplating all that we do and all that I'm happy with about it, but how much destruction it causes. It's yet again one of those socially conscious songs. I just had to say it.

'I'LL NEVER GET TIRED OF YOU'

DOUG PINNICK Another four-track demo. I had the basic song down; Sam and Ty came up with the '*ahhh*' part. I remember Sam had his portable piano there, which was the only time he ever brought it. I think he sensed we didn't want it there, and he was very sensitive about it. Sam came up with a riff that was actually a popular song, and he and Ty had an argument about it. So they settled on Ty's idea. Sam never brought his piano back to a rehearsal again!

I always wanted it to be a love song—about somebody that you'd be in love with. And then as I was writing it, I thought, *This should be a wedding song or something.* So, it's a love song to whatever you're inspired by, or love.

JERRY GASKILL I remember my toe hurt so bad that I could barely walk on it—my big toe, I forget which foot. I do remember being in the studio, doing vocals—I think it was for 'I'll Never Get Tired Of You'—and I had my foot in this tub of water. Just something to ease the pain and help me make it through. And I think it helped bring some emotion into the vocals.

'FINE ART OF FRIENDSHIP'

TY TABOR 'Fine Art Of Friendship' was a Doug song that we worked on in the studio—that all of us pitched in on.

DOUG PINNICK I remember we had gotten some money that Sam let us have from the business. I bought a six-track cassette recorder and a drum machine for my demos. My demos started to sound a little better, so I was extra-inspired for *Faith Hope Love*. I noticed that, since I've been single all my life, I've been able to watch relationships and watch people who care for each other, and the dynamics. I've come to learn that being a friend to someone is an art. You have to learn how to do it. And you can be good at it. But it's not something that you just are. *It's a fine art of friendship.* That's why I say, '*Meaning of love / Understanding / Growing old.*' It's like, how do you get inside someone's head and how do you learn to tolerate them? How do you put up with them and how do they put up with you, and figure out the best ways to do that, instead of conflict?

I'm a very peaceful person. I am not a 'conflict' type of person. I hold my anger in. I probably have a violent temper, but I've only seen it twice in my life. And I decided I would never go there again. One time, I was really mad when I was a teenager, and I went up to my room and slammed the door, and the door fell off the hinges. I slammed it *so hard*, the whole house shook! And I didn't realize I had that much adrenaline and could be that angry. The other time, I remember I was so angry that I couldn't control myself. I said something stupid, but I can't remember what it was. I think I said something horrible, and I've regretted it ever since. To this day, whenever I feel angry or I want to say something horrible, I stop and think and think, I hold it back, and I don't even say anything. I'll just take the shit that somebody is giving me and not say anything back—until I can calm down and come back with something that is going to help, rather than make them hate me more or bring a bigger wall up. Because I think words can kill. When someone says something terrible to me, I never forget it, and it affects my life forever. So, I try to stay away from those situations.

'MR. WILSON'

TY TABOR That one was about a lawsuit, actually. Another associate of Sam's was under the impression that he was actually a co-owner of King's X. I can't speak to whatever was represented to him—I have no idea—all I know was that we, as a band, had never made him a member of the band or a co-owner in any way. He worked for Sam's other company, Wilde Silas, which we hired occasionally to do videos and stuff. So we had to go to court over it and everything—and leave a tour to deal with it. But this was my song to the other person, because he was a friend. And as a friend—despite whatever Sam may have done to him—he sued me, too, and he sued Doug, and he sued Jerry. So, as far as I was concerned, he sued my wife and son, and tried to take money from my family—for something that I didn't do. And so, as a friend, it was disheartening. So that was my song to him.

'MOANJAM'

JERRY GASKILL 'Moanjam' was a song we just jammed on. I don't think we even used a click—we went in there and played the song, jammed it, and said, 'OK. *That's the song.*' I would imagine if you heard some of the tracks by themselves, you'd go, 'Oh my God … that is live, isn't it?'

TY TABOR I wrote 'Moanjam' with no lyrics. I was beating on a Styrofoam cooler, and I beat the drumbeat out on that, and then I played guitar along to it, and wrote the music like that, and had it on a cassette. I played it for the guys and everybody loved it.

DOUG PINNICK I call it our Motörhead song. But it has a gospel kind of thing—with a fast beat. And when we started working on it, I remember … I don't know who wrote what or how we started with that song. We used to call it 'The Moanjam,' because I didn't have words for it. We did it when we would do cover music—we would jam it out, and I would hum it. I'd go, '*Hmmm-mmm-mmm*'—like old black ladies do at church, when they're all excited and happy, but they've got no words. In a black church, they say, 'Well, if you ain't got no words, *then you moan.*' But when we went into the studio to record it, we had to write lyrics—so it's sort of like a prayer. It's sort of appreciation for God and the universe.

'SIX BROKEN SOLDIERS'

JERRY GASKILL It's always hard for me to talk about lyrics, because I don't like to say exactly what I'm thinking, because then that takes away from anything that you may get from it. When I write, I put everything I feel and think into each line, so it comes off very ambiguous sometimes, and even unintelligible sometimes. But I have specific things I'm thinking when I wrote that. Basically, it's just me talking about me.

'I CAN'T HELP IT'

TY TABOR I wrote the lyrics and melody; the music is something that Doug came up with a while back. We used to have another song that we all wrote parts to, actually—I came up with the musical middle part to it. And I think Doug came up with the initial riff, and then I came up with the other parts. And then we wrote the lyrics, and we—as a band—worked on it together. It was a different song altogether that I kind of stole from Doug, and made it a different song. It's a song about having to write music. It's a song about that thing that you can't control, and if you don't release it, you'll go nuts. And that's why people have to do art.

'TALK TO YOU'

DOUG PINNICK I remember I was learning how to program my new drum machine, and I think I went overboard. That's why there are so many unrelated parts on that tune. The guys reeled it in, and made it a King's X song. I was trying to sound like Billy Gibbons on the verses. Lyrically, that was about everything that was going on in my life one day—from my neighbor coming by to the phone ringing. Every verse on that song is literally something that happened that day, or the day before. And the chorus, Sam came up with: '*So how are you today?*'

'EVERYWHERE I GO'

DOUG PINNICK I think Ty wrote that. I wrote the lyrics about Jesus, but it is a love song to somebody who is in love, too. So, it's sort of twofold. That one was a pretty religious song.

'WE WERE BORN TO BE LOVED'

JERRY GASKILL That's a track that we worked very, very hard on. Especially the ending. It's a song that Doug came up with. And it was not the ending that he had. I think it was mainly Sam and Ty, with a little bit of me in there, that came up with that ending. That was something that was totally ridiculous—just trying to come up with something that was ridiculous. And I think we kind of accomplished that. Now that we've learned it and we've done it for so many years now, it's like second nature. It seems to other people that it's very hard for them to figure out.

DOUG PINNICK It's pretty close to the demo. But the ending—Ty, Jerry, and Sam came up with while I sat there. I couldn't understand what they were doing and thought they were messing my song up. But it's become the showstopper. I'm a dumbass!

I remember back in high school, when I learned what a cluster chord was, I thought I'd try it in this song with the harmonies. Something reminiscent of the Andrews Sisters from the 1940s. And the chorus is a vocal sound I learned in my school choir.

Again, that comes from my childhood—feeling like I wasn't cared about or no one loved me. So, I had to write a song about how we were born to be loved—to tell everyone that we were *all* born to be loved, and anybody out there who feels like they weren't, just let them know that they were, and you will find that peace somewhere and sometime in our life. There's always a light at the end of the tunnel.

I was a pretty depressed person back then, and very down on myself. I didn't feel like I had any self-worth, and I was pretty much a basket case in many ways. Instead of writing about the dark side of it, I always wrote about trying to get out, and what it must be like to get past it. I've overcome depression, for the most part, and I've learned to understand it. And I've learned to understand how to not let it into my life, and how not to feed it. It's not going to go away, but I've learned—like everybody else—to live with shit, and you get on with your life, and have a good time.

'FAITH HOPE LOVE'

DOUG PINNICK I had become obsessed with my new six-track recorder. The freedom to make up many parts for a song was so exciting, so I got my twelve-string bass out and wrote basically this whole boring song! The parts were so long and drawn out, we got to the studio and Sam put the cellos in, and we all built the song to what it became. I still think it is too long and very boring. And so naïve to say, '*There's more heaven than hell.*' But I believed it at the time. That's what the whole song was about—that there's got to be more good than bad, there's got to be more happy than sad. That's what I felt at the time. Since then, I've grown up and learned a lot about life, and the dark side and the light side, and we need both. But back then, I hopelessly believed that the world could all fall in love with each other.

'LEGAL KILL'

TY TABOR I wrote that song, and I don't want to add it. It says what it says.

FAITH HOPE LOVE PEAKED AT #85 ON THE BILLBOARD 200, AND
YIELDED THE BAND'S BIGGEST RADIO/MTV HIT, 'IT'S LOVE.'

TY TABOR I know there was a bigger budget, because of *Gretchen* being a lot bigger than *Out Of The Silent Planet*. I remember we had a much bigger video budget, and we had more money to record the album. I remember that pressure. But I do remember we went for it, and that included the video production and everything.

JERRY GASKILL The *Faith Hope Love* cover was done by a guy named Randy Rogers. I'm not exactly sure how he came into the picture. Possibly through Sam. But my understanding is that the cover is a depiction of the stories in the Bible. I believe each letter tells a story. And, if nothing else, I think it looks pretty cool.

We have the original paintings of the first four records. When the dissolution came about with Sam, we were each awarded one of those paintings. I got *Faith Hope Love*. It hangs prominently on the wall as you go upstairs in my house. It's a great piece of art.

REX BROWN If you go back and listen to *Out Of The Silent Planet* and *Gretchen Goes To Nebraska*, and then listen to *Faith Hope Love*, *Faith Hope Love* was a constitution of the first two records.

SHANNON LARKIN *Faith Hope Love* killed me—as it did everybody in my circle—as this big, epic album. It wasn't as commercial as their first two. It was deeper on many levels—lyrically and musically. It was more *epic*—that's the best word for it.

CHARLIE BENANTE It's a continuation basically, of the *Gretchen* type of sound. 'It's Love' is on there, which is awesome. 'Six Broken Soldiers,' 'I'll Never Get Tired of You' is a great song. 'Moanjam' was a good one—I always liked that song. 'We Are Finding Who We Are'—great fucking song. And then there is another song on the album that has a very proggy feel—'We Were Born to Be Loved.' I *love* that song.

MIKE PORTNOY *Faith Hope Love* is my favorite, because it had the catchy, memorable songs of *Gretchen*, but it went a little deeper. Like, the ending of 'We Were Born To Be Loved' was really musical. And they had a lot of moments on the album—like 'Moanjam' or the title track—where they stretched out a bit. The prog fan in me appreciated that they were stretching a bit. They were taking the blueprint of great, catchy songs with three-part harmonies, but they were stretching a little bit more and getting a little more progressive.

JEFF AMENT The *Faith Hope Love* album, I think I was less into some of the poppier tunes. I think a couple of those songs broke them a little bit—'It's Love.' I was sort of confused. I know there were some talk about 'Legal Kill' being anti-abortion, and I remember being a little confused by that. I remember, at that point, I went back and looked at the other lyrics, and I could sort of see some of the religious overtones. Lyrically, I was pretty confused by it, because it seemed like there was definitely some internal [conflict] about how they felt about God.

It seemed liked there was a period where Doug was definitely fighting everything he grew up with, which I can relate to, because I grew up in a Catholic family, and I was going through my own issues with that stuff. I think the thing with that *Faith Hope Love* record, some of the lyrics were more obvious, and it made me go back and pay more attention to the lyrics. But, *man*, there are some great Ty songs on that record. And 'Fine Art Of Friendship'; 'We Are Finding Who We Are' is amazing. That record really flows together. With 'It's Love,' it's probably the same people that skipped over 'Jeremy' or 'Even

Flow' on our [first] record—I was skipping over 'It's Love.' For some reason, it didn't fit for me, because there was a video of it.

ROBERT DeLEO [Stone Temple Pilots bassist] The first time I heard them, it was the *Faith Hope Love* record. It was 1990, so I was working at a guitar store on Sunset Boulevard. And that was one of the regular CDs that we had, and we would crank that. We had a PA system in there, and we would play that CD a lot. The owner of the store was a born-again Christian, and he played a lot of Phil Keaggy and had a lot of good music in there. I think my initial reaction to hearing that was, *Here's a band that's got great songs, great vocals, great guitar tones ... just a lot of soul.* It kind of encompassed everything that you'd want in a band. That was one of those albums that it was a complete journey. Growing up in the 70s, *that's* what I was used to hearing and digesting. And that album hit me in that kind of way—where it was kind of a journey from start to finish. We used to listen to the whole record. That was a complete journey for me, that record.

MATT PINFIELD [DJ; VJ; MTV *120 Minutes* host] The thing about King's X that I love is *Gretchen Goes To Nebraska* ... or *Faith Hope Love*. I love both those albums. One of the things that I started doing—that I loved doing—when I became music director on the rock station on the Jersey Shore [WHTG-FM], was embracing and playing King's X. I felt like there was something so fucking *real* about those guys. The songwriting was great; it wasn't about being fashionable in any way. They just played and wrote really great, intense songs. I played 'We Are Finding Who We Are' and 'It's Love.' I played them in heavy rotation, because I thought they were so good and powerful sounding. I've always loved that band.

NUNO BETTENCOURT [Extreme guitarist] I think the first time I heard them was probably on MTV, around *Gretchen Goes To Nebraska*. I might have seen the video for 'Over My Head,' and I thought it was an interesting band—mainly because of Doug's vocals. But it wasn't really until *Faith Hope Love* that I realized what they were and who they became. I think special bands—great bands—have certain things they touch on that they probably don't even know they're doing. It was kind of effortless. But I had never heard anything like that.

I'm obviously a big fan of vocals, but I never heard that combination. Every great band, I don't think anybody reinvents the wheel—so to speak—I think they have their own version of 'the soup' that they have.

ALAIN JOHANNES We were on tour, and *Faith Hope Love* and Soundgarden's *Badmotorfinger* were what we used to listen to. Besides a tape of the usual Stevie Wonder, Beatles, Zeppelin—pretty much all of the things that defined the inspirations I'm sure King's X and Eleven have, as well.

TY TABOR We stretched ourselves hard, because when we finished the album, we went into video production, and we flew out to a really remote area of Colorado. We based ourselves in Telluride, and then flew in a helicopter—a really pretty good journey—out to the top of a mountain, that was surrounded by no signs of civilization. It was complete desolation, out in the middle of the mountains. No buildings or towns or anything in view or sight. And we shot some of the video from up there on top of this mountain. I remember we did other shots where we had a whole caravan of people in four-wheel-drive Jeeps, loaded down with camera gear and all kinds of production stuff. Driving along a mountainside, hugging the mountainside, where the door is right up against the mountainside, and there's just sheer cliff to the right. And *I'm* driving one of the Jeeps! I remember us crossing sections of wooden planks, where the road had washed out and wood had been thrown across the washout, and we drove across that crap to get to where we wanted to film.

And then, when we got to where Sam wanted to film, there was this ... nodule thing sticking up with a sheer drop cliff all the way around it—except for a one-foot-wide sheer drop ledge that led out to the nodule. And the top of the nodule was maybe two feet by two feet, but it was flat. But you had to traverse this one-foot kind of walkway—with sheer drops to either side—to get out to the thing. And Sam wanted me to go out there to play the solo, for that shot. So I got out there, climbed up on the thing, and they had to throw me the guitar, because there was no way to do it without holding on for dear life. And we're filming the thing, and I'm sitting there on this nodule and looking around, and it's like, a thousand feet down behind me—straight down—to rocks. We're filming this, and I'm thinking, *This better be the most spectacular shot on earth, because this is stupid to risk life for this stupid shot.* I was getting pissed off.

And then a bird swooped at my head, and I nearly lost my balance off the thing. I told Sam, '*You get just one more take! Roll it! Period!*' And I threw that damn guitar back at him and climbed back off of that thing. And then, if you see the shot in the video, they filmed it in a way that you don't even see that I'm sitting on a ledge that is dangerous. You don't see it at all. From that moment on, I refused. I said, 'I will *never* do anything stupid like that again, for your stupid video shots.' That's one of the things that I remember the most from doing that—it being dangerous and risking life to get stupid shots.

At one point in the video, we're dealing with a live cougar—which is two hundred pounds or so—and we're around a campfire. And they have this rope around the cougar's leg, and they want us to do this scene, where my back is to the cougar, and Doug and Jerry are facing me, and they're supposed to look scared while I'm telling a story, and as soon as I say, 'Boo,' I think they're scared at my story, but a cougar is supposed to run across the campfire at them. So, the way they got the cougar to run at the right time was to dangle this fake chicken thing that was his favorite toy. Well, they dangle the thing, I go, 'Boo,' the cougar comes running right by me and right after Jerry, snaps the rope, jumps on Jerry, pulls him down to the ground, and is inches from his face and his neck. But he suddenly looks around, realizes he's free, and takes off! Boom—*gone*. There was stuff like that happening, just to shoot a video. It was a long list of stupid things. And we no longer did any more of those videos.

JERRY GASKILL We took a helicopter up to the top of this mountain, where we were, and I remember coming up, and it was incredibly beautiful up there. And as we were about to land, we're coming down on this piece of rock that, to me, seemed too small for us to be on. But finally, we did—they let us down and we got out. And here's the three of us, still on the top of this mountain, and they left us there. And they circled around and filmed, while we stood on the top of this mountain, looking at this unbelievable scenery, in Telluride, Colorado.

DOUG PINNICK That was a three-day shoot. We went to three different states to do that, and it was tedious and long, and it cost *a lot* of money. I think it was a good video, if you want to say it was a big production. But other than that, it's what it was—for me. At that point—and with the band—I was kind of tired of everything, because we weren't selling a lot of records, I didn't feel happy, and

I felt like my whole life was controlled by the record company and the manager, and I was trapped.

TY TABOR But that video became the video to the biggest hit we ever had as a band—still to this day. 'It's Love' went all the way to #6 on *Billboard*'s Mainstream Rock charts and #1 on the FM Radio Airplay charts. It was our highest-ranking single, ever.

LEA PISACANE The closest we got to real commercial success was 'It's Love.' We got the video on MTV—MTV still played videos then and had much more of an effect on whether a developing act broke. 'It's Love' got on MTV and the radio. It attained a higher position than anything else we worked from King's X.

MARIA FERRERO One of the ways, back in the day, to try to break a band was MTV. MTV was *huge*. Radio or MTV—if you didn't have that, then you weren't going to have success. You could have all the press in the world and, as my bosses and those who came before or after said, 'Press doesn't really sell records.' No, it doesn't sell records, but it's a great way to build perception for an artist and make awareness. And everybody was aware of King's X. There was a great perception of their music out there. There were some really big supporters in the media at the time. David Fricke at *Rolling Stone*, he reached out and wanted to cover the band, which was really great—to have someone of that caliber recognize King's X and want to cover them was a really big deal.

But, at the time, radio and MTV was the way to break them. So, during that time, there was the show *Dial MTV*, where you would call in and request videos, and they would have a top-ten countdown of the day. Every day, Megaforce would pretty much close down doing whatever we were doing, and everybody would dial in to request King's X. So, if we could make them the most requested, they're going to play the hell out of their video, and then it's going to build momentum—more people will see it, more people will be turned on to them, more people will potentially buy their records. It just never ever clicked. It never connected. I don't know why. They were voted always, every day, one of the top bands on MTV—because we made sure that we were voting to get them in—but it never connected, and they never ended up selling a ton of records like they really should have.

RICHARD CHRISTY I remember 'It's Love' was always on *Dial MTV*, and I used to call *Dial MTV* every freaking day, because I'd call and vote for King's X on there. I thought the video was really cool. I'd come home from school and call *Dial MTV*. I think that was right around my senior year of high school. But also, in high school, I was diehard into *Dial MTV* because Stryper was on there all the time, and I'd ask my parents if I could call, because I think it cost you, like, two dollars a minute or something to call and vote.

JERRY GASKILL We also did a video for 'We Are Finding Who We Are,' which I think was all shot at a show we did in Houston—at the Tower Theatre, which is no longer the Tower Theatre. It was a great show, a sold-out show, and I think all the footage came from that. But I remember when the 'It's Love' video came out, going to a hotel, and we walked in, and the maid looked at us and said, 'Hey ... you guys are the guys on top of that mountain, right?'

10 HITTING THE ROAD, HARD–PART 2

WITH STARDOM SEEMINGLY AROUND THE CORNER,
THE MEMBERS OF KING'S X SACRIFICED THEIR
HOME LIVES IN FAVOR OF A LIFE ON THE ROAD.

TY TABOR We went to Europe for a bit, because Europe was very good for us. And we did a tour—it was very brief, but huge—in Germany, with Iron Maiden and Anthrax. It was a *Metal Hammer* thing, and we did more than one show with Iron Maiden, and that was awesome. For us, that was big—we got in with *Metal Hammer* in Europe. So now we're playing places there that are bigger than the places we played in America.

CHARLIE BENANTE We were on the whole tour with Iron Maiden, and King's X were added to just a few shows [five dates in Europe during December 1990, on Maiden's *No Prayer On The Road* tour]. I remember I was so happy about it, because I hadn't seen those guys in a little bit, and it was great to see them and reconnect. And, of course, watch them.

DOUG PINNICK Iron Maiden, I had never met them and had never seen them, and I remember going out front to watch them after Anthrax played. I was mesmerized by the energy that they had! The bass player, Steve Harris, was amazing—galloping all over the place. I'm going, 'Where do all these guys get all this energy from?' We've gotten to know the guys now, and we're fans and they're fans.

JERRY GASKILL Then we did a US tour opening for AC/DC, which was truly incredible. Every single night I watched those guys play. And every single night they were incredible. I remember when Sam Taylor came to us and said, 'Hey, we've got the AC/DC tour!' It almost didn't feel real at first. At the same time, in that period of our career, things were moving so fast and so upward, that it almost seemed natural that we would do that. Everything was happening, and the tour with AC/DC was like the cherry on the top. It was almost like the next natural progression. Those guys were so nice—they were so kind to us.

They took us out to dinner one night in Europe. We were in Hamburg. It was all the guys in the band, and Angus Young's wife. I remember they sent a car—it was a really nice Mercedes—and we got on the Autobahn. I wasn't familiar with the Autobahn at the time. The first time I'd been there, and we get on, and all of a sudden, the driver is going so fast, I started freaking out. I looked at Ty—who I was sitting next to—and said, 'Ty … are we not going a little bit fast?' And he goes, 'Yeah! I think we are!'

I had to lean up and talk to the driver, and say, 'Excuse me, sir, but are we not going a little fast?' And then he explained to me the whole system and how it works. There is no speed limit, and how they signal and they understand. So, I was able to relax. And he told me that we were going *140 miles an hour*. And then we got to the place, had dinner, Angus told all kinds of great stories, and Brian Johnson was telling jokes. It was incredible. A really, really beautiful time. The whole tour was like that.

DOUG PINNICK Probably one of the best times of my life was touring with AC/DC. One of my favorite bands in the whole world. I would watch them every night and they were *amazing*. We got to hang out with them, and got to play a song at soundcheck with Brian and Chris [Slade]—the drummer at the time—when the bass player [Cliff Williams], Angus, and Malcolm Young didn't show up. So, I don't know if anybody can say they got to jam with AC/DC … but I did, sort of!

I call that tour the Rolls-Royce of touring—it was a top-of-the-line tour. We were treated like we were a part of it—tour bus, catering. It was *so* cool. And we thought, *Wow, if this what it's like, we can deal with this!*

TY TABOR Huge tour. That was major for us. We did about two months in America and about two months in Europe. Four months straight of touring with AC/DC—that was pretty amazing. We played only the very biggest venues everywhere, and all of Europe was sold out before it was even announced who was opening, because it doesn't even matter who's opening for AC/DC. It has no bearing on their sales—people don't care who's opening.

You usually have to pay a lot of money to get on a tour like that. Atlantic stepped up and gave us some big tour support, which allowed us to do that, which is very big promotion and support for us. It really helped us. It was during all that, 'It's Love' went to #6 in America.

JAY PHEBUS That was probably the best tour we ever did. And the Living Colour tour we did in between those two legs was pretty cool, too. The AC/DC tour was playing basically every NBA arena—the one dark spot on that was the crowd casualties in Salt Lake City, at the old Salt Palace. [Three fans were crushed to death during the show there on January 18, 1991.] We came offstage, got all the gear off, we were backstage, and, like, ten or fifteen minutes into the set, they stopped, and the lights came on in the arena. I'm going, 'That's not good.' And the next thing I know, paramedics are bringing people through the backstage area. So that was obviously a dark spot on that tour. But everything else was phenomenal.

We had started in Tacoma with AC/DC, and went all the way down to Tampa—all across the US. AC/DC had a month off, and Atlantic got us the opening slot with Living Colour. We started right there in Florida and worked our way all the way back to California. So, while AC/DC took a month off before the six-week leg in Europe started, we just kept touring with Living Colour. We were playing smaller places, but their record was so hot, it was a highlight. The guys all treated us well. The genre of music was closer, so it was a good match and good timing. We played a lot of colleges on that tour. I've always been an Alabama Crimson Tide fan, and we played Tuscaloosa, at the University of Alabama, and recently I went back and took my nephew—who is possibly going to Alabama for football—to the hall we played, and showed him how, twenty, thirty years ago, King's X played there with Living Colour.

TY TABOR We had really not yet made a splash in Germany—at all. Nothing was really happening there … until we did a very extensive run through Germany with AC/DC. And, by the time we left Germany, our video was actually above theirs on whatever the video playlist was at the time. I remember being surprised by that—that we finally had something catch on in Germany. And that changed everything for us in Germany—to this day. It was also the most difficult tour we've ever done in our lives, because when we got to Europe, to walk out in front of a stadium full of hardcore AC/DC fans that are—in unison—like an army, with their fists pumping, going, '*ANGUS! ANGUS! ANGUS!*' before you even come on, trying to intentionally drown out any chance of you even being heard. And they throw things at you—shoes, toilet plungers. But the worst thing is that they threw coins, and coins can break fingers. I remember getting hit in the hands with coins, and getting swollen fingers and swollen hands. And people booing. We'd step out onstage, and they'd turn their backs to us—'*ANGUS! ANGUS! ANGUS!*'

We got to Germany, and it was like nothing we'd ever seen—that kind of unified hatred and that unified vibe. We'd never seen humans act like that before. And not anywhere else since—it's never happened again. But on that tour, before anybody knew who we were, it was the most hardcore thing I personally have ever experienced from a stage. Physical abuse and mental abuse—to be able to step out there, knowing what you were stepping out to each night, was brutal beyond words. I don't think anyone can understand how brutal it can be until you're put in that position and you have to humiliate yourself by doing it. But, that's how the first three songs or so would be.

Here was our game plan—we were like, 'We don't care what we have to do, we're going to have them cheering for us by the end of this show. We don't care what we have to do.' So, we started stepping out onstage, and we're looking right down front, and whoever was shooting the bird to us or throwing objects at us, we would look right at them, smile, and point, and play a solo *straight at them.* And everybody around them would start looking at them, like, 'What the hell is going on?' And, all of a sudden, people started paying attention. The next thing we know, everybody is turning around—and we were doing the same thing, every single night.

Like I said, it took about three songs of doing stuff. For instance, somebody threw a lighter at me one night—right as I stepped up to do my solo. So, I picked up the lighter, kept the solo going, I lit it, and lit my strings as I played the solo! And then I threw it right back at the dude as hard as I could—and people were fighting over it, all of a sudden. Everything we did made them turn around and pay attention. We were running up on the big side barrier things that we weren't supposed to—that only Angus runs up on. I mean, we were owning the place, like, 'This is *my* stinking show. You're going to pay attention.'

And, like I said, it's boos and getting pelted at first, but I kid you not, every single show, by the last song, we had the crowd on their feet, cheering for us. *Every single show*. So we knew, each time we stepped out, it was going to be the most brutal thing ever. We were going to face it night after night. But by God, by the end of the night, we were going to get them on their feet and pay attention. So, we laid down the heaviest, most energetic, show-off stuff that we could for the last ten minutes of the show. And it worked every time. Like I said, we left Germany with a video that actually went up over AC/DC, and we won over the place. And, ever since then, it's been the #1 place for us to go in Europe.

AC/DC were super-cool. They treated us like we mattered, and we absolutely did *not* matter. We didn't sell a ticket on that European tour, because, like I said, it was sold out before they even announced who was on the tour. We had nothing to do with it. They were gentlemen. It was a gift to us that they gave us, for the privilege to get to go out and try to win over their audience every night. That's worth more money than you can possibly say. And they knew us all by name right off the bat—they did their homework—and gave us full sound, everything. No headlining band ever does that. They knew they had nothing to worry about, and they gave us everything to do our best. It just made the show better. Which, we never run into that in situations where we're opening. That just doesn't happen. They were as good as it gets.

There was one night on a night off when they sent drivers for us and drove us like a hundred kilometers away to meet them at some favorite little private pub they liked to hang out at, and bought us an amazing meal, sat around all night, talking and sharing books—we ended up buying books for each other on the tour! Talking about all kinds of stuff. Heavy stuff. It was an amazing, amazing tour. It was the best experience with a band—as far as opening for a headliner—we've ever had.

JON ZAZULA I got to tour with them a bit with AC/DC. And … what I know remains with me. [*Laughs*]

DOUG PINNICK 'Junior's Gone Wild' was a demo I submitted for *Gretchen*, and got rejected. I was bummed. I really liked it. And then we were on the road with AC/DC in France, and we had the opportunity to get a King's X song on the *Bill & Ted's Bogus Journey* soundtrack, and Sam said, 'We don't have any new songs. Let's give them "Junior."' So we went into this studio in France and recorded that song, and gave it to the movie people. I remember the engineer couldn't speak English. It was about a kid I know who was always in trouble—and I was worried about him.

AND THEN … A FATEFUL INTERVIEW WITH *ROLLING STONE.*

JERRY GASKILL I remember David Fricke came on the road with us for a few days, for an article in *Rolling Stone*. He talked to all of us, and I really wanted to stay away from any Christian things. I felt like that was where we needed to be. And it seemed as though the whole article ended up being about the whole Christian thing! I don't know if that hurt us or helped us or did nothing at all. But that's my memory—thinking, *That's not what the focus of this band should be right now*. And it seemed like that is exactly what happened. There were some great pictures in the article, though.

TY TABOR This is what I observed through that whole *Rolling Stone* article thing. First of all, there was starting to be a rumor that we were this Christian rock band—which was not true. We just wanted to be *artists*. We wanted our music to inspire anyone—whoever they are—in whatever way that it can. That was our only goal as a band. And we saw any label calling us a 'Christian band' as a horrible thing—that would be the end of our band, because we know what that world is like, and what a wall there is against that, and rightfully so. That's why we didn't want to be a part of it. We wanted to be not associated with that label or that industry in any way, because we weren't. That's not who we are as people, and we didn't want to be. We honestly were just trying to be artists. We would write things about what we would spiritually think or believe at the time—that was just being artists. It was just being a person. Not preaching—not telling them how they should think or what is right or wrong—but just sharing life experience. *Period*. Because we all knew it.

I remember, before David came down, we had a meeting as a band. It was mostly through the instruction of our manager at the time, Sam, but I agreed with him 100 percent; he said, 'Guys, if you talk about spiritual beliefs, and in particular Christianity, in this article, the first shot to be recognized as the artists you are, it will be the end of your career. And the end of your radio play. It will be *the end*.' And we all agreed: 'OK. We'll just talk about the music and talk about it as artists, and be honest. But let's not let this turn into some BS Christian band article.'

So we spent two or three days with David, and we did interviews and whatever. The truth is, he didn't really want to talk to me at all—he talked to me maybe a total of thirty minutes. I don't think he even realized I wrote half of all the music and had a lot to say about it. So he had good interviews with Doug, and Doug keeps it from being that stuff that can be misread.

And David decides, 'Hey Doug, let's go to lunch, and kind of talk off the record.' So Doug opens up to him at lunch—about all his beliefs. And, suddenly, *that* is the article. And we are a Christian band all of a sudden—which we were not. And all of a sudden—instantly—from #6 on the charts with 'It's Love' and there are major doors opening for us … after that came out, we started seeing doors shut real quick. And I specifically called our A&R radio guy, Bill McGathy, who was the #1 radio guy in the country, and who had helped us get all this success on radio, and said, 'Hey man, what's going on?' He said, 'Man, I'm calling radio stations, and they're telling me, No, we're not going to play them. They're a *God band*.'

What I witnessed was, that article stopped radio play—and thus the growth of the band—overnight. It was all perfectly timed with when that came out. Everything was so much more of an uphill battle after that. When the fourth album came out, to get stuff on the radio … I can't possibly tell you the difference after the *Rolling Stone* article. It was entirely a different world for us from that moment forward. People labeled us a Christian band.

JERRY GASKILL I totally understand where the Christian thing came from, because we did come from Christian backgrounds—all three of us. If we deny it, then we're not telling the truth. But, at a certain point, we realized that is not who we are, that's not where we belong, and that's not what we want to project. And, as time has gone on, further and further, I can't put myself in any category or any box whatsoever, saying, 'I am this' or 'I am that.' And in many ways, I feel more 'Christian,' if you will—not that I am by any means a Christian—now than I've ever been, even when I professed to be a Christian. Just by life happenings as you go along. People will always put some label on you, I guess—because they have to in order to have some kind of understanding as to what is going on. Just like religion and everything that is—we have to have something that gives us some kind of a reason for things. And I think the same thing happened with us. Now, we gave people some of that ammunition, too—in the early days. We gave them a little piece of that, because it was a piece of us.

CHARLIE BENANTE I was thinking about the lyrics, and I don't know if it was so much them or the influence Sam Taylor had on them—with the Christian type of vibe. But I think it's apparent. I often thought, *What if they were promoted in that way? Would things have been a little different?* They would have been labeled as a Christian act, but if you promoted it toward the Christian side of thing with the rock feel … if you remember, in the late 80s/early 90s, the Christian rock thing started to become a little more mainstream. And bands who were looking more 'rock' were starting to go that route. Later on, you had bands like Jars Of Clay, and even Creed. Creed broke out of that mold, but the first album was more directed toward Christian rock radio.

JERRY GASKILL Any time that you define who you are, and say, '*This* is who I am. *This* is where I am. *This* is what I think. *This* is how I am,' then you are not going to be the very thing that you say you are. You can't be, because to be that thing, you can't be that closed—you have to be completely open to others and to life, and any change that can happen. That's the problem with religion. I think that's one of the reasons why the world is the way it is today—because of religion. Religion is a horrible thing, to me. It's the exact opposite of what religion teaches itself to be. And we all know that. It's obvious, right? Religion and politics are my least favorite things. That is why the world is in the shape that it's in—religion and politics go hand in hand.

MARSHA ZAZULA We weren't getting the radio hits we needed. Atlantic, in those days—I don't know what they are like today—would give you X-amount of time to push radio and promote radio. And if it didn't hit by their time frame, they were on to the next. And somebody had brought them Marc Cohn, and this song—which to this day, haunts me—'Walking In Memphis,' was the first single that Atlantic put out from him. And it clicked, and they saw that it was doing well, so Atlantic dropped all its commitments for radio by King's X to chase 'Walking In Memphis.' Sadly, that hurt the band.

DURING THE SUMMER OF 1991, KING'S X TOOK PART IN A GATHERING
OF THE TRIBES, A MULTI-BAND TRAVELING TOUR THAT ALSO FEATURED
X, FISHBONE, PRIMUS, AND STEVE EARLE, AMONG OTHERS.

DOUG PINNICK That was the first tour that we'd ever been on like that. Lollapalooza was happening, and other stuff was going on. When I found out about the Gathering Of The Tribes, I thought, *This is going to be great!* Because it's great exposure. For me, it was playing shows and playing in front of people that had never seen us before, so that's a 'commercial.' I was very excited.

JERRY GASKILL On that tour, Doug came up to me and Ty and said, 'Hey man, I just met *Neil Young!* You've got to come meet him!' And at that point, I'm thinking, *Everybody seems to know who King's X is, so it will be cool and we can hang out with him.* So we went over there and we wound up taking a picture. It was actually just Doug and me—I think Ty took the picture, for some reason. And I leaned my head on Neil's shoulder, thinking, *Oh, this is nice!* He had no idea who we were. [*Laughs*]

TY TABOR Gathering Of The Tribes got cut short—I think we only did two or three shows. And I think it was supposed to be two or three more. I don't know why they cut them short, because the two that we did were packed. They were good crowds.

DOUG PINNICK After it lasted only a few shows and it was over, I thought, *Here we go again. Whatever we do ends up falling apart. And here we go back to the drawing board, trying to write another record.*

TY TABOR I remember being above Madonna and Janet Jackson on the video charts at one time, and laughing to myself how absolutely ludicrous this was— because they were selling millions of albums … *and we didn't even matter.* It seemed like complete nonsense.

DOUG PINNICK I remember living in an apartment, driving a piece-of-shit car that I could stick my feet through the floorboard. I was in Texas, in 110-degree weather, with no air conditioning, miserable, and pissed, and walking in the door, and seeing 'It's Love' played next to Mötley Crüe and Madonna. I would sit there and be completely confused. We were told we had no money—my paycheck was so small I could barely pay my bills, and I'm seeing us next to Mötley Crüe and Madonna, and I didn't know what to think about it. And I *still* don't know what to think about it, because I noticed the record didn't sell a whole lot. I felt like, *Is this all a joke? What's going on?* I started to lose my faith in the energy of rock'n'roll—not the music or going out and playing for people, but the whole bullshit of MTV and radio.

TY TABOR I was driving a used Hyundai—that was in the early years, when they first came out and were the cheapest thing you could possibly buy. Well, mine was already rundown, beat-up, and used. That's how broke I was, when we were all over MTV. And when we went out on that tour, we were selling out everywhere we went. Big shows. We were headlining places like the Ritz in New York on that tour and selling out. We did nothing but big shows, sold out, on that tour.

JERRY GASKILL It was very sad and very hard, being away from my family while on tour. But it was something that we needed to do. To this day, it's something that I feel—the sadness of being away for so long. But, at the same time, we believed it's what we needed to do for the long run. And we went out for like, *nine months*, and I remember Sam coming to us and saying, 'We have another tour we can do—with The Black Crowes.' And, actually, my ex-wife was pregnant at the time. I remember saying to him, 'Look, I can't do it, man. I can't go back out again. I have to go home. I have to be home with my family. I can't do this anymore right now.' So I went home for a while.

It's a hard thing. I think about that—I think about the time I spent away from my kids. I think they're OK now—we joke about things. I wasn't there all the time, but I was there for them, and I think they know that. And, when I did come home, I was there 24/7. So I think there was a good balance.

TY TABOR It was very difficult. And we had a manager who had no care for that, whatsoever. There was one time when we were out for almost nine months straight, where we only came home for one week or two weeks during the entire nine months. My son was becoming a year older without me even seeing him, and not being there for my family. All the things that happen in a year that you need to be there for, to take care of.

So, we're at the end of these nine months, and we're finally going to get to go home and take care of some things, and The Black Crowes call up and want us to do a tour with them. They were hitting big, and it was a big deal. But none of us wanted to do it. We were about to break up as a band if we couldn't get home. I remember telling that to Sam on the phone, and his reaction—after me giving my blood for nine months and dying on the road and not seeing my family, while he's sitting at home on his ass, all comfortable—is, 'Oh, boo-hoo. You don't get to tour and play in front of thousands of people.'

I hung up on him. From basically that moment forward—as far as I was concerned—I couldn't wait for him to be gone. I was done with him. It took a little longer for the other two.

11 KING'S X

THE STORY BEHIND THE BAND'S SELF-TITLED FOURTH
STUDIO ALBUM–THEIR FIRST SOLELY FOR ATLANTIC
RECORDS–RELEASED ON MARCH 10, 1992.

JERRY GASKILL Going to Atlantic only, it was almost like going from the minor leagues to the major leagues.

TY TABOR Every single album, the deal was much bigger—from album one all the way up to this point. By the time we got to the fourth one, the deal was *huge*. It was a large amount of money, making an album and doing videos and stuff. We were now in the hundreds of thousands of dollars to do an album. So, things were getting *massive*—we were signing merchandise deals that were massive, for hundreds of thousands of dollars. The numbers that we were hearing being thrown around were beyond our wildest dreams.

JERRY GASKILL Megaforce let us do our thing. Megaforce signed us because they liked what we were doing already. They didn't really want to affect that or change that—but they didn't really know what to do with us because it wasn't their normal thing. But they were happy we were not in their normal thing, so they let us be. The first three albums, we handed them whatever we had, and they put it out. There was no involvement with the label in choosing songs or what the album was going to be. We sort of all had that idea that that was our deal—that we could turn in whatever we wanted to.

When we got strictly with Atlantic, they're not a hands-off company—especially when big money starts getting involved. Suddenly, everybody there is involved. But the thing is, you *want* everybody there involved, so that it will work. It became 'corporate'—moving into Atlantic. It became big machine money and teams of people. I remember being in, I think it was Doug Morris's office—all of us—and, somehow, the conversation got to the point where Sam said, '*I am indebted to you for life now.*' And I think that had something to do with being on Atlantic. But I remember Sam saying that, and I'm going, 'Whoa. Now, I'm not saying that. I'm not indebted to *anybody* for life.'

TY TABOR I thought Doug Morris was amazing, and a great support for us. And so was Tunc Erim, who was our A&R guy, who was the #1 A&R guy at Atlantic since the very beginning. Tunc was our guy and Doug was our guy. Doug believed and wanted us on the label for credibility. He wanted us on the label for all of the amazing press and cred. They really liked having King's X on the label, because King's X was getting a whole lot of really good press and really good props from all over the industry. And they felt proud having us.

EDDIE TRUNK I left Megaforce around 1990. King's X would continue on, and then King's X would segue directly over to being on Atlantic. But, to this day, I'm still in touch with the guys.

TY TABOR We loved being on Megaforce, because Megaforce was in cooperation with Atlantic, so everything we put out had the Atlantic label symbol on it— along with Megaforce. It was considered *Megaforce–Atlantic*, even though we signed with Megaforce all the way from the beginning. So we had this association with Atlantic, but we weren't just on Atlantic only.

Little known to us, Megaforce has a deal with Atlantic, apparently, that after certain options of whatever, they could buy a band—or take them—if they want them fully on Atlantic. And that's what happened to us. We actually didn't pursue that. It just happened to be something that Atlantic wanted.

It happened while we were recording the fourth album, because we were in the studio recording, when our manager wanted to make an announcement. He said, 'Just to let you know, you are now officially on Atlantic Records.' We were like, '*What*?!' He was like, 'Yeah, they decided to take you off of the Megaforce–Atlantic deal, and make it solely Atlantic.' We had no idea.

Doug immediately said, 'I want the old Atlantic symbol on our albums—the one that is no longer being used.'

DOUG PINNICK I do remember asking Atlantic to give us the logo that they had for Ray Charles, back in the 60s.

We were looking at pictures, to see what kind of a cover we wanted, and I remember when I saw the little girl under the table with the bread and wine, I thought, *That is the greatest picture I have ever seen*. It had so much symbolism. I asked the guy [the artist, Randy Rogers] to spill the wine, and the little girl would be picking up the crumbs under the table. There's a scripture in the Bible that says that when Jesus was at these rich people's house and they were eating, some poor man came and asked for some food, and they turned him away. And Jesus said, 'Even the crumbs under the table the dogs eat,' basically. I forget exactly what it was, but it was sort of like, 'Hey, have some sympathy, bitch!' So that picture was a little girl under the table with the crumbs. And I wanted the wine to be spilled, because I kind of wanted it to be a little sacrilegious. Because that was basically the bread and wine that Jesus did—the whole sacrament thing. I kind of wanted it fallen and the wine dripping, to say, *I'm not completely into this anymore*. It had a little symbolism for me, personally. I really pushed hard for this particular cover.

I remember I also asked for our album not to have our name on the front cover—like *Led Zeppelin IV*. I thought it would be really cool. But Atlantic said, 'It has to be *somewhere* on the front cover,' because they're all about marketing. So they put the King's X logo in the tile on the floor—a little one—where you could see it. Where the little girl's hand is, you can see the King's X logo. I even have the painting at my house. The four paintings that we had for the first four records, each of us has one: Sam has, I think, *Out Of The Silent Planet*; Jerry has *Faith Hope Love*; I think Ty has *Gretchen*; and I have the fourth one. And they're huge pictures—framed and everything.

TY TABOR I remember us all being in agreement and thinking it was not that unusual to call the album *King's X*. I mean, *The White Album* is not called *The White Album*—it's just *The Beatles*, a self-titled album. And we called it *The White Album*, and it has been deemed that since. But it came out as just *The Beatles*. There have been a whole lot of albums like that—*Led Zeppelin IV* is not *Led Zeppelin IV*, it's just untitled, right? So, we probably couldn't think of a good title, and said, 'Why don't we do that this time?' But I honestly don't remember.

The recording was the same as usual. It was hard work. It was stressful. Always kind of like walking on eggshells, working with Sam, because you never knew what was going to set him off, and how far off he was going to go.

He was a time bomb waiting to go at any time, and you always felt that pressure. There was always that, working with him—that pressure … horrible pressure. But it was the same as usual, except I found myself feeling like we were being pushed into some mold that we had created by the first three albums, of what we were supposed to be. And I felt that was a mistake.

And this is where I started becoming very unhappy with things, and started voicing it. Saying, 'I feel like we're starting to imitate ourselves now, because we don't know what else to do—instead of trying to reach for new things that we don't know what it's going to be.' This is how we came up with this in the first place—not imitation or setting rules of who we are supposed to be. It was not knowing who we were going to be, and going for it. And I felt we were losing touch with that on the fourth album. Although it has moments and some highlights, and I was proud of the album overall, it was yet another one where time constraints, pressure from Atlantic … things were just *different*. I wasn't quite as happy with that one.

DOUG PINNICK I don't remember a whole lot about recording that record. Ty and I both at that point were writing almost complete demos. Ty's were always perfect and complete, really. There was nothing for King's X to do but record them. I had worked very hard at these tunes I had written, also, so I think it was more like all of us were going into the studio and just recording them. Doing our thing. I do like most of that record. Lots of good songs.

THE SONGS

'THE WORLD AROUND ME'

DOUG PINNICK I remember my demo sounded crappy—with a one-beat drum machine and a simple harmony part. I wanted to come up with a weird riff that grooved. I listen to Carl Stalling—the guy who wrote all the Looney Tunes music. *Bugs Bunny* cartoon music. I made it up in my head, but it took me forever to figure out how to play the riff, because it was very unnatural to play. I still have a hard time with it, but I love doing it.

I used to take walks back in the day every night, and watch the sunset and listen to mixes. I would write all day long and then I'd grab a joint, go for a walk, get high, and listen to whatever song I was writing—to hear it 'under the influence.' It was like listening to it for the first time, so I'd *really* get it.

When I work all day on a song, I begin to hate it, but I remember I was walking along, and I had written the song but I didn't have lyrics for it. It was like a waterway that I'd walk along—a ditch or a reservoir that went for miles. And it had a sidewalk on it. I'd walk for a long, long ways—until the sun went down—with my headphones on, listening to what I did all day. And I was walking and listening, thinking, '*One morning walking down the street / Where nobody walks nobody can hear / I started listening to a sound so clear / To the world around me.*' When I walked out there, I could hear the birds and the crickets and everything. It was away from the city. And it was about that period of nature and looking around and realizing that this was something special— and we don't pay attention to it much.

'PRISONER'

TY TABOR I wrote that song so fast that I don't even recall any memory of writing the lyrics or what I was thinking at the time, to be honest. I really don't.

'THE BIG PICTURE'

DOUG PINNICK When I was a kid back in the 50s, I loved the music intro to the TV show *American Bandstand*. The saxophone riff sounded so big and powerful. I played baritone sax in grade school—there's a tone that you get that's really great. I think of those two things sometimes when I make up a riff. It's a slow march with a fat sax riff, like slow marching down the street in New Orleans, going to a funeral. And, when I sang it, I wanted to sound like Curtis Mayfield in a falsetto. If I'm going to imitate somebody, I want to go back to the original, so I was trying to sound like Curtis Mayfield.

The chorus vocal is the actual demo on my six-track in my house. I remember we had had a meeting at my apartment, and I had not gotten stoned all day. So, when everyone left, I went for my usual walk, and listened to what I was working on the day before—with no vocals. I came home and plugged my mic into a Pignose amp, and I screamed the choruses out at the top of my lungs, and felt every moment of that one take. I couldn't sing a note after that to do another take, so I just kept it. I'm surprised the neighbors didn't call the police for how loud I was screaming! I could not reproduce the distortion or the way I attacked the chorus when we were in the studio, so we flew it from the six-track cassette onto the twenty-four-track.

To backtrack a little bit, at the gospel church I grew up in—where I learned a lot of how to sing soulful—there was a guy named Donny Ray Thompson who would get up maybe every other Sunday and sing a song. *The boy could sing his butt off.* But the PA at the church was a bad PA, so his voice was distorted when he sang. So what I actually did was, on that song, I tried to emulate exactly the feeling I got and what I had heard when I sat in one of those church services. No one else would ever know that, and no one else would understand that, but my goal was to do that—just for me. It's a glimpse of when I sat in the pew at church, experiencing these amazing, young, local gospel singers when I was fourteen. That church rocked and grooved *so* hard—it was aggressive gospel music. I went there in my teenage years with my mom. Mount Zion Missionary Baptist Church. It was a great learning experience for me. And, lyrically, it's sort of like a prayer, saying, 'I don't understand what the fuck is going on, so can you tell me the big picture?'

'LOST IN GERMANY'

TY TABOR That one is the only song I have ever written in my head in its entirety. While I was taking a shower, I heard all these parts—the guitar parts, the harmonies. I heard everything. We were on the road, and we had just gotten back from Europe—from being on tour with AC/DC. As successful as it was for us, the way we turned the crowd around every night, it still was brutal in a way that I never can explain to somebody. I remember when we got out of there, I felt like I'd been dragged behind a truck emotionally and felt almost dead inside. *It killed us.* We were glad it was over—even though we were thankful for the opportunity. And, like I said, AC/DC themselves were awesome. But we were glad that trial was over.

We get back to America, I write this song in my head, we're getting ready to hop on the bus, we're late for running to soundcheck, and I yell to my tech at the time, James Senter, and asked him to grab a guitar. James passed away recently—we miss him, he was a special person. He dug out my guitar and brought it up to me, while everybody waited for me to figure out the guitar part and play it enough times in my head to where I wouldn't forget it. And then I demoed it when I got home.

'CHARIOT SONG'

DOUG PINNICK One of my favorite songs is by Kansas—it's called 'Magnum Opus.' It's one of the greatest prog songs *ever*. It starts out with an intro, then Steve Walsh wails for a very passionate verse, and then they go into this ten-minute-plus song that has a thousand parts. I always loved that song. So, when I wrote 'Chariot Song,' I thought about that. I thought, *Let me try to write me a 'Magnum Opus.'* It has a lot of parts and harmonies. I made up a whole lot of parts with my drum machine, and I memorized all the changing parts for one take, because, back then, there was no digital copy-and-paste. It was a lot of work. And I'll never write a 'Magnum Opus' again—the demo was a lot of work. But we did it very close to my demo version.

I had all the vocals worked out, pretty much, too. I was just listening to that demo, to refresh my memory. There are parts of it where I wanted it to sound like we're doing a march in New Orleans to a funeral again, but faster. And again, this particular time, I was coming up with 'high-school glee club' type choir harmony parts in my demos. I don't even know if anyone would notice those things that I was trying to create. I think I put the most thought into this song than I ever have done. One of my favorite songs—which we'll never do live. Also, that song, I dropped the tuning down to C—which we had never done before. We worked hard on this one in the studio. Ty and Jerry's 'special sauce' and input always saves the day.

'OOH SONG'

TY TABOR I know that it started with Doug, but that we all worked on it. And the same thing with 'Chariot Song'—all of these, we worked a whole lot. Because when Doug brings in songs, they're normally not finished songs. He'll have verse and chorus ideas—not necessarily complete. So they'll come from him, and then we'll work them a bit and add some tweaks. That's a lot of the time how Doug's stuff comes in. When Jerry brings something in, it's usually just on acoustic guitar—but it's the full song. And when I bring something in, it's a full demo—all harmonies, all parts totally worked out. That's sort of the normal way of things for us. However, that isn't always the case. Doug sometimes demos his songs to a more finished state. But even if we bring something in that is totally worked out, it is still subject to being torn apart and worked on—no matter who's song it originally is. We try to make sure everyone is happy with whatever they are playing and feeling about the song.

DOUG PINNICK I vividly remember writing that in my apartment. It had such a dark groove to it—I had been trying to get darker, because I wasn't feeling positive any more. A sort of personal wake up call. That's why there are no real words in the chorus—it was another cluster chord thing I was into at the time. Just the word *ooh*. I remember the demo was very simple, but with all the vocal harmonies and all the starts and stops. It was fun to write. It was more the vocals and the *oohs* I was into. Lyrically, it's just words and thoughts to ponder on.

'NOT JUST FOR THE DEAD'

TY TABOR Lyrically, I think it was [based on] something I read by C.S. Lewis, but I can't remember exactly what it was, to be honest. That's another old one I kind of let go.

'WHAT I KNOW ABOUT LOVE'

DOUG PINNICK My whole struggle in life was to understand what love is. It's an obsession with me, to really figure out what it is, because I think most of us get it wrong. So, that song is the things that I've learned about love. It's more like saying, *This is what I know about it, but this is nothing compared to what it really is. And what I can still learn.* But now, looking back, I realize I didn't know a thing about love.

When I wrote the song, I was trying to make up a Dokken-type guitar part, with a bass line that didn't follow the guitar. I was thinking of George Lynch at the time when I came up with the guitar part. I had never even met George at the time. I remember that I kind of didn't like the song, and I didn't want to do it at first, because I had changed the chorus two times—the other chorus had swirling harmonies and a lot of words. But I never played that version for the band—I didn't like the lyrics I wrote, or my delivery of the lyrics. It still annoys me. But I think it's the loudest bass on a recording for King's X at that time! I played it for the guys and they all liked it, so we put it on the record.

'BLACK FLAG'

TY TABOR That again came from the whole trip through Germany that just sucked my soul. [*Laughs*] The song was about me making the decision that I'm over it—life is different, starting this second. It was my own self-realization—to stop wallowing and get the hell over it.

'DREAM IN MY LIFE'

TY TABOR That one I actually wrote while I was in Germany. At the time, I was married, with my son, and my home life was wonderful. I was really thinking about that—and wishing I could be home.

'SILENT WIND'

TY TABOR It's one of those I wish I could throw away. I don't care for the song *at all*. And we actually recorded it wrong. When I heard the original demo, after we recorded it, I was like, 'Oh, man … we did it *wrong*!' We did the harmonies wrong, and it was way better the way it was written. And it was my fault that we did it wrong. I didn't remember the right harmonies in the studio, and did it wrong. I always looked at that song like, *I blew that one*. But the song is about being quiet, and letting things come to you.

DESPITE ITS MAJOR-LABEL BACKING, *KING'S X* SURPRISINGLY DID NOT SERVE AS THE TRIO'S EXPECTED COMMERCIAL BREAKTHROUGH, RISING NO HIGHER THAN #138 ON THE *BILLBOARD* 200.

CHARLIE BENANTE The fourth album … it was kind of a 'silent release.' That's a weird album, too. I love that album, but it's the start of something turning and changing. Whereas *Faith Hope Love* is King's X, the fourth album is King's X … but it's one of those moments where you can tell something is changing.

JEFF AMENT It felt like the self-titled record was sort of more a return to the heavier King's X. Was 'Lost In Germany' the single? 'Black Flag' is kind of a crazy choice. It's an obvious chorus, but it seems like there were other songs on that record that might have been more single-y. 'The World Around Me' could have been a single, too.

TY TABOR I never thought of 'Not Just For The Dead' as [a song] that should have been a single. I thought 'Black Flag' should have been a single, and I thought it was an obvious one—because it was more straight-ahead and hooky. Come to think of it, I only thought that 'Black Flag' would be a good single—on the entire album. But I did feel like it was a pretty good, strong group of songs. 'Prisoner' I liked, 'Big Picture' I liked, 'Lost In Germany' I like a lot. I even like 'What I Know About Love'—that's a pretty cool song.

ROD MORGENSTEIN The song that I've loved the handful of times I've gotten to see them live is 'Lost In Germany.' Everything about it is cool, the riffs and and another thing—being a drummer, where you're always tuned in to timing and counting, that's a song that is, while it's not complicated timing, the fact that an extra beat or two or three will pass by as a chord is being held out, that can add so much to a song. That otherwise might not seem all that amazing. Not that 'Lost In Germany' isn't amazing, but I think they are so clever in their use of adding an extra beat or two here or there.

TY TABOR The 'Black Flag' video was filmed more than once. We went to LA and shot it with some dude—in some nuclear-holocaust-looking place. It was a place where some filming would happen for weird movies—zombie stuff and whatever. But it was a strictly off-limits place, where you weren't supposed to be, unless you had permission. And you were supposed to go in, do your thing, and get out, because it's chemically not a good place.

So we filmed the video out there in this stupid place, and we see the video, and we're like, 'There is *no way* we are ever letting anybody see that!' We wasted an entire other video budget on completely starting from scratch and re-filming it and redoing it. Then we released our version of it. But boy, *that cost us*.

DOUG PINNICK I remember it took us a couple of days to do the 'Black Flag' video. We had to do acting, and we had costumes and all kinds of stuff. It was fun. When Sam did videos for us, they were like movies—he'd take you all over the United States and film you from a helicopter, on top of a mountain! He was very grandiose with that. And he made some great videos for us. And they were very expensive. Nowadays, things are different—if they had given us $250,000 to do a video today, we'd do the video for $5,000 and keep the rest!

JERRY GASKILL We used some of the footage that the original people shot—I can't remember who they were—but Sam added a lot of the color scenes, with Doug in the bed, and Ty and me in whatever uniforms we had, with makeup on, standing by a casket. We put some kind of flag over it, and then we folded it afterward.

TY TABOR I remember shooting the video for the second version wasn't as bad as shooting other videos. I remember enjoying that one somewhat, because, for one thing, we did it in front of a blue screen. If there was any scenic wonderfulness, we didn't have to drive up dangerous mountains and climb out on ledges to get a stupid shot that didn't even show it properly. For me, standing in front of a blue screen is always way, way better. It was simple—our family hanging out, good food, just, 'Shoot this. OK, take a break! Now, put this latex on your face and do this.' It was a whole lot of 'do something quick' and then wait. So, during all the waiting, everyone is hanging out, eating, and having fun. It was an enjoyable shoot because it was all in one little place.

JERRY GASKILL That video eventually got played on *Beavis & Butt-Head*, and I remember Doug is in bed and has got this red pajama thing on, and I think it was Butt-Head who said, 'Oh, he's got morning wood!' It was cool—they didn't dog us, they didn't put us down.

RICHARD CHRISTY 'Black Flag' was awesome, and that was back in the days when MTV played videos. I feel so fortunate that I grew up in the 80s, where I got introduced to these amazing bands like King's X by seeing their videos on *Headbangers Ball*. There was no internet or anything to hear about bands from. King's X had these really cool videos. Almost a little bit artsy and surreal videos—some of them were. They really caught my attention. Plus, the songs were great. They were super-catchy songs. I'm so fortunate that I was able to discover them by watching *Headbangers Ball* and *Dial MTV*.

IN APRIL 1992, KING'S X FLEW TO LOS ANGELES FOR A TELEVISION
TAPING TO FIND THE CITY IN LOCKDOWN FOLLOWING A SERIES OF RIOTS
PROMPTED BY THE ACQUITTAL OF FOUR LAPD OFFICERS ACCUSED OF
ASSAULT AND USE OF EXCESSIVE FORCE IN THE ARREST OF RODNEY KING.

DOUG PINNICK We had flown into town to perform on *The Dennis Miller Show*, and the riots had started in LA, so they wouldn't let people come down, because there were fires, like, *six blocks away*. But they wanted to still video the show— so we did it without an audience. It's crazy—we're the only band to do that, I guess. I was wearing a Martin Luther King shirt for that reason—I just wanted to make a statement with my T-shirt.

JERRY GASKILL We went in there, quickly performed, and it was aired later. And then, going back to the hotel, I remember standing on the balcony of the room and watching the city *burn*. It felt like we were in one of the Middle Eastern countries, where so much was going on there at the time. It was crazy— it was like a ghost town … as the city burned.

TY TABOR That was one heck of an experience, man. We experienced it first-hand, seeing it with our own eyes. Some amazing things we saw with our own eyes. But basically, how it started is all of us were aware there was going to be a verdict that day. The whole United States was aware. Waiting for it. And I believe that the verdict was made right as we were leaving for the *Dennis Miller Show* studio. We were in this limo, they drive us over, we get out, and, apparently, it was somewhere around the area where a lot of people started getting up on their roofs with guns. So we were in there, waiting to film, getting ready to shoot the show, when somebody runs in and says, 'There is gun fire in the parking lot, and the police want us to clear out of here now.'

The producer looks at us, and says, 'Look, we're going to roll tape on you right now. Just play the song twice, we'll do it, and then we'll get the hell out of here.' So we played them straight through, quick, grabbed our stuff, and got out of there as quick as we could. And, by now, they're showing on the news stuff that is looking like things are getting out of control. And we're like, 'Man ... *get us out of this limo.*' But we didn't encounter anything—they drove us to the Sunset Strip, to the hotel we were at. At this point, there are some fires that are starting to break out. We turn on the TV, and then we start seeing people get beat up and fire after fire after fire, crowds of angry mobs. So we get out on our balcony—we're about ten floors up—and we basically spent the whole night in shifts, watching to make sure that our block didn't have a fire on it, and we didn't need to evacuate. Because in every direction, we could see there were fires. Countless fires. By nighttime, *the whole city* was lit up—as if it had been bombed all over the city. The sky was getting black from the fires—like there is a lid on things. I remember all of that very vividly.

I remember our soundman and I seeing somebody with a gas can running between buildings, and thinking, *Oh, crap.* Nothing happened to our building, but we didn't get any sleep, because there were whole blocks going up in fire, so we had to be aware of our surroundings and make sure we didn't need to run. It was a scary night of watching the city burn. The next day, there was smoke rising everywhere—from all over the city. Just like bombs had been dropped. I've never seen anything like that in my life. And I've never seen video of it that shows it like that. The video will always just show one block burning and then another one and then another one. I've never seen a video showing across the landscape, the whole black sky above the city from all the smoke, and all the fires coming up in all directions. I've never seen that picture ever before. And it surprised me that there hasn't been a whole of video of that, because it was one of the most amazing things I've ever seen with my eyes.

DOUG PINNICK I don't remember a whole lot about the tour. All those tours are a big blur of tour buses and fans, and every day getting up, going to sleep, talking to people, and playing music. I wish I could remember more of it, only because a lot of people have said in the past—and I agree with them—that when you're in the middle of it all, you don't realize what's going on until it's over, and then you can look back. And the things that happened in our lives and experiences that we had, they're only memories now. But when they're happening, I didn't even realize it—I was busy making sure my hair was looking good and I was singing on pitch. [*Laughs*]

TY TABOR I remember we continued hearing, 'They don't want to play you. They're saying you're a God band.' And we were also about to split up after touring so much on the last album, so we had to give our families a little priority … or there wasn't going to be any more band. So, that album, there was a little backing off.

DOUG PINNICK Fans told me that it was like a two-story different thing here. A lot of people said they thought it was our best record from the four of the Sam Taylor years. But there are other people who thought we were at the end of it, and that was just a rehash of the first three records. So … I don't know. I like the record, because I felt like that record finally was the crux of the Sam Taylor era.

TY TABOR I think we were about cycled out of that album when the band split with Sam Taylor. We were kind of in that grey area where you could pick up another tour or two and keep going, or you can lay back and start writing music, take some time off, and think about the next one. I think we were at that point when things happened.

DOUG PINNICK Somewhere in there, Sam had quit, and Sam took care of everything. Sam took control of the band, and everything we did was his doing. We just sat there and he did everything. We had no say-so in much of anything, and when Sam left, we were kind of there with nothing—no manager, nobody to tell us what to do. At that point, I think everybody dropped the ball. No one was pushing Atlantic for another video, and we didn't have a manager, so it was time to move on. And I think Atlantic said, 'Look, this record is not really doing anything, so let's go for the next one.' And we did. Doug Morris told me as long as he was the CEO of Atlantic, we would always be on Atlantic—no matter how many records we sold.

JERRY GASKILL I would never discount anything that Sam did, because he helped us, he motivated us, he worked us, and brought the best out of us—I do believe. And that kind of catapulted us to what King's X became. There's no doubt about it. But at one point, I realized that there was a lot of money going to Sam's company, Wilde Silas. I mean *a lot* of money. We had a lot of money coming through, and we never saw it. There were hundreds upon hundreds of thousands of dollars coming through, and I remember one incident—I was getting ready to go on tour, and I couldn't even pay my bills. I went to Sam and said, 'Look, I'm not even going to go on tour, man. I can't do this, because I can't even pay my bills. I need to pay my light bill, for like, a couple hundred dollars.' And I remember the answer being, 'Absolutely not.' And I'm thinking, *Hmmm*.

And then I realized there was a lot of money going into the Wilde Silas account—something like $30,000 a month, when we were getting, like, $300 a week. But we believed in Sam—we believed in the vision together.

Finally, I called the accountant, and said, 'Hey, what's going on here?' Because I was curious. I said, 'There is a lot of money going into Wilde Silas. What is this all about?' And they said, 'Well, do you want us to stop doing that?' I said, 'I think I do. Until we find out what's going on.' So we had a meeting with Sam, just to talk to him and see what was going on, and said, 'Hey, maybe you can explain this to us so we can understand what's happening here. We're not accusing anybody of anything, but it seems a little odd that I'm making $300 a week and you're getting $30,000 a month.'

So we got together for the meeting, and at that meeting … he quits.

DOUG PINNICK We were making no money. Sam was barely paying us anything, and telling us that we were broke. When we would ask for money, he would accuse us of being greedy, and that he never got a paycheck, so why should we be complaining? People don't realize, we were making three to four to five hundred dollars a week. Jerry had two kids and a wife, and Ty was married and had a kid. The wives were working, everyone was struggling, and here we are on MTV, with four records out, doing major tours, and all this money is going through the camp. We didn't know what was going on, and he kept it from us. But he remodeled his house, had a new car, a huge complex with his office in it, a receptionist, and a secretary.

One day, we got all the information on the money spent from the new accountants we had just hired for our books. And we saw thousands of dollars of checks written out to people we didn't know. Plus we were getting huge advances back then—for everything. So we asked him what was going on, and he quit. We asked him about it, and he quit. He never gave us an explanation. And that was that. He said to talk to his lawyer, and he wanted severance pay. I was shocked!

So that era was done. Quite frankly, we were glad.

TY TABOR We had a situation where King's X and Sam Taylor's company, Wilde Silas, worked very closely together. We would hire Wilde Silas to do the videos, so King's X would get a budget, which would actually go to Wilde Silas. It was not unusual, in our accountant's eyes, for a hundred grand to go to his company, and things like that. And Sam was the manager who would make those requests.

I think there was a time when King's X was completely out of money, and the balance between the companies was … very unbalanced. We three guys were starving to death, and there should have been a whole lot of money. That's when a meeting was called, and when we called the meeting, it was just to start discussing some of this, and figure out how we could finally start getting a paycheck after all this touring, and all these sold-out shows.

Management during that time was not in the same situation as us. Management was able to afford to buy a building, a house, add on to that house, buy cars—do all kinds of things while we could do none of those things on that list. *Not a single thing.* Including buy a car. We were broke. So we wanted to have a meeting about it, because at this time … the balance of money was massive. And also, a whole lot of it that had gone, which we were not aware of until we talked to our accountants. They told us what the balance was, and that we didn't have any money. So we told our accountants, 'This is directly from the owners of the band, and you don't listen to anyone else—don't give one more penny to Sam Taylor, to his company, or to any of his employees. Not one more cent of our money.' And then we called this meeting. Sam comes in, and of all things—I'll always remember this—says he can no longer afford to work with us, and that he's quitting.

DOUG VAN PELT [Sam] managed three bands at the time—that I knew of—and he approached me about giving him a business plan or giving him a proposal if I ever needed some money. Because sometimes, a lot of money came through because of the success of those three bands—specifically King's X. I never took him up on that opportunity, but at one point, he approached me about letting him know if I needed some investment capital or even kind of like a grant situation—money that came in, that I could use.

JERRY GASKILL Sam called me when I was in the hospital, about twenty years after the split, and that's pretty much the last time I spoke with him. I hadn't spoken to him before that—since all this happened. So basically, no, I have no contact with Sam Taylor.

JAY PHEBUS Sam Taylor was a brilliant producer. In my opinion, a horrible manager, but a brilliant producer. Just like Dr. Jekyll and Mr. Hyde—you never knew what you were going to get. I mean, one day, I was his #1 right-hand man, and then, the next day, he's trying to crucify me in front of the band. It was very schizophrenic—how things were hot and cold with him. But I was there before Sam *and* after Sam, so I saw it all. For every bad thing I've got to say, I've got one or two conversely phenomenal things to say. But it boils down to: he was an amazing producer. I learned a lot—especially in the studio—from him.

JERRY GASKILL I know a lot more now—I'm much more in tune now than I was then. I was younger, it was new to me. I was believing in people and trusting people before I knew not to trust people.

SAM TAYLOR WOULD EVENTUALLY BE REPLACED AS MANAGER
OF KING'S X BY RAY DANNIELS, RUSH'S LONGTIME MANAGER.
(TAYLOR DECLINED TO BE INTERVIEWED FOR THIS BOOK.)

TY TABOR I don't think Atlantic said anything about Sam leaving. They were OK with it. I remember when we mentioned it to certain people there, that's when stories started coming out to us about things he had done there, and they were very glad that he was going to be out of the picture. That's the kind of response we were getting.

At first, after Sam left, *I* was acting as the band's manager—just for the lack of having anyone. I did that for a little while, but it was not possible to keep it up. At one point, we had to start getting the word out in the industry that we were looking for a manager. We had different people drive to Houston to meet us, and we made it be like that—we figured, if anybody wants to manager us, they need to show that they really want to do it, and they need to see us and spend some time at their own expense. That will show us if they mean business or not.

Ray Danniels was a great manager, and got some great things done for us. I enjoyed working with him, too. He would have been the next manager after Sam, because he was our manager during *Dogman*, and he was the manager during *Ear Candy*. There was talk of [King's X touring with Rush], it's just that Rush would only tour in the summer, and somehow things were never timed out right. But I have met them more than once and gotten to hang out and everything—which was a dream come true for me, to hang out with Alex Lifeson, because he is a huge influence on me. So we ended up getting to know them a little bit and meet them, but we never got to tour.

Ray was a businessman, and that's what I loved about him. He came in to make the band work monetarily for us—as opposed to Sam, who was the producer, manager, mentor, controller, and whatever else you want to call him. Sam engulfed us with everything. He controlled every little aspect—he even told us what to say and what not to say in the media, even though we didn't listen to him. But Ray Danniels gave us freedom. He said, 'Hey, man, *you're King's X*. Let me see if I can make it work for you.' He went to bat for us, and he's the guy that would make great deals. He's known in the music business for making great deals for bands. And he went in and did some good stuff for us, monetarily.

Afterward, we made more money than when we were with Sam, but it still wasn't much, because we were already past the 'heyday' of our selling out three-thousand-seat places. By the time Sam left, we were playing House Of Blues and stuff like that. They're good gigs and decent pay, so we were able to pay ourselves more. But, at the same time, bus expenses went way up during that time period, gas went way up during that time period—so, all of a sudden, what used to be not a big expense was almost something that could cripple an entire tour. This was back in the super-expensive gas days. There was a lot to it, where we were barely staying afloat, but we were getting a little bit bigger paychecks, because nobody else was taking our money.

JERRY GASKILL It's always a funny thing with King's X—it feels like something always blocked everything that was going on with us. I mean, we catapulted to this place, but something always stopped it. And, like I said earlier, I wasn't as in tune with things back then as I would be now.

12 DOGMAN

THE STORY BEHIND KING'S X'S FIFTH STUDIO
ALBUM, RELEASED ON JANUARY 18, 1994.

TY TABOR I think around *Dogman* is when I started being unhappy. When we went to Atlantic is when I started becoming unhappy. The further it went at Atlantic, the more unhappy I got—until we got to *Ear Candy*. We literally got ourselves off the label at that point.

DOUG PINNICK I remember Atlantic said, 'All right, who do you want to produce this record?' I wanted Brendan O'Brien, and everybody said, 'Yeah!' Because Brendan was doing everybody, and everything was sounding great. Everybody sounded the way we wanted it to sound, sonically. On the first four records … I'm not going to say they were *over-produced*, but they were produced like an 80s record. It was a whole different era, and we wanted to be in the new era.

I remember making *Dogman*, and how different it was making that record as opposed to making the first four, because Brendan did things quick. He didn't waste time. He knew what he wanted—you went in, you played the song, it sounded great, and you went on to the next one. We didn't break things down and dissect things and tear things apart, like we did with the earlier songs.

We had gone through a lot of emotional trauma—trying to get the emotion out of a tune—on the first four records. I'm not complaining—that's what producers are supposed to do—they bring out what they feel that is in you. Sam did that, which I was happy with. But Brendan was a completely different guy—he let everyone do what they wanted, and be free. So, when we made that record, it was such a freedom. And, listening to the tracks back, as soon as we did, we'd go, 'Whoa … this sounds great!' With the first four records, we'd listen to a track before it was mixed, and it sounded like shit, because it wasn't mixed. But Brendan had this great way of making everything sound great from the beginning. It was a culture shock for us. In fact, we took about twenty minutes for us to get a drum sound—when it used to take *a week* to get a drum sound for the earlier records. It was a whole new era of recording—with compression, and 'off-the-cuff.' Brendan was a new guy on the block, and it was pretty cool.

TY TABOR Things kind of changed in the writing of the *Dogman* album. Doug sang more of my songs on that album than usual. I didn't sing any of my songs on that album. I was thinking at the time that we needed to be more focused as a band, and that the idea of me singing some lead songs and Doug singing most of the lead songs—and our biggest video being of me singing—was actually confusing.

I remember, when we got to *Dogman*, I actually went to Doug, and said, 'How do you feel about singing everything on this record, just so it's all focused and not confusing?' And he said, 'Sure. I'll try.' The way we had done it in the past is, I would write a song, and I would give Doug the first chance at it. And if he wasn't feeling it, then I would go ahead and sing it. So I was hoping he would feel everything. And he did on that one, because we worked on it, and we made him be able to sing things the way he felt OK singing to what I was writing. That was the difference in *Dogman*—we wanted to focus on Doug being the lead singer.

Our sound and vibe changed pretty radically on this album. That happened *before* we met Brendan O'Brien. And it happened on purpose. After we'd done several albums, I felt that we were starting to imitate ourselves—we were using all the same amps, the same mics, the same sounds, locking in to this same thing that we felt that we had to do, and what people knew as 'King's X.' But, in the beginning, that's not how we became what we were. We became what we were by experimenting, and *not* knowing what it was going to be. So, when it came to *Dogman*, I said to the guys, 'Let's quit making the same album, and see who we are now. Quit imitating. What do we want to do *now*?' We went into rehearsal, and I intentionally changed amps—I started playing Boogies and Marshalls—to force myself to sound different, play different, and think about it differently, and force me out of the same mold.

We started doing demos, and we actually released those demos [in 2005], if anyone wants to hear what it sounded like before Brendan—because it's very, very close to what the album came out as. The only reason I bring that up is because a lot of people may assume that, by having a new producer, the new producer forced that on us. But that's not true. All you have to do is listen to *Dogman Demos*, which is released online, to know where we were at before we met Brendan. We were already there. We were already in that change of style and vibe, on purpose. And then Brendan came in and really put on some fine touches, put on his magical recording sounds, and how he captures vibe. Brendan is a great producer. The atmosphere he makes for everyone playing in is so relaxed and fun. We took breaks to play basketball a lot, and do fun things—to keep ourselves light. And then, when we went in, we just knocked it out. He worked fast. We like to work fast, too, so it was a great situation.

The way it happened was, Brendan went to Atlantic Records and basically told them he had worked with everybody he had wanted to, and now he wanted to do an album with King's X. That was the last thing he really wanted to do, and to ask us if we would be willing to do an album with him. And it didn't take us any time to say, '*Absolutely*.' Our only worry was, 'Can we afford to work with him?' At the time, he was the biggest producer on the earth—by far. He was the man everybody wanted to work with. The fact that he wanted to work with us was an honor. We of course said yes, and we worked out financially how to do it. That's how it came together. But working with Brendan was absolutely fantastic. However, it was kind of a tough time for Jerry—there was a lot going on at home. Things were pretty crappy for him. It was a dark time for him.

JERRY GASKILL Here's what I remember about the *Dogman* record—my life was in shambles. But I had some great times *because* my life was in shambles. And I remember going to the studio earlier than everybody else, and going over all the songs—by myself—with a click track. Just to get the groove happening myself, so that when we all got in there, I felt it—I had the groove happening.

I remember, when Brendan first came to work with us, he came to Houston. We played some songs for him and we hung out together. At that point—right before he came—I remember my ex-wife punched me in the face. I'm sure she did it just to shut me up! And I had a big fat lip. I even went to the hospital, to see if I might need stitches.

Mostly, what put the strain on my first marriage was our relationship. The two of us. The touring may have had something to do with it, but I'm in a marriage now that, if that was happening now, I don't think it would be a strain on the marriage. I think it would be something that we would continually focus on working out.

I believe that divorce starts the day you get married, and there's something inside you that knows that something is not 100 percent right. Therefore, eventually, it's going to grow and make its way to the surface, until you finally say, 'Look, we have to break this thing up.' Those are my thoughts. And that's the way it was with my first marriage. And when that's the case, then everything puts a strain on the marriage—unless it's exactly the perfect thing that you both want. Which, most often, is not the case … *ever*. [*Laughs*]

TY TABOR Southern Tracks was a little more modern. A nicer place with a little more room. It was a little more 'live' of a room—there was more wood, to give a more live kind of sound, whereas the place that we recorded the first four albums was like one big, carpeted, dead room, and there was no life to it at all.

JERRY GASKILL I remember talking to Brendan, and telling him, 'I want this record to be so heavy, that it sounds like big monster creatures are walking through the town, and they're crushing everything as they walk through it.' I think all three of us wanted it to be a real *heavy* record. I guess we accomplished that.

THE SONGS
'DOGMAN'

DOUG PINNICK I remember Ty said he set out to write the baddest riff he could ever write in his life … *and he did*. [*Laughs*]

TY TABOR I wrote it, demoed it, and brought it in. So it was already done. We just learned it. The only thing we changed was something that I asked to change when I brought it in. I said, 'I like this song, but the only thing I don't like about it is what it's called, and the main catchphrase of the song.' Because, originally, it was, '*To be a* good *man*.' And it didn't fit what I was trying to say. So I remember, in rehearsal, we were all sitting around trying to think of things to come up with. I think I just thought about the fact that I love dogs, and always have. I have three right now—I always have dogs. They're family to me.

I threw out 'Dogman,' and everybody thought it sounded good—but none of us knew what it meant. Then, when Doug started singing it, it all of a sudden made perfect sense. It was a lucky accident. Lyrically, I'm not exactly sure—it's kind of disjointed artistically, on purpose. And trying to express that feeling of not standing on solid ground—although that's a bad way to put it. The thing is, I write lyrics because I don't know how to explain what I'm feeling. The lyrics say it best on that song. I don't really know how to add to them. It wasn't about Sam at all. It was totally about a personal self-struggle. There is a song on the album about Sam—but it's not this one.

'SHOES'

TY TABOR I love that song. It's super-heavy.

DOUG PINNICK We were going through that whole time of feeling betrayed with Sam and all that stuff that went on with him. And Jerry was in the middle of a divorce, and things were changing for us. We saw the world as it was, instead of through this little fantasy world that Sam had kept us in. He protected us. So, anyway, what happened was we were a bit angrier and a bit betrayed and a bit frustrated. We had put four records out, and everyone had said we were going to be the next big thing in the world—and nobody gave a fuck about us. So we're going, 'Well, what the hell is going on here?' I don't know about Ty, but I wrote the angriest songs I've ever written—in the best way I could.

Also, grunge had happened, and grunge was rocking the world. And I felt our songs sounded wimpy compared to Alice In Chains and Soundgarden. We needed Brendan O'Brien to do that, because that's what we sounded like, anyway. We sounded fat and thick and powerful like those bands did, but we never got it on a record. And that was the biggest reason why we wanted Brendan to do that. So, when I wrote 'Shoes,' that's another song that I dropped the guitars down to C on. I had never done that, other than on 'Chariot Song.' I wrote several songs on that record in drop-C, which made it even heavier.

'PRETEND'

DOUG PINNICK It was my poor attempt at a pop song. It's so happy—with dark lyrics. Probably my least favorite tune on the record … and I wrote it! It's close to the demo, but the last verse/bridge-type part, Ty came up with that to give the song a boost out of boredom. He's a genius on things like that.

That was about a friend of mine that I felt was using me, and I didn't know how to deal with it—so I just acted like everything was fine. He heard it, and was pissed!

JERRY GASKILL I remember doing the vocals for 'Pretend.' I had a harmony part, and we got in there and I started singing, and they stopped the tape, and Brendan said, 'That was really great … but you are singing *Doug's* part.' [*Laughs*]

'FLIES AND BLUE SKIES'

TY TABOR I don't remember where that one came from. I don't really remember what the inspiration was. But I remember it must have been something heavy—because it's one of the heaviest things I've ever written. But I honestly don't remember where it came from. I remember sitting down and writing it, and it coming out very fast.

'BLACK THE SKY'

DOUG PINNICK That was another drop-C tune with a different tuning. I wrote several *Dogman* tunes in that tuning. C-G-D-C-B-E—I think that's it. I was going for a very dark, ZZ Top, grungy type of groove. I remember Brendan said to do a key change in the chorus, and Ty changed the riff a bit—to make it more him—and it made it so much better. I remember Ty suggested a few kicks and accents, which made it badass. It's one of my favorite songs I wrote. And it was mixed perfectly, in my opinion.

I was down in a deep depression—really bummed out about everything in my life. It was about wanting to die, but knowing I'm too chicken to do it, and it would be just plain stupid for me to do.

TY TABOR We were in the studio in Atlanta, with Brendan O'Brien, doing *Dogman*. And we were recording the song 'Black The Sky,' and it was a real funky tune. I didn't have a wah-wah pedal with me—I didn't bring one. I had been using it too much, and intentionally had not brought one for those sessions. But when it came to that song, I was like, 'This has to be a wah.' So, we sent out for a wah, and I believe Jay Phebus—our soundman at the time—is who went and got it. Jay drove to the nearest store, grabbed a wah pedal, and came running in. We just happened to be listening to the song from the beginning when he walked in with it in the box. I plugged my guitar into it—I didn't even check my tuning—and it just happened to be coming up to right where the solo was, and I looked over at Brendan, and said, '*Hit record!*' And I played that solo—not even hearing what the wah was going to sound like or anything. It was just a few seconds, *boom*, he stopped, I unplugged it, handed the wah back to Jay, and said, '*You can take it back.*' [*Laughs*]

'FOOL YOU'

TY TABOR *That's* the song I wrote about Sam. I think everything I write is therapeutic—for one reason or another. It has to do with something. I think that is why I write—for therapy. It helps. There was plenty to say about Sam, and I didn't really know how to say it. So, I thought about putting his own words in there, and letting him speak for himself. The choruses are him, basically. The verses are me telling about our friendship, and the choruses are actually what he had to say.

'DON'T CARE'

TY TABOR That one I'm pretty sure was one of the ones Doug demoed almost completely, and we just did it.

DOUG PINNICK That was about a person who I thought was the greatest person in the world, and then I found out that they played a game on me, and really tried to make a fool of me. And it really was the truth—it wasn't me being paranoid. Just some terrible stuff happened from this person. At that point, I realized, *I don't care about you like I used to*—and that's what that song is about. And again, that song was in drop-C tuning—which gave it a whole new vibe for me, the way I was writing at the time.

JERRY GASKILL 'Don't Care' is a song that I think I do some pretty cool drum stuff on. It was something that I did on my own, because it wasn't on the demo that way. I remember playing the drums on that, and everyone was excited afterward. And Brendan O'Brien—when I came back into the control room—said, 'Man … the cover of *Modern Drummer*!' Of course, that didn't happen, either.

'SUNSHINE RAIN'

TY TABOR That was Doug, too. The more I think about it, *Dogman* is 75/25 Doug, possibly.

DOUG PINNICK I was completely depressed and crying—feeling down, as usual, and I was feeling like an idiot. The sun always shines in Houston, but all I could see was rain … blah blah blah. So, I had to get it out somehow. And it's the same kind of vibe. The funny thing is, all the songs that I wrote on *Dogman* are all kind of the same songs—with just a different paintjob, you know? That whole record is like that. But there's a sound that we have on that record that is very coherent.

'COMPLAIN'

TY TABOR That one, I was listening to a radio program about the guys that first tried the attempt to make it to the North Pole and then back to their original base camp. And they died just a few miles away from making it back to the camp. There was a radio program where they were reading the diary of the last guy— the head of the expedition—who died last, and what he was writing the whole time and at the end. I remember them reading that, and it having a big effect on me—as to how petty everything in the day that I had been upset about actually was. Just about how easy it is to complain about stuff that isn't a real problem at all. And, musically, I actually was thinking of—even though it doesn't sound anything like them or what they would play—the high tempo was because I was listening to some Galactic Cowboys, and I wanted to write something that was a little faster tempo.

'HUMAN BEHAVIOR'

TY TABOR That's another Doug one. We used a whole bunch of different guitar tunings on this record. Like, for instance, 'Fool You' is one tuning that is different from 'Shoes,' that's different from 'Black The Sky,' which is a different tuning from 'Human Behavior.' 'Human Behavior' is the only song on the album tuned in that tuning, and there was a good bit of that stuff going on—on *Dogman*—which made touring a nightmare. I had to bring *so many* guitars. It was stupid. But 'Human Behavior' was Doug. I remember thinking it was a little Led Zeppelin-ish and really digging it.

DOUG PINNICK I wrote that one on my twelve-string bass—in a different tuning, actually. It was a complete demo. It had some specific accents through the whole song that had to be there, and it just rocked. We went in and killed it, sonically. *It's brutal*. Wish I had come up with a better vocal line, but that's life.

King's X, our thing is to groove things and push the beat—play the upbeat instead of the downbeat. And I wanted to write a whole song that was on the upbeat. And I loved that song—except I hated the lyrics and I hated the melody. I wish I could have come up with a better hook vocally, and different lyrics. I think the reason why is because I was kind of drained when it came to words, and I think I was searching for things to sing about. And as a result of it, I think I didn't do my best. It's probably *someone's* favorite lyrics! But I love the music.

'CIGARETTES'

TY TABOR That's me, and I can't really explain those lyrics. I really can't. There's no possible way I could explain those lyrics—I'm sorry! It was stream-of-consciousness, and portraying feelings that are real from real circumstances, but they're disjointed and will make no sense if you take them away from the song.

'GO TO HELL'

DOUG PINNICK That was written back in '81 or '82. We had just got together, and we decided to write a punk song. And I don't know who came up with what—who came up with the chords or anything, because it's so simple. But I remember we did it, and that was back in Springfield. We weren't even doing cover music at that time—we were a brand new band, writing crappy songs. But when we were doing *Dogman*, when we got done with all the songs, Brendan said, 'Do you have anything else?' And we go, 'Well, we've done everything we really know.' Then somebody came up with, 'Well, what about "Go To Hell"?'

We went in and did two takes of it, and when we came back in and listened, Brendan said, 'Can you believe this? I put two mics on the drums. That's it!' He wanted to make it real punk-rock-sounding, and it came across that way. The lyrics are really dogmatically Christian. That's what we were into at the time. But when we put the song out, I thought, *I don't believe in those lyrics anymore. I can't be behind them.* We didn't have time to write new lyrics, so I said, 'Well, let me sing the lyrics, and then we'll distort the lyrics so they'll be inaudible, and we'll never tell anybody what it really means.' And, to this day, we've never told anybody.

'PILLOW'

TY TABOR 'Pillow' is Doug, and he didn't have any idea what to write for the chorus. And he *still* thinks it's nonsense. [*Laughs*]

DOUG PINNICK Again, it was that era of trying to write these really heavy songs. So that's all I can say about that—it's a heavy fucking song. Lyrically, though, I was going to a church at the time where I sat down in the pew, the preacher started preaching about stuff that was so mundane and had been said so many times before. It was nothing new. I was like, 'OK. Come on. I *know* Jesus loves me. Everything you're telling me … I've heard this sermon for the last four years.' So, I came up with, '*Listening to words that seem to bounce right off my chest / Like I heard it all before / Teach an old dog the same old trick.*'

The second verse is '*I ate the crumbs and I spilled the wine / The thought that counts*'—because we take communion at this church. We go up every Sunday and eat this bread and wine, and it was the same old thing. And then there are candles shining as you're doing your communion. It was sort of a Catholic-based church. And I looked up and was like, 'OK. There are these candles shining and this incense—supposedly a sweet savor to God or something. This is crazy.' So, the chorus was, '*Tide underside my pillow / Willow thundering.*' I woke up and I heard that melody in my head. And the words make no sense, but I put them on there, anyway.

'MANIC DEPRESSION'

DOUG PINNICK I think Brendan said, 'Why don't you do a cover?' And somebody came up with 'Manic Depression.' So we sent somebody to the store to get the record [the landmark debut from the Jimi Hendrix Experience, 1967's *Are You Experienced?*], and when he brought it back, we played it a couple of times in the upstairs reception area. Then we went in the studio and just did it. We went over our parts like … one time, by ourselves, and then went in and knocked it out in two takes.

The first time we did it, I sang it so much like Hendrix, Brendan made me do it again and sing it more like me. I did, and that is the take that they got. And then, after we did it, we decided to put crowd noise on it—to make it sound like it was live. So Brendan dug out this twenty-four-track of The Atlanta Rhythm Section at Carnegie Hall, and took the crowd response track and put it on the song. And then, he took another one from a philharmonic orchestra, and took the crowd applause from that, mixed the two together, and put it on the song. It was funny.

DOGMAN BECAME THE BAND'S SECOND-HIGHEST-CHARTING
ALBUM ON THE *BILLBOARD* 200, HITTING #88.

TY TABOR I'm not sure who came up with the 'dog' idea for the album cover. Because there were all these different covers that were being come up with. And I think I just said to them, 'Can't you just put a dog's face on the cover, and let it be that?' And then the wheels started turning: 'Well, let's release it in different colors in different parts of the country, and then people will want to collect all of them.' It became this thing, then. The photo came from somebody at Atlantic—I don't know if it was their dog or a stock photo.

JERRY GASKILL For the 'Dogman' video shoot, we were in Harlem, and it was very, very cold. We were able to pick out some cool clothes. I picked out cool boots—which I still have to this day! I remember when we did *The Dennis Miller Show* a while earlier, we heard it back, and I thought, *Oh … my harmony is off*. And one of the crew guys on the 'Dogman' video said, 'Hey, sorry about *The Dennis Miller Show*, man.' [*Laughs*]

DOUG PINNICK We did that video in the middle of winter. It was, like, *below zero* in the evening. We had fun because we knew it was going to be a badass video, and we loved the song. We thought we had finally nailed the record we wanted the world to hear—so we were very excited, and we had high hopes for that record and video.

TY TABOR I remember freezing our butts off! We did a couple of daytime shots, but most of it was nighttime shots. Between takes, we would jump into the trailers as fast as possible—because of the agony and pain of our fingers and faces—until they would say, 'OK … *ready*!' And we would run out, do another cut, and then run back in the trailer. It was absolute misery. I was glad when that one was over. But, at the same time, it was kind of fun. We tried to make the best of it, and everybody had good attitudes. I remember enjoying it—despite how cold it was.

SHANNON LARKIN When *Dogman* came out, it was shorter songs, it was a heavier record. It fused all of their influences—whether it be blues, gospel, metal, rock, funk. It seemed like *Dogman* was the culmination of all the best moments of the first four records, and they put that into a set of perfect songs.

NUNO BETTENCOURT *Dogman* was incredible to me, as well. It was uniquely different from *Faith Hope Love*—it wasn't as bright, it was a bit darker, meaner, tougher. But when I heard that, I couldn't believe it.

MIKE PORTNOY When *Dogman* came out, I was convinced that they were going to blow up. I thought that was 'the album.' They finally were on a major label, Brendan O'Brien produced that, and he was like 'the hot producer' at the time. I thought that *Dogman* was going to be their breakthrough, and they were going to be as big as Stone Temple Pilots or Pantera at the time. And, sure enough—in true King's X fashion—it never materialized to everybody's expectations. But I remember when that album came out, I had the song 'Dogman' on Dream Theater's house music mix tape that whole tour, so I remember hearing it every night from the dressing room, and always trying to support them. No matter how much success and notoriety I got—either myself or within Dream Theater—I always carried the King's X flag, and I always tried to mention them in interviews, wear their T-shirts, and bring more attention to them.

RICHARD CHRISTY I remember that was sort of my soundtrack for when I first moved to Florida. I *constantly* listened to the *Dogman* album. Music brings back memories, and when I hear *Dogman*, it brings back memories of when I ended up joining the band Death. I moved from Springfield, Missouri to Orlando, Florida, and I had a long drive—I think seventeen hours or something—in my old '73 Ford LTD. And I remember I must have listened to *Dogman* about twenty times on that trip. That album helped me get through a long drive in a crappy old car down to Florida … so, thank you, King's X!

BRIAN SLAGEL The one song that is one of my all-time favorite King's X songs—that I still try and get them to play—is 'Complain.' I *love* that song. I can listen to that song over and over again. 'Cigarettes' is another one that I love. That's one of my favorite King's X records—it's super-heavy.

CHARLIE BENANTE So … here's where it got a little weird for me. I didn't really like the sound of that record. It didn't sound like King's X anymore, and it took me a while to struggle with it, because of the amount of love and how much I really enjoyed the sound of those other records, and it *was* King's X. That was their sound and that was their style. So, *Dogman* comes out, and I remember feeling a bit like, 'I don't know, man. I don't know about this.' I think that was the turning point, where things started to change a lot. Sam Taylor was not there anymore, and I think … this may come out wrong, but … when they started to get a bit lost.

MICK MARS Probably my favorite one is *Dogman*. That's the one I remember the most, and *Dogman* had some really great songs. That's still my favorite album by them. I feel that they were more like brothers, instead of sitting there and going like, *We're just a bunch of musicians we put together.* They were like one person playing this music that, in my opinion, is incredible.

GEORGE LYNCH There was a KXM bonus track that we wrote after we had done the first record. We realized we needed a bonus track. We were already done with the album, and we needed this for Japan. So, I went back to *Dogman*, and listened to *Dogman* over and over again, and used that inspiration and wrote something that was kind of 'in the spirit of.' It's called 'Big Rocks,' and it's on the Japanese version of the *KXM* record. Honestly, it's my favorite KXM song. Unfortunately, it's only on the Japanese record, so nobody else got to hear it!

JEFF AMENT I'm a sucker for Brendan's production. I don't know the details of that record, but I think the guitar sounds different. It sounds a little bit more direct and dry. I think Doug was the main singer on most of that record, which I always loved when Ty had a song or two, but I think sometimes, when Ty had half the record, it wasn't as strong, personally. So I think I was probably psyched about that part of it. But part of what made that band great was, they had three guys writing songs, and two guys writing a lot of the songs. There is probably a natural internal competitiveness, where they're trying to outdo each other. I think that stuff always makes bands great. And Ty wrote two or three of my favorite King's X songs. But, for me, that was the height of Brendan's production. I think he really had a good balance of his imprint and then letting the band do their thing. I think he knew how to make things powerful, and I think we learned a lot about that—how to really bring the 'rock' out of the songs.

TY TABOR We still were on an incline at that point. But the way I remember it, *Dogman* was the first leveling off—instead of continuing to get bigger. The previous album had way more press and worldwide hype. It might have been different in America for *Dogman*—a little more high profile. But worldwide— which is really all that we ever thought about—*Dogman* plateaued just short of the album before that. So, it was the very first time ever that things didn't ramp up to 'bigger' for us.

Back in the old days, if you ran ads in certain magazines I won't name … in other words, *gave them money*, they would tell you where you were going to be on the charts in two or three weeks. None of that was real. All of that was BS. When we charted with *XV* in 2008, that was the first actual *real* charting we've ever had—where it showed where we should have been on the charts.

The fact is, as far as I believe and I'm concerned, we were selling enough records on *Faith Hope Love* at one time, where I actually saw—on a piece of paper, from Atlantic themselves—what the ten-day sales were. And that amount of sales in ten days is a Top 10 record right now. And we never got anywhere close to that on the charts. We were never given that. So none of the charting back then—as far as I'm concerned—was real. When we sold the most records, it did not reflect on the charts. The only time things looked good on the charts is when we took ads out. It was all total BS.

13 THE TIMES THEY ARE A-CHANGIN'

GRUNGE AND ALTERNATIVE ROCK SEEMED TO INSTANTLY
SHIFT THE DIRECTION OF ROCK MUSIC DURING THE EARLY
90s. BUT DESPITE SEVERAL OF THE ERA'S TOP BANDS
LISTING KING'S X AS AN INFLUENCE, THE RECORD-BUYING
PUBLIC REMAINED FICKLE WHEN IT CAME TO THE TRIO.

JERRY GASKILL I thought grunge was a breath of fresh air, because the whole 80s hair metal thing, I never really got it. I get it more now than I did when it was happening. So, to me, the whole grunge thing felt like *real* music. It felt like people who were just making music because this is the music that was inside of them and it's what they had to do. And I found that very refreshing. And to find out that these people looked to us as an inspiration, is beyond what I can really know how to know, if it makes any sense.

I remember Layne Staley coming up to me one time—I think we were recording *Dogman* at the time—and said, 'Man, I can't wait for that new record to come out, so we can learn how to do it again!' During the tour of the first record, I think, I was walking down the street to eat at McDonald's—I don't eat McDonald's anymore, by the way!—but Layne ran down the street, to catch up to talk to me. I can't remember the conversation, but I remember that happening.

When we met the guys in Pearl Jam, they were just starting Pearl Jam, and Mother Love Bone was no more. They were not even Pearl Jam, yet. I think we were on tour with AC/DC, and Eddie Vedder came to a show, and he was backstage with us. They were still going by the name Mookie Blaylock. I remember Eddie talking to me, and I wasn't really sure exactly who he was. I knew that he was playing with Jeff Ament and his band was about to happen. And he was asking me, 'How do you do it, man? How do you get out there and make it happen?' He was talking to me like that! I think I said something to him like, 'You just got to get out there, you just got to do it. You've got to be yourself and do it.' *He figured it out, didn't he? [Laughs]*

JEFF AMENT To this day, I still feel the same way—there are bands that baffle you as to why they're not bigger than they are. And, at that time, I felt King's X was one of those bands. I remember being in New York around that first album time, and they played acoustic. It was downtown ... I can't remember the name of the club. But I remember they were touring and doing an unplugged kind of a thing. And it was *insane*. Because it took a little bit of the heaviness out of the music, and it really showcased how well they could sing. It was, like, full CSNY harmonies. And it showed you how great those songs were. I think I have always heard them a different way after that show, because it was so stripped down, and with minimal instrumentation.

KIM THAYIL [Soundgarden guitarist] I met King's X in the early 90s. Doug Pinnick and Ty Tabor came to a show in Houston. There was a festival atmosphere to the show—I don't think it was Lollapalooza ... it could have been, but I also know we played a few shows in Texas around that period of time with Pearl Jam. One of the shows was at the Bronco Bowl—it was some bowl-shaped amphitheater. But during this particular tour, the King's X guys came to the show, and I met Doug. I think Chris [Cornell] introduced me.

DOUG PINNICK I was told that the second Lollapalooza, in 1992—that had Pearl Jam, Soundgarden, Ministry, and the Red Hot Chili Peppers—since Perry Farrell ran it, it was *his* thing. A member of one of those bands told me, 'Lots of those bands suggested, 'Why don't you have King's X on Lollapalooza'?' And Perry said, 'No. They are pretentious bullshit.' And I have never had any respect for Perry Farrell from that day on. Every time I'm around him, I won't speak to him. I know the guys in his band, and I'm on the guest list when they come to town, and I hang out with Stephen Perkins all the time. Great bunch of guys— the whole band are cool people. But for me, I have an attitude with Perry. I could walk up to him and say, 'Dude, did you really say this? Why did you do that?' But actually ... *he may have been right*. I feel that way about *Faith Hope Love*.

JEFF AMENT We were so *not* a part of that world—I mean, we barely got on that Lollapalooza. And I think it was mostly because of Perry and Stone, and I had a long relationship with Jane's Addiction and Perry. Green River did shows with Jane's Addiction, and Mother Love Bone did shows with Jane's Addiction. Jane's was a huge influence on us. But I think Perry's partner, Ted [Gardner], and those people—I don't think they cared anything really about Pearl Jam. I mean, we were on that bill for a few months, and then we sort of 'broke' between when we got added to that tour and the tour actually happening.

I remember they came back to us and said, 'Hey, we want to move you guys up more in the middle to the top of the bill.' And we were like, 'Nah. We want to be early in the show, because we want to hang out and watch our friends.' And we didn't want to feel any pressure. We sort of felt that if we played early on in the festival, it took a lot of the pressure off. And we had been touring a ton up until that point. We were sort of ready to just be hanging out with our friends. In retrospect, I think because King's X was on Megaforce, they sort of got lumped into the 'heavy metal zone.' And I think it hurt them—in terms of the time and how things were changing at that point. By 1991, 1992, if you had any connection to the heavy metal world, you sort of had the mark of blood on your forehead.

MARSHA ZAZULA Of course, a year or so later, in marches the grunge scene, and kind of leaves King's X—who started that sound—behind. That whole Seattle grunge scene started to rise up, and the record companies jumped out of metal into that. And nobody really ever gave King's X their due for having explored and started that kind of a sound. They had to fight tooth and nail to stay alive, and, unfortunately, the grunge scene grew by such leaps and bounds that they sort of got left in the dust. It was very sad.

IN THE SPRING OF 1994, BETWEEN MARCH 24 AND APRIL 3,
KING'S X OPENED FOR PEARL JAM AT SEVEN SHOWS.

JEFF AMENT They were one of my two or three favorite contemporary bands at the time. So, for me, I was stoked to be able to watch them every night. And there were a handful of shows where they would come out and played with us, and Doug singing on 'WMA' with us. There were some pretty special moments. I think, somewhere, I played 'Manic Depression' with them—I don't think I knew the song very well at that time.

DOUG PINNICK Knowing Jeff for so long—I knew Jeff before there was a Pearl Jam, when it was Mother Love Bone. He would fly out to New York, come to King's X shows, and hang out at Megaforce. I didn't know him that well. I was like, 'Who is this guy, always hanging out?' [*Laughs*] From that point on, Jeff and I became friends. I remember he sent me the Mookie Blaylock cassette, which was a demo, and I've known those guys *forever*. And touring with them, they were so popular and they wanted to take so many bands out with them that weren't just commercial bands—they were bands that they loved. They would only take a band out for a week and then get another band, so they took us out for the week. It was really great—we had a great time and saw some great shows. What a great band they were live. *Geez*.

I remember my rig went out on me the night they broadcast Pearl Jam live from the Fox Theatre [April 3]. Pearl Jam always loved to have people come get up and jam with them, so Eddie said, 'Hey, do you want to sing the second part to "WMA"?' So I learned it, went out there, and screamed it the best I could. By the way, that was a live broadcast to the world. Pearl Jam had bought the license to broadcast that show to anybody who could broadcast. Commercial free. So that was a pretty interesting thing—a band to play a live show for free for anybody on any radio station that wanted to broadcast it.

JERRY GASKILL I played the Octobans [drums] on 'WMA' at the Fox Theatre. I remember Pearl Jam's drummer, Dave Abbruzzese, said, 'Come on, you've got to do this—we never did this song live. We never had this part.' He showed me the part, and I got up there and did it. I remember, after the song, Eddie is up there introducing us, and he goes, 'We've got Doug Pinnick' and whatever … and he never said anything about me. And Dave was back there, going, 'And we've got goddamned Jerry Gaskill, too!' Of course, nobody heard that, but it is true—I played, and it was awesome. It was the encore, and the ovation as they walked back onstage was overwhelming.

TY TABOR That was absolutely phenomenal. I felt kind of weird, going out and opening for Pearl Jam—only because of what a strange kind of mismatch, vibe-wise, it was. But they wanted us to do it, and we weren't about to say no. So we did. It's hard for me to overemphasize what that tour did for me. I remember feeling a bit disillusioned at this point. I was really hating the industry, thinking all of it is crap, all of it is just a game, none of it is real anymore, none of it really matters anymore. All these terrible things I was feeling.

And then we went on the road with Pearl Jam. The first night, we go out and play, and the crowd response is great. Really great. I'm thinking, *Well ... that's cool. These people don't know us at all, and they're pretty open to it.* I wasn't really expecting that. And this crowd was like no crowd I'd ever seen before. Pretty much everybody was the same age, everybody looked very similar, they all had the same look in their eyes. It was a very strange experience. *It was like seeing the 60s again.* It was like seeing young hippies. Young free spirits.

And then Pearl Jam comes out—with no mega light show, no pyrotechnics, no BS of any kind. Just playing music from the heart, and not trying to do acrobatics and show off or anything. Sometimes just standing there with their eyes closed, playing the music. And the crowd was *engulfed* in it, and singing every word. The vibe of it was like the 60s—which I lived through and saw with my own eyes, when I went to park concerts and saw it when it happened for real. I honestly had not seen this since then.

That changed me. It really affected me, in a way that—to this day—I've never let go of. Because I had given up on music mattering—music really being able to have an effect anymore. It was all a game of money to me. And I saw first-hand—Pearl Jam connecting on a different level the way it's supposed to, the way I believed in and thought was dead. And that let me know, *No. You can hold that torch and be real still—and screw the industry.* That's how I felt from that moment forward, and I didn't give a flying crap about what they wanted or what the industry was doing.

JERRY GASKILL Pearl Jam, I felt like we were in the midst of watching history being made. Because they were touring behind *Vs.*, and they were at the top of their game. But they weren't doing the big, big arenas—they were doing smaller places, but two or three nights in those places. It was incredible. We'd known those guys for years, and to see them achieve what they achieved and to be a part of it ... it was incredible, man.

One night, Jeff Ament got up and played onstage with us. I think we did 'Manic Depression.' I think he later told us, 'I was so nervous playing with you guys.' Which has always amazed me—that that's the case.

JAY PHEBUS That tour was *phenomenal*—I wish it would have lasted two months ... or two years! Because that was a perfect match. Unfortunately, [it was] way too short. We only did two weeks. It was during that time where

Pearl Jam were fighting Ticketmaster, so we were playing all the 'previous' arenas. In Memphis, for instance, instead of playing the Pyramid—which was the big arena to play at the time—we played the old Mid-South Coliseum, at the Fairgrounds. It was all the ones that Ticketmaster didn't have control of. And there are recordings of the Fox Theatre in Atlanta, where that was the one where they did a free worldwide broadcast of.

By the way, in Memphis, it was the first time ever—to my knowledge—that Eddie Vedder beat a hole in the stage, and the band all exited through that hole that he beat through the decking! It was one of the coolest things I'd ever seen. He did it subsequently other times, but used the butt of the mic stand, beat a hole into the decking, and then all five band members went through that hole to exit the stage at the end of the show. That was pretty dang cool.

TY TABOR There was some hanging out with Pearl Jam—not a whole lot—backstage. We were all in the same area. They built this whole backstage area every day with tapestries hanging and lava lamps and posters. They created this whole 'backstage home' every day, and hung around in it. Eddie would wear a wig all day, and skateboard around the venue—trying not to be bothered by venue workers, because they were playing much smaller venues than they could. On purpose. They wanted that contact with the people, so they were playing ten-thousand-seaters instead of thirty thousand or stadiums. And they could have played stadiums.

The reason I know this is because every single show on the tour was selling out in thirty, forty-five minutes. We showed up in Miami, and there are twenty to twenty-five thousand people outside the venue, hanging out—who actually busted down the fences and broke into the concert at one point. And we were at one city where the entire downtown was pretty much shut down by the thousands of kids who weren't at the show, just wanting to see them.

It was like absolute Beatlemania. Like nothing I'd ever seen before. When they would leave the gig, there would be cops lined up—like with The Beatles—on both sides of the walkway, holding people back with all their might, and Eddie would run to the open door of the van, while people would try to pull his hair out and his clothes off. That was his existence. He'd spend time hanging out with Jerry's son, Jerrimy, who was on tour with us at the time, roadie-ing. They would skateboard around the venue, hanging out. And I think that was like a real relief for Eddie—to have a second of normality. Because, I'm telling you, what is surrounding those guys was complete Beatlemania—just like movies. *Out-of-control insanity.* So they lived and hibernated in the venues in the little world they created for themselves. And we were there for a little bit.

DOUG PINNICK I hung out with Eddie a lot. Eddie's a cool, cool guy. A very heartfelt person. He's a very sober, thinking person. We talked about politics, religion, and life in general. He's a very deep thinker. That's what was so great about him. And he was a great performer in his own right. Some of the things that he did … I remember one night, he came up to me, and said, 'I feel like I just don't give enough. I'm not giving enough. This is not good enough. I don't know what to do.' And I gave him a hug, and said, 'Dude … *you already did it.* You put that record out and they all love you. They just want to see you perform. Don't worry about what they think—they're already here.'

And that was when he was jumping off the rafters and climbing things. I remember, after we talked, he went onstage that night and stood in front of his mic the whole night and never left it. And everything he did in front of that mic was just as much he would have done if he ran all over the place and jumped off the rafters. I cried. I saw how great that guy was. What a great performer. Boy, the energy and the vibe and the thing that he did with his hands, his mouth, and his body, just standing in front of a mic, was really phenomenal.

JERRY GASKILL I do believe that Eddie or one of the guys came knocking on our door of the bus—I had my oldest son out with me, I think he was fifteen at the time—and said, 'Hey Jerrimy, let's go play some basketball!' And he'd just hang out with the guys. I also remember the very last day of the tour, Eddie was walking down the stairs, and I was at the top, and he turns around and looks at me, and says, 'Hey, tell Jerrimy any time we're playing anywhere, he's welcome. Let him know that.' It was a cool thing. And I remember, too, we were back home after that tour, and I was driving Jerrimy to school one day, and he said, 'You know what, dad? Everybody in my school would give their right arm to do what we just did. *But that's just what we do.*'

ON APRIL 8, 1994—THE DAY THAT KURT COBAIN'S DEATH WAS ANNOUNCED
TO THE WORLD—KING'S X TAPED AN APPEARANCE ON MTV'S *HEADBANGERS*

BALL. THE FOLLOWING NIGHT, THE BAND PLAYED THE BIGGEST NEW
YORK HEADLINING SHOW OF THEIR CAREER AT THE 3,200-CAPACITY
ROSELAND BALLROOM. THE SHOW WAS ELECTRIC—AND INCLUDED ONE
OF THE BEST PERFORMANCES I'VE EVER WITNESSED OF 'MOANJAM.'

DOUG PINNICK We did a couple of appearances on *Headbangers Ball*—I
remember hanging out with Riki Rachtman and talking to him. One of the times,
in the middle of the taping, we found out that Kurt Cobain had killed himself.
So, when we went in to do the live section of the songs, Riki was so bummed out
that he could barely say, 'Ladies and gentlemen … King's X.' He said it really
sad. At first, it looks like he just doesn't care, but nobody had realized we had
just found out that Kurt Cobain had killed himself.

We did the MTV thing, and then went over and did Roseland. It was all that
vibe. There was a lot going on. It didn't have anything to do with Kurt's death,
though. I'm weird about that—I come from a very huge family, and people die
in my family almost every year. So, when someone dies, it's like, OK, they're
gone, and you've got to move on. But I hate when people kill themselves. I
don't understand.

TY TABOR When we get onstage and do a show, we sort of get into a trance—a
zone—where we are completely self-absorbed, in order to pull it off. Because
that's what it requires. I can remember doing the Roseland show wide open, like
a King's X show, as usual—because there was no time to think about anything
else for a second onstage with King's X. With all the vocals and guitar parts
I was trying to cover at the same time, and keep the show flowing and have
the energy, that takes 100 percent of focus—every time we get onstage. Other
things just have to go away during that time.

Before the Pearl Jam dates, we did a tour with the Scorpions—which we
were very thankful to be on, and very happy to be a part of. So I don't want to
disparage them in any way. But I will say the culture shock of coming from a
Scorpions tour to a Pearl Jam tour is hardcore. It's an entirely different vibe of
performing, you know? Choreographed guitar moves at certain times—the kind
of stuff that Pearl Jam would run in horror from. But it was one side of the rock
spectrum to the other—as far on the other end of the spectrum as possible. It
was a culture shock.

JERRY GASKILL Playing with the Scorpions was great. I remember one time, walking backstage—we played these big arenas—and walked past Herman Rarebell. And, as I walked by, he says, 'Hey Jerry!' I thought that was pretty cool—he actually knew my name. And they used to have these stripper-type girls come up onstage, and I would just walk around all the time. Again, my life was in a place where it was all becoming 'new.' I would just walk into the room where the girls were changing, and hang out with the girls. That was amazing to me—here I am, hanging out with the girls, they didn't think anything of it, as they're changing their clothes. That to me was a pretty cool thing at the time!

DOUG PINNICK That was like a real quick kind of thing. It was the arena thing, like with AC/DC—big tour buses and the whole deal. But we never talked to those guys much, and never got to see them very much. It was just a tour—we'd play for a whole bunch of people, then got in the bus, and went to the next city. The only thing I remember really about it is that we played San Diego, and I said, '*San Antonio.*' I heard a bunch of booing! At that point, Ty went to the tech and said, 'Every time we play any town, put a big note on the floor, to tell him where we're at.' [*Laughs*]

TY TABOR Mötley Crüe had asked us to tour, also. We had actually been in touch with them for a while—sending messages back and forth. They let us know early on that they loved the band, so we were very thankful for that. We were always thanking them whenever they reached out. Eventually, they said, 'Hey, do this tour with us.' And we said, 'Absolutely'—because they had always supported us. And it was a fantastic, fun tour for us. There were things that happened on that tour that I'll never forget. Just road experiences that were the epitome of road stories—*the absolute epitome*—true rock life to the hilt. Wide open beyond your wildest imagination. I was expecting crazy … and it surprised me! And I'm not joking—it was absolutely crazy. So much fun.

JERRY GASKILL That was probably the lowest point in Mötley Crüe's career—which is in line with most of King's X history. [*Laughs*] But I got to meet some people, and got to be great friends with Johnny Kelly and Kenny Hickey from Type O Negative, who were also on that tour, and Tommy Lee. On the Mötley Crüe tour, every show, they had these bleachers set up behind the band, and they would invite people up from the crowd to stand behind them as they did this acoustic thing. I would always try to find a girl—because my marriage was basically over—to come sit with me. And this one night I was sitting back there, and I thought, *I need to play with these guys!* There was a break, so I tapped Tommy on the shoulder, and said, 'Tommy, I need to play.' And he says, '*YEAH!*'

So, there's a break in the song, he gets off the drums—I don't even remember what song—I sit down, the song comes back in, and all three of the other guys, Nikki, Mick, and John, simultaneously looked back at me. Because something was obviously different. They saw it was me, and they all took it as, 'Oh. *OK.*' And went back to playing again. I remember afterward, Tommy was so excited. He would get so excited about things. He gave me a great big hug, and was like, 'Oh man! That was great! YEAH!' Later, his tech said, 'Tommy has never let anybody do anything like that before.'

TY TABOR Here's something that Tommy liked to do on many nights—and he got in trouble for it, because it's totally illegal—he would order I don't know how many thousands of dollars of fireworks. Very often, in the middle of the parking lot, surrounded by buses and people, there would be thousands and thousands of Black Cat firecrackers. They would pour gas over whatever and light them. This thing would become a glowing white orb that was maybe about eight to ten feet circular—of white noise and blinding white light, from all of the firecrackers going off simultaneously. It was so loud it was absolutely ear-crushing. And Tommy would get as close to that orb—walking right up to it, with this white ball of fire in his face. Just going, 'YEAHHH!' Screaming at the top of his lungs and pumping his fists and jumping up and down, like a five-year-old at Disneyland. And he would do that just for his own personal pleasure—how close he could get to it. So I couldn't wait to watch that, whenever it happened.

One time, we were at this speedway doing a show, and the next thing I know, there is a bus racing around the speedway, and they're telling me Tommy is driving it. The bus driver goes out on the speedway, trying to jump in front of the bus to make it stop—because he's trying to actually get it to slide around the corners. He had the bus pinned and was being completely reckless with it. That's the kind of stuff that goes on, on a Mötley Crüe tour.

DOUG PINNICK Loved it. I hung out with Tommy Lee every night, just about—playing new music on the bus and smoking weed. It was so much fun. Mick was awesome. They all were. Just hanging out—they were fans of ours and we were fans of theirs. No drunken debauchery or stories that you hear about Mötley Crüe—it was pretty sober. But in the way of attitude, there was still a lot of partying going on.

Type O Negative were awesome, too. The guys in the band were great—we would hang out and talk. Pete Steele was so hilarious. He'd tell me so many funny stories, and getting to know those guys and where they came from and their whole lifestyles helped me understand their music, and it was really cool. It was a good time.

I remember we were doing 'Moanjam' one night, and Tommy Lee runs on the stage and grabs my mic and starts screaming at the audience how great we were, and how come nobody was freaking out. [*Laughs*] *Screaming* at them. I remember on the last night, they put a bunch of chickens on the stage—bands always do crazy things at the last show. We were onstage, playing, and there were a whole bunch of chickens walking around. So, that night, to get them back, somebody in Mötley Crüe did a solo, and Tommy left his drum set for a minute, and Jerry went up and put a bunch of talcum powder on his snare. So, when he sat back down and hit the snare, talcum powder flew *everywhere*. Tommy cracked up laughing—it was so much fun.

MICK MARS I got to talk to Doug—I didn't get to talk much to Ty and Jerry. But I talked to Doug a lot, and I got to know him pretty well. We became friends. Not, like, real tight, but we still stay in touch and talk to each other and see what everyone is up to. But that was a good time. And I was going like—well, I can say it now, because I don't care—'My band sucks, and these guys opening have all this stuff.' Not only musically, but the way they delivered was, like, *Wow*. How I felt, it was like, 'Goddamn … my band sucks.'

JOHN CORABI Right before we went out with them on the Mötley tour, I really started getting into them, because we watched them play every night for the whole tour. That's when they had the *Dogman* record, and that song would come on, and I was like, 'Oh, God … I want to rip the dashboard out of my car!' It was so great.

JERRY GASKILL I don't recall a lot about Type O Negative, but they recall a lot. I've talked to them since, and they tell me that we partied a lot together. We went out a lot, they said. Jay—our tour manager at the time—would say, 'Hey. Make sure you get him back at this certain time.' And they would all say, 'OK. We'll have him back!'

JOHNNY KELLY Jerry and I became fast friends. Jerry and Doug would hang out. We'd see each other in each other's dressing rooms, and then after the shows, staying in town overnight or whatever. Kenny from Type O and I would grab Jerry and he would come out with us. Every night. Jerry is very calm, and he's quiet—he's very 'below the radar.' And, every night, Jerry would want to come out with us. So, we were like, 'All right, let's go!' We'd jump into a car with some people, and I'd always ask their tour manager, 'What time does Jerry have to be back?' We always made sure that he got to his bus on time.

MICK MARS When they went on it was still pretty much daytime, and people were still coming in, so the crowd was pretty small. But let me put it this way: King's X should have had a way bigger break than they got. A *way* bigger break.

JOHN CORABI What's funny is, Tommy and I would watch a little bit of Type O Negative, then we'd go get ready, and then we would take two hoodies and hats, and we would go out and sit on the lawn—because we were playing a lot of outdoor amphitheaters—and watch those guys. Almost every day. Even today, I still go see them. I saw them not that long ago, when they played in Nashville, and I did the Kiss Kruise with them. It's so powerful—three guys making that wall of sound. All three voices, and, for the life of me, I sit and listen to them, and I go, 'Why are these guys not bigger?' Tommy and I would say the same thing. He'd say, 'God. These fucking guys are great.'

Like I said, we'd watch them do their set and all the hits, and Tommy and I would get chills when they did 'Over My Head.' That was the last song in the set, and we were like, 'Doug's voice and the intensity that he sings with in that tune is unmatched.' And we would sit there and scratch our heads, and go, 'Why are these guys not bigger?' They're one of those bands … it goes across the board. If you talk to Mötley Crüe, Poison, Ratt, or Extreme, and ask, 'What do you think of King's X?' They're like, '*Love that band!*' But then you ask

Metallica, Sevendust—the heavier guys—it's the same thing. I can't figure out why they're not bigger. It's like the secret sauce on a Big Mac!

JOHNNY KELLY By far, they were the most superior musicians on that whole tour. That went without saying. And they did three-part harmonies live with no tracks, no nothing. Three guys go out there and kill it every night. And it was consistent, as well. There was never, 'Somebody had a bad night,' or one of the harmonies was bad or something. There was nothing you could say about it. It was great *every night.* I loved it. The only thing that I was bummed out about it was it was too short—because they were a support act.

JAY PHEBUS The Mötley Crüe tour, I wasn't very happy. I told the guys up front that their front-of-house guy was squashing us on the sound system—basically, he had a limiter on it, and there was no way for me to mix King's X powerfully, because if I got to a certain power threshold, it squashed it and made the band sound small. I was aggravated. The next thing I know, Doug is talking to Tommy, and Tommy is going like, 'Nah, man, that ain't gonna happen.' So they kind of reprimanded the front-of-house guy, and told him to open the system up for us, and things got better.

The actual Mötley Crüe guys were phenomenal—they were great to us. And, oddly enough, that was probably their best incarnation of Mötley Crüe, because Corabi could sing circles around Vince Neil. But, ultimately, we all know how that panned out—nobody wanted to see Mötley Crüe, and nobody wanted to see Vince on his own. Put them back together, and they're dynamite again.

ON AUGUST 12, 1994, KING'S X PLAYED THE OPENING NIGHT OF WOODSTOCK
'94, A HUGE MUSIC FESTIVAL IN NEW YORK STATE THAT MARKED THE
TWENTY-FIFTH ANNIVERSARY OF THE ORIGINAL WOODSTOCK IN 1969.

TY TABOR Way back in the very beginning, when we did that show in New York, at the Cat Club, we met Jeff Rowland, who was the head of ICM Booking at the time. He was the main guy—either the president or at least the #1 agent at the agency. But we always heard he was 'the dude' at ICM. And Jeff is who asked us to play Woodstock, and he put us in a super-primetime spot—on purpose. We were the first band when the sun went down, and we used the stage lights.

That's usually a real impactful moment. He gave us that spot, which was a headline spot—right before Sheryl Crow, and right after Live. I remember being really excited about it, because this was the only other time—at this point—that Woodstock had ever even been thought about doing. And it was the twenty-fifth anniversary, so we knew it would be a big deal. We knew it would be hundreds of thousands of people, and the biggest thing we'd ever been a part of.

We bused it in. They had special busways for all the bands. And that's another thing—when you have that many bands and that many buses, that alone gives you an idea of how enormous the back area had to be, because not only did you have to get countless busses in, but they all had to have plenty of room to maneuver and get around, and go to this site or that site. It was totally nuts. I remember the backstage area was an entire city of its own, with countless tents, sheds, trailers, mega-tents for a press area, and all these different paths and roads with golf carts going in every direction, shuttling from this spot to that spot, to the MTV tent, to the whatever tent.

We were getting shuttled around, and the enormity of it before we even got onstage was ridiculous. And then, after we got offstage, we pretty much got the heck out of there, because we had a gig the next night in another city. But we spent a full day—from morning until late night—there. I got to hang out with Crosby, Stills & Nash, and it was kind of by accident. They thought I was someone else, because Graham Nash came up to me and asked if my dad was so-and-so in the army, and I said, 'No … but he is Colonel Tabor, from the air force.' And he goes, 'Oh OK, I'm sorry. I thought it was someone else.' But that was how our conversation started—by accident. We were in the same tent, doing a photo shoot, so we got to hang with them for a second. It was just one thing after another—the whole time we were there.

JAY PHEBUS One of the largest crowds in rock'n'roll history. I heard some people say that it was close to half a million people there. The one thing that they planned on doing was digging a tunnel from the stage to front of house. But because of budget or time restraints, they weren't able to complete that. So, knowing that, I left thirty minutes before our set—so I could get out to front of house—because I had to go, like, a hundred yards to the right, go to a fence, and then go out another couple hundred yards, and then go way back into the crowd and cut through to the tower.

It was a phenomenal show. We were added on late. Originally, it was scheduled for just Saturday and Sunday. But by the time things were going, there was so much interest and success that they added a Friday. And they ended up putting on the main stage all these newly platinum—especially Atlantic—artists. The only band that I know that toured on any kind of a scale at the time would probably be Queen down in South America, where they were playing to a hundred thousand people a night. Well, this surpassed that.

DOUG PINNICK It was the biggest deal for me in my life—the anticipation, the excitement, knowing what it was. Being around when the first one happened and wishing I could have gone—I was nineteen at the time of the first Woodstock—and seeing how it changed the world and all those bands, it was such a big 'commercial' for all of them. And it was the catalyst for them to get huge. And I thought, *We're going to play for three hundred thousand people or more. This is our chance.* Now *they're going to hear us—and hear us live. Everybody's going to get it.* The crowd went nuts. The response, the comments … MTV, Howard Stern, *USA Today*—everybody raved.

JAY PHEBUS The crowd was totally into King's X. It's hard for any crowd that is exposed to 'Over My Head' to not be totally into it, and moved. So, do that times five hundred thousand. That was probably one of the nearest religious experiences that you could have at a concert—that many people into that song.

JERRY GASKILL I remember a couple of nights before that show, I was hanging out with some friends, I think in Connecticut, and I drank a lot with them. They had this whole pitcher of something—some fruity drink—so I drank a bunch of that with them, and I had a great time. And I ended up in their hotel—completely sick. Have you ever been to that place, where you're like, 'Oh my God … *I'm actually going to die.*' I was laying in the bathroom, thinking, *Two days before Woodstock, there is going to be an article in the paper, saying, 'DRUMMER DIES TWO DAYS BEFORE WOODSTOCK PERFORMANCE.'* That's how bad I felt. But it turned out I was OK—we did the show, and it was great.

DOUG PINNICK I had never played in front of that many people before, and I'm used to intimate crowds where I can see people and sing to them and look at people in the eye. Woodstock, it was so big, and people were so far away because of the cameras in the pit and all the stuff in front with the press—you couldn't see people, really. It was a wall of flesh. It was like a soft roar all the time, because people are talking—no matter how loud the band is. It really threw me off—I wasn't used to it. So I thought that I had completely ruined the band, and our career was over. But time tells.

DEVIN TOWNSEND [Doug told me] that he was going to approach Woodstock like a U2 concert—like trying to unite people. I don't know if he has ever mentioned that he would do it differently, but I think more than anything else, what he had suggested was, the way he did it just didn't work.

TY TABOR The performance was kind of impersonal, because when it's that big of a crowd … and the truth is, because of all the trackways for all the different contraptions they had built in front of the stage for the filming, there was probably a seventy-to-a-hundred-foot gap between the stage and the very first person in the crowd. It was a *huge* gap—with other people running in and out of there. It was far enough away for us to have really no contact with the crowd. It was totally impersonal. So, it struck me, like, 'OK, we're not going to feed off the crowd at all. We're on our own.' I remember we locked in together and gave it our all, because it was like playing in a room with nobody, to be honest.

We realized it was Woodstock and we were going to be filmed, so Doug and I both decided to do something with our guitars at the end of the performance. I don't know if he slammed his on the ground or what, but I chucked mine up in the air, because it was a guitar just for destroying. I threw it up in the air—to see what would happen. Howard Stern had said that we were one of the best things there, *USA Today* had listed us as one of the best things there, MTV called us 'the highlight of Woodstock.' There were, like, four or five major, great things that came out about us.

And I think our appearance on *The Jon Stewart Show* was only a few days after Woodstock. I had cut my hair because of a bet with Tommy from Mötley Crüe. We both said at the end of that tour together, we were going to shave our hair off. Because Stone from Pearl Jam had just cut his hair off, and we both thought it looked cool. We were like, 'Man, that dude can wear whatever he wants and do his hair however he wants, and looks cool as could be.' And one of us dared the other: 'I dare you to cut off all your hair off.' I believe I dared him, and then Tommy said, 'I'll do it if you will.' I was like, 'Really?' And he said, 'I will!' I don't know if you noticed, but he cut his hair off exactly at the same time. We shaved it.

I remember Jon Stewart was really, really cool to us. He came to the dressing room to hang out, and was super-nice. He raved about what everybody had been telling him about us at Woodstock. So we go out to do the thing, he announces us, we come on to play ... and Doug's bass amp dies about ten seconds in. We had to cut the taping to where they would have to edit later, and we reshoot the whole little section. But other than that, it went great, and Jon was super-nice.

Here's the thing ... and it's also an amazing thing—to give people perspective, I guess, because this is the reality of what can happen to you as a band, no matter what kind of exposure or press you're getting. First of all, on that Friday night, we were the one and only band that MTV played a full live song, broadcast to MTV worldwide, on regular MTV. They did highlights of it all while it was going on, but they didn't just stop and broadcast a performance. Because it was pay-per-view to see all the performances. But MTV was only interviewing bands, and the bands would be playing in the background. I think they had the rights to show small clips, but other than us, they didn't play full performance stuff. And they put us on, and I think they showed the entire Hendrix cover we did ['Manic Depression'], and they were talking about how the crowd was going nuts and all this stuff. I think that's partly why we got all the rave reviews—because it was a pretty exciting moment on TV.

So we get all this exposure worldwide. Who knows how many millions are watching MTV on that night, because it was a big deal. And we were in front of over three hundred thousand people at the place itself.

Well, the week of Woodstock, *Dogman* was really slowing down in sales, to where it was only selling about 350 albums per week. And that's normal. We would come out, and it might sell several thousand the first few weeks, and then it slows down a lot to a few hundred, and then it slowly trickles down to less and less. Well, we were down to the 300/350-a-week range, so we had dropped off of the 'mega-hit' of sales, and were trickling down by that point. But we got all this huge exposure, so we had a real, concrete way of seeing what the difference would be in record sales, by checking our reports. Because the reports would tell you how many you sold in Austin—how many you sold in whatever. You could even break it down to chains of stores. You could get all the information. So, we knew exactly our sales and exactly where they were. And we were in the 300-something range for about two weeks, before we hit Woodstock.

OK, we do this, we're in front of millions of people—including the three hundred thousand there at Woodstock. The following week, all the press, we film *The Jon Stewart Show,* we get our record sales … *350 sales again.* We did not sell one more record—with all of that huge exposure. We were shocked that you could be in front of that many people on MTV broadcasting everywhere, primetime on a Friday night, an event that people were tuning into in huge numbers worldwide. And to have no bump whatsoever. It was incredible to us. Shocking. Astounding.

Dogman was the place where I quit believing it was getting bigger and started getting disillusioned about it. Well, that was the big punch in the stomach, where I felt like, 'Man. What is any of this worth, if it has absolutely zero effect for us?' At that point, I remember things going grey in life, and going, 'What the hell? What's it all worth? If you work so hard to get there, and it means nothing at all? What makes something happen? If that doesn't, we give up.'

DOUG PINNICK I felt like, 'Why am I doing this? What's the purpose?' I kind of went inside myself a little bit more, and kind of gave up in certain aspects of fame, fortune, and all that kind of stuff. I felt, 'I'll just keep doing what I do. We ain't the shit, like they all thought we were.'

Before they were Kings … **TOP** Ty, Jerry, and Doug rocking in Springfield, Missouri, in 1984, during the Sneak Preview era. **LEFT** Doug rocking a Fedora, 1984. **ABOVE** Ty rocking a mullet in his bedroom studio, 1986.

ABOVE Sneak Preview's sonically subpar lone album. RIGHT An ad for The Edge featuring the shortlived Kirk Henderson lineup. BELOW A publicity shot for Sneak Preview. OPPOSITE Snapshots of all three members from an early tour … and the trusty ol' Chuck Wagon.

sneak preview

ABOVE *Out Of The Silent Planet.* **RIGHT** Doug on bass at the Ritz in New York City, August 1988. **BELOW** Jerry on drums at the Cat Club, New York City, May 1988.

ABOVE *Gretchen Goes To Nebraska* and two covers for the 'Over My Head' single. LEFT King's X and the Megaforce crew (including Jonny and Marsha Zazula). BELOW The band's first ever magazine cover (*Kerrang!*, February 20, 1988).

OPPOSITE AND TOP Doug and Ty shredding … and a triumphant
ending at the Chance, Poughkeepsie, New York, October
1989. ABOVE *Faith Hope Love* and its two singles, 'It's Love'
and 'We Are Finding Who We Are.'

ABOVE Ty playing his once-trademark Fender Elite Stratocaster—a shortlived model only manufactured from 1983 to '84. **BELOW** The band's self-titled album. **RIGHT** An advert for the *King's X* album and tour.

BELOW Doug and Jerry in July 1992. **BOTTOM** The 'Black Flag' single, and two releases from Molken Music linked to this era: *The Bigger Picture: 4th Album Pre-Production Recordings* and *Tales from the Empire: Cleveland 6.26.92*.

ABOVE Doug and Ty let it rip at the mammoth Woodstock '94 festival.
RIGHT The four shades of *Dogman*.

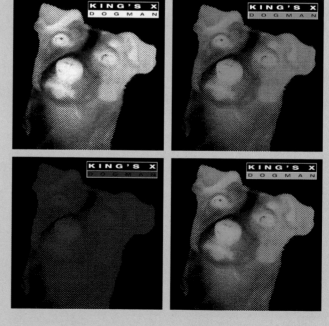

ABOVE The promo-only *Building Blox* compilation (autographed by the band). **LEFT** An image from inside the *Dogman* CD booklet. **BELOW** An early '94 feature from *Raw Magazine*.

RIGHT An outtake from the photo session for *Ear Candy*, taken near the band's rehearsal space in downtown Houston, with new hairdos. **BELOW** *Ear Candy*. **BOTTOM** Plugging in.

LEFT Ty at Millbrook Sound Studio in New York, during an early recording session for the Jelly Jam. **BELOW** *Tape Head*, *Please Come Home ... Mr. Bulbous*, and *Manic Moonlight*.

TOP AND LEFT Doug (note the upside-down pentagram belt buckle, later replaced by a marijuana leaf buckle) and Ty in 2008. **ABOVE** *Black Like Sunday*, *Ogre Tones*, and *XV*.

LEFT The 'King's X choir' sing 'Goldilox' to the band (note Doug and Ty's mics pointed toward the audience).
BELOW Jerry bashing the beat.

TOP King's X, still rocking in 2017. **ABOVE** Doug, Jerry, and Ty about to meet fans/shake hands post-performance.
LEFT Doug lets the audience strum sum up.

14 EAR CANDY

THE STORY BEHIND THE BAND'S SIXTH STUDIO
ALBUM, RELEASED ON MAY 20, 1996.

JERRY GASKILL We all had long hair during Woodstock. And, shortly thereafter, I remember going to Ty's house for something, and he answers the door … and he had no hair! Then we played *The Jon Stewart Show,* and Ty had no hair, but both Doug and I had hair. And I think shortly after that, Doug cut his hair off. So now, Ty and Doug had no hair, and we went into the *Ear Candy* record, and I had hair almost down to my back. But I didn't feel that I was in the place I should I be. So, one night, I said, 'Doug, *shave my head.*' I'm sitting in the apartment in LA, and he shaved my head. And that was it. I remember after doing that, thinking, *I need to go on a crusade now, to tell everybody to shave their head, because it's incredible! You don't have to deal with your hair—you have nothing there anymore.* And that's how the 'no hair' thing came about.

TY TABOR I felt pressure from Atlantic—and this was the icing on the cake for me. Ray was our manager at the time, and Ray was just conveying the message—I'm not blaming him. But Ray came in to tell us that he was getting some pressure from Atlantic for things that were more 'single-minded'—for radio. And we, of course, pushed back on it, like, 'That's not why we make music and not how we approach anything, and not what has worked for us so far, and not what we want to do.' I remember it being a thing that kept coming up, and being pressured.

So, I remember offering up some songs that I probably never would have before—like 'Mississippi Moon'—because I thought they were pretty 'radio.' And Doug did the same thing. We pulled out a bunch of old songs, actually, that we used to do a long time ago, and we kind of reworked them. And Doug did new lyrics. But they were a lot of old songs that were more commercial, I think.

Anyway, we go in and record this album. We get Arnold Lanni to co-produce with us. Working with Arnold is great. He had done some stuff that became pretty big hits on the radio, and some albums that were doing real well. So we met him up in Canada and decided to work with him. He came down, and we went out to California, to a place called Milagro Sound Recorders. We record the album, and Atlantic comes back excited about the song 'Mississippi Moon,' and they say they want to do a video. I remember talking to Ray, saying, 'You know what? We're going to have the same "It's Love" syndrome again—where, all of a sudden, there's this song where the guy singing is not the lead singer, getting the exposure, just causing more confusion. *I don't think it's a good idea.*'

DOUG PINNICK I never knew that. I guess they kept that from me. [*Laughs*] I wish it could have been a single … but I would have had a hard time with it—I really would have—because when we put 'It's Love' out, and Ty sang it and it became our biggest hit, it really made me question my role in the band. And maybe it's my fault that this band isn't successful. I still struggle with that—to this day. Luckily, Jerry and Ty like my singing and want me to sing. But it seems like the hit songs are what Ty sings.

It makes me feel like I'm .38 Special—they had Donnie Van Zant singing everything, but the only two hits they had, the guitar player [Don Barnes] sung. And I thought to myself, *Wow, what a slap in the face.* That's a public slap in the face—you put a song out and everybody buys the song the guitar player sings. That means something. That tells you something.

In a way, I wish they had put 'Mississippi Moon' out—I would have had to deal with it, but they could have had a hit. Life goes on, and you deal with things; you get humble, you get up, and you keep going.

JERRY GASKILL I never felt those things. I think probably Ty and Doug would have different stories about that. I guess Atlantic was probably looking for a hit. I guess we just didn't write hits. [*Laughs*] I mean, I like the songs. I think sometimes, if one of our songs could become a legitimate hit, then we'd have a catalogue of hits all the way back. Because if there's one song people of the world could tap into, then they're going to tap into *all* the songs—of this whole treasure house of music. But the chances of that happening are very slim, I think.

DOUG PINNICK I felt pressure. They didn't say it, but I felt it—because I knew that *Dogman* didn't sell well, and we all figured they were waiting for us to do something … or else they're going to drop us.

The other thing is, Doug Morris told me that as long as he was with Atlantic, King's X would always be there—no matter how well or bad we sold. He was a fan. And then, about three or four years later, he left. And the new guy that came in, the rumor was that he came in and fired forty bands from the get-go—because Atlantic wasn't doing too well. He started cleaning things up. We figured that we would be one to go, so we decided to go on our own—but that was after *Ear Candy*. But I think that we decided in the middle of, or a little before, *Ear Candy* that it was probably our last record with Atlantic … so let's go *balls out*. We rented condos and cars and went out to LA. We spent *a lot* of money making that record. [*Laughs*] Just to do it.

JERRY GASKILL I liked working with Arnold Lanni. The *Ear Candy* record is a bit of a different experience for me—I didn't do any vocals on that record, except for the song 'Sometime.' And there's a song on there that I wrote, called 'American Cheese,' where I did the vocals, but we actually did that later at another studio. We went up to LA—that's where we recorded the album—and we worked with Arnold a little bit before we went out there. But, in the middle of it, my ex-wife had a really, really bad car accident. We didn't even know if she was going to live or die. Fortunately, the kids weren't with her.

So I got the phone call—I was just about ready to sing, I think—saying, 'There is a phone call from a Houston hospital.' And of course, the first thing I think of is, 'There is something wrong with my kids.' But she had an accident, so I had to fly home and be with the kids. So I ended up not singing on any of the songs—being as I wasn't there.

I think the guy from Toad The Wet Sprocket, Glen Phillips, did a lot of the background vocals. That whole record, I think I played OK on it. I don't feel like I played everything really the way I wanted to play.

THE SONGS
'THE TRAIN'

TY TABOR Even though I didn't tell anyone yet, it was my way of saying, 'I think this is the last album and last tour I'm doing. *I'm gone.*' Because I was unhappy with Atlantic. I knew that the soul of the band was dying, and *Ear Candy* was pretty good proof of it. And it was only going to keep getting worse. There was no reason to keep going, if we were going to be pressured to not be ourselves. I didn't want to live that way. I didn't get into this for that. I'd rather work anywhere else than be a whore with music and things that mean that much to me. A lot of that album is going to be Doug, because I had almost checked out at this point, when Atlantic wanted a bunch of 'singles.' This is the album I am least involved in bringing songs to—even though all of us had to work everything very hard.

'(THINKING AND WONDERING) WHAT I'M GONNA DO'

DOUG PINNICK My demo was as full-on brutal as 'Pillow,' and the vocal harmonies were full-on, but when we got to the studio, I said, 'Let's scrap this and do it acoustic—with a South Africa vibe.'

I love doing that song. It's very peaceful. I thought it turned out perfect. Ty built a landscape of guitars on it, and it's one of my favorite tunes on *Ear Candy*. But I was at a place where I was dealing with my personal life, the band's life— we all were dealing with some really crazy stuff. I was trying to find a place to feel safe—and I always write lyrics from how I'm feeling. This was exactly what I was thinking at the time. And I know there are people who relate to that.

TY TABOR That's an old one of Doug's. But I will say that with every song on this album, all of us—along with Arnold Lanni—worked them into final pieces and worked groove, tempo, everything about it together. Because a lot of stuff is old stuff that wasn't all that great, but had potential—had good riffs and good ideas—but weren't totally complete. Or the lyrics weren't OK.

'SOMETIME'

DOUG PINNICK That was the place in my life where I was getting away from Christianity, and I was trying to be honest about how I felt. All these feelings and thoughts were racing through my head—the fear of going to hell, because when I wrote 'Black The Sky,' it was just after I had come to a frightening realization that the Bible said that I was an abomination to God, and that it was the only sin you can't be forgiven for besides blaspheming the holy spirit. And then I read that God makes vessels for his glory and those for destruction. I was gay, so that stuff was driving me crazy. I was walking away from my religion at that time—I was terrified, but didn't know what to do. So, as usual, I wrote a song about it!

'A BOX'

DOUG PINNICK I remember my demo was 'mechanically sterile.' But together, we did put life into it, and it turned out great, and a good live song. The ending jam is hypnotic. This record I had fun doing, actually. *'There is no room inside a box'*—I had to get out of it. The song is about me being trapped in this world that I was unhappy in.

'LOOKING FOR LOVE'

DOUG PINNICK Things were not making any sense anymore to me—concerning my faith in God and the church. Way too much talk and very little doing—especially things that a person full of love should be doing, according to the Bible. When you have too many bad examples, you have to find your own way—it's logical to me. So I thought, *I'm looking for love outside the box*. Looking for it inside the world that I was living in was hypocritical, and I thought it's got to be better outside of the evangelical world, and it was for me. And, again, I wanted to write a real simple rock'n'roll song that could be a hit song. I wanted it to be a radio-friendly song. But the thing is, I don't know how to write a radio-friendly song. Plus, the lyrics are not very relatable!

'MISSISSIPPI MOON'

TY TABOR When I wrote it, I didn't even know what it was for. I was just trying to come up with a guitar part in D that was a very melodic, straight-ahead kind of thing, but that was not the same old, same old, if you try to figure out how to play it. That's where the guitar part comes from. It's slightly different than anything I'd ever heard people playing rhythm at that time doing. But it sounds straight-ahead. I'm kind of singing about Mississippi—where I grew up. I reference blue and gold—that's my high-school colors. It's all referencing old Mississippi stuff from growing up, riding motorcycles—everything is covered.

DOUG PINNICK That's probably one of my favorite songs that Ty has ever written, because it's a happy, bouncing song … that's dark, at the same time. And I love playing it. I love standing on the other side of the stage and bouncing with Jerry. Ty doesn't like to do the song much, but I do. I love it.

'67'

DOUG PINNICK I was writing this groovy song that went nowhere. The demo was a long, drawn-out vibe. No hit-song potential here. This one truly had a strong stoner vibe to it! A fun jam to play live, also. I had just got cable TV about a week before I wrote the lyrics, and it had sixty-seven stations. I was going through every channel and finding nothing interesting, and I was totally depressed. Dying was all I could think about. It was a dark song, for sure. But it has a badass groove! We took some badass takes, I remember.

TY TABOR Here's a really interesting thing about it—we decided to call it '67' because Doug refers to sixty-seven stations on his TV. And we sequenced the album and didn't think anything of it. And then a fan reaches out to us, and goes, 'Wow. Your sixty-seventh song is called "67." How strange.' Apparently, chronologically, it is the sixty-seventh song we released.

'LIES IN THE SAND (THE BALLAD OF …)'

TY TABOR I read a book called *The Satan Seller*, and I recommend it to anyone so they can really pay attention to the Christian industry and beware. There's a lot of fraud and a lot of BS in the Christian world that goes unchecked. And, thank God, there is one group of people up in Chicago, they're actually part of this Christian community, called JPUSA—Jesus People USA. They've been there forever, and I've known about them since the 70s.

There is a band from their community who have been touring since the 70s, that I've been a fan of—the Rez Band [aka the Resurrection Band]. Super-hard rock/heavy rock band. The first time I saw them, they were these longhaired hippies with long beards, Sound City amps, playing loud on a street corner in Utica, Mississippi—on a flatbed trailer. Rocking *hard*. I was thinking, *Man, this band is unbelievable!*

The Rez Band had two great lead players and a killer lead singer. More than one lead singer, actually—a female and male. And the female sounded very much like Grace Slick from Jefferson Airplane. Trippy. Just a unique band. So, I saw them and started following them then and kept up with them, and they started putting albums out a few years later. Eventually, several years later, I produced one of their albums [*Lament*, 1997] and went up to JPUSA for a couple of months with them. I actually lived at the studio!

Anyway, this one group of guys up there do journalism like *real* journalists, but they do it to the Christian world, trying to hold people accountable. And there's this dude named Mike Warnke, who built a small empire and name for himself by being this supposed ex-high-level satanic priest who had become a Christian, apparently. And he was on *60 Minutes* and *20/20* as an expert—any time they wanted to bring in people on any kind of story concerning satanic cults or Satanism. So, Mike Warnke was this accepted dude. And I even had his albums—he was a standup Christian comedian when I was a kid.

Anyway, the guys in JPUSA started looking into him, because they had been around him enough that things weren't adding up, and some things ... you really need to read the story, because it is too unbelievable to tell. Basically, these good people at JPUSA exposed Mike Warnke, and they were almost destroyed for it. The whole Christian community rebelled against them, like, 'How dare you speak against this man of God?' It was this whole big cloud of absolute irony. It affected me hard—including the fact that I had believed this guy. There is so much to it I can't even get into. But I had to write a song about it.

'RUN'

DOUG PINNICK The words are totally self-explanatory—no mystery at all. I was going for a hard rock/Pentecostal/raw-funk type of vibe. A very simple song.

'FATHERS'

DOUG PINNICK I remember that I didn't like the chorus on my demo, so we built it up in the studio. I have fourteen siblings: some have different fathers and some different mothers, some of them I know well and most of them I didn't grow up with. Our fathers were never there. So, the chorus is, *'Every one of us loves every one of us.'* It's a dark, family kind of song, about family dysfunction and love. Family ties.

'AMERICAN CHEESE (JERRY'S PIANTO)'

JERRY GASKILL It's a song that I wrote on the piano, and I took it to the guys. I think the title comes from Ty thinking that the song was kind of cheesy. So, he said, 'Hey, let's just call it "American Cheese."' And then they added 'Jerry's Pianto' at the end—the story about that is from many years ago, I was in church with my ex-wife, Grace, who is a piano player. The pastor's wife was praying one day, and she was very stoic, and said, 'Lord, please bless Grace … at the pianto! So I told that story, and we decided to call the song 'American Cheese (Jerry's Pianto).'

TY TABOR We self-produced that one—along with '(Thinking And Wondering) What I'm Gonna Do.' We just went into a studio in Houston and did those ourselves.

'PICTURE'

DOUG PINNICK It was an old Edge tune I wrote called 'The Door.' We all built that one into a nice journey, and I changed the words from the original. That's about my mom and my dad. What happened was, at the end of the song, I say, *'We all got together for the first time last September,'* and on my birthday, I went to Chicago to visit family. We have a family reunion around the time of my birthday. They didn't do it because of my birthday—there's a lot of us, and my birthday is on Labor Day weekend.

So I went, and my dad was down the street at his daughter's house—my half-sister's house. I seldom saw him, but for some reason he drove down the road to my cousin's house, where I was having my mom's family get-together, and said, 'Hey, is Doug here? I want to say hi to him.' One of my cousins ran up and said, 'Hey, this guy says he's your dad, and he wants to say hi.' So, I went out to the street where he parked, and I said hey to him. And I thought, *I need to do this now*—I said, 'Can I take a picture with you, me, and my mom?' He agreed.

So, I went and got my mom, and said, 'Mom, would you take a picture with me and Herman?' I went and got her, and we took the picture, and I stood between the two and put my arms around them, and my cousin took the picture. I had to develop the picture, and when I got it developed and looked at it, I burst out crying, because I saw myself in both my mom and my dad, and we had never had been in the same place—all three of us—in my life. That was the first time—and only time—we'd ever been in one place at the same time. So, that picture means a lot to me. The picture is sitting on my mantle, right here.

'LIFE GOING BY'

TY TABOR I was being reflective, because I felt like I was getting older and things had not happened the way I thought—all these mega-breaks had turned out to be zero. I was disillusioned, and thinking, *I'm getting older and I'm not sure where things are going.*

'FREEDOM' (JAPANESE BONUS TRACK)

TY TABOR It's an old one. We do it live sometimes. People request it a lot. We re-recorded it and put it on *Ogre Tones*, many years later. The truth is, I wrote it basically saying freedom is the ultimate wonderful thing, but it comes with a price in all directions.

EAR CANDY PEAKED AT #105 ON THE *BILLBOARD* 200—KING'S
X'S LAST APPEARANCE ON THE CHART UNTIL 2008'S *XV*.

DOUG PINNICK I was the one that named that album. I thought *Ear Candy* would be a neat name for an album, after we got done with *Dogman*. And I wanted the cover to look really psychedelic—real bright. So we got ahold of the guy that did the Haight-Ashbury posters back in the day [Alton Kelley]—he did Grateful Dead stuff and things like that. An older guy. He did great artwork, so we got a hold of him at my request, and he made a cover for us.

JERRY GASKILL There are no official videos for that record whatsoever. I guess we were on our way out at that point.

DOUG PINNICK Atlantic did nothing with that record—it wasn't promoted much.

TY TABOR What it sounds like, to me, is neutered King's X—not going full into what we need to be doing, and not being able to do what we're asked to do.

RAY LUZIER *Ear Candy* is one of my favorite records. There are so many great songs on that record. The start-off riff for 'The Train,' I don't know, a lot of people say it sounds too much like The Beatles. I'm like, *I don't think so*. Yeah, it's influenced, but it's one of those special records.

Around that time is when a friend of mine got to know Doug really well. And Doug is such a great, humble guy that he ended up giving the demos of *Ear Candy* to my friend, and my friend calls me up, and goes, 'Dude, I got the demos for *Ear Candy*!' One of my favorite songs on there is '(Thinking And Wondering) What I'm Gonna Do.' A lot of people don't know, but the original version of that song is really heavy—it's distorted guitars. What you hear on the record is an acoustic, broken-down version of it. Which is great, but the initial way they wrote it was super-heavy guitars and full blast. I love hearing stuff like that—that's a little different.

TY TABOR We definitely did an extensive amount of touring for *Ear Candy*. And I remember some of the shows being good ones. I remember California being great. New York—the East Coast is always great. Chicago area is always great. A lot of the North is always great … a lot of the South is always great. All of Texas is unbelievable—such a rocking state. So, we were touring a lot, and the shows were going good at that point.

WALLY FARKAS I remember one time—I think it was the *Ear Candy* tour—we didn't have cell phones and laptops or anything like that. We had really tight budgets. A lot of times on the road, it's like, you've got your hour or two of doing a show, and then, like, twenty hours of boredom. We'd have to entertain ourselves a lot. Ty had gotten—I think at RadioShack—a little crystal radio kit, where you can put in the different little crystals and pick up whatever in the area. We were sitting outside a club, bored silly, waiting for our times to do soundchecks. And some car I guess had driven past us that had one of those old school car phones or something, and it all of a sudden—loud and clear—came through somebody leaving a message on someone's old answering machine. They left a message saying they needed to call them back, and left their number. And, at the exact same moment, we both looked at each other, and said, '*Let's call it!*' We went and found a payphone, and we dialed this number we'd memorized that came over this crystal radio … and prank-called them. [*Laughs*]

Personality-wise, they're all very, very different from each other, and very unique. Jerry has a very dry wit. When you least expect it, he would come out with something that was just crazy, but he's very intellectual and very well-read. Ty is very practical, logical the way his thought processes work, but real playful. And Doug is *what you see is what you get*. As far as whatever image fans have of him—that's who he is. He's the bubbly, extroverted person that's the light in the room that everybody wants to go to. But, at the same time, Doug's personality is very complicated. I guess we all are, but Doug doesn't hide as much of it. So, at the same time, he's this outgoing guy but he has a lot of self-doubt and that sort of thing, too—and shyness, too, that maybe people don't see that much of. I don't want to say he has insecurity issues or anything, but has self-doubt, and it's interesting to see him go from that to the front man that he is onstage.

AROUND THIS TIME, DOUG CAME OUT AS A GAY
MAN DURING AN INTERVIEW WITH *HM*.

DOUG PINNICK It wasn't something I thought about. If I had thought about it, I may have done it a little differently. It was a Christian magazine, and I just wanted to get it over with, because I was tired of the scrutiny that the Christian music scene was putting on us. And I wanted to let them know: 'This is who I am, and we say *fuck* and we smoke weed. So … *fuck you*.' [*Laughs*]

DOUG VAN PELT The story on that is, about a year or two previously, he told me that he was gay, and I kept that under wraps. I didn't write about it because I figured that was Doug's personal life, and if he was struggling or not struggling with it, it was his own deal, and I didn't feel like it was my duty to put that out there in the public. I was never gung-ho about exposing somebody. In fact, my tendency would be to be the last person to expose somebody, or the last person to bring up something like that—just for the sake of a juicy story.

But a website, a guy named Mark Joseph, he read between the lines of Doug's lyrics and asked Doug if he was gay, straight up on a website interview [in *RQ* magazine]. And because that was online, I realized that, with my platform, people were going to start hearing about it, and because they trusted me as a media source, it was probably a good idea to approach Doug about making the story public. So that's kind of how it happened—coming into the interview with Doug's blessing, mindset, and permission that we were going to talk about this issue, and he was ready to talk at that point. I believe I was the first magazine that printed the issue, so technically, yeah, he did come out in the pages of *HM Magazine*. I think that was 1998.

JERRY GASKILL We'd known for many, many years. Back in probably the early 80s, we discovered that fact. And we've grown and learned together. I'm very thankful to be a part of his growing and learning about himself, because it has helped me learn about myself, too. Just to accept people for who they are. What greater thing is there in all of life than to just accept people for who they are? And not judge them, and say, 'Oh, that's got to be wrong. You should change that. You shouldn't feel that way.' Because the way we feel, that's what we have. We feel what we feel because we do.

DOUG VAN PELT I got a lot of positive feedback on it, because I tried to present it from a balanced viewpoint. Because I actually gave a shit about the person I was writing about—he was a friend, so I wasn't interested in getting accolades from my readers or the press for doing a great journalistic job at the expense of my friend. So, I treated it delicately, as best I could, and I got a lot of positive feedback—people that appreciated it. And I heard feedback from fans, some of whom were turned off by that revelation, and maybe turned off by the rainbow sticker on his bass guitar on the subsequent tours after that. But I think, by and large, the vast majority on all the feedback I got was really positive, and appreciating how I handled it. I probably got a letter or two that wanted to take that moment to remind me or my readers what the Bible said about homosexuality. So there were probably a few harshly written, judgmental letters to editors, as well.

JERRY GASKILL He has no qualms about any of that. But I know that he struggled with that all of his life, because of religion teaching you how you feel is wrong. You can't feel certain ways, because that's 'wrong.' And I believe he's expressed that it's something he's always struggled with. Now he's free. He is not religious, he doesn't have any of that in his life anymore. He's free. And he's probably closer to being a Christian than he ever was as a Christian—if that makes any sense. He's free now—he doesn't profess to be anything.

You have to use certain words to express things, like, that's the most Godly place to be, by not believing in anything, sometimes. I hate to even talk about God, because what is God? God is whatever God is. [*Laughs*] That one thing that we don't know—that's what God is. The thing that we have no right to talk about—that's what God is. If there even is a God—that we don't know, either!

TY TABOR The truth is, I don't remember there being any repercussions—except for in the Christian world, of course. Suddenly, champions of the band were no longer champions of the band. I remember us feeling it was kind of funny, really, because before Doug announced … he didn't really *announce* he was gay, he just happened to mention it to somebody in an interview, and it came out. I don't think it was planned or anything.

I remember the *Ear Candy* album has the song 'Looking For Love,' where Doug declares he guesses he lost his faith—and that wasn't enough to turn anybody against him … but being gay was! I remember rolling my eyes, and thinking, *Typical*. That's one of the reasons why I like to keep my distance from the Christian world. Just completely typical. But thinking nothing of it, other than, *Whatever*, and moving on.

DOUG PINNICK They banned our records. I know that a lot of Christians were disappointed in me and turned their backs on me.

JERRY GASKILL I heard something about *Ear Candy* doing well in the Christian market. [It peaked at #4 on the Christian Music Charts.] I didn't know it made it that high on the charts. I think that's great. I think it's funny, because we were never a Christian band. We never presented ourselves as a Christian band. We had some kind of Christian lyrics, and we came from Christian backgrounds, but we never—as a band—portray ourselves or present ourselves as a Christian band. That was all put on us by others. But as long as people bought the record, I thought that was great—whether they were Christians or non-Christians or whatever they are. So I guess somebody bought it. But when Doug came out as being gay, I think they took all the records out of the stores! [*Laughs*] I heard they took all the King's X records out of the Christian music stores—which I think is great. That's greater than being #4 on the Christian charts, to me.

DOUG PINNICK It was kind of like, 'OK. I did it.' And hardly anybody made a big deal about it, so I just went on, like, 'OK. Whatever.' I wasn't hiding it, but how does anybody know your private life unless they're *in* your private life? Nobody knew my private life but what I said in songs, pretty much.

REX BROWN I think they got frustrated in the middle of the 90s, when they put out such great material, that they felt that they weren't going anywhere and it made them … I don't know, it was a weird period. That was a time when we were touring constantly. I talked to Doug all the time, but when you're on the road, you don't talk to him every day like you used to.

BRIAN SLAGEL Someone showed me an article the other day about metal in the 90s, and there are so many great records that came out of that time period, where the metal scene was deemed to be a little bit dead. Some of the records that came out then really didn't get their due, because nobody paid attention—it was all about nu metal, grunge. And the albums King's X put out around then I thought were just as good as their earlier stuff. People go back now and listen to that stuff—especially now, with the advent of Spotify and all the streaming stuff—and people say, 'Oh, those records really *are* good.' There is definitely a bit of a resurgence there—which is nice.

TY TABOR I think, during that whole stretch from once things started happening on *Gretchen*, from then all the way through *Ear Candy*, I think we had big expectations every time. Always expecting something bigger. And it was after *Ear Candy* that we quit expecting that. But at least for me, it was all the way up to then—every album after things started getting going on *Gretchen*. I fully expected bigger, better things. Almost assumed it, naïvely, because things were getting bigger and bigger around us. It just was our reality.

15 BEST OF KING'S X

THE STORY BEHIND THE BAND'S FIRST EVER
COMPILATION–AND LAST EVER ATLANTIC RECORDS
ALBUM–RELEASED ON NOVEMBER 11, 1997.
PLUS, A SWITCH TO METAL BLADE RECORDS.

TY TABOR Doug Morris left [Atlantic] around this time, and somebody who used to be the vice president under Ray Danniels, at his management company, ended up taking Doug's place at Atlantic. At one point—and I know people find this hard to believe—Atlantic did let us go. They did drop us. But one of the reasons they dropped us is that we expressed being very unhappy being on their label. I had a very long talk with Ray about it, and I told him, 'If they want us to do this sellout thing, then I don't want to be on Atlantic. I want us to be somewhere else, where we can be free to be ourselves again. I didn't get into this to do this. This is not what I want. I'm unhappy, and I don't want to do this.'

So Ray expressed that to him, and they had a big budget planned for doing a 'Mississippi Moon' video. They just dropped it instantly and dropped us instantly. And that was it. Ray was able to work out a package where they let us put out a 'best-of' CD and gave us a budget for it. I don't know how he did it, but he actually worked out a way for them to end up giving us more money for us to leave—and put out a greatest hits. So we took the deal and walked. It was announced that they let us go, but that's what happened—we were telling them we were very unhappy being there, and they probably felt we were being ungrateful, and said, 'OK.'

JERRY GASKILL We did the three songs that were new on the record in our rehearsal space. We recorded those on an eight-track, and that was kind of fun. We went in there, jammed a little bit, and put some new songs together. It was kind of exciting, to put that out like that. I don't remember a lot about that record—I guess it must have been in the contract to put out one more record with Atlantic, so we put out *Best Of King's X*. They didn't call it 'greatest hits,' because we didn't have any hits! [*Laughs*] It is what it is. It served its purpose.

TY TABOR I wrote 'Sally.' I wrote that one so fast that I barely remembered that I wrote it! I knew that we were getting ready to go into the studio, and I wrote that really quick.

DOUG PINNICK Those I think were demos of older songs that were floating around. I had written 'April Showers' and we recorded it, but we never put it on a record.

TY TABOR I remember pressuring Doug to do that one, because I thought it was a great song … and 'Lover.' I thought both of those were really good, hook-y songs. I thought 'Sally' was, too—it luckily fit with that group of tunes. I don't think it was anything intentional—it just happened to be the three most recent songs that we did.

DOUG PINNICK 'April Showers,' I used to sing about being lonely and looking for someone to connect with. And the chorus is sort of a hopeful thing. It's '*April showers bring May flowers*'—maybe next month somebody will come along.

'Lover' was another demo that I did. It was a 3/4 type song—a waltz—that I liked. I don't use 3/4 timing very often. And the song, I think it's a universal song—'*You want to be my friend and I want to be your lover.*' That's pretty much what the whole song was—I think it speaks for itself.

JOHN CORABI I have the *Best Of King's X* on my iPod—because it gives me a little bit of everything across their career. I love 'Dogman,' 'King,' and one of my favorite songs is 'Goldilox.' Doug's vocal delivery is amazing on that song. There is a great live performance of 'Over My Head' from Woodstock. The whole record is great. I also love that song 'Sally.' That's definitely a record that you put on and you don't skip a song.

MARSHA ZAZULA It's so funny, because as much as Atlantic wanted to drop the ball on King's X when Megaforce and Atlantic severed their relationship, they fought to keep King's X, and we were going on to another distribution deal with Polygram. And I would have loved to have had them with us, because the people at Polygram really got it and were willing to go the distance for them. But Atlantic would not allow us to keep King's X in our stable. They took it—and they did nothing with it.

DOUG PINNICK I love Megaforce, don't get me wrong—they were great people, and they worked so hard for us—but they were still a *subsidiary* label. They were a label of a label. And, no matter what was going on, we were still considered a metal band on a metal label.

When we got on Atlantic, it gave us a little bit better clout. Jonny Z. told me that Atlantic paid a lot of money for us. He didn't tell me how much. I would love to know all the stuff that went on back in the day, when they thought we were going to be 'the next Beatles.'

BILLY SHEEHAN I attended a King's X show with Pat Torpey, and we went down into this little room, and King's X was set up. We had tears in our eyes—this band was *so* great. It was just so awesome. And we kept looking around like, 'Why isn't everybody in the building in this room? This is a crime!' Atlantic didn't get it. Well, Atlantic didn't get Mr. Big, either. They refused to release the *Lean Into It* record because 'there were no good songs on it.' Doug Morris at Atlantic Records refused to release it. It wasn't until our management went and threatened him that he finally decided to release it, but they weren't going to do anything to help it out. And they didn't. And then 'To Be With You' went to #1 all by its little self. So, the same atmosphere at Atlantic Records was the same that King's X was against. The label did not know what they had. They had no idea. And whoever was at the head of the record label didn't know a hit if it came and bit him in the ass.

So, unfortunately, a different set of circumstances—maybe being at Warner Bros or another more musician-friendly label—might have changed history. It would have changed history for the whole world, too, because King's X would have had a huge impact not only on music, but on life and culture, too. They were *that big* in my mind. So it's sad to see them in a situation where the label had no idea what they had.

I was at the show that King's X did in LA, at the House of Blues, when, during the day, they got dropped by Atlantic. And that night they had a show in

LA. The place was sold out to the rafters, and it was like a religious experience. The entire place sang along and had their hearts torn out for this band. It was amazing. I got up, and I think Carmine Appice joined me, too—we played 'Closer To Home,' the Grand Funk Railroad song. I remember being torn apart inside. *Look at this place. Completely sold out. Everybody in here rabid, willing to give up anything to help this band out*. And that was the night Atlantic decided to drop them. *Unbelievable.*

JERRY GASKILL There were some great people at Atlantic that really believed in us. And Atlantic, I believe, did everything they could to push King's X as far as they could go. I really do believe they did everything they could. You can't force people to buy records. I don't think you can make them like something … unless you pay people enough where it gets played on the radio so much that you learn to like it, because you hear it every day. I don't think it was like, 'OK, you guys are dropped from the label.'

It seems to me that it felt like a natural progression: there was not much left that we could do. It didn't take off like everybody had hoped, I guess. So we were let go, and we looked for another label. And we went with Metal Blade. I think Metal Blade had wanted to work with us even before that. And now they had the opportunity, and the deal worked out where we said, 'OK, let's do this,' and we made a few records with them.

TY TABOR The guys at Metal Blade decided to fly to Houston and go out to eat with us and talk in person about it. Of all the people we spoke to, they were the only label that said to us, 'We don't really want to interfere with your music. We want you to do what it is that you do, and we'll put it out—that's our job.' So, we talked about it, and I think because of coming out of that situation and feeling like things were trying to get out of our control and that the pressure to write in a different way and all that crap, to hear those words from Metal Blade was like a relief.

BRIAN SLAGEL Over the years, I became good friends with them, and we had heard that they weren't on Atlantic. The first thing I did was call up one of the guys, and said, 'Hey, we'd love to do something with you guys, if you haven't signed with anybody yet.' Luckily, we were able to do a deal with them, and we did quite a few records with them. Which was a dream come true for me, because I was a massive fan of theirs, and being friends with them—and being able to work with them on some really great records—is really awesome.

DOUG PINNICK We'd known Brian forever. Brian has been a big King's X fan since day one. I would always go out to Metal Blade and hang out, and go to shows and have dinner. It finally got to the point where we were away from Atlantic, and we were looking for a label. So, Brian popped up, and said, 'Hey, sign with *us*.' We did, and that's how we got those five records out.

TY TABOR The truth is, we started on an independent label—Megaforce. Megaforce is the label that broke us, and Megaforce worked as a team—much harder for our band—than anything we ever saw at Atlantic. I'm not knocking Atlantic—they had a smooth-running, professional machine—but the people at Megaforce were *in the trenches*. I mean, they were on the phone—we saw their hard work all the time. Way beyond what was reasonable, at times. Staying way past hours at work to continue doing things and making calls. So our personal experience with the smaller label was that they worked harder, and that's who broke us. I don't think we even thought on those terms at all—as far as which would be better for us, as far as which label. I felt like, at that point, we had already made our name. Whoever we signed with, it wasn't going to be like it was in the beginning—whether it was that important or not. It was more of, 'We get to be King's X again, and whichever label will allow that, we'll go with you.' Because the label almost *didn't matter* at that point.

16 TAPE HEAD

THE STORY BEHIND THE BAND'S SEVENTH STUDIO
ALBUM—THEIR FIRST FULLY SELF-PRODUCED
ALBUM, AND THEIR FIRST FOR METAL BLADE
RECORDS—RELEASED ON OCTOBER 20, 1998.

DOUG PINNICK That was a fun record to make. That was the first record we ever wrote together. I think there were a few songs that I had written earlier, but the rest of the record was all songs written from scratch in my brand new studio I had just put together, Hound Pound. It was a place in downtown Houston, back then. Three big rooms—a band room, a drum room … basically, it was a full-blown studio in a big complex. I forget how much I rented it for, but I rented it with a friend, so we brought bands in to record. Not much happening. We did do *Tape Head* there, and I think I did my first Poundhound record there, too [*Massive Grooves From The Electric Church Of Psychofunkadelic Grungelism Rock Music*, 1998]. I got rid of it a couple of years later, because I couldn't afford the rent, and I wasn't making any money.

TY TABOR At that time, Alien Beans Studios was part of my house. I had a large place in Houston where I dedicated a good chunk of the house to just being a studio. So I operated out of home for a few years. It's currently in a separate building away from home, but for the first fifteen, twenty years, it was in my house.

Whenever we would work at Alien Beans, we would set up a mini–drum kit and some small amps in my living room of my house, and we would make that the band preproduction/rehearsal space, before we would step into a studio and record. So we were recording in the house. There were some pictures of us on I think it was *Tape Head*, where Doug is wearing an afro, and we're all dressed up silly—but that's in my living room, at Alien Beans.

JERRY GASKILL The Hound Pound Studio was in a different building, so Doug had a building where his studio was set up. It was sort of like going into a studio to make a record. But again, it was a different thing, because it was just the three of us. I'd have to emphasize that the most—just the three of us were in there, making those records, and nobody else telling us anything. And that's how they came about. The Alien Beans Studio was part of Ty's house, so we would go over Ty's house and make some music. Which was very relaxed and very comfortable.

DOUG PINNICK We are so used to doing stuff on our own, anyway—I don't think it made a lot of difference. We've been so jaded with producers that we just wanted to do it ourselves, to see if we could do it and have fun. There was no pressure. There was no set time that we had to have it done by, so it was a pretty easy record to make—we did it at our own leisure.

TY TABOR I think we wanted to get back to see what would happen without the influence of others. All of the original songs in the beginning that we built it all on didn't really have anything to do with any direction of any producers. It was just what came from *us*, so we kind of just wanted to see what would happen if we did that again. We sometimes like to have somebody there to push us, but at that particular phase, we wanted to see who we were again, and what would we do if we had no other influence, and were progressing into whoever we are as musicians at that moment. And find it purely in the same way [as we did] in the early days. I think that was the intention on that one. I think it kind of evolved into something a little more straight-ahead.

JERRY GASKILL It was great. I felt the freedom that I never felt before. I didn't feel the pressure of even having to learn a song, because the songs weren't even written yet! We wrote all the songs together. And that was a great thing. That was a great era for me—to do that. It was like the start of a new era for us. I think we did three records where we got together with no preconceived ideas, and wrote music together.

That record, *Mr. Bulbous*, *Manic Moonlight*—those three records, we came in, just the three of us, made those records together, wrote together, and that's how those records came about. And that's kind of a nice period for me—to think just the three of us can do that. They are three of my favorite records.

THE SONGS
'GROOVE MACHINE'

DOUG PINNICK We wrote that together. Ty started playing the riff and Jerry and I fell in place. It's fun writing from scratch with these guys, because whatever someone starts playing first, the rest will immediately find something to play with it, then we immediately track it—while it is new to us. There's something magical about this band when we're all playing together as one—the song usually writes itself. And I think it's my favorite King's X song. It's the purest King's X music we can create. There are no home demos to compare them to, or the struggle to reproduce or change someone's original demo to fit the band. And everyone's playing what they want to play. I remember when I was writing the lyrics, I thought, *The song grooves hard*. I was thinking, *This might be a nice intro song—'Welcome to the groove machine'—and we could probably do it live, too*. It's the song we start the show off with—every time we play.

'FADE'

DOUG PINNICK Same as 'Groove Machine,' Ty started playing a guitar riff, and we fell into it. Before you knew it, we all were pitching in, and we had another song. I think I was about fifty years old at the time, and it was starting to hit me: *I'm getting older, and soon, it will be over. So I'm dedicated to living my life to its fullest, until it's over*. I'm at the age where death is a very common thing in my age bracket. 'Fade' is a 'celebration of life' song. I wouldn't mind doing that song live again—everything has to be *if I can sing it*. That's the bottom line on every song nowadays, because my voice has dropped so much since thirty years ago, when I could sing a lot higher. I'm sixty-seven years old now, and my voice doesn't do what it used to, so there are a lot of songs we can't do. If we can figure out a way to pull them off, I'll do it.

'OVER AND OVER'

DOUG PINNICK Ty started playing this beautiful slow guitar part in 6/8. It was the verse—we all fell into it, and the song wrote itself like the others. This was a whole new thing for us, and I loved it! A friend told me that expectations only let you down. And I realized that everything that let me down, I had high expectations. So I stopped expecting things from life and people, and my life became stress and drama free. People are who they are, so let them be who they are—but we can't, for some reason. And I *will* let you down, because I'm human. It reminds me of an old gospel type song, so, vocally, I wanted it to be like a Curtis Mayfield–type old soul song. I remember Ty played the chords, and for bass all I could hear in my head was a Hammond B3–type bass line. Jerry had that perfect feel … and that was it!

'ONO'

DOUG PINNICK I was watching a lot of drama going on around me, and it was obvious to me that no one would take blame, and they couldn't get past that to figure out what the real problem was. '*It's always everybody else's fault*'—that seems to be the problem with people that have a lot of drama in their life. This whole song is about that kind of person. And it's reflective of me, also. I think about myself when I sing these lyrics. Am I like that? I've had my moments!

'CUPID'

DOUG PINNICK That was a finished demo from the batch of stuff I was writing between *Dogman* and *Ear Candy*. It was an extra to fill up the CD. '*Cupid shot the wrong guy.*' I've fallen in love so many times in my life, and it's always the wrong person. King's X did it as a demo after that, and put it away until *Tape Head*. I'm glad we did, because I like that song a lot.

TY TABOR That one was one that Doug wrote that I insisted we do. He had a demo of that one, and I insisted we put that one on the record, because I thought it was a super-cool song.

'OCEAN'

TY TABOR I wrote that one. Everything was written quickly and recorded quickly, and then you move on. It's like when you cram for a test and then have no idea ten years later what the test was. That album is that for me.

'LITTLE BIT OF SOUL'

DOUG PINNICK We all wrote that together. And the same thing—it's kind of a Curtis Mayfield vibe, again—that whole kind of soul thing. The guitar parts lend to an old soul/60s/R&B thing, and the lyrics were inspired from the vibe I was feeling from the music. I wrote all the lyrics after the songs were done, and that's usually how we do it when we write together. The music dictates the vocals and words—in many cases. Again, I was trying to sing like Curtis Mayfield.

TY TABOR I believe that one started with Doug, and then we all collaborated on it. But I remember really loving that one, too, and pushing hard for that one to end up on the record with my vote, because I thought it was one of Doug's coolest, funkiest riffs. At the same time, I think I came up with the verses, too. I don't remember who wrote what. I just know we all wrote stuff on this.

'HATE YOU'

DOUG PINNICK I wrote that song from scratch. I intentionally went for happy music—but with angry lyrics. The band made a demo of it, that we never put on a record. It was another extra to fill up the CD. It's a true story about the first person I truly hated. Those who intentionally go out of their way to hurt someone, I have absolutely no respect for.

'HIGHER THAN GOD'

TY TABOR I wrote the music, and I remember I wrote the chorus. I think Doug probably came up with the verses. As a matter of fact, I think he came up with everything except for the line 'Higher Than God.' I think that all that I had was that line and the music, and then he came up with everything else.

That's how songs come sometimes, for both of us, I'm sure Jerry, too—a phrase will be there and you don't know why, and there's nothing you can do about it but try to make a song around it, because it's been forced into your mind as something that needs to be.

DOUG PINNICK I wrote the words in the verses, and Ty wrote the chorus. It's about my one-sided attraction I was having with someone. Yes, I used to be a man of expectations. I write a lot about love—but way more about love that didn't happen.

'HAPPY'

DOUG PINNICK That was a dUg demo [Doug began going by 'dUg' around this time], and the chorus was '*Quality control / Say what you'd like / But get the fuck out of my way.*' I was tired of everyone condemning me or going down the rule book of Christianity, and saying, 'You've got to do this, you've go look this way, you've got to act this way.' And I thought, '*Quality control / Say what you'd like / But get the fuck out of my way.*' Then I felt like it might be a little bit too much to put 'fuck' in a King's X song at that time, and everyone agreed. So we never put it out. And later, when we decided to do it for the *Tape Head* record, I changed the lyrics. So lyrically, I was telling myself, 'It's time to be happy. No more trauma and drama, and get rid of all the crap in your life.'

'MR. EVIL'

TY TABOR I remember coming up with the guitars on it, but the lyrics are most definitely Doug. And they're a real story. Usually, if it's drop-D and kind of 'swamp rock,' it's something I'm coming up with—and then Doug puts the melody and stuff on it.

DOUG PINNICK It was another quick collaboration. It's a true story about a person who threatened to kill me once.

'WORLD'

DOUG PINNICK That was a song I wrote back when we were Sneak Preview. It had different lyrics. I changed them for *Tape Head*. The world keeps going, no matter how long we're going to be here. Once we're gone, it's still going to keep going.

'WALTER BELA FARKAS (LIVE PEACE IN NEW YORK)'

WALLY FARKAS That started out as a private joke. Even though that came out on *Tape Head*, it was recorded on the *Ear Candy* tour at Tramps in New York. What had happened was, several weeks before that, I don't even remember where we were, but we were somewhere in the US on tour, and they had finished their set, walked offstage, and they were waiting on the side of the stage to come back out for their encore. So they walk back out for the encore, throw their instruments on, they were going to play 'Mission,' and, like most people do, they start to move their fingers around to warm up. They noodled around for a second, and were all doing their own little thing—in different rhythms and keys. It wasn't even a jam—they were noodling around for a minute. After about twenty seconds of it, they stop, and the crowd is like, *Ahhh*. The crowd acted like they were witnessing Mahavishnu Orchestra throwing down some heavy shit!

I'm a huge fan of Yoko Ono, and I was talking to them and joking. I was talking about her first solo album, *Plastic Ono Band*, and there is a track on there called 'AOS,' where she has Ornette Coleman's band on a track. The great jazz group, with Charlie Haden on upright bass and Ornette Coleman on trumpet. And they're playing this avant-garde jazz stuff, and then all of a sudden, out of nowhere on the top, is just [*shrieking/singing sound*]. And I was laughing, going, 'The only thing missing from that thing you guys did was some Yoko.' And one of them—it was either Jerry or Ty—turned to me, and said, '*You* should do that.'

So, a night or two later, they come back out for an encore, and they start doing it again. We're in a different town, but the town has kind of the same reaction, and I'm standing on the side of the stage nervous, going, 'Well ... did they really want me to do that? Or were they just joking?'

I just said, '*Fuck it*,' ran out there, grabbed the mic, did it for a couple of seconds, and ran back off. Afterward, they got offstage, and they were dying laughing. They were like, 'Why did you leave? You should have stayed out there!' So, we started this thing—and it didn't happen every single night, but it was most of the nights on that tour—where it was our little humorous inside prank joke, where they would go out and start doing this weird improv stuff. If we thought the crowd was into it—like they thought this was really something special—then I would come out while they were doing it, and grab the mic. And the fans would get really upset, because they thought I came out there and ruined some magical musical masterpiece—that wasn't even happening! Our joke was, if the crowd had a negative reaction to it, we'd do it more, and longer. It was very Andy Kaufman–esque.

DOUG PINNICK I remember going to a club one night and watching a jazz band get up and improvise, and I started laughing out loud. And a couple of people with me were like, 'What are you laughing at?' I didn't tell them, but in my mind, I was thinking, *Man, that sounds* exactly *like what we were doing! [Laughs]*

WALLY FARKAS But the funny thing is—check out this irony—they put it out on *Tape Head*, we go back out on tour for *Tape Head* … and people are *requesting* the fucking song!

'TWO' (BONUS TRACK)

DOUG PINNICK I wrote that song the day after I wrote 'Down.' It's a pretty depressing song, actually.

THOUGH *TAPE HEAD* DID NOT REGISTER ON THE CHARTS, THE QUALITY OF THE MATERIAL WAS CERTAINLY NOT AT FAULT.

BRIAN SLAGEL *Tape Head* is the first thing we did with them, and I remember hearing the early stuff, and again, everything they do is so good. I was blown away by how amazing the songs were, the riffs were, the sound was. They had done the first few records with Sam Taylor, and they had a certain style to them. But then they kind of grew into their own way after that.

TY TABOR At that time, I had a much bigger weight on my shoulders, because I was sort of producing, mixing, engineering, *and* recording everything at the moment—including management, for a while. And I remember telling Doug during some of that time, 'Man, you guys are going to have to pick up some slack. *I can't be three people.*'

I think Doug was actually happy to be able to do it that way, and come up with more of the lyrics. I was very thankful he was willing to, because, first of all, I love his lyrics, and it relieved a tiny bit of pressure on me. Because I love coming up with music, and lyrics are like pulling teeth for me. I wouldn't say I prefer [working quickly], I think it was more a matter of it was the only way we could do it at the moment, because we were shouldering everything. It was *too much* to shoulder.

DOUG PINNICK Ty took me in the front door of his house and wrapped my face with recording tape, and took a picture of it! [*Laughs*] And said, 'Let's call it *Tape Head*.'

JERRY GASKILL 'Fade' was a *no budget* video! That was fun.

TY TABOR I remember we did the 'Fade' video with Frank Hart of Atomic Opera. It was kind of done in one day—jumping from location to location, not really with any real plans. We would get somewhere, we would see something and say, 'Let's film there!' It was all very spontaneous and quick. I don't remember who the little kid was in the video, but I know Frank was responsible for bringing him in. I think he was from his local church or something, possibly.

DOUG PINNICK That was a lot of fun. We went underneath a bridge in downtown Houston, and did the video in a couple of hours. It was a couple of takes. We trusted Frank to edit it, and he did a great job with it. I really liked the video. It's kind of cheap but endearing.

TY TABOR The entire period of Metal Blade—which was three albums and a live album—is all the same for me. Because during that time, like I said, I was doing the engineering, recording, mixing, mastering, and trying to be an artist and write and tour and manage. On all of those, it was a blur of way too much pressure, and way too much responsibility. That's all I could remember during that time—I couldn't wait for it to be over. As far as touring, we did a lot of extensive touring. We were constantly on the road, so people were still coming out. There's never been a period of time where people weren't coming out. So we always have toured.

17 | PLEASE COME HOME ... MR. BULBOUS

THE STORY BEHIND THE BAND'S EIGHTH STUDIO
ALBUM, RELEASED ON MAY 23, 2000.

TY TABOR I remember enjoying that one, because we went in with the idea once again that we would all collaborate and write together. And we would start from scratch on that album. Just, 'Don't bring demos in, don't bring *anything*. We're going to write together and see what happens. And not only that, we're going to come up with some progressions that are outside of the box, that would be difficult to write melodies to. And see where it stretches us and what new ideas we can come up with.'

So, I remember, on that one, if you take the vocals off and think about the chord progressions, there are some very difficult to predict chord progression things going on in places. With the vocals, it all seems to make sense, so it was kind of hard to separate it, if you never heard it by itself. But some of that stuff was almost impossible to come up with a melody on top of. And then, once we did, it totally made sense. So that was the fun part of the album—stretching ourselves musically to do some different ideas, and making ourselves go outside the box. And starting from scratch with zero and doing it all together.

JERRY GASKILL I really enjoyed the way I played on that record. I enjoyed the freedom I felt on that record. The same with *Tape Head* and even *Manic Moonlight*—I felt free to play the way I felt to play. And I think those three records may represent the way I feel to play drums the best of all the King's X records. Because it was just me *playing*—not having demos for me to listen to, not having pre-drum beats to learn, or anything like that. That was a great time.

TY TABOR The title is just another stupid phrase floating around from somewhere. We tended to lean on those things whenever we were needing ideas. I mean,

Gretchen Goes To Nebraska was the worst album title we could possibly think of. So, *Please Come Home ... Mr. Bulbous* was another one of those: *It doesn't really matter what we call it, so let's call it something completely ridiculous.* And then that kind of gave us the image idea for the cover.

JERRY GASKILL I don't even know where the album title came from! It's probably something really silly. I think the word 'bulbous' was a word that Ty had in his mind ... or a word that he thought is funny or liked. We somehow put these words together and came up with *Please Come Home ... Mr. Bulbous*. Which means, really, absolutely nothing. Or, it means *everything*.

DOUG PINNICK I remember we got together to make that record, and I think we were all at a place where we were disillusioned, like, 'Why are we even doing this? Nobody cares about our music.' And I remember Ty was saying, 'This sucks. We suck. I don't even care anymore. I don't even want to be in this band.' And we all were feeling the same way: 'Why are we even doing this?'

I remember Ty said, 'Well ... what do we do?' And I said, '*Let's make a fucking record!* [*Laughs*] Let's take our drop-B guitars and drop them down to A, and write an album of some of the most fucked up chord progressions we can come up with.' And we wrote 'Julia.' At that point, we got excited, and we kept going—so that's how that record came about. I wish we had worked on it a little bit more—I feel it's a little bit incomplete. But I'm real proud of that record, because it's a deliberate experiment.

THE SONGS
'FISH BOWL MAN'

TY TABOR On every one of these songs, I believe it's going to be, 'We all wrote them together.' I remember I came up with the riff of the chorus for 'Fish Bowl Man,' and I think we all came up with everything else on it. But that's what it was—this one was totally collaborative, all the way. Even lyrics. There was a time where, on some songs, I would write one lyric line, Doug would write one lyric line, Jerry would write one lyric line, then it would come back to me, and we did the verses of the whole song that way. It was the most collaborative thing we've ever done.

DOUG PINNICK 'Fish Bowl Man,' I think Ty wrote those lyrics, and I remember we thought some of it was stupid. '*Fish Bowl Man* … that's ridiculous!' And the middle part, when Jerry talks? We thought the song was so horrible, we thought, *Let's put it on first, so we get through it. It will only get better after this!* And we did. But a lot of people love that song.

'JULIA'

DOUG PINNICK I think it was the first song we came up with. I remember saying, 'Let's make up progressions that go anywhere they're not naturally supposed to.' And we went for it. 'Julia' is a fictitious song about a girl. I was just trying to tell some kind of story, but I hadn't figured out what the story was about yet.

TY TABOR I remember coming up with the most unpredictable chord progression ever, and then working with Doug on making a melody make it make sense. And there were times when we were recording the melody, and Doug couldn't even think of the right note! So, what I would do is, I would hum the right note in his ear, and we would punch the one note and he would sing it. It took him a while to learn what the melody was—it was so stupidly unpredictable as it went down. I remember we did whatever we had to do to get the line down, and then he could hear it back and familiarize himself and learn it, and go, 'Oh, *OK.*' So it was tedious work on the melody on that one. But it turned out being super-cool when it finally clicked.

'SHE'S GONE AWAY'

TY TABOR I think I came up with pretty much all of that—even though we were all there together. I believe I wrote that one. It was about my separation and divorce from my wife at the time. It's all about re-telling the truth … without actually saying the truth.

DOUG PINNICK I remember specifically, when we worked that song up, Ty played the lead as we were recording the song—just to have a scratch track where the lead was. But the one-take lead was so good, we wouldn't let him redo it. And it's probably one of the best leads I've ever heard him do.

'MARSH MELLOW FIELD'

TY TABOR I remember coming up with a whole lot of that one, too. And with the same idea of a chord progression that doesn't go where it should in places, but, somehow, comes back together. It's the same idea—another direction to take that idea. I remember us making it be wrong, and then making the vocals make it right.

DOUG PINNICK That was a jam song. I think Ty came up with 'Marsh Mellow Field,' because we were making up rhymes, and Ty said, *'Beautiful marsh mellow field.'* As we wrote the song, we kept coming back to marsh mellow field—every fourth line of every verse—until we realized that must be the song title, so we left it. For us, writing music is sort of like art—we throw things in the pile to see how it looks and how it sounds. We have no fear when it comes to trying shit—whether it works or not.

'WHEN YOU'RE SCARED'

TY TABOR I don't even remember where the initial idea came on that one. Something tells me it was mostly Doug, but I don't remember.

DOUG PINNICK That's another one of those songs where we didn't have any lyrics, so everybody came up with a line. And I think every line has a different meaning to each of us.

'CHARLIE SHEEN'

DOUG PINNICK I remember when we were making up lyrics, Ty kept coming back to, *'Are you my friend, Charlie Sheen?'* And I'm going, 'What the fuck is that?' And he's going, 'It rhymes … *let's keep it*!'

TY TABOR The song actually had nothing to do whatsoever—in any way—with Charlie Sheen. I just happened to see him on some tabloid TV show, and the song was finished—except for the lines about Charlie Sheen. There was nothing there. And I saw him on the screen, and just stuck him in the song. That's the honest truth. I have no idea if Charlie has ever heard the song. [*Laughs*]

'SMUDGE'

DOUG PINNICK That was again one of those songs where we went line by line. There are four lines on every verse, and I would make up the first, Jerry would make up the second, and Ty would make up the third one, and we'd all make the fourth one up. That's how it came about lyrically, and every line is about something that happened to us in our past that you wouldn't understand. Jerry had a grandmother who … I don't know if she was crazy, but she used to say crazy things, and there is a line about, '*Hey Betty May, it's summertime in Jersey / Don't you know the kids will freeze*,' because he said she would yell at his mom to get the kids in the house because it was freezing outside—*when it was in the middle of the summer*! Ty had a line that he saw a picture on his wall when he was a kid, and when he fell asleep, he thought the painting was melting or something, and it was going to come get him—that there was a demon in it. I sang about being abducted by an alien.

'BITTER SWEET'

TY TABOR I came up with that one. Everything I was writing at that time was all from the same place—about the same thing. That was all basically what I had to write about—including 'Charlie Sheen.' It wasn't about anything but my marriage breaking up.

'MOVE ME'

DOUG PINNICK Again, musically, we threw it together like we did all the songs in that three-album Metal Blade era. Ty, Jerry, or I would come up with a part, and we'd fall in with our own parts.

I think it kind of sounds like a religious song. It's sort of like a prayer *and* a disclaimer—at the same time. I came up with the lyrics. More about my faith and losing it.

TY TABOR I know that one was a collaborative thing. I think I came up with guitar parts, then we all worked on where it was going melody-wise and structure-wise, and created it into this thing all together.

INSTEAD OF TRYING TO SCORE THAT ELUSIVE BREAKTHROUGH RADIO
HIT, KING'S X WENT IN THE OPPOSITE DIRECTION WITH *BULBOUS*—
ONE OF THEIR MOST EXPERIMENTAL RELEASES TO DATE. AS USUAL,
THEY THEN LAUNCHED A TOUR IN SUPPORT OF THE ALBUM.

TY TABOR The tour was more of exactly the same—for all three of those albums, it could have been one album and one period for me. It all was the same thing. Christian Nesmith toured around I think Europe with us, and recorded us doing the song 'Smudge' every night, and got a whole bunch of different angles and stuff, and a bunch of other footage, and threw it together as a music video.

CHRISTIAN NESMITH [video director] 'Smudge' was the first video I did. They were doing a European tour, and it just so happened I was doing this other musical project, and I was doing it in France. The day after I was finished was when they happened to be the closest they were going to be to me on their entire tour. I had my video camera with me, and they said, 'Why don't you come jump on the bus? We have an extra bunk.' I had nowhere to go and I didn't have a gig to go back to, so I said *sure*. I jumped on the bus, and the first thing I started doing was shooting. And because I'd known them for ten years, almost, they were very comfortable with me with the camera around. I held it low at my hip and let it roll pretty much all the time. I got some great stuff.

And, as I was hanging out, I would film the soundchecks, and I would film some of the shows. I really took a liking to 'Smudge.' I said, 'Why don't I capture every single performance of at least this song, all the way through—in whatever venue we're at, and the soundchecks.' So they finished up that tour; I wound up leaving them in London, flew back, and hooked up with a buddy of mine, Kurt Bonnem. I didn't really have the editing skills at that time, and he knew Adobe Premiere pretty good.

So we hauled them all in and started cutting together some stuff. If you look at the video, it's all grainy and lo-fi. But because King's X are so consistent in their tempo and the way they play, it was very easy to cut against the recording of the song. I took all their live performances and would cut it together, and the next thing we knew, we had a little 'behind the scenes/chase King's X around Europe' music video for 'Smudge.'

Ty has pretty much been my closest friend—although I love them all—so I sent him the video, and he said, 'Man, out of all the videos that have ever been done for us, this shows who we are. *Exactly* who we are.'

CHARLIE BENANTE I'm still a fan, of course, and I remember having this deep conversation with Doug about the *Mr. Bulbous* record. I didn't get it, and he kept saying, 'No, dude—give it another chance!' I remember following their next couple of records and picking out songs that I did like, but it wasn't the same anymore.

DEVIN TOWNSEND I guess it must have been 1997 or 1998, I had put out an album called *Infinity*, and my wife was doing our sort of fan-club/mailing-list thing. And she said, 'You know, there is a guy in Texas that is signed up to your mailing list. Isn't this the singer from that band you like?' And it was Doug's name! I was like, 'Yeah, but it doesn't strike me as being realistic that it's actually him.' But then, when we played in Texas on that Superjoint Ritual tour—probably around 2000 or so—Doug came out to the show. And that was the first time that I met him. And it turned out that it *was* him on the mailing list! Since that meeting with him, we have become good friends.

IN 2000, KING'S X CAME IN AT #83 ON VH1'S *100 GREATEST
ARTISTS OF HARD ROCK* COUNTDOWN.

TY TABOR I remember we were pretty stunned to be acknowledged. There are a lot of rock bands out there, and everyone else on the list are people who sold albums. So, to be mentioned, we were pretty stunned.

JERRY GASKILL I remember when that came out, it was going to air tomorrow, and the cable system I had didn't have VH1. So, I went out that day and got Dish Network, because they had that. I got it just so I could watch that. And, when I saw it, it made me think almost in some ways for the first time that we were a valid band. That there's validity to what we've done in our career. It was a really good thing to see—it really helped me to feel a part of the whole rock universe. And people said some great things about us. People who obviously are valid in the music world said some *really* nice things—like Nile Rodgers. Who would have guessed? It was incredible.

18 MANIC MOONLIGHT

THE STORY BEHIND THE BAND'S NINTH STUDIO
ALBUM, RELEASED ON SEPTEMBER 25, 2001.

JERRY GASKILL We kind of experimented with that one. We experimented with some drum loops and things like that. Just, 'Hey, let's try something different.' But that record came about the same as the *Tape Head* and *Bulbous* records came about, too—we came together and wrote songs from nothing, and added a bunch of drum loops.

DOUG PINNICK All I remember was, we were at the end of our rope, and didn't know what to do, what to play, what people wanted, or what they didn't want. We knew we had to make a record—because that's what we do. And we're not going to break up or stop. So, we just said, 'Time to make a record. *Let's go do it*.' I remember we went into the studio and wrote everything together. I think it's one of our least 'worked on' records. I think there were some really good songs on it, and I also think there were songs that were kind of a waste—or that we could have worked on some more. But that was sort of a low period for us. Lyrically, I was talking about things that I felt and believed. I remember I did a lot of slap-plucking on my bass on that CD. That was something I didn't do much.

TY TABOR We recorded it entirely at Alien Beans. We decided to move into my place and do everything from beginning to end there. And that we worked with loops for the first time—to see what it would inspire. We wanted to see what would happen—to experiment with it, to see where it would take us. And, by the way, that particular album, at the time it came out, because it was so different, there were a lot of King's X fans who weren't too into it, and were pretty vocal about it, and were dogging the band pretty heavily about it.

And, at the same time, there was this new group of fans that heard that album, that it was their favorite thing we've ever done. I don't make any apologies for that album. We all three felt it was a good album. We knew it was different, we knew King's X fans who wanted us to stay in this box weren't going to dig it. But it turned out to be a turning point for things to come, because it brought us some new fans, and the King's X fans that did like it, *really* loved it. So it was a moment where something changed.

DOUG PINNICK At the time, there were noises people were putting in their music, and we thought, *Hey, let's give that a try.* I don't think we were all excited about it. To this day, I don't think it was a real great idea. But we all agreed on it, and we worked real hard on getting the right sounds—even though I think we could have done without it.

TY TABOR [In response to my question, 'Is *Manic Moonlight* King's X's equivalent of Kiss's *(Music From) The Elder*?'] Um … I don't know—I think *Bulbous* and *Moonlight* could possibly be that! Because neither one of them broke any records on the charts—as far as sales. People scratch their heads on *Mr. Bulbous* a bit, but when it got to *Manic Moonlight*, there were some people who were just like, 'What the heck?' But we were into it.

CHARLIE BENANTE I remember the biggest thing was, Ty's guitar sound was drastically different. And it was a big thing for me. And maybe I'm being so fuckin' impartial to it, but whatever—*I missed it*. It's a strange thing when that gum that you've chewed for so many years completely goes out, and you don't have that taste anymore. Like I said, there were moments on different records that I really loved. Especially the *Manic Moonlight* record, which had some good tunes—there is a song called 'False Alarm,' and the song 'Manic Moonlight.'

DOUG PINNICK I've been going through dark times all my life, so it's nothing new. I think it was a different dark time. My journey has been one darkness to the next—trying to figure everything out. And that was another phase, I think.

TY TABOR I came up with the album cover. Just trying to come up with something that gave an uneasy feeling—even if you didn't quite know why. That was the intent, anyway. But I think the title came from the song 'Manic

Moonlight.' There's a lot of different images put together on the album cover and it's discolored. I hate to try to explain visuals, because people get different things from it. All I know is that I did things until it felt like what I wanted it to feel like.

THE SONGS
'BELIEVE'

TY TABOR I remember it being a pretty encouraging song. This is another one of those albums where we came in and worked on everything together. So, I don't know where ideas started or ended on that album, because it was so collaborative.

DOUG PINNICK 'Believe' was something that I had to write, because I was having a hard time with my self-hate. And I like to sing songs about things that I want to be doing—not that I'm doing. I was telling *myself*. But a couple of people have come to me and told me they didn't kill themselves because of that song. So that meant a lot to me.

'MANIC MOONLIGHT'

DOUG PINNICK When we wrote that song, I remember, when I had to write lyrics, all I could think about was Oasis, and 'Champagne Supernova.' That was such a beautiful melody, and it was so long. And it didn't really have much meaning to it—I didn't really understand what they were saying—but it was a great hook. So I took that approach on the song 'Manic Moonlight'—'*Let's pretend it's tomorrow / And we borrowed / The life of a perfect circus / In a manic moonlight*.' That was my way of trying to do an Oasis song.

TY TABOR That one was kind of like the progression of *Mr. Bulbous*, because *Manic Moonlight* also had a couple of chord things that were slightly wrong, but the vocals made them right. Without the vocals, it would be nonsense. I remember feeling that on that, too, so that song might have been *Bulbous Part II*—as far as trying different things. But, vibe-wise, it was in a totally different direction. And I don't understand why the vibe is so different on that album. It is where we were at, because we didn't intentionally have an idea of what we wanted to do—we went in and did it, and that's what came out.

'YEAH'

TY TABOR I remember it being funky and digging it. The loops were kind of vital in the funkiness of that one. There was a great bass part that we were cracking up over.

DOUG PINNICK That was just a jam. And couldn't really come up with a chorus, so I just went, 'Yeah, yeah, yeah.' I didn't have much to say.

'FALSE ALARM'

DOUG PINNICK I think I had fallen in love with this person who didn't feel the same way about me, and I thought they did. I was verbally led on. I was led to believe there was something there, when there really wasn't. He just wanted to be my friend but was afraid to tell me. It really broke my heart, and I felt stupid, also. It took me two years to get over it. Lyrically, it's so self-explanatory, it's almost stupid.

'STATIC'

DOUG PINNICK Musically, we wrote it all together, so I don't have much recollection about how we wrote it. But lyrically, it was a song about a friend of mine who I let live with me; I went on tour, and he went on a crack binge and sold or pawned almost everything in my house. And he got most of it back from the pawnshop, when I got back! But there are a few things that I never got back—to this day, when there's certain things I can't find, I think of him.

'*I don't wanna do this anymore / I really wanna do it*'—I know it's kind of a tongue-twister, but '*I don't wanna do this anymore*' means I don't want to be this person's friend and have this person use me like that. And when I put '*I really wanna do it*'—the 'really' actually means you have to do this, because I always say things but I never go into action and do it, when it comes to dealing with people. I kind of let people walk all over me. So, the chorus is, '*I don't wanna do this anymore / I really wanna do it*': This time, I'm going to do this, I'm not going to let this happen again.

'SKEPTICAL WINDS'

JERRY GASKILL I had some lyrics that I really liked, that I wrote when I was seventeen years old. Those lyrics became the basis for that song. Doug rearranged them a little bit … or maybe Ty helped, too. I'm not quite sure.

TY TABOR That is probably my favorite song on the record. Just super-crazy, funky, weird.

DOUG PINNICK That was one song where we didn't have any lyrics—*nothing*—and we just made stuff up. We wrote about four or five verses, and, for some reason, one of the verses became the chorus. And every time we got to the chorus, we did the verse that didn't become a verse. Which was really cool, because I remember when we got to that place, Ty looked up and said the same line again, and we said, 'OK. *That's* the chorus.' It was really a no-brainer when we wrote it. It was a lot of fun.

'THE OTHER SIDE'

DOUG PINNICK My brother had told me he was dying of an incurable disease. It's about how I felt right after he told me.

'VEGETABLE'

TY TABOR 'Vegetable' is one we still play live to this day. It's one of the highlights of the show, and it's evolved now into a jam that goes into more different places than the album. But it's a straight-ahead, funky tune that has survived from that album to this day.

'JENNA'

TY TABOR There's some funny stuff in there … if you pay attention. [*Laughs*]

DOUG PINNICK We didn't have a chorus, and I said, '*Jenna tell ya something*,' and I thought, *Genitalia*. So basically, we thought of the word genitalia, and used it as a chorus! It's a play on words that most people don't know, so we called it 'Jenna.'

'WATER CEREMONY'

DOUG PINNICK I was drinking some water, getting ready to sing, and Ty said, 'Damn, that sounds good. Let's record it!' And I did, and I belched at the end. We both cracked up laughing, so we put it at the end of the record. If it's stupid or goofy, we're going to do it.

MANIC MOONLIGHT WAS RELEASED JUST TWO WEEKS AFTER THE 9/11 TERROR ATTACKS ON NEW YORK AND WASHINGTON, D.C.

JERRY GASKILL I do know 9/11 affected everything in life. I remember I was at some car place—a garage—doing something with my car. I was sitting in the waiting room, and a TV was on, and I see this plane hit into the first building, and I think, *Oh my God. A terrible accident happened.* And then I saw it happen again, and I go, 'Oh my God … we're being attacked!' And I felt like everybody else probably in the whole world—that everything in life at that moment changed. Life will never be the same again. Something has happened unlike anything that has ever happened in the history of our country. I'm sure that's how everybody felt.

How it affected the band, I don't know. As a band, we somewhat try to stay away from the political things and religious things. But it all affected us individually, I'm sure, equally. I don't remember a time thinking, *We can't travel now because of that.* I don't remember that.

DOUG PINNICK I remember I woke up and I went into the office in my house, when I lived in Texas. I always turned on *Good Morning America*, and, for some reason, that morning, something kept telling me, 'Turn it on, now.' Usually, I get up and brush my teeth and do my thing—get my coffee. But for some reason, something was telling me, 'Turn it on, now.' And when I turned it on, there was the tower and it was on fire. And I'm going, 'What the fuck?!' And then, a few minutes later, the other one went down. I sat there, going, 'What the hell is going on?' It was a big shock. I never wrote any songs about it, though.

TY TABOR I remember that we went to New York and played—we were one of the first shows in the city after all these other bands had cancelled all their shows, and there was nothing happening in the city. We said, 'We're going. If there ever was a time to go and refuse to let fear win, *it's now*. And maybe these people need some relief for a minute.'

So we headed our butts up to New York to play, and I remember it was one of the heaviest experiences—there was still smoke coming from the buildings. It's when there were lights—night and day—and, at night, huge lights up into the sky, where you could see smoke. It was like that for a while. It was like that when we came to play.

I remember it was a huge show, and the people thanking us so much for being there. We felt very touched by the whole thing. I remember police coming on the bus and offering to take us to Ground Zero. I remember so much about the city being so unified, and American flags everywhere. Just a feeling that was hard to put into words. I mean, *everybody* was completely devastated by 9/11. But one of the first things that I did was, I got on a plane with my son. As soon as the planes started running again, we hopped on a plane and flew to Florida, did some scuba diving, flew back, and I was on the plane—me and him—with maybe fifteen people. But it was our way of saying, 'We are not letting one thing in our life change because of this. That's how fear wins—*screw that*.' And then, the next thing I did was hop on the tour bus and head out with King's X—and do the shows in New York.

DOUG PINNICK I figured I'm not going to stop, and terrorism is made to scare people and stop them from doing what they do. It's like getting struck by lightning—well, if it happens, it's going to happen … but I'm not going to stop doing what I'm doing.

IN THE SUMMER OF 2002, KING'S X EMBARKED ON A US
TOUR WITH DREAM THEATER AND JOE SATRIANI.

MIKE PORTNOY They were on the opening slot, Dream Theater was in the middle, and Joe Satriani was closing the show—so it was a three-band tour. The memories were we were always hanging out with those guys backstage and after the shows. None of the other Dream Theater guys mixed and socialized that much, but I always did. I was always going into their dressing room and mainly talking Beatles trivia with those guys, because all three of them are such big Beatles fans. I used to love shooting the shit with them about that kind of stuff.

TY TABOR It was fun. I remember being amazed at how Joe was so unbelievably consistent, night after night after night. Just never missed a thing. I'm sure he thought he did, but his consistency was ridiculous. And, of course, Dream Theater is like a machine of consistency, also. I remember that tour as an onslaught of musicianship. [*Laughs*]

RICHARD CHRISTY I didn't get to see King's X live until I moved to Florida. If I remember right, they were on tour with Galactic Cowboys, and I remember freaking out that I was going to get to see King's X *with* Galactic Cowboys. They sounded incredible live. And Doug's bass sound sounded just as great live … all the guys sounded amazing. The harmonies were beautiful—this was long before people could Auto-Tune stuff. They had voices of angels, these guys. But it was rocking, pretty heavy music—with these kind of angelic voices over the music. And I loved that.

I think that show was around 2002, at the House of Blues in Orlando. And then I got to see—I think around 2003, 2004—King's X in LA, on the Sunset Strip, at—I think it used to be called Gazzarri's, but it was called something else after that. It was right next to where the Rainbow is. I remember being in LA with my buddy, who is a big King's X fan. I remember freaking out, because King's X is one of those bands that a lot of musicians love—famous musicians.

I remember seeing Eric Singer from Badlands and Kiss at the show, and freaking out. I went up to say hi, and he was really super-nice. I don't remember who else, but there were a lot of big-time musicians from LA that were at this King's X show. And it was a pretty intimate show. You know a band is really cool when other huge musicians will come to a small club show and see them.

19 BLACK LIKE SUNDAY &
LIVE ALL OVER THE PLACE

THE STORIES BEHIND THE BAND'S TENTH STUDIO
ALBUM, RELEASED ON MAY 20, 2003, AND THEIR FIRST
EVER LIVE ALBUM, RELEASED ON NOVEMBER 2, 2004.

JERRY GASKILL [*Black Like Sunday*] is a record of songs that we wrote before we were even King's X. They are all songs from way back when we were the Edge, and some of the first songs that we ever wrote and performed together. And we thought, 'Hey, let's bring back all these old songs that we loved at the time, and make a record.' That's exactly what we did with *Black Like Sunday*.

TY TABOR It was probably the quickest of all our albums to record … I don't really have much to say about that album. [*Laughs*]

DOUG PINNICK I remember we were getting ready to make that record, and we didn't have any songs again. It was like, 'We're going to get together and make up stuff.' And I said, 'Let's do a whole bunch of old songs that we did way back in the Edge days—when we first got together. And I said, 'Let's do them all in drop-C or drop-A—a lot lower, so it will sound heavier.' So we went into the studio and did them all, and I kept the lyrics the way they were originally. I thought about changing the lyrics, but I left them as they were, and at that point, I wrote some pretty naïve—to me—immature lyrics. But we kept them, and, as a result, I can barely listen to that record. [*Laughs*] I think the music is great, buy lyrically, I think, *Oh my God. Why didn't I work on some better choruses and melodies?* But that's what that record is. It kind of came and went—nobody talks about that record very much. We put it out on Ty's label, Brop! Records.

TY TABOR Brop! Records was us licensing a record to Metal Blade, rather than doing a normal record deal. That way, we kept ownership of it. If it says 'Brop!' on it, but it's totally owned by King's X.

We had been together for many years before we recorded our first album. And, during those years, we had written countless songs that whenever we were out playing the bars, there were certain songs that were people's favorites—that they wanted to hear all the time—that never ended up on an album. So, we got to thinking about it—it's a shame to just let all that stuff go to waste. We thought, *Why don't we do one album, where we pick a lot of the songs that used to be those songs that were people's favorites—before anybody even knew who we were?*

JERRY GASKILL My songs weren't very 'considered' in those days. But, at the same time, we were all putting ourselves into the songs equally, so we felt like they were all our own songs. That's the way it was, working back then.

TY TABOR We had a contest online and let fans come up with covers for *Black Like Sunday*, and that was the one [drawn by Danny Wilson] that we chose as the winning cover.

THE SONGS
'BLACK LIKE SUNDAY'

DOUG PINNICK 'Black Like Sunday' was called 'The Dog' originally. It was a tune I wrote back in the early Edge days. My four-track demo was a total AC/DC rip-off, recorded with Drumdrops [a collection of drum loops and samples]. Just terrible! So, we did it in drop-B, which made it nice and heavy. I changed the words when we re-recorded it, too.

'ROCK PILE'

DOUG PINNICK I really loved the music of that song. Another four-track with Drumdrops. I had an old SG, and I could barely play guitar. I was making these very badly played and terrible sounding four-track demos back in the Edge days. There was this album of several standard drumbeats that were complete songs, so I'd play along and ignore the drum changes. Vocally, I was trying to sound like Johnny Rotten … what was I thinking? And that was basically about how rock stars come and go—they rise and they fall. I had no clue—I was stuck in Springfield, but I was singing about it. [*Laughs*]

TY TABOR That was one of the first songs we ever did as a band. The very first show we ever did, that was one of the songs in the set. Doug wrote it. Another one of those songs that used to be people's favorites—one that they wanted to hear.

'DANGER ZONE'

DOUG PINNICK It's a simple song, a fictitious song about a teenager who is dealing with growing up. I wrote it when Dan was living with me, before everyone else moved in my house back then. Dan was the first guitarist—he left shortly after. He might have had some input, because we used to jam on our guitars in my room back then. I know he was there when I wrote it.

'WORKING MAN'

DOUG PINNICK This is another song from the time Dan was living with me. Dan had a lot to do with writing this song—I can't remember details. Lyrics are self-explanatory.

TY TABOR 'Working Man' was another one of the very first songs we did as a band. We all liked that one a lot. It used to immediately get people on the floor. And it was back during the time when Gary Numan had the song 'Cars'—I think it was written around the same time, and had the same kind of vibe as that song.

We knew Rush had a song called 'Working Man'—I had been familiar with Rush since their first album, and that was the biggest song on it. I was familiar with it, but Doug wrote that one, and wasn't thinking about Rush at all—so we didn't worry about it much.

'DREAMS'

DOUG PINNICK That was a funk song that I came up with—with the slap/pluck thing. It's sort of a holistic type of song—just encouraging.

TY TABOR That one was written after we were called Sneak Preview, and I think we were doing that when we had just become a three-piece, and we were in Springfield—doing all different kinds of music. But that one was our attempt at sort of a reggae-ish song. Doug was into the Police quite a bit when they came out. It took me a little while to get into them. But we were more influenced by *actual* reggae—like Bob Marley.

'FINISHED'

DOUG PINNICK I remember vividly everything about writing this song, because I was using the Drumdrops album, and it had a shuffle on it, so I had just put all the parts down on it, and I was excited, because it was the first song that actually sounded like a good song. Back then, whenever I learned a new finger position on my guitar, I'd try and write a song. I was in my room, listening to the whole song, and our manager came in, and I said, 'Hey! Listen to this tune I just finished.' He said that Jerry, Ty, and the several others who worked with the band were in the living room, and they wanted to talk to me. That's the night that he asked me if I was gay. Ty and Jerry didn't care, but everyone else moved out. We were all Evangelical Christians, and that was a very, very big deal in that world. Not something you wanted people to know about you back then. It was not accepted *at all*. It was definitely one of the worst things that happened in my life, so I'll never forget writing that.

Then, somewhere in Missouri, there was a festival going on—some type of food festival or something. My friend and I were walking down the street with all these vendors and people buying stuff, and this guy walked past me, looked up at me, I looked at him, and we both kind of caught each other's eye for a minute. It was like one of those looks when you meet somebody, and you go, 'Oh my God. This is the person that I've been looking for all my life.' And I was too shy and afraid to say anything—if I was wrong I could get beat up, or killed. So, I just kept walking. *'Finished before it started.'*

TY TABOR That one was another one of those heavy rock songs that used to bring the house down and everybody wanted to hear. That was another one that was in the first couple of years in the band.

'SCREAMER'

DOUG PINNICK We all wrote that one from scratch, back in the Edge days, jamming in my kitchen. I remember Ty was playing that bending note, and Jerry and I started grooving together under it. Before we knew it, we had a song.

The words came easy, because it's a true story—sort of. I have night-terror episodes a lot when I sleep. I scream and yell at night, a lot of people have told me. Ty has some stories that still freak me out—people have to wake me up. Sometimes, I don't even remember the nightmares. Sometimes, I speak in another language—people have told me that I spoke in Latin. *And I've never spoke another language.*

One of my roommates said I sat up and screamed at the top of my lungs, then sang a full three-octave scale, then started laughing, and then fell asleep—right after a gig, where I wouldn't be able to sing that at all.

'BAD LUCK'

DOUG PINNICK I had been listening to the album *Lovedrive* by Scorpions. I wrote it during Christmas break, when Jerry and Ty went back to their hometowns for the holidays. We had just committed to being a band. It's about the antichrist: 666, the number of the beast.

'DOWN'

DOUG PINNICK That was a demo from around the *Dogman* period. We recorded it for an extra track, I think. It was at a time when I was in full-on 'hate myself' mode. I woke up on a hot Texas morning, and, as usual, the phone rings, and I don't feel like answering. I didn't want to talk to anybody, because I never could hide my feelings, and trying to act like I was OK was impossible for me to do then. I wanted to be alone in my self-misery.

Some things never change—but I was tired of always waking up in this depressed mood. That knot in my stomach was always there when I woke up. And the only thing that would help me come out of those feelings was to write a song about it. I think working on the music and parts helped me not feel so bad inside about the things that depressed me. It was like medicine. It still is—I think that's why I write so much. The chorus is '*Feeling down again.*' It's one of my favorite songs, only because it's lyrically accurate to what happened that morning. Probably one of the saddest songs I've ever written.

'WON'T TURN BACK'

DOUG PINNICK This is from 1981 or 1982 … maybe 1983. Most of the bands were playing this power/new-wave/punk-type stuff, and I thought I'd take a stab at writing one. Kind of goofy, I think. But it was all about learning from my mistakes, and not leaving my faith.

The hardest thing about some of these old songs for me is I don't believe or feel the same way anymore, but a lot of people want to hold me to these old lyrics. But … I sang them! I was listening to it a few days ago, and was reminded of how hard it rocked.

TY TABOR When we first came out, we were a lot more eclectic and weird. By the time we were doing stuff like 'Won't Turn Back,' we were just trying to get people on the dance floor.

'TWO'

DOUG PINNICK That was the other demo from the *Dogman* era. Musically, there wasn't much to that song, but there's a lot of vibe to it. We did it simple—like my demo. It was just for another extra track we needed.

Back in the day, I had thought about Eddie Vedder singing the verses—years later, we recorded it for *Black Like Sunday*. I tried to emulate his style of singing on the verses. My favorite part is the *a capella* part. It's a song about longing for that special one to come find you.

'YOU'RE THE ONLY ONE'

DOUG PINNICK It's a love song. A fictitious song about being in love, and, '*You're the only one that can make me happy.*' It was a cute little Elvis Costello–type pop song I was trying to write. I hate it now!

'JOHNNY'

DOUG PINNICK I was really obsessed with the Police at the time. So, it's basically a Police rip-off—with a long lead at the end. And it's a song about following trends, and trying to be like someone else, when you need to find yourself, which is exactly what I was trying to do—sound like the Police! I think I was really speaking to myself.

TY TABOR That one was probably the biggest hit on the record—as far as songs that people loved and requested all the time. People always wanted to hear 'Johnny.' It was another reggae song—a reggae-rock song. That one is probably more Police influenced.

'SAVE US'

DOUG PINNICK That's another prayer. Another quick, fast pop song. I actually think this song and 'Won't Turn Back' are the same song with different words!

TY TABOR That was another one of our high-energy/punk kinds of things. We had a lot of three-chord, wide-open, in-your-face, punk-ish stuff for the time. Because that was what was going on in Springfield. We didn't actually start drawing crowds until we started doing that kind of stuff. It was just in that time period—another one of those.

DURING THE ENSUING TOUR, KING'S X RECORDED THEIR FIRST EVER LIVE ALBUM (AND LAST METAL BLADE RELEASE), LIVE ALL OVER THE PLACE.

TY TABOR It was exactly that—it was taken from tapes and recordings from everywhere. Just *all over the place*. And I don't really remember much about it otherwise, because I was playing all those songs every night.

BRIAN SLAGEL They are such a great live band, and we were like, 'King's X doesn't have a live record yet? How is that possible?' The timing was right to do it, and the band was still playing at a super-high level, so we thought it would be the perfect time to finally capture what the band was like live.

DEVIN TOWNSEND I ended up playing with them with the Devin Townsend Band—not Project—in Vancouver [around this time]. That was the first time I had actually seen them. It was really cool. I think the thing I liked about them …

there is an element to them that they remained relatively underground, but there is something about that, that even when we got a chance to play with them, it felt like it was 'my band' still. And there was something—selfishly—about that, that I really appreciated.

JERRY GASKILL What I recall about that is, we must have needed to make another record, and we decided to make a live record. My feeling about that is that, in some ways, it was one of the lower points of our playing history. It may have been different tours—that's why we called it *Live All Over The Place*, because it's from … all over the place. Different times, different cities, whatever. But I remember a good portion of that being from what I called 'The Drunk Tour'—where all three of us, by the end of the show, had drunk quite a bit when we were onstage. [*Laughs*]

I actually remember having shots of Raspberry Kamikaze lined up on my drum riser. And there were nights—by the end of the show—where I could barely even see straight! As we were listening back to the recordings, they start off sounding pretty good. *Oh, this isn't bad. It's pretty good.* But by the end of the show, it's like, *What happened? We're all fucking drunk!*

I think Jay Phebus, who was our tour manager at the time, and who was with us for many years, said, 'You guys have to got to stop doing that. You've got to stop drinking so much. You're starting to sound *bad*.'

DOUG PINNICK We decided to put a live record out, and we went out on tour and recorded every show, and all of our techs at that time were alcoholics—they drank from the time they woke up until the time they went to bed. And we all were drinking onstage—some of us way more than others. They would bring us drinks—Jerry would have five or six shots of Patrón, and I would have my pitcher of Raspberry Kamikazes. It wasn't good for the show. We listened back to every concert, and, at the beginning, it rocked. The first couple of songs were cooking … and then, all of a sudden, we start getting worse and worse. And we could barely find enough songs to put on that record that we didn't sound like shit—because we were *so* drunk.

I was singing pretty bad at the time—my throat was starting to change. The older I get, the harder it is for me to sing certain things. Like anybody would. But what happened was, it was my worst time of singing, so we had to really doctor the vocals up to make it work. It was a rough record, putting that out. I forgot about that record! These days, I'm probably the only one who drinks when we're playing. I remember saying, 'Let's call it *Live All Over The Place*.'

TY TABOR That might have been *Doug and Jerry* sort of drinking heavily on the tour. I've never been a heavy drinker on tour. I drink wine; I don't drink like Doug does, and like Jerry did back in those days. They would drink Patrón and hard liquor, and I didn't have any of that. *At all*. It wasn't my deal.

I actually didn't like it when Doug and Jerry were drinking too much. Especially Jerry. Jerry is not a good drunk. He's lucky to have not gotten his butt whooped by several people during that time, and lucky to have not gotten hurt—or died. But he was going through some heavy stuff. I've never blamed Jerry, because he's had to deal with and gone through a lot more than I can ever dream of. But, yeah, he did have some low points with the drinking.

DOUG PINNICK That's my preaching [in the middle of 'Believe']. I'm always preaching about something. When I was a little kid, this lady said to me that I was going to be a preacher. I looked at her, like, 'I don't know what you're talking about.' But I guess that's kind of what I've become in rock'n'roll—preaching love.

JERRY GASKILL I do remember liking the acoustic part of that record—I think it was really nice and really done well. It was pretty good for a live representation of us.

TY TABOR I personally hated doing the stuff acoustic. As a matter of fact, all of us did. None of us liked it. We used to do acoustic tours because we could do radio appearances with a couple of acoustics and a bongo. We did a whole tour of radio stations doing that, and doing live performances in each town. So we had this acoustic stuff worked up. I remember when MTV started doing *Unplugged*, we'd already been doing that forever. We didn't like doing it, but a lot of people asked for it, so we decided to do a tour one time that was going to be some acoustic shows and some electric shows. And, as it turned out, because of confusion, we ended up doing a few songs acoustic, and then doing an electric show.

20 IN CONCERT

WHAT MAKES A KING'S X CONCERT SUCH
A DARNED SPECIAL EVENT?

EDDIE TRUNK Live, they were *unbelievable*. To this day, people can't believe the sound that these three guys put down. And how great they are vocally. So that pushed it over the edge, where, all of a sudden, 'Oh, these records are really good'—then people went and saw them live, and their jaw was on the floor.

MARIA FERRERO The most impressive thing I ever saw   and will ever see in any band, and I've been doing this thirty-four years—was to see King's X live. It was *so* special. The fan/band exchange was unlike any other band I ever saw. They wouldn't even have to sing the lyrics to their songs. They would get up there, start playing the music, and everybody in the crowd sang every single word. It was this 'love exchange'—that's the only way I could describe it. Love between the fans and the band. It was magical. I'd never seen it. I've seen many concerts, and yep, fans stand up and they sing the words and know all the lyrics. But nothing is like a King's X show.

JON ZAZULA I saw King's X either the week or the day before I saw Nirvana in London, at a little place that held about a thousand people. And it was very weird—while Nirvana had a great, intense show, King's X was like going to see a Pink Floyd show … without all the lights. I find King's X live to be a religious experience. I find King's X to be very spiritual. A song like 'Pray' takes me to the moon and back. Those guys are monolithic.

REX BROWN The three-part harmonies, it was so Beatles. It made you feel at home. When you heard those choruses, they were layered—impeccable vocals. And they could pull it off live. That's the thing that always amazed me.

JEFF AMENT I saw them twenty times, probably. Because they probably did ten shows with us, and I probably watched every minute of those shows, because you feel lucky when a band you really, really love is opening up for you. But, to me, that acoustic show, and that first show at the Central, and I saw a show about ten years ago—I think they'd been taking a break, and the venue might have had a different name, but it was the Phoenix Underground. That was the first time I'd seen them in a few years, and I remember thinking how great they were. Sometimes, you drift from something, and then you see something, and you're like, 'My God, this band is so great.' It's so incredibly unfair that they weren't massive. And, at that show, there was probably four hundred, five hundred people, and they were all *in*, man. There wasn't a wishy-washy fan in the room. Which I think is true to this day. I think they have some pretty hardcore fans.

RAY LUZIER I lived in LA for twenty-seven years—I've been in Nashville for the last three. But when I lived out there, my buddy Joe Lester—he plays for the Van Halen tribute band, Atomic Punks, and a Mötley Crüe tribute band—he's a great bass player. Doesn't do too much original stuff, but he's still on the scene out there. He's probably a little bit bigger King's X fan than me, because there were times he would call me up and say, 'Dude, they're in San Francisco tonight.' And we'd buy a flight on Southwest and fly to Frisco—go see them, get a cheap hotel, then fly back the next day! He'd call me up, and go, 'Dude, they're playing this place in San Diego. It's a two-hour drive—I'm picking you up in ten minutes!' He and I would go back and forth a lot, or vice versa—I'd find out about something before he would. There was probably a five- or six-year span where we would fly to Vegas, Frisco, drive to San Diego. I remember even a Phoenix show.

NUNO BETTENCOURT I'm not exactly sure, but I want to say that I saw them live first on the *Faith Hope Love* tour—before I even heard the album. I think it was at the Astoria in London. And, once again, I was like, 'Are you fucking kidding me?' I couldn't believe that a three-piece could sound like that. It wasn't just something that they did in the studio, and, 'Oh, that's cute and that's great … but how are they going to do this live?' But then … *they did it.*

It wasn't like they were the most physical band to watch—they were a 'player's band' to watch. They were performing with what they did, talent-wise. They didn't have to run around stage and be crazy. [When Extreme and King's X toured together in 2008] that was one of my favorite tours. That, to me, was probably one of the ultimate connections of two bands that could do a tour and give a great night of music, and a great night of vocals and harmonies and players.

WALLY FARKAS A lot of rock bands that have big followings, girls are throwing their bras or panties onstage—not at King's X concerts, obviously—but a lot of rock bands, some chick jumps up onstage and wants to get a kiss on the cheek from one of them, and get off the stage. With King's X, dudes jumped onstage with little throwaway flash cameras, and they wouldn't try to tap Ty on the shoulder or whatever. No. They'd jump up onstage and run straight to the rack of equipment that was on the side of the stage, and take pictures of all the gear and settings … and then jump offstage!

GEORGE LYNCH I've seen them many times. We've actually played shows with them occasionally, here and there—sharing the bill and so forth. They're one of my favorite bands live. They really are. They're old-school enough that I really appreciate their improvisational tendencies, where, live, they also take off and elaborate on studio songs. They would make it more of an experience—rather than reciting the songs they wrote. They took the live approach as a different animal.

JERRY GASKILL Nowadays, for tours, we just show up and play, and hopefully do a little rehearsal on our own. But I think that we kind of know the songs enough that even when we don't rehearse, we'll somehow pull it off. [Sometimes] I haven't even seen the guys since the last time we did a show … then we land in [say] Dusseldorf together, and we have a show the next day at a festival—with thousands of people!

REX BROWN Going to so many shows and seeing those guys, we went out of our way. I can't remember when this was, but I went to see them, and Doug asked me, 'Do you want to get up and play "King"?' And they never let hardly anybody get up and jam on a song. That's one of those bands that just didn't do it. We were like that for a long time, then it became a big free-for-all, so that Dime could get some entertainment. But Doug called and asked if I'd like to play 'King,' and I said, 'It's the biggest honor of my fucking life'—to play the first song I heard off that first record, twenty years ago. And then, every time they're in town, they do the same thing.

So I got up and played with them. I've done it two or three times. And I've played with Jerry in some jazz club that we took over one night. Playing bass with someone that tight, and the way that he hits the drums, there was just something special about each and every one of them. And you put those three together—that was the chemistry. And it's the same thing with me, Dime, and Vinnie—any nucleus of a really good rock band, you've got to have that solid core. But they did it *and* sang it. I've always admired guys that do that. They can do it all. That's the way rock'n'roll was meant to be.

TY TABOR We believe in that contact with people being the thing that is more important than anything—after seeing it on a mass scale. And we started trying to reach out emotionally. 'Screw everything else. Nothing else matters.' It has become that now. It has become the first church of rock'n'roll.

Before, there were elements of that, and, yes, there was the love and people singing, but we weren't fully on board. We were still 'performers.' After the Pearl Jam tour, I got real—and did not give a damn about what anybody else wanted, ever again.

21 OGRE TONES

THE STORY BEHIND THE BAND'S ELEVENTH
STUDIO ALBUM–THEIR FIRST FOR INSIDEOUT
MUSIC–RELEASED ON SEPTEMBER 27, 2006.

TY TABOR I was already dealing with InsideOut for my solo stuff and other bands I am in—Jelly Jam and Platypus. I was good friends with Thomas Waber, who was at the top of the label, and had done many albums with him with the other projects. At one point, we approached them to see if they were interested in doing some King's X, and they were.

DOUG PINNICK I remember, when we signed with InsideOut Music, somehow we got wind that Michael Wagener was a King's X fan. And we thought, *Wow. Why don't we get him to do records for us?* We were really excited about it.

MICHAEL WAGENER [*Ogre Tones, XV* producer] I crossed paths with them right before we did the *Ogre Tones* album. I saw them at a concert here in Nashville, we got to talking, and, 'Hey, let's do something together!' I love King's X, and I think they're amazing. I think it must be somewhere in 2005, and then we got together and did the record together.

TY TABOR Accept's *Balls To The Wall* was the first thing he worked on that we were aware of. But by the time we worked with him, we knew of him working with all kinds of people and all kinds of things. But that was the initial thing that made us think, *Man, this sounds amazing. He's good.*

MICHAEL WAGENER I ended up mixing *Balls To The Wall*. We talked about it when we first met, and you try to find out what the band wants to go for. I guess we talked about it then. With King's X, I produced; with Accept, I just mixed. But they kind of liked the sound that we got on the Accept album. There's nothing in particular that you go for—you just want the overall tone. King's X totally has their own sound—with the guitar tone and the way they play, it's totally their own thing. But I think what they liked was more the energy and the overall picture of the song.

JERRY GASKILL Michael does these workshops where people pay a certain amount of money, they come to his studio, watch him work, and they can be sort of 'hands on' and learn from him. And he asked us if we wanted to be 'the band'—because he would record a band and let people be involved. And we thought, *Oh, this might be a good idea to get involved with Michael, and do this*. So, we did. We did a couple of songs with him at this workshop thing, and we really loved what came out of it. So we decided to make a record, and the first record was *Ogre Tones*.

TY TABOR Michael does these recording things, where people come in for two or three days, and he schools them. Something gets recorded, and he schools everybody on all of his techniques of what he's doing, while things are being recorded. So, somehow, the idea got passed around—*Why don't we try working together and see what we think? And let's do it in a way that doesn't cost us money*. We decided to do one of those two or three-day seminar things with him, where we would work on and record a couple of songs, and there would be a small group of people paying to get to watch and learn. So that is what we did, and we recorded a couple of songs, and it went real well. The record company was behind it with a budget, so we decided to go ahead and work with him to do an album … and we ended up doing two albums.

DOUG PINNICK We had a lot of fun doing the record in Nashville and hanging out in the studio. We spent a whole month there. It was like making a *real* record, because we hadn't done that in a good while. Since *Ear Candy*, we really hadn't been to a studio with a producer. So it was pretty cool.

MICHAEL WAGENER King's X was one of the very few bands in my career that recorded pretty much everything live—where they all play at the same time. And it's mostly keeper tracks. We don't have to redo something … maybe just do the vocals afterward, just because of the acoustics in the room. But, so far,

I think I've only had three bands in my career where that really happened, and King's X are one of them. They're amazing musicians.

JERRY GASKILL I love Michael. And I love working with Michael. He makes me feel comfortable, he makes me feel valid, and I think I love working with him because he loved working with us. And he's so knowledgeable. He has many years behind him of making records, and that's what he loves more than anything. And he has great stories to tell from throughout the years. So all those things make it a really great working situation for me.

TY TABOR I'll say that no other producer that I've ever worked with is anything like Sam. Even remotely anything like him. No other people were ever like him! He's on his own. But Brendan O'Brien was super-easy and nice to work with and fast and killer, and so was Arnold Lanni—he was great. And Michael was super-fun to work with, because he too is meticulous, but he's a very funny guy, so the kind of vibe in the studio is always light and funny, and of a good energy, and getting the job done. He seemed to be impressed that we spend most of our time working on what we wanted to record, and then, when it came time to hit the button, we played it once and that was it. He's used to it being the opposite. So he was really loving it. And as far as how the recording went, just getting the parts down was the easiest part of everything.

JERRY GASKILL I didn't really write anything on that record, but I felt like the songs were songs that we all put ourselves into. Like all King's X songs—we all put ourselves into them, and, therefore, they become all of our songs. And that's been that way throughout our entire history.

MICHAEL WAGENER It was a wonderful session. They would just do their thing—play their instruments—and there was not much I had to say to that.

THE SONGS

'ALONE'

DOUG PINNICK On this album, we brought finished basic demos in. I had a pile of tunes, as usual, because I never stop writing. I was experiencing and watching how terrible people treat each other, so the lyrics are '*No one should be made to feel alone*'—like, why do people make people feel bad? Why do people hurt people for no reason?

U2 was one of my favorite bands back in the day, and this sort of has a 'U2 vibe' to it—like an 'I Will Follow'–type thing. My demo was a long, drawn-out version—with a long funeral-type march for about eight measures, before it kicked into the U2 vibe. It was *so* boring! We took out all the crappy parts and turned it into what it is. I'm glad we did.

TY TABOR It was very easy. It's a simple, straight-ahead song. The time it took us to learn it and play it was nothing. That one happened so fast I don't remember recording it. That's a Doug song. I sang the intro … I don't even know why I did the intro, to be honest—instead of Doug just doing it.

'STAY'

DOUG PINNICK I wrote that. It's a very simple tune that stayed close to the original demo. It's a sad song, lyrically. But it's how I felt all the time.

'HURRICANE'

DOUG PINNICK That song was a dUg demo. I was proud of that one! It wasn't as boring as some of the other ones I wrote for the album. Allison was this tropical storm that came into Houston. It wasn't a hurricane, actually—it was a tropical storm. But it flew into Houston, dumped I don't know how many tons of water—the whole city was underwater. Literally, the highways, everything was underwater—tractor-trailers were floating. And it went back out into sea, came back, and did it again. It really devastated the whole Houston area.

TY TABOR 'Hurricane' is one that Doug originally wrote. I changed it a bit from how he wrote it. The way he wrote it, the chorus was all one note. There were no chord changes in the chorus—it was just a drone. And I felt that it should go somewhere, instead of just droning. So I changed the chorus to have the chords in it that it has in it. But that's a Doug song, otherwise.

'FLY'

DOUG PINNICK That was another one from a while back that I wrote. It's pretty close to the demo. '*No matter what you do / Always somebody who doesn't like it.*'

TY TABOR That is another really old one—we actually recorded it when we were doing *Ear Candy*, and it didn't make it on the album. But it was a song that I always thought was a good song, and just wanted to give it another shot. And, this time, it came together.

'IF'

DOUG PINNICK It was a simple tune I wrote about how I was feeling. I didn't realize though that it was the same chorus as 'Man In The Mirror' by Michael Jackson—until the record came out. I was listening to it one day, going, *Man, that sounds like, 'I'm starting with the man in the mirror.'* And I'm going, *What the fuck?!* Nobody said nothing to me, so, at this point, that's life. But I didn't realize that.

'BEBOP'

DOUG PINNICK That was the last song I wrote before we went to make that record. I was thinking about Little Richard—'*bop bop-a-lu a whop bam boo*' ['Tutti Frutti']. 'Bebop' was sort of like a celebration. I wanted this four-on-the-floor-type beat for people to dance to. But yet the verses were all fucked up, so you couldn't dance to it. The crazy ending happened in the studio as we were tracking it. We used to do that song live, which was a lot of fun. Especially the crazy ending.

TY TABOR That's another one of Doug's—we were a little stumped on this one, and Doug went out to his car to work on it a little. He came in and got me to go to the parking lot to hear what he was thinking for the chorus. He was almost afraid to sing it to me, thinking I would think it was stupid. I thought it was awesome!

'HONESTY'

TY TABOR That one was written in the studio. I think I was in the lobby with an acoustic guitar, waiting for Mike [Wagener] to do some editing or something. I wrote it on the spot, and we decided to record it. To be honest, I don't remember what the lyrics are about. I remember it was deep introspection—whatever was happening with life at the moment.

'OPEN MY EYES'

DOUG PINNICK That was a song I was recording for my solo album, *Emotional Animal*. Jerry's son, Joey, played drums on the original track. Then we decided that King's X should do it. Again, I questioned the horrible nature of man. And the chorus is, '*What does it take to get to the point / Where you want to kill someone?*' I didn't have any answers. I wanted to make a statement of the question.

'FREEDOM'

TY TABOR I think we just played a lot of stuff for Michael, and gravitated toward anything that he felt strong about. I think that was one of the ones that he liked a lot, so we did it. There is a lyric in the song 'Freedom' that uses Jay Phebus's name. It's '*Freedom to terminate Jay Phebus if he don't fit in.*' Jay was adopted, and was always very thankful to whoever his parents were for not aborting him. And that one line in the song is directly referring to conversations I've had with Jay about that, and about him being happy to be here. I wanted to throw out the dichotomy of, *You very easily could not have been here. You could just be considered an inconvenience*. But it's someone's freedom to do that. So, I'm spouting all kinds of 'freedoms,' and I used Jay to spout that particular one.

'GET AWAY'

DOUG PINNICK My demo was originally a heavy rock tune, with none of the beautiful vocal harmonies it has now. It reminds me of the Carpenters. I said, 'Let's do it acoustically, instead—just for variety.'

'SOONER OR LATER'

DOUG PINNICK That was another basic verse-and-chorus tune I had written. I wasn't too crazy about it. But it came out great. It's about everybody leaving in my life. It seems like from the day I was born, somebody left. It's about how everybody that came into my life that I attached myself to and that I loved deeply, they would leave. I never could understand why, and I thought personally that there was something wrong with me. I was pushing them away, I think. That's where that came from. It's another psychological song.

'MUDD'

DOUG PINNICK I had an uncle, and we called him 'Mudd'—he died at ninety-seven years old. I remember, when I would drive to Chicago to see my family, I would drive through my hometown of Braidwood, Illinois, to see my uncle Mudd. And the last time I went up there, before he died, I was getting ready to drive back to Texas, and I drove through Braidwood, but I just kept going. I figured I'd see him next time I was in town, but he died the year after. I didn't get to go to the funeral.

'GOLDILOX (REPRISE)'

TY TABOR Believe it or not, it was Jay Phebus's idea. I never thought it was a good idea to re-record it. But we did it, based on the heavy suggestion of Jay Phebus ... so, it's on there. [*Laughs*]

'BAM'

DOUG PINNICK I said, 'Let's take one note—*bam!*—and then let it ring out.' So we did. We put that on the record just for fun.

TY TABOR We had this wall of amps that were locked in a room with everything turned wide open, and we wanted to see what it would sound like to hit a chord and let it absolutely roar, to the point of moving me out of the building. And I did it probably five or six times—hit the chord and let it ring for eternity. That's really all it is—an attempt to just be a massive, massive power chord.

AFTER A FEW EXPERIMENTAL STUDIO ALBUMS, *OGRE TONES*

SAW KING'S X RETURN TO STRAIGHT-UP ROCK'N'ROLL.

TY TABOR With *Ogre Tones*, we went with an artist, Jeff Wood, and, through conversations on the phone, came up with an idea for the cover.

JERRY GASKILL I remember we did the 'Alone' video in Houston. We worked with a rap director [Dr. Teeth], who had worked with rap artists. I was living in New Jersey at the time, so I flew to Houston and stayed with my oldest son. And we had girls in the video—which we'd never had before. It was a little strange … but it was kind of fun, at the same time—to do a little 'girl thing.' But when I see the video, it seems a little out of place—it doesn't seem necessary. It seems like they were just thrown in there, to be in there for some reason. It was fun, but it had no real purpose. And then I saw a video that somebody did, where, instead of having the girls, they inserted Chris Farley doing the Chippendales dance thing with Patrick Swayze! Somebody had taken the girls out and put him in there instead—doing the Chippendales stuff. I thought *that* should have been the damn video. [*Laughs*]

DOUG PINNICK I think that's the stupidest decision we've ever made—to put them [the female dancers] in there. I didn't like it from the beginning, and, to this day, I'm still embarrassed by it. But Ty and Jerry didn't mind, and at the time, we were putting videos out and nobody was paying attention, so we said, 'Well … put some chicks in there, and see if that helps'—which didn't seem to do anything. I think it was a bad decision.

TY TABOR As far as I'm concerned, nothing we do is a mistake or matters. I mean, after playing at Woodstock in front of three hundred thousand people, live broadcast to millions around the world, to the next week not selling one additional album, I don't think *anything* matters. I don't even think about that stuff anymore. That cured me of worrying about anything. [*Laughs*]

I remember we went with a hip-hop guy that had some top videos on MTV, and had a huge name at the moment, and he happened to live in Houston. So we went with it, because he was absolutely the guy everybody wanted to work with at that moment. It was entirely his idea to put the girls in. We just said, 'Do whatever you do, because what you do gets played on MTV.' We didn't care what he did.

DOUG PINNICK We're kind of like the kids in the field, chasing butterflies—whatever fits our fancy at the moment, we just do it.

RAY LUZIER I remember the video for 'Alone' coming out, and again, every record, I think, *This is going to be the one that will bring them more recognition and will take them over the top.*

To me, you, and a bunch of other fans, all of the records are a huge success. But having such a great love for the band, you want to see them succeed and make a lot of money—like everybody else. There is no reason that they shouldn't.

That song 'Mudd' hit me hard, because it's about someone who's passed. What strong lyrics, like, '*You said you were tired / Then you went away up into the sky.*' That's something that everyone can relate to. The songs 'If' and 'Stay,' there is no reason why they shouldn't have been all over the radio. It's like, 'Come on, how much more commercial appeal do you want?' I think some of us will never really understand that.

22 XV & LIVE LOVE IN LONDON

THE STORIES BEHIND THE BAND'S TWELFTH STUDIO
ALBUM, RELEASED ON MAY 20, 2008, AND THEIR SECOND
LIVE ALBUM, RELEASED ON NOVEMBER 22, 2010.

JERRY GASKILL I thought *XV*—at the time—felt like it was going to be a record reminiscent of the early albums. With the same kind of vibe—but still completely different and completely new. And I felt very excited about that record. I still think it's a pretty good record. I have a song on the record—maybe that's why I like it! But that felt like it could be ... I don't know if *revival* is the right word, but *introducing* King's X to the world again. And that record felt like that to me. It felt like we were taking time enough to put it together well—with the sequence and everything—to make it a real record. But still, it's just another King's X record.

MICHAEL WAGENER In terms of recording, it was done fairly similarly to *Ogre Tones*. But on *XV*, we had already done *Ogre Tones* together, so we kind of knew each other better, and knew how people would react, and so on and so forth. So it was a little bit easier.

DOUG PINNICK I have always had a hard time with this album, so, just before this interview, I pulled it out, after not listening to it for years. I didn't understand what had happened.

Here's my take on it—Ty had three songs, Jerry had one, and I had a demo of fifteen songs on a CD. I remember we agreed to make this a great record. Put our heart and heads in it. Everyone had a say-so in everything going down, so we were all happy with what we were individually doing in every song. Throw out ideas, fight for our ideas like we used to do, back in the day. I personally feel like we did it.

The three albums we made writing almost everything from scratch we found worked really well for us. And, even though I wrote ten of the thirteen songs on *Ogre Tones*, I felt we connected and made those tunes really good. There's something special that happens when a song comes together when we put our hearts into it—especially live.

In my opinion, we are three alpha males, and very passionate, highly emotional—we're very different as people. This combination of energy together, I believe, is the heart of King's X—what people are drawn to. And we all have the power to veto a decision if we simply can't deal with it. We won't make anyone do anything in this band against his will. And there's always that power struggle, emotionally, when someone feels like they can make a song or part better than it is. Even though I used to be totally devastated when parts or whole songs were rejected, which caused my mind to walk down the wall of shame and my mind beating myself up—I'm not good at accepting criticism—and when they wanted to change my songs. Even though I know especially those first four albums would not be classic albums if they had not made my tunes better songs, and it's magic when it becomes a King's X song. It was the struggle—that's how we got the best out of us, especially back in the Sam Taylor days.

So I thought we were going to do it the same way again, and was prepared in my mind to be open to anything and everything changing in my demos. And to not be afraid to put my input into Ty's songs, also, because it's something that I usually never did. His songs were usually a done deal, and very well thought-out. There wasn't much to do but learn them usually, and enjoy the playing. He's a great songwriter. But I felt that mine were always torn apart. And I always had so many to choose from. I have never thought I was a great songwriter, but I love writing songs more than anything I do. If I ever write a huge hit song, I'll probably quit!

My mom once told me when I was sixteen that I couldn't sing. Well, let me explain—I used to sing all day long at the top of my lungs, like there was no one around. But, in reality, I was just annoying my mom when she was taking a nap. When I was sixteen, I had just found my vibrato, and I was learning. But I believed her, and I've never liked my voice. Can't stand it ever since. So, be careful what you say to your kids, because it means way more than you think. And, when someone picks at everything you do, you tend to shy away from them. I have a very difficult time with people who always find the flaw in another person but never compliment them on their good qualities. Especially when they point out the very things that they are themselves guilty of doing, and, when you confront them, they immediately try to make you look like the bad guy. Make you feel helpless. But singing is what I'm driven to do. And yeah … I need therapy! [*Laughs*]

Anyway, I played the CD of songs on a ghetto blaster in the studio, to choose what they liked or passed on. We always did this before the Metal Blade era. So I purposely wrote a batch of songs mainly to be simple with room to create—very simple, with a drum machine with no fills. The songs were very sterile on my demo, as opposed to me putting all my emotions into my previous demos—which didn't help my insecurities, when parts were changed or reinterpreted. These songs I purposely wrote for us to tear apart. I felt mentally ready for the month of working on the record in the studio. There were two things I was specific about that I wanted to keep in two songs, but that was it. So I was thinking I was not gonna be the crybaby, and hang with the big boys. [*Laughs*] But I felt like we just ended up playing them like the demos. Very little input. We would track songs usually in two takes, and move on to the next. It was like nobody cared, I thought. So I lost interest early on. Jerry left a few days earlier. And when I was done with my overdubbing, I left, too. Ty told us he stayed until the end, because they were mixing his tunes. There was absolutely no need to be there. Maybe that's why we haven't made another album—I don't know.

TY TABOR It was like a continuation of *Ogre Tones*—with the exception that Doug's and Jerry's heads were not quite in it as much. Jerry had to fly out in the middle of us recording tracks for the weekend, to do some kind of cover gig he had committed to. So his mind was on some of that. Like, there would be times we would be working on things, and he would be tapping around on the drums on the songs he'd be trying to remember for his weekend gig. And Doug just wanted the hell out of there—he wanted to get whatever he had to do over with and leave. Which is exactly what he and Jerry both did. They kind of stuck me with the record, and I stayed for a few days with Michael, and I just said, 'Screw it. If the guys aren't going to be here to be a part of all of this, then I'll just let Michael do this. I don't want to be the one that's responsible for everything by myself.' So I left, too. That's what I remember most about the album—feeling disappointed, feeling that, in my mind, it was the end of King's X. I didn't say anything to those guys, but that album is the reason we have never done another album.

And that's the reason I have refused to even talk about doing another album—until Doug and Jerry are at a place in their lives where they're ready again to really commit themselves to doing an album, and doing it right, because it's hard to do an album. I understand, after so many albums and everything, just being tired of it. And I think that's where we got, by the time we got to *XV*. Just tired of doing the records. And Doug and Jerry got there faster than me. But I had the full realization of it, too, by the end of it. So, we just said, 'OK, we're done with records—until we all feel good about doing it again.' Which is where we're at now, and why we're finally—after a decade—talking about doing another album. But that's really what that album represents to me, and it's why we quit recording.

DOUG PINNICK People asked me why I was wearing a pentagram belt buckle on the front cover. They didn't notice the cross or other symbols for some reason. [*Laughs*] I don't know … I just do things like that.

TY TABOR We did the album cover photo in New Jersey with Mark Weiss. We wanted him to do it just because he's a fantastic photographer, and he had become friends with Jerry. Jerry had moved back to Jersey, and Mark is right there, close to Jerry. So we wanted to use somebody who's legit, and get some cool shots for promotion and the album. He took us around to a few sites and we did it all in one day. It was a dreary, kind of half-rainy, crappy day—but it all ended up looking right.

THE SONGS
'PRAY'

DOUG PINNICK The music was inspired by a band called The St. Louis Sheiks from the 70s. I used to go see them when I was just starting to play bass, when I was around twenty-four. They never got a record deal. They were a hard rock four-piece band—the singer was black, and his performance and their music was straight out of a black Pentecostal church. It was like going to a Holy Roller service, but in a bar, drinking, doing drugs, and singing about sex! And playing really aggressive—it grooved hard. They were *amazing*.

As for the lyrics—I don't care what religion you have, if it works for you, then that's awesome. If you've got a problem with the way I believe, then just pray for me. I got no problem with that. But when you condemn someone for anything you do in secret, or in your mind, you immediately become a hypocrite. 'Let he who is without sin cast the first stone.'

TY TABOR It was one of my favorite songs on the record, because it's a song that, in my opinion, calls out hypocrites. It basically says to every religious group that Doug could name, 'If you believe so strongly that you have the truth, then don't hate me—*pray for me*. Don't be a hypocrite, do what you preach. All of you. Every one of you. Every religion.' And I thought that was a great message.

'BLUE'

DOUG PINNICK That was about a friend of mine—out of the blue, she decided she wasn't in love with her husband anymore. It was something she was dealing with for years, but when she finally stepped up and said, 'I'm done,' everyone was shocked, because nobody knew.

'REPEATING MYSELF'

TY TABOR I think I may have written that before we got in the studio. I just brought a demo in and we learned it. I do know that I wrote some of it about a couple of dear friends of mine whose marriage was breaking up. And that was the inspiration for some of it. And, in my own life, some of it is inspiration, too. But the thing that sticks out most is thinking about my friends—their relationship was ending.

'ROCKET SHIP'

DOUG PINNICK '*Let's take a ride in my rocket ship to another planet, and screw it up like we've done to this one. Let's go make a mess somewhere.*' George Carlin is my pastor! [In response to me saying that Carlin once did a comedy routine about man's desire to inhabit Mars, and we'd probably screw up that planet, too.] He always makes sense to me—even though I'm not an atheist. Everything he said totally made sense to me.

JERRY GASKILL It's a song that I had worked on with my friend, D.A. Karkos, who I did my second solo record with, *Love & Scars*. He came to my house and we recorded it together, I presented it to the band, and they said, 'OK, let's do it.' I was very happy about that, because I liked the song. It was a song inspired by tequila. That's the lyrics—'*Sorry Julie / Sorry that I made you cry*.' It was a horrible, horrible time and experience for me and for her—something that I would never want to repeat, and something that I was very sorry ever happened. So that's where the lyrics for that song came from.

JULIE GASKILL [Jerry Gaskill's wife] I think it's a very pretty song. I like the song. It was based on a night of … I guess Jerry had a little too much to drink. He doesn't drink Patrón anymore, because when he does, if he gets to a certain point, he's having the best time of his life, and then it's like you flip a switch, and it's the worst night of his life. It was one of those incidents. And, in the morning, he didn't even remember what had happened, and I said, 'Look, I've been through my whole life. I don't need to deal with this. If you don't stop what you're doing, you can just go back to Houston. I can't do this.' And that's when he wrote the song. [*Laughs*] I don't like the memory, but I like the song.

JERRY GASKILL I never thought I had a drinking problem. Nobody ever thinks they have a drinking problem. And it never got to the point where I had to go to rehab or anything. I wasn't drinking every single day. I wasn't waking up drinking. I didn't feel like I had to drink. It was just something I did on the road. But I did enjoy drinking—and continue to enjoy drinking. And I discovered Patrón tequila at one point in my life, and that became 'my' drink. I *loved* Patrón—it was on our rider and everything. I'd drink it quite a bit. But what happens is, when I drink, I'm having the best time of my life, and then, all of a sudden, at one point, one shot or whatever would take me to another place, and I become a different person. I become mean. And that's where the song 'Julie' came from.

It was a tequila thing, and I realized, *I can't be doing that stuff. I can't allow myself to get to that place.* But I still continue to drink—I discovered red wine. I love red wine. I don't drink that much anymore—I'll drink a glass or two, or have a beer or two. I don't do tequila anymore. And I remember there was a time when I wasn't drinking at all, and I said, 'I'm probably never going to drink again.' What I loved most about not drinking was waking up the next day and not having to wonder if I ruined my life the night before. It was an incredible feeling, to think, *Wow. I don't have to wonder about that now*. Because that's what happens when you drink—you wake up the next day, and go, *Oh my God ... what did I do? I might have ruined my life and not even know it*. I've seen that look in people's eyes before—especially Julie's eyes.

DOUG PINNICK I love Jerry's song. I wish he would have submitted more. He's never really pushed any of his tunes on us. He thinks we won't like them, I think. It's fun to play, also, but at the end of the song, I always wish we attached another verse and chorus at the end of the song. It's such an interesting and fun song to play.

'ALRIGHT'

DOUG PINNICK I love songs that rock hard. I was thinking a vibe like [Billy Idol's] 'Rebel Yell.' I think the Iraq War was happening, and everyone was freaking out over it. All I could think about are soldiers getting ready to go fight in a war that came from a lie. I have two nephews in the armed services. The stories they tell me are overwhelming. All I could think about is, *One day, it's gonna be all right*. And '*When I was crawling along on the way side / I saw the dead in the street*'—I could imagine a soldier in a house that had just been bombed, he has his gun on the ground, and insurgents are coming after him. The song was a picture in my mind—of a soldier fighting for his life. I had a video in my head the whole time I was writing it. But it would have been expensive and a lot of work, and we didn't have a budget that big.

TY TABOR That's probably my favorite song on the record, musically. It's a straight-ahead rock bash. It wears Doug out, but we sometimes do it live. I love that one.

'BROKE'

DOUG PINNICK I was going for a Free type of vibe. Ty was rediscovering Paul

Kossoff from Free, and we were talking a lot about the magic of that whole band—Paul Rodgers is one of my all-time favorite singers. 'Broke' from credit cards—I totally abused mine. Now I don't have one.

WALLY FARKAS I think Ty was doing guitar overdubs at the time, and they were doing gang chorus/backup vocals [for 'Broke'], and they were like, 'Come on!' I ran in there with them and we did all the parts. It was not a stressful vibe—everybody was enjoying what they were doing. Jerry wasn't there—he had to go back to New Jersey for something—so it was the other two and Michael.

'I JUST WANT TO LIVE'

TY TABOR I wrote that one before we got in. I'm not sure how old it was, but I do remember when I wrote it—it was when I got tired of how life had been for a long time. First of all, my marriage had broken up, then I was in another relationship a little later … I was in *a couple* of relationships after my marriage broke up. One of them turned out to be a nightmare to me. So I quit dating and quit wanting to even be in a relationship. After that relationship, I felt like life would be a whole lot better alone, and I'm OK with that. I was alone for a while, and I wrote that around that time, saying, 'I am tired of all this crap. I am ready to live again. I'm ready to be over the drama and BS, and move forward to good things.'

'MOVE'

DOUG PINNICK God, wars, and system beliefs. Seems like these days, it's the main thing—the world is killing each other. When religion controls politics, there can be no freedom or peace. We worked on this one a bit. I think we captured a good vibe.

'I DON'T KNOW'

TY TABOR I wrote that one just a couple of weeks before we got in the studio. I think it's self-explanatory, too—it's saying if I ever said I knew what I was talking about, *forget it.*

'STUCK'

DOUG PINNICK I feel like there are two sides to everything when there's a conflict between me and another person—across to world conflicts between nations. Being too far left or too far right in anything can only create conflict. It seems like the middle ground isn't even considered—because of religious and cultural tradition. So I feel stuck in the middle.

'GO TELL SOMEBODY'

DOUG PINNICK That was the only song we wrote from scratch. Ty started playing a riff, and we fell in. The song wrote itself after that. I love that song. It's fun to play, also. After we had finished recording all the songs, Michael said, 'We need one more song. Why don't you guys write one more song—*quick*.'

We came up with 'Go Tell Somebody' within ten minutes. It never takes us long to write a song together. We didn't have any lyrics. I remember, two days later, I was riding in my car, going down to the studio, and the words and melody came to me—'*If you like what you hear / Go tell somebody*.' I got really excited about it, and I came back to the studio, and I told Ty and Jerry. I brought them out to the car and sang the chorus to them while I played the rough tracks we had just recorded. They both got excited about it. It's a good song.

'LOVE AND ROCKETS (HELL'S SCREAMING)' (BONUS TRACK)

DOUG PINNICK I wrote the music way back in the early days—probably around the *Gretchen* or *Faith Hope Love* period. Just couldn't find lyrics for it for all those years, but I liked the music, so I held on to the demo. That song is about people who abuse children. Especially the very young and innocent. It overwhelms me that people actually do horrific things to the young and innocent. And you hear about it in the news almost every day. It gets to me sometimes.

'NO LIE' (BONUS TRACK)

DOUG PINNICK I wrote a goofy song, and we recorded it. Nothing special.

XV PEAKED AT #145 ON THE *BILLBOARD* 200—MAKING IT THE
BAND'S FIRST ALBUM TO CHART SINCE *EAR CANDY*.

TY TABOR Basically, all albums that come out sell 90 percent of everything that they will sell in the first week. That's been the trend for a very, very long time now—probably fifteen years. So, when that album came out, I expected it to spike for one week and then go away. And that's exactly what it did.

JEFF AMENT I think I have all those [post-*Ear Candy*] records. There was a record called *XV*—I was into that record for a while. There was a record where they did another version of 'Goldilox,' too—*Ogre Tones*. And Doug is a buddy, so whenever he puts out any record, I pick it up or download it—I'm curious to hear what he's up to. I love to hear his voice.

GUNTER FORD [King's X manager, 2007–present] I was managing another band, Tapping The Vein. I had heard of a King's X show that was being put together for New York for B.B. King's, and the agent that was representing King's X at the time was representing Tapping The Vein. And he did me a favor and got Tapping The Vein a support slot. I went to the show, and I met somebody who at that point was Jerry's girlfriend, Julie—who happened to be a Tapping The Vein fan. We were chatting, and we hit it off pretty well. Eventually, it turns out that she suggested to them—via Jerry—to take a meeting with me. She had heard about me and other bands that I managed for my company, World Entertainment Inc.

I wasn't a real expert on King's X at that point. So, for me, it was a brand new band, in a way. I get what they're doing, I get who they are as people, and then we work on it from there. You work on your planning, whether you're making records or touring, or even looking at past business—trying to get that up to speed. In some cases, you inherit some nightmares, and in some cases, you don't. You have to know the big picture. And that's why I say it's very much like having a family or a relationship—there are some dysfunctional elements to all bands, and there are great things to all bands. But, mostly, you start off with the artistry, you start off with, 'Do I like this? Do I want to work with this?' And then you work on the other little facets along the way.

ALEXANDER FORD [King's X management and merchandising] I got involved with King's X first through the label side. I was working at the time for SPV Marketing, the marketing branch of SPV and InsideOut Records, which was based in Germany at the time. We were kind of running the US branch of their marketing team here, when the *XV* album came out on InsideOut. That was my first introduction really, in 2007, 2008, when I was first turned on to the band, and then, simultaneously, I also worked that particular album.

After the marketing company dissolved, years later, I got involved with them through the management side, because I'm Gunter Ford's son. I work also with him on the management side of things, so, as a result, I was working behind the scenes a little bit with the band—kind of doing more or less the day-to-day maintenance and interview scheduling. And then there came a point where we had a major problem on the road, and the people that were doing the merchandise for us at the time, *disappeared*—in the middle of the tour, with the merch money! When that happened, we re-started the crew after that tour, and, as a result, I ended up going out as the merchandise person on that next leg. And, from that point forward, I have been the band's merchandiser and multi-tasker for the better part of five or six years now.

DOUG PINNICK Christian Nesmith came out on the road, and took it upon himself to make videos for us [for 'Go Tell Somebody' and 'Pray']. They came out pretty good.

TY TABOR They were basically shot live on tour—over a period of several days, by Christian Nesmith. He edited it and everything.

CHRISTIAN NESMITH They wanted to do another little promotional thing. They said, 'Let's do it again. Jump on the bus!' I said OK, and I followed them around for a whole bunch more shows, and I had a better camera at that time, and that yielded 'Go Tell Somebody' and 'Pray.' And, as you can see, it's very much the same sort of trip. You can tell that a lot of the shots from both of those videos are from the same shows.

ON JANUARY 22, 2009, KING'S X RECORDED THEIR SECOND
ALBUM LIVE ALBUM, THE CD/DVD SET *LIVE LOVE IN
LONDON*, AT THE ELECTRIC BALLROOM IN CAMDEN.

TY TABOR I think that I may have expressed to Thomas Waber at InsideOut Music, 'I don't know how much longer we're going to do this, so I think the time is right to do a proper live DVD—or it will never happen.' That kind of kicked him into gear, and he came up with a budget and plan, and we did it.

That show, I'll be honest with you, I was *so* miserable on that entire tour—because of a really bad hip injury. And the injury had been lasting for about six months, and doctors could not quite figure out what was causing me so much pain. But that entire tour, I was walking around with a cane, and I barely walked at all. And I remember standing onstage, trying to act like I wasn't hurting—for what seemed like an eternity. Such a long show. And every show was long.

That's all I remember about it, to be honest with you. I know that it was sold out, I know that the crowd was screaming and yelling as usual, but I barely remember playing the show. I remember extreme pain, and trying not to show it, and trying to get through it. That's all I think about when I see that show—it gives me a dark, horrible feeling in my stomach, because of how terrible it was at the time, trying to play that show. It took about a year to a year and a half for the pain to work itself out, and, luckily, I haven't had that kind of problem since.

DOUG PINNICK I've always wanted to do a proper video, like just about every band out there. Specifically in London. Even overdub parts, like they did on all the live recordings on nationally released live videos. I think the whole band was not up to full potential. Maybe it was because we knew this was a big deal and it was forever—I have no clue. But I can't watch it. *Ever*. All I can think about is what it's not. But that's how I see a lot of things in life. I really wish we had done a live video from back in our prime. We never really got to capture some of those great moments on film back then. But it is what it is—like everything we do.

23 MOLKEN MUSIC

INSIDE THE BIRTH OF A LABEL SPECIALIZING
IN KING'S X-RELATED DEMOS, LIVE
RECORDINGS, AND SOLO MATERIAL.

WALLY FARKAS Ty had already put out some *Dogman* demos—just on CD-Rs—on his own label at the time. Plus some King's X rehearsal tapes and stuff like that. I had been working with some local and regional rap artists, and King's X saw what kind of promotion I was doing for some of these other guys, and it seemed to be working pretty successfully. So they were like, 'Hey, can you do some of that for us?'

The next thing I know, I'm getting trash bags and shoeboxes full of tapes! A lot of them were even unmarked. Just kind of went through, and, *What do I have here?* The first thing was a bunch of Doug's old four-track cassette demos. So, I compiled one release out of it and put that out [*Songs From The Closet*]. It was going direct to consumer, and it was a big deal. A month or two later, Ty is like, 'Well, here's all of my four and eight-track cassette demos.' And it had a few unreleased songs [resulting in *Tacklebox*].

It grew from there—doing archival things. Ty also brought three solo records [*Balance*, *Something's Coming*, and *Nobody Wins When Nobody Plays*]—newly recorded albums—to me, and one of the Jelly Jam records [*Shall We Descend*]. It has kind of grown organically like that the last ten years.

DOUG PINNICK If you want to hear how the songs sounded in the raw, before King's X put the 'mojo' on—plus tunes we never got to record—it is a treat for fans. I personally love that stuff—I've got tons of old U2 demos. We planned to do *Songs From The Closet #2*, but it hasn't happened yet.

TY TABOR *Tacklebox* was all the original demos of a whole lot of the songs that ended up being on King's X records. Just letting people hear how they were originally written, before the band did our own versions. We just wanted to put that out for interest. Anytime I've played that for people, they seemed to dig it, so I decided to put it out. To me, the actual best live show released is *Tales From The Empire*—Molken Music released it online only. That's a good live show. That was at a time when we were tight as a band. I believe that was recorded in the middle of a very extensive tour, so we were on top of our game—probably at our all-time height—during that time period. And that captured a pretty good show.

WALLY FARKAS *Tales From The Empire: Cleveland 6.26.92*, in my opinion, that is the single best King's X show, *ever*. And, in a way, I hate saying that, because some people might mistake that as a connotation as being *it was all downhill after that* or *they were never as good again*. No, they were always great. But I'm saying that show … you've got to understand, these are soundboard DATs and cassette tapes and bootleg stuff. I don't have multitrack stuff. I can't go in and fix. I can do some hard edits or EQ stuff or compression—just overall shaping and mastering—but if they're singing all out of tune and fucking up everywhere, I can't fix it. *And it is flawless.*

I'll tell you this, too—back then, King's X used to always get accused of using backing tapes for vocals. Because a lot of bands back then *did*. King's X never did. I used to watch them while standing at the board, and people used to always come up, straining their neck around, looking for the tape machine. They swore the backing vocals were coming off tape. There was no tape. But that performance, you've got to remember, it's live and three dudes, and they're nailing it, on fire, from start to finish. It's the fourth album tour, and it's the majority of the shit you'd want to hear from those four albums. It hits like a sledgehammer. That is my favorite thing I've ever heard of King's X.

JERRY GASKILL *Tales From The Empire* was a show that was recorded for live radio in Cleveland. And the Empire was the name of the venue we were playing. It was really just aired live on the radio—I don't know the name of the station—and we decided to release it ourselves, through Molken. It was a good show.

The Dallas show, *Live And Live Some More*—I forgot that even happened! There was a time when we were having Molken put some stuff out—archive things—and that's what that was. I thought that was a good show. It was a good period in our career to capture. I think we probably thought it should be captured somehow and released. That's most likely why we did that record.

Rehearsal CD Vol. 1 is basically us rehearsing for a tour, and we recorded some things. I think there's a pretty cool jam on there. And there's one part at the end—we were at Ty's house, and I was in his garage, away from everybody else. That's where the drum room was. And I remember it was going on and on. We were jamming and doing whatever—not really even doing anything at that point. So I just got up and left. And, on the CD itself, the other guys are going, 'Jerry? Where are you? Jerry?' And I guess I had left! 'I don't need to be here anymore. This is going nowhere.' So, I left the room, and that was that. [*Laughs*]

Here's the deal with the *Burning Down Boston* release—I have no recollection of any of that stuff for the most part, because that was something released after I had my first heart attack. It was released for download to help to pay my medical bills. It was overwhelming, all the love I felt and concern from people all over the world. To this very day, it's helped me to move forward and be strong and be the person that I am today.

The *Gretchen Goes To London* DVD is stuff with a handheld camera, no professional quality to it whatsoever. Wally Farkas went and edited it, and made it into this thing that was watchable and listenable. That was a good period in our career, and a good period to have captured. And I think that's the best we had from that period, so we released it. I think it's pretty cool—it has an exciting vibe. And we were playing good back then—we were totally on the top of our game. And we were *looking* good! We had the look, the sound, the crowd—the whole thing going. It was a great, great period to capture. I felt like we were on our way at that point. Which, in a sense, we were. We still had *somewhat* of a career. [*Laughs*]

DOUG PINNICK We were broke. [*Laughs*] At that point, we were just trying to figure out some way to make money. There was no money coming in. We were really, really struggling hard. So we decided to just start doing stuff—put stuff out on our own, trying to make a little extra money, releasing old band and personal demos.

24 THE THREE KINGS
FURTHER INSIGHT INTO DOUG, TY, AND JERRY.

THE MAN ON THE FOUR-STRING, EIGHT-STRING,

AND TWELVE-STRING BASS, MR. PINNICK.

DOUG PINNICK I've never had a relationship. I've watched everybody else fuck theirs up, so I guess I'm doing OK! [*Laughs*] It's bittersweet. I have fourteen half-brothers and sisters—I met my dad and his wife and kids around the same time I moved in with my mom, who lived on the other side of town. I grew up with my great grandmother raising me—I was fourteen when I left. I left my mom's when I was twenty, and went on the road with a musical group, and moved in and out of her house until I was twenty-five and I decided I needed to grow up.

We just laugh and have a good time nowadays. They are really proud of me. And they get a lot of attention from their friends and co-workers, and they love it. My mom absolutely loves Jerry's drumming. She's got good taste! My family, we don't really verbally let each other know how we feel about each other, but they always come to all King's X shows when we play the Chicago area. We don't really compliment each other. And it doesn't matter, anyway. We're family.

I struggle with depression, but it's not something that debilitates me. There was a time when it did, and I would walk in circles in my house, because I couldn't focus or do anything. It comes and goes now. I think that's OK—maybe normal. I know it's gonna go away. I'm a chronic loner. Every morning I wake up and say to myself, 'What did I do wrong?' I mean, everyone seems to find *someone* in their life. I don't think that there's anything wrong with me. I don't think that I'm the type of person that a person wouldn't be attracted to, so I don't know what happened. But, one day, it dawned on me, and I realized the reason I was depressed was because, 'You wouldn't let anybody into your life.' And I'm going, 'Oh, wow. I fucked that up really bad.' I remember, the few times there was a possibility of a relationship, I would shut down. Yeah, I need therapy! [*Laughs*]

But at my age now, it's like, *What am I doing to do?* I can't go back to sow my wild oats in my twenties. I can't go back to my childhood for the parental nurturing that I didn't get. I went from believing that nobody wants me to where I wouldn't let anybody into my life. At this point, I can't go back. And the future is … well, I'm old. Who wants an old person? So I kind of gave up, and I'm going to do the best I can to get through this awesome adventure of a life I'm having, until I die. I've made it alone so far. I've had a chance to observe everyone else. I watched so many of my friends fall in love, get married, get divorced, have kids, love and abandon their kids, their kids have kids … I'm seeing generations of people coming and going. I guess I consider myself an observer. That's what I sing about—what I see.

Lots of people texted me [when Chris Cornell died], saying, 'Are you OK?' Here's how I look at it—I made it this far, I'm going to ride this bitch out. I have no desire to leave now. After all I've been through, and after all I've had to fight for in my own self, to get myself to the point where I can actually look in the mirror and not think I'm a stupid idiot and I'm ugly, I don't want to kill myself over depression. But as for Chris, I knew him—he was a good guy. I miss him. I don't understand what happened. One day we'll find out, hopefully … or maybe we never will. I don't believe he killed himself, but if he did, he wasn't in his right mind when he did it. There's no way he would have left his wife and kids at this time in his life.

I don't hide the fact that I smoke pot. I've been busted a few times—it's on my permanent record. But that's just what I do. It's legal here in California. I sing about, I talk about it, I write songs about it. As for the other drugs? I've watched what they have done to some of my best friends. It truly does ruin people's lives, and they end up the opposite of where they hoped to be later in life. Prescription pills, crack, meth, heroin—you can go down the line and see the destruction that it causes. And we know what alcohol does and doesn't do. I drink—way more on the road than home. But I haven't seen any kind of real negative effects with weed. The more you study about it, the more you find out how good it is—in so many different uses. I was busted when I was twenty-two—back in '72—for having a joint. Almost every song I've ever written for

King's X, I was stoned. And every record I've made, during the recording, I was stoned. I quit between 1974 and 1987 … then started up again.

WALLY FARKAS One thing I'll say about how Doug works—this is a little insight into his creativity—is that, remember how I told you how quickly Doug likes to work and record to get things down? Something to do with—I don't know if it's the self-doubt or he's feeling like he's not good enough, but something that Doug usually has a knack for doing is, he'll throw something down and demo it, and it will be amazing. And then, a day later, he'll go, 'Hey, check this out,' and he'll send me the same song, and he has re-recorded all his vocals and changed some stuff. And I'm like, 'What did you do? *You just ruined the fucking song!*' And he's like, 'Oh, really? Well, why do you feel that way?' And I'll tell him exactly—what he was doing with the delivery and this and that. I'm like, 'The original demo was raw. It was your soul communicating. And you now brought it more into something more plain.' And then he'd find his old vocal tracks that he almost shit-canned and put that back on.

BILLY SHEEHAN *Grand champion.* He has got a tone and a feel that is just supreme. I know he's got a new amp now [the Tech 21 dUg Pinnick Ultra Bass 1000 Signature Bass Amp], and I'm so glad—people are flocking to buy the amp to get the 'Doug tone.' And I don't blame them. He's such a great, solid, huge … one note of Doug's is worth about fifty of most every other bass player.

And, on top of it, he sings. His voice … I even told him, 'Now that you're out in LA, you should do voiceovers, man. Just your speaking voice, you should just get on that mic and do voiceovers for TV and movies! You're worth a million bucks with that, bro.' What a great voice he has. But his bass playing is rock solid. One note says it all. Some of his bass intros, like the song 'Out Of The Silent Planet,' is just an awesome bass tone. He used a twelve-string for a while, but he doesn't even need to. A single, low E note on one bass by Doug Pinnick to me is worth about a thousand dollars right there. The tone of Doug … one of the grand masters of all time. I have such high regard for him.

RITA HANEY To this day, Doug is like my brother. He's always there for everything. He's always got a big smile on his face, and he's always so positive. And, both of us being out in the LA area most of the time, we get to see each other quite a bit more than we did in Texas. He would even come and spend Thanksgiving with us at Darrell and Vinnie's mom's house. He spent several holidays with us over the years.

There was a little club that Darrell and I had for a little while, called the Tattoo Bar, and Doug and Darrell got up and jammed together there, and that's where a cover of 'Born Under A Bad Sign' was recorded. And then I think they laid it down on a four-track as well. But the live version was there at the club. It was awesome. I remember Darrell sitting around with Doug, playing him new Pantera music, and vice versa—Doug playing him new King's X music or solo. They've always shared that love and have been big fans of music. King's X was one of his favorite bands.

REX BROWN Doug was such a mentor to me. I tried forever to try and get Doug's tone, and I would sit and pick and pick and pick. 'What are you playing through, man?' Of course, he wouldn't tell me! Because the way he ran his rig was completely the opposite of what you would think—he'd run all the lows through a thinner bass, and then the highs through an Ampeg, which you would think would go the other way around. But his tone has always been a mystery—nobody has really captured it. *It's the way that he hits the strings.* As a bass player, I was always trying to strive to get that ... *I've got to get that 'piano-sounding thing' to come out.* With Pantera, it was so hard to get the bass in the mix, because the guitars were so big, and there was so much reverb on the snare that you could hardly hear the bass in the mix. But Doug's place was always impeccable, and the way that he sang.

ROBERT DeLEO *Amazing.* There's guys that play a lot of notes, and there's guys that play less notes with a tone. Doug encompasses it all. He's got tone, he's a great player, he's a great songwriter, and he's a hell of a singer. He's got it all. He's got a lot of soul in that cat. And, upon that, he's one of the nicest people I know in this business—or anywhere. You meet someone like him, and you're like, 'Wow. This guy has been around for a long time, he's real, he knows where it's at, he knows where it's been at.' He's one of those cats. Very honorable— musically and personally.

I have the same interests in bass that Doug has. When you're a musical three-piece, you're trying to fill in as much as you can. And Doug always really had that down—to really act as not only the basis of holding it down, but also, as a rhythm guitar. It just had that thing. That's what Tom Petersson had, too—he just had that *thing*. Robin Zander didn't play a lot of guitar, so it was mostly Rick Nielsen, and Tom had the room and space and freedom to do that. And more so with Doug. I think what he had going on there with the twelve-string was perfect for the band.

KIP WINGER Well … left-handed, for one thing, so you immediately associate him with McCartney. Not that he is anything like McCartney, but Doug is one of these talents … he's set apart, because there is no pretense with Doug. He is completely 1,000 percent genuine. And when you see him play live, he can create the 'moment' with most authenticity than any performer that I've ever seen. He's completely vulnerable and in the moment—he exposes himself 1,000 percent to the performance at hand. I had him in the studio when we did The Mob record, and it was the same way. The second the guy hits the microphone, he gives it everything he's got. There's no holding back. And you can't really say that about too many performers. You can really understand his soul the second he opens his mouth. And I think that really is an underpinning of a true artist and a great artist.

RICHARD CHRISTY As far as playing with Doug, Kirk Hammett, and Robert Trujillo, out at Comic-Con, it was 2014 and was a small club show. I was terrified, because these are my musical heroes, and I'm some dweeb that happens to play drums. But they were nice enough to invite me to jam with them. I remember showing up at the club, and Doug was standing outside the club. I went up to him and he was just the nicest guy in the world. And I kind of geeked out on him—I started talking to him about how I had lived in Springfield, Missouri. And we really hit it off, because we started talking about all the things we loved about Springfield, Missouri—like there's this restaurant called Mexican Villa. And Springfield is famous for their cashew chicken—it was invented in Springfield.

It was really cool to break the ice with Doug, because I'm a fan, and I didn't want to 'fanboy-out' too much. But we did have something in common, with living in Springfield. Just a lot of fun to talk with him about the time he lived there, and to hear the stories about King's X when they lived there. I remember I talked to him and I knew they played the skating rink back then, and he remembered my buddy Joe, who had told me all those King's X stories from back then. So, it was really cool—in addition to playing with my musical idols, it was a lot of fun to talk to Doug about the early days of King's X, and also to build a bond with him over Springfield, Missouri, and cashew chicken, Mexican Villa, and Andy's Frozen Custard. [*Laughs*]

We got to do 'Jailbreak' by Thin Lizzy, and Doug sang on that—he sounded amazing. It was so surreal to be behind the kit, and watching Doug singing. I could have never have imagined, while watching King's X on *Headbangers Ball* when I was in high school, that one day, I would actually be jamming with Doug. It was *so* cool. And I got to do [Metallica's] 'Trapped Under Ice' with Kirk and Robert—and that's always been one of my favorite songs, from *Ride The Lightning*. Just the whole night, I remember I couldn't sleep afterward, and going back to the hotel, it had to all sink in, what had happened—that I had just jammed with Doug from King's X and Kirk and Robert from Metallica, and also Mark Osegueda from Death Angel sang some songs with us. It was awesome. Definitely one of the best nights of my life.

BOB KULICK [Meat Loaf guitarist; Kiss session guitarist; solo artist; producer]
He's an amazing singer, an amazing writer, an amazing bass player. A *personality* onstage … to stand next to him is not like watching somebody play. When you stand next to somebody under that circumstance, at Lemmy's seventieth birthday party—I'm standing to his right, Steve Vai is standing to his left. Do you know what the vibe was like on that stage? The aura of what everybody was putting out? His was as large as anybody's on that stage that night. Zakk Wylde, Slash, Steve Vai—any of them. He totally crushed, totally killed. *Always*. One of my favorite singers.

THE MAN ON GUITAR, MR. TABOR.

TY TABOR When I got married, I instantly became a father. Josh was three when we got married, but I was around him since he was two. When we got married, we were very poor, and King's X didn't have a record deal yet. We were married for twenty years, and then we got divorced. I dated a couple of times after that, briefly, but I decided I really just wanted to be alone and not worry about relationships for a while. And then I met Michelle.

MICHELLE THOMAS [Ty Tabor's long-time significant other] I was a casual fan of King's X. I was aware of them, respected the band, and I think I had their 'greatest hits' record. I am a huge lover of live music—I love seeing live music. I was talking with a friend that turned out to be mutual friend between me and the band one day, and I heard something that sounded like King's X, and I said, 'Oh, this sounds like King's X.' And he was like, 'Oh my God, I was just hanging out with them! I think they're coming to Kansas City. You should come see them.' It was this weird alignment of stars, and I went down to the show. I'm petite—I'm very short—and I knew the venue was a flat-floored venue, so, if you're short, you are aware of such things. I got down there really early, and wound up in front of the stage—right in front of Ty's side.

They do the meet-and-greet after every show, so I went through the line, and mentioned that we have some mutual friends, and I didn't really think that much of any of it. This was the night before Thanksgiving in 2005. I had coincidentally gotten a new camera that day, and I never really did a lot of picture taking at shows. So I messaged Ty on MySpace, and was like, 'I don't know if you remember me, but I met you in Kansas City a few nights ago. I wound up getting some good pictures of you—if you would like to use them, you're welcome to.' I didn't hear from him for a couple of weeks, but finally I did, and he said, 'I'd love to see the pictures.' I emailed them to him, and we struck up a really casual email conversation. We would talk about our gardens and our dogs.

Every few months we would email and check in with each other. He came back through town about six months after that first meeting, and it's kind of rough when you're on the road and can't get a decent meal, so I asked if he wanted to meet before his show and grab a bite to eat. Again, completely platonic—I was thinking he was married, because we hadn't even talked about anything like that. He took me up on that, and we went out to lunch. He likes to eat late afternoon when he's on tour, so we met and had some Mediterranean food. And it was at that point that I was like, 'Oh. He's really cute … and he doesn't have a ring on!' [*Laughs*] We had this awesome conversation, and we were kind of together from there. I went to Houston about a month later, coincidentally, and he was off tour at that point. So we met up and had our real first date.

We did the long-distance thing for about five years—between Houston and Kansas City. And the last year of that was trying to sell his house. It took us a few years to figure out who was going to move, and what direction we were going to go with the relationship. And finally we decided that, as much as he's gone, it made more sense for him to move to Kansas City. I've got a huge family, and they're all here, and I just wanted to be home and not be in Houston and not know anybody when he wasn't on tour on New Year's Eve or whatever.

How much do fans really know him? He's considered kind of 'the quiet one.' We've got a good garden in the back, with tomatoes, peppers. We try to eat pretty cleanly. We very much are only about eating humanely raised meat. Which is very expensive, so we don't eat that much of it. A lot of our friends and family consider us vegetarians, but we're not—we do eat meat, but we are really selective about the source of it. We're very much about clean living. We live in a pretty urban environment. Ty is really handy—he builds all kinds of things. He built a raised bed for us, for all the vegetables, and it's enclosed. We have a lot of squirrels here, so it's all enclosed so the squirrels can't get into it. He's got so much creativity—it comes out every way that it can. He takes pallet wood and breaks pallets down, and he's got all kinds of woodworking tools, and he makes beautiful things.

How I would describe him off the road … I don't know if he's that different, to be honest. He's a shy person—he's an introvert. Very much a typical artist. He's a thinker—he's extremely intelligent. He's constantly watching documentaries and always learning—taking online classes. He loves to write code and program and do web design, which I've always found very unique about him, because usually programmers don't have an artistic side. I have an IP background, and I know and work with a lot of nerds and geeks and people who are very much into computers, and he gets that—he can write in code, and that's pretty unique for someone who also expresses themselves musically—at least in the way that he does.

He's in a band with John Myung, Jelly Jam, and John … they are so different artistically, the way that they approach music. John is so schooled, and he practices constantly. And Ty has never had any kind of formal training or learning with his guitar playing. And he always jokes that he does stuff the wrong way, but it works for him. I see those two guys as such opposites when it comes to that. If somebody like John was into computer programming, that would almost make sense. But the type of musician that Ty is, he feels his music so much more than he learns and practices it—if that makes sense. It always has impressed me that he has both sides of his brain going. But he's kind of the same guy on the road—he's quiet, has a few close friends, and he's a creature of habit. He has his routine every day that he likes.

CHARLIE BENANTE Ty had this signature sound that was completely 'Ty Tabor.'

NUNO BETTENCOURT For a guy to say somebody is underrated is kind of ridiculous—because whoever loves him, loves him, and that's all that matters. Right? But in the sense of within the realms of the greats, I think Ty is super, super-underrated. His tone and his sound is so unique to me. Once again, you can be a great guitarist, you can play circles around people, you can do anything, but when you hear somebody playing and you know it's them within one or two notes, *that's* special. And I think Ty has that. The second you hear him play, you know it is him. His rhythm sound, his solo sound, his tone, his choice of everything he did was unique to him. I'd never heard, like, a George Harrison/ Jimi Hendrix mix. It was really cool and bizarre to me. Just great. And he had the chops, as well—it was beyond what those guys I just mentioned did. Pretty special player, I think.

BUMBLEFOOT For one thing, he is so tasteful and hummable and sing-able. He comes up with these rhythms that start with a sound—he has a very unique sound. You can hear just two seconds of his playing, and you know it's him—in his tone, in the clarity. He sounds like something unique. And the rhythms that he puts into songs, where the stops are, where everything goes tight, and where it chops up—it's very him. And you add to that his tasty, perfect playing— and perfectly bending in key and all of that—and then his vocals. And his solo albums—I was happily a guest on one of his solo albums … I have actually individually worked with each member!

MICK MARS I thought Ty was really good. I was kind of going like, *I wish I had stuck with that style!*—instead of doing some of the stuff that we were doing. He also plays a lot of different … not just phrasing, but it's his chords. The licks that he does were not all the same. He changed them up and did something else with them. He takes you on a journey with his stuff.

MARTY FRIEDMAN [ex Megadeth, Cacophony guitarist; solo artist] I really, really liked the guitar player in that band. The guitar player is amazing. I remember his playing did stand out—it didn't sound like all the other guys out at the time. When I heard it, in the early 90s, all of the 'good' guitar players were playing at warp speed, and with very little content of interest. But King's X's guitarist was super-tasty, and he had a really nice pitch and intonation of the notes, and his interpretation was very nice. He stood out as [being] *really* on the ball. I was really impressed with his guitar playing—so much that I remember it now!

REX BROWN Dime went through a phase where he was all Randy Rhoads and flash, and Eddie Van Halen. And then Ty came around, so he started to get more feel. About that time, I think we were on tour, and doing *Vulgar Display Of Power*, and I think Blues Saraceno came around, and they became great pals, and Blues would come on the road for a long time, and they would just sit and play licks. But I think that style of playing … if you listen to a lead like 'Planet Caravan'—of that period of time—that's what Dime is going for. If you listen to 'Floods,' that's what Dime was going for. He was going for that style and feel … not Ty's, but this own interpretation. It's all the blues, man. It's just simple blues. But instead of throwing so many notes in it, you really don't have to. That was the whole feel. I think Dime was starting to go in that process of everything was well thought out—instead of just flying off the cuff. I remember him going down for 'Caravan'—I was there when he was doing it—and he did, like, three different takes, and, 'Which one do you guys like better?' I said, 'The first one.' The first one just nailed it. That was definitely Ty-influenced. *Absolutely*. Ty was a big influence on Dime.

RITA HANEY Dime loved the way Ty played, and his melodies, and just the way he could move you with a single note. It wasn't about trying to cram how many notes he could fit into one bar. He really liked that fluidity of his playing. And singing. Darrell said, 'All the dudes in that band have got pipes. The way they come together is just amazing.' He was right—they had some of the best harmonizing on a record. And when you saw them live, it was like you were listening to the record. No Pro Tools, no tricks and licks—it was what they were about, and they could pull it off live, too.

ROD MORGENSTEIN Ty is so fast with coming up with ideas. When we first started doing the Jelly Jam, I remember on that first record, I wanted to see if I could create standalone, one-of-a-kind, signature drum grooves. I teach at Berklee College of Music, so I'm driving 240 miles each way, thirty weeks a year—I'm in the midst of completing my twentieth year doing it. So, sometimes I'll set the cruise control, and the steering wheel and your feet are your 'drum set.' I remember it took probably two or three hours, and I came up with what I thought was a really cool, syncopated pattern.

A few days later, Ty and John came over, so we could start throwing around ideas, before we'd get in the studio a couple of weeks later. I said, 'Hey, guys, what do you think of this groove?' And, I swear, within five or ten seconds, Ty is like, 'Hey, what do you think of *this?*' It was freaky how fast he came up with this thing. And then, by the end of the day, the song was ready for lyrics. It's the first track of that first Jelly Jam album—'I Can't Help You.'

The thing is that the drumming is very syncopated—the snare is not on the backbeat, so if you just heard the drumbeat, it wouldn't be obvious to most people, like, 'Where am I supposed to tap my foot?' But Ty ingeniously came up with a vocal line where he was singing very straight on top of it—and that is what tied it all together, to sell the song. Very much like the cleverness and the genius of King's X—how someone who doesn't know music, they will be bopping their heads to this really off-beat, syncopated drumming, because it's tied together with a more normal, regular-sounding vocal. Ty seems to do that a lot. It always amazes me, when we get together, how fast his mind operates, and how fast whatever is going on in his head makes it to the fingers.

WALLY FARKAS It's true what they say—it's really not the gear that produces that sound, because, yeah, Ty is known for his special little green Mel Bay picks or whatever they are that he can't play without—he's got to have that pick—but I've played into his rig, playing his guitar, his pick … and I did *not* sound like Ty! And, at the same time, I've handed Ty my Les Paul a few years ago when they were in town, and he used it for the whole soundcheck—and it sounded like Ty and that Strat Elite.

TY TABOR I think one of the most key things to my sound back then was something called the Lab Series L5 amplifier—that nobody played. It was a very unpopular amp. They quit making it not long after they started making it. So it never was a popular amp or a known amp at all, until a few people—like me—started using them, and then people heard of them. I found out B.B. King used L5s and liked them, and also Eric Johnson. And Allan Holdsworth, at one point, used an L5, but I didn't know that back then.

When I was using them, I thought I was the only person on earth using them. *Honestly*. I bought my first one in 1980, so that's how long I've been using L5s. The first time I heard the L5 though was in the 70s, in Jackson, Mississippi. There was a place called the Musician's Shop that was a music store that had a back warehouse area that they would turn into a small concert area on Saturday nights. And they would have bands come in and play a show using their gear. And they had L5s that they were selling there. I heard this band play through the L5s, and I remember thinking, *Wow. That is an incredibly unique guitar tone. I like that amp*. It was my goal to buy one whenever I could afford one.

I ended up going to college in 1980, and I had joined a band where the keyboardist had an L5 he was playing through. He had left the band at one point and asked me if I wanted to buy the L5 from him—because I was always raving about what a great amp it is. So I bought it from him, and I kind of built my tone around that amp. I was using Les Pauls at the time, and then I switched to an Ampeg guitar that was like a Les Paul Jr., and then, in 1985, we got hired to do that album with that Christian artist, Morgan Cryar. We were listening to a lot of Gino Vanelli at the time, and there was this one album in particular, *Black Cars*, that we were really studying the sonic characteristics on the record—really listening to the production. And there were some guitar tones on that album that were really beautiful.

Morgan asked me, 'How can you get a sound like that?' And I said, 'Well, the first thing we need to do is probably go buy a really nice Strat. That will help to get those type of tones.' So we went to a place called Rockin' Robin in Houston, and there was this Strat with gold hardware, way up on the ceiling, out of reach from everybody, that looked different than all of the other Strats. I thought, *It's got a different bridge, it's got locking tuners, it has a different kind of pickups than I've ever seen on a Strat before*. I asked them to get it down, so I could see what it sounded like. We plugged it in, and the first second I started playing through it … we bought the thing, *instantly*. And that's the guitar that became the Strat that I'm known for, that's on all of the early King's X albums.

It was a brand new guitar when we bought it. I had never even seen one, never heard of one, nobody played them, and the thing weighed more than my Les Paul. It was like a complete lead brick of a guitar. And it's part of the reason why it had such a great tone. I fell in love with it for its sound alone. But as far as how the guitar played, it was one of the most difficult to play guitars—still to this day—that I've ever played in my life. I never touch the thing anymore—unless I'm playing rhythm guitar in the studio. Because it is the most *unplayable* Strat on earth. It just happened to sound so good that I put up with it. Using the Strat with the L5 were the key elements of all the tone that everybody loved.

What I would do is, I would not use the L5 speakers—I would just use the L5 as a head. We would unplug the whole power section of the amp, get rid of it, and simply use it as a preamp. And then I would run it into big power amps, and then use the big power amps to run several cabinets onstage. And that was part of another thing that just brought it to a new level, because the coloration of the power amps smoothed out the Lab a little bit, and then running them through Marshall cabinets with Celestion speakers instead of the Lab speakers was yet another part of the key that changed the tone a little bit. And there were also a series of pedals I would run through that colored things a little bit.

It was mostly a bunch of junky, noisy gear, to be honest, but it was just magic together. As far as distortion or clean sounds, all of that was straight into the amp, being controlled with the volume knob on the guitar. I've never used a distortion pedal or fuzz pedal or anything like that with King's X live. I use boost pedals—to boost the signal into the amp a little harder once in a while, for a lead. But that's not a distortion pedal. I always was a purest as far as *let the amp have the tone—don't get it with pedals.* That was my philosophy in the old days. I depend a little more on pedals now, but I still to this day only use natural amp tone for my distortion. I've never used a pedal with distortion. So it was a purist, straight-into-the-amp thing. And what I would do is, I had a MIDI controller on the ground, and the MIDI controller would control all my effects—which were back by the amp, running in a loop in the head. In other words, it would come out of the head, through the effects, and then right back into the head.

The effects weren't at my feet. And the effects loop was after the preamp section, instead of on the floor before it. Having them after the preamp section always made the effects way more clean and pro-sounding, like they are in the studio. I did do that for effects, and I would use a couple of delays and a slight chorus on guitar every once in a while. But that's about all I used. It was very basic. And I had a rack-mounted Dunlop wah in the rack, controlled with a pedal up front, because I didn't run signal through the pedal—it was just a controller—so I didn't have all of these cables running through all this crap before it gets to the amp, to kill the signal. I did that on purpose. I wanted as little cable as possible, and then all of the effects would be in a tiny loop, with hardly any cable at all. It was a very purist way of doing things.

I quit using the Elites before *Dogman*, because the Elites—despite how good they sound—are one of the noisiest, horrible guitars on earth, if you're in a situation with bad electricity. Two of the most popular type of pickups on guitars are humbuckers and single coils. Strats have their unique tone because they use single-coil pickups—most of them—and the single coils have a unique tone that can only be gotten by making it a single-coil pickup. But the drawback is that they're extremely receptive to electrical disruptions. And there would be times I'd show up at a show, plug in my Strat, and the buzz coming through the guitar would be just as loud as when I would hit a power chord! Meaning the guitar was unusable in that venue.

I then started working with other companies that were trying to do things like stack pickups that have a single-coil sound but don't make as much noise. And I tried with Zion, Yamaha, and Hamer—all of them made great guitars that sounded great, but none of them sounded anything like the Elite. Not even close. I spent years trying this and that to have a guitar I could play venue to venue, without all the technical problems of that type of pickup. And I never did get it, and never could get it, because nothing really sounds like a Strat but a Strat. So, a few years ago, I just said, 'Screw it. I'm going to go back to a Strat.' It sounds better than anything else I play … other than my Les Pauls, which sound immaculate, also. I decided to go back to singles. And, lately, I've been using Fender noiseless singles, and Fishman Fluence pickups are also noiseless. So now, I have the single coil tones without the noise. They finally—after almost thirty years—have figured it out. It doesn't sound quite as good as the old single coils by itself, but it sounds very close now. And that's good enough to be worth using—without all the noise.

JOHN MYUNG I see it as a blessing in my life—being able to work with Ty and really get to know him. He's one of the best people that you'll ever meet. And

Jelly Jam is still going. It's one of these sorts of things in life that you don't really plan—but it turns out to be something that you really appreciate and feel very fortunate to have in your life. There are certain things that are priceless. It's not just all about making money, you know? I tend to think, if you do things for money, the results tend to be disappointing. It's much better to go with what feels right for the right reasons. And when I look back at the things that I cherish the most in my life, it's the people I got to meet and the relationships that I got to have—it has nothing to do with any materialistic possessions at all. So I see getting to know Ty as one of those moments.

THE MAN BEHIND THE DRUM SET, MR. GASKILL.

JERRY GASKILL I love the story of meeting Julie. It's a beautiful story. I was completely done with women. Up to that point, I had been divorced, I had been in other relationships that weren't the best ... *I was done with women.* And I discovered prostitutes. Prostitutes were my girlfriend, and I was happy with that!

And then we were playing this place called the Tradewinds in Sea Bright, New Jersey. It's no longer there. We finished the show, and I walked off the stage, and I'm walking to the bus to change my clothes, and off in the distance on the street, I saw this girl standing there. It was like I was seeing the most beautiful girl I've ever seen in my life. It was overwhelming. I kind of waved to her, and she waved back to me. She was standing all by herself—just her, standing on the street. And I got on the bus, and our merch guy was on the bus. I got on the bus, and I said, 'Hey, look, there's a girl out there. I want you to go out there right now, and tell her I'll change my clothes and be right out there to talk to her.' And, less than a second later, I said, 'No, no, no. Don't do anything. *I'm going to take care of this all myself.*'

So I changed my clothes, and I walked off the bus, and there was a line of people all the way down the street, waiting to talk to us. As soon as I get off the bus, they start chanting my name—*JERRY! JERRY! JERRY!*—like people do, for some reason. I'm going, 'Oh my God ... I can't fuckin' win.' [*Laughs*] I signed everything for people and talked to them, and then finally Doug or somebody came off the bus, and I said, 'Hey, here's Doug!' So then I walked over to Julie—of course, I didn't know her name at the time, because I hadn't met her yet. And now, she's standing with her sister. So I walk over to her, and the very first thing I say to her is, 'So … who's your boyfriend or your husband?' I wanted to get that out of the way, because if that's involved, then see you guys later! And she looks over to her sister, looks back to me, and says, '*Not applicable.*' So, I walked over to her, as close as I could without touching her, and in my mind, I'm thinking, *You belong to me now.* [*Laughs*]

That night, we went to the bar, we had a drink together, we hung out, and as we were leaving, I look at her and say, 'I think you're the most beautiful girl I've ever seen.' And she looks at me and says, 'You're full of shit.' And I looked up, and with all sincerity said, 'Am I?' I never got her number or anything, and she just left. I thought, *Well, I might not ever see her again.* But she emailed me through some address she found online, I gave her my number, she called me, and we've been together ever since. It was February 8, 2002, and we've been together since that day. Every single year we celebrate that day. It's the day that everything in my life changed—for the better.

JULIE GASKILL I had seen them before probably seven or eight times. I'm from rural New York State, so there really wasn't much of an opportunity to see too many bands. I was recruiting some people to go see the Seabright show, funny enough. It's a funny kind of thing between me and Jerry—I don't know if you'd call it a karma or cosmic thing. They were always my favorite band, and for some weird reason I can remember the exact moment when I first popped their cassette tape in my car—where I was going, what I was doing, and I don't know why I have that memory. I don't have it for any other album, cassette, or CD I've ever purchased.

I'd seen them seven or eight times, but I had no desire to speak with them or meet them. I loved the music. I loved the band. But that particular night, I went to see them, and I had my sister and my brother-in-law with me, who had never seen them before. I was excited about that, because of how much I loved them—I wanted them to see them, too.

So we went to the show, and my brother-in-law is famous for sometimes having a few too many drinks, and he gets funny and wants to do certain things. As the night went on, he started pushing my sister and me up to the front—we had a great time. And, at the end of the night, he said, 'I want to go back out there to the buses and talk to those guys.' And I said, 'Ah, I don't want to go out there. I don't have anything to say to them. I love their band, I love the music, but I don't have anything to say. I don't want to go out there and do that.'

He kept insisting, and we ended up out there with the crowd—just kind of standing there, quite a distance away from the bus. And it's funny—again, like I said, those cosmic things, Jerry was getting on the bus, and he looked in our direction and waved. It's such a weird memory, like the cassette tape moment—I can very clearly remember that exact moment, when he looked in our direction and waved. I thought that he couldn't possibly be waving at me/ us, but a snapshot of that moment is burned into my brain, and I can see it very clearly. It was weird. Ultimately, he did come over and start talking to us. We had a little conversation, and we went in to the bar with them and my sister and brother-in-law, and ended up talking for a while, before they had to leave. That's how we met. When he left, he said goodnight, and they all left … and it kind of bothered me, because it felt like he was very familiar to me—like I'd known him all my life. It was really weird.

So, I sent an email to their website, to say, 'Hey, it was nice meeting you.' And the website said, 'They are on tour, so don't be surprised if they don't get back to you right away.' And he immediately wrote back within the hour, and gave me his phone number. I called him and we met up at the New York show— at the Knitting Factory, I think it was, maybe a few days later. And then, after that, we exchanged numbers and we were talking a long time, long distance. And he ended up coming to visit the following month.

In the beginning, when we first started dating, I said something like, I want to get married, because I'd never been married before, and he said, 'Well, I have. I don't want to get married again.' So we were kind of playing it by ear. And then he worked it out with my family—we had my sister, brother-in-law, mom, and my two nephews come over one day. We were having brunch. And, all of a sudden, my little nephew appeared with a ring in his hand, and he said, 'Will you make Jerry my real uncle?' I said, '*What?!*' I was kind of taken aback by it. Then Jerry knelt down and asked me to marry him, and, of course, I said yes.

JERRY GASKILL We got married September 1, 2012, and Julie says that was a banner year for us. She said, 'First you died, then we got married, and then we became homeless.' [*Laughs*] My first heart attack happened on February 26, 2012. I remember that weekend feeling a little weird. It wasn't anything where I thought, *I think I'm dying*. Nothing totally out of the ordinary. Just a different kind of feeling that we feel sometimes. And the weekend ended with us going to a little club right down the street from where we live. And I sat in with the band there—they were friends of ours—and we rocked. Afterward, I went to the bar and sat with Julie. And I said, 'I feel like I pulled a muscle or something right around my chest area. It kind of hurts.' That's pretty much all I remember.

JULIE GASKILL Jerry has a hiatal hernia—he had been bothered for a while with it, but never knew what it was. He had been taking medication when he finally got diagnosed with it, because he was having chest pains, and it finally took the pain away. So, a few weeks before the heart attack, he was saying how it was bothering him—his hiatal hernia. He went and had a scope, and they said, 'Well, it's not this, it looks fine. But your cholesterol is really high.' Before we could even move on, that is when the heart attack happened. And, in hindsight, I think everything he was feeling was probably chest pain. But we both mistook it for the hiatal hernia that we knew he had.

So, the night that it happened … it's almost like it's given me posttraumatic stress disorder—I don't like to think about it. We went out that night, and he sat in with a local band that we know. He got done playing and said, 'I don't really feel good. I feel like I pulled something. I think I need to go home and lie down.' We left, and he ended up throwing up outside. We got back to our house, and he was like, 'I don't know what this is.' He had put his pajamas on, and he was walking around, rubbing his chest. I was like, 'I don't like the way this is going. I think we need to go to the hospital. Put your shoes on, I'm going to call the ambulance.' Then he said, 'No, no, no,' and went to the bathroom. I was of course following him every step of the way; he wanted to go toward the toilet and fell forward on his knees, and then he fell backward. He seized up and the back of his head smacked against the cement floor, and he started turning purple and his eyes rolled toward the back of his head. He was gurgling and making these awful noises. I knew immediately what was happening.

I ran to the kitchen, got my cell phone, called 911, and ran back to the bathroom, screaming his name. I held him upright to a sitting position, and I tried to do CPR. The police came first, and they had to shock him—I think two or three times—in the bathroom. I went out and tried to flag down the ambulance. The ambulance finally came. Jerry never spoke or opened his eyes. They dragged him out of the bathroom like you would drag a body—because our bathroom is very small—put him into the ambulance, went to the hospital, my sister met me there, and they ended up doing the catheterization, and he ended up having what they call the widow-maker—his artery was 100 percent blocked. Most people don't survive that. But they did the catheterization at four in the morning. The doctor came out, and he said, 'I think he's going to be OK.' Then, after that, he was on a ventilator, and he had the balloon pump—that pumps your heart for you—for a day or so. They took him off that, and I think he was in a medically induced coma for two weeks, and he was on a ventilator. Eventually, they had to trach him, because they wanted to get him off the ventilator. So they gave him a trach for a while. And, ultimately, he started healing up after that.

While he was in the hospital, still on the ventilator, he got what they call ARDS—Acute Respiratory Distress Syndrome—and it's either, you die or you don't die. He developed that, which was another complication. I think maybe, during the catheterization, he vomited and aspirated, and maybe a little bit went into his lungs. So that was the worst. The heart attack, once they did the catheterization, it cleared that out, but, in the meantime, he had done the aspirating and his lungs got all … it was kind of like pneumonia. That's why he was on the ventilator for two weeks—to clear up the ARDS. He had a feeding tube—he had everything under the sun. And then he finally made his way out of it and came home. So easily, things can turn on a dime. And Jerry tells everybody: you always have to stay up with your physicals and your blood work. Because Jerry was running before that. He was fine. He was lean. He doesn't smoke, doesn't drink that much, eats well—and it took him out.

JERRY GASKILL I have absolutely no recollection of any of that. During that time, I was dreaming I was living an entirely different life. At one point, I was dreaming I was living in an apartment in LA—I was living with my son at one point, I was about to be on *American Idol* with Steven Tyler, and we were in the dressing room. We were going to do some Aerosmith tunes, and I thought, *I don't really sing Aerosmith tunes. But if that's the gig, I guess I'll do it.* And, the whole time, I was never on my feet—I was either sitting or lying down—and I'm in the dressing room with Steven Tyler, and we both have hospital gowns on!

That was my reality. It was kind of like *The Wizard Of Oz*, because all the characters in this life I was living were people that were visiting me in the hospital, and people that I knew. And they all sort of appeared at different times in this other life I was living. And it still feels like reality to me. I have no recollection [of 'dying']. But it's inspiring to me to know that I can be in so much pain—like my wife said—and it took my life away, that I can enter into death without even knowing. Without any knowledge of pain or any knowledge of discomfort. That I can just enter into death. Had she not been there, I would be dead. I kind of feel like I have this kinship with death. Not that I know anything about it, but I feel like I have a bit of a kinship.

Then, later that same year, we had four feet of water throughout our entire house [as a result of Hurricane Sandy]. Fortunately, we were renting at the time, but we lost everything we had, and we had to live with my sister-in-law and her husband for two months. But everything worked out great—because of Sandy, we were able to buy this house that we absolutely loved, which is right down the street from her sister. It turned into the best thing ever. So, you just have to keep moving on, man.

JULIE GASKILL Two years later, he had a nodule on his thyroid. So they did a needle biopsy, and the doctor said, 'It's 80 percent benign, but I don't feel comfortable leaving it in there, when there's a 20 percent chance it could be something different. I'd like to take it out.' So he was cleared for surgery. He had the surgery, they took it out, but he kept saying after the surgery, 'I feel horrible. I feel nauseous.' And they said, 'It's probably just the anesthesia.' And I'm thinking, *With his history, I'm sure they know what's going on with him. He should be monitored.* Ultimately, the next morning, they call me at seven in the morning, and said he was having heart issues, and was going to have to be transferred.

He ended up having a heart attack for quite a few hours, I think—that's why he was so nauseous. Then they did the catheterization again, and the doctor did it to relieve the blockage. But he said, 'Where the blockage is, it's on a curve or something. He's going to have to have bypass surgery.' And his mom had had it in her forties, as well. He ended up with a double bypass a few days after. But the worst part is, they were giving him blood thinners because of the surgery, and when they found out he was having a heart attack, they had put him in Jersey Shore—this hospital to monitor him—so he could have the bypass. And the incision on his neck suddenly developed a hematoma, due to the blood thinners, and it cut off his breathing. There was a nurse there, and if he had been alone, he would have died—because he couldn't breathe. He doesn't even remember this happening, either. They had to hurry up and intubate him and take care of his neck. It was just a nightmare—it was one thing after another. Then, when he healed up from that a little bit, he had the bypass, which went very well—thankfully.

JERRY GASKILL The second one was September 11, 2014. I went in and had the thyroid surgery—I was cleared for everything. Then, during the recovery from that, I started feeling really, really bad. Really nauseous. Really not well. Sweating. I remember calling Julie and saying, 'I really don't feel good.' And I told the doctors, and they said, 'Well, that's what happens sometimes when you're recovering. It should go away.' And then, finally, this team of doctors rush into my room, and said, '*You're having a heart attack!*' So they rushed me down again, my cardiologist came, he put a catheterization in, to open up the blockage that had formed, and I immediately felt better. And, as he was doing that, he looks at me, and says, 'You're going to need open-heart surgery.' I thought he was joking to make me feel better. And that's exactly what happened—five days later, I had open-heart surgery. Double bypass. It's a bit of a hard time to recover from a lot of that—when they rip your whole chest open, take your organs out, and put new arteries in. But I did have Percocet, which was really great. [*Laughs*] And I kind of got addicted to it, without realizing it.

The first time I was in the hospital, after the first heart attack, I determined that I was going to be better than ever. And I thought I was kind of doing OK. Then I had the second heart attack, and there are parts of me thinking, *Well, maybe I'm* not *going to be better than ever. I don't know*. But I knew I had to fight. I finally came home three or four days after the surgery. Two days after that, I went to the bathroom and I could barely even breath. I couldn't breathe. I called the doctor and they had me come back in, and I had fluid in my lungs. They had to put these tubes in my back—I already had this done once in the hospital, it was horrible. So I had to go back in—after being released—and they put two tubes in this time. I remember doing that and going back to my room, and I was laying with my head on a table, thinking, *I can't fucking do this, man*. And I asked them, 'Is there anything you can give me to help me get through this? Can you just give me some Percocet?' And they allowed me to have Percocet.

As soon as it kicked in, I thought, *OK ... I can do this. I'll be all right*. I made it through that, and I continued with the Percocet for however long.

Now, I am better than ever. First off, after the first heart attack, Doug sent me this link to a video called *Forks Over Knives*. It's basically just a plant-based diet. And, when I watched it, I thought, *OK, I'm doing to do that. I'm going to stop eating all animal products and eat plant-based stuff*. For a couple of years, I kind of did that. Until I had the second heart attack. After the surgery, I woke up, and it wasn't like an epiphany or anything, but I just started eating whatever was there. And, now, I've learned to listen to my body. Because our bodies always tell us what we want and what it doesn't want. We just have to listen to it. And that's what I'm doing. I'll eat some animal products now, but if it doesn't feel right to me, I won't eat it. That's where I'm at with my food—I feel really good about it. And I also work out six days a week.

I started seeing a personal trainer, as well—his name is Danny Weltman— whom I love—totally changed my life. He used to train Jon Bon Jovi, as a matter of fact! I started off seeing him three days a week, and he kicks my ass every time. He never lets up on me. He knows my whole history, and he watches me closely. Now, I'm seeing him twice a month. He came to my house, helped set up my basement, gave me a routine to do. I do that six days a week. I can't wait to do it. I go to bed waiting to wake up in the morning, so I can go work out. Every day, I wake up, go into my basement, and kick my own ass. I'm so far into it that I can't imagine my life without it now. I feel better, I'm stronger, and I think I'm healthier probably than I've ever been in my life.

If it wasn't for the heart attacks, I wouldn't have known now ... well, it was going to happen anyway—I'm inevitably going to die. It's going to happen, no matter what. So I'm very thankful for that. And that's where I'm at now, man.

JULIE GASKILL I do go on tour with them sometimes. I have a day job, and I use my vacation time. When they're not on a bus, it's better, because we get to sleep in a hotel room every night instead of on the bus. But it's hard on the bus. I don't mind sleeping on the bus, but it's hard trying to do what I need to do with a bus full of guys. Sometimes I travel on a bus with them, and sometimes I don't—it depends on the location. But after what has happened with Jerry, we both don't like it when we're not together. I think he likes that I'm there to watch over him, and I like that I can see him. Sometimes it's difficult for me—if

I call and he doesn't answer for a long time, I start getting freaked out. *Why isn't he answering?* Sometimes it's easier if I just go—for the both of us.

CHARLIE BENANTE I've always loved Jerry's drumming. Jerry comes from a different place, where I don't know if he is playing with the song or if the song is playing with Jerry. In his syncopated fashion, he's not a very fast type of drummer or anything like that, but the things that he contributes to the songs make me go, *Oh, yeah, that was really tasty right there.* Just great.

RICHARD CHRISTY I've always loved drummers that sing. And for somebody to sing as well as Jerry … and he is just an incredible drummer. I've always admired that. I remember being in high school and practicing along to *Gretchen Goes To Nebraska* on the drums. Jerry kind of taught me how to sing and play drums at the same time, because I used to practice to their album and try to sing their songs—while I was playing drums. And, from seeing their videos, I knew that all three guys sang. So I really have to thank Jerry for teaching me, 'Hey, *drummers can sing.*' When I joined the band Iced Earth, I sang backup vocals, and I was confident enough to do that from practicing along to King's X albums and singing, and learning how to do that by listening to Jerry.

And just his drumming style—he had such a great groove. He was so tasteful. I always loved his drum sound—his drum sound was amazing. Jerry is a big influence on my drumming, for sure. I actually got to meet Jerry in person about four years ago, at a comedy show in Jersey—because Jerry lives in Jersey. And he's also friends with my buddy, Don Jamieson, who's a comedian. I went to one of Don's shows, where he was recording a live album for Metal Blade, and Jerry was at the show, and I was freaking out. I was so nervous to go up and meet him, and he was the nicest guy in the world. It was so cool to know that he was a fan of comedy, as well.

ROD MORGENSTEIN First off, he's a lovely guy. I think he's got one of the best dry senses of humor of anybody I've ever met. I remember hanging out on their tour bus one time. I was sitting in the back, talking to Jerry, and when I got up to leave, he said, 'Hey man, *it was so great that you got to see me.*' [*Laughs*] He is like a 'team player' musician, where it's not about him—it's about coming up with the parts that make the song pop. Everything that he plays seems like it's supposed to be there. And he has a great sense of time, which is really important for a drummer. He's an all-around strong player, and you never hear anything that was not supposed to be there. And he also has that 'musician sense' where he will throw in things in places where a straight-ahead rock drummer would never think to do.

KIP WINGER I don't think there's anyone else that could have filled that role in that band anywhere near as well as Jerry did. His kick-and-snare interaction with the music is very unique and very well thought out. And there is a lot of intention behind his drumming that is probably missed by the average listener. That's a really key element. He is as important to that band as Ringo was to The Beatles.

MIKE PORTNOY Jerry is a great drummer in the Ringo sense. Ringo is one of my favorite drummers of all-time—not for technical reasons, but because Ringo always played the most perfect thing for every Beatles song. And Jerry is very much that type of drummer—he's perfect for *everything* King's X does. And I can't picture anybody else playing drums in that band. Jerry is the perfect guy for their music. And it's funny, because the last time I saw Ringo live, I was sitting with Jerry! It was kind of funny, because I always compared him to Ringo in a very positive, complimentary way.

RAY LUZIER I can hear one bar of his playing and know it is Jerry Gaskill. *Done.* He's got the groove, his laidback feel, but yet there is a different energy that he hits. And his style is so unique that it drove that band. He has this thing where he hits the hi-hats really light in certain sections, and it's all textures and nuances and flavors. It's very unique. You can't really compare him to anyone. Someone said he's got that [John] Bonham kind of feel. And there are definitely elements there. But he's got his own thing.

There are records that I've done where I'll listen to them, and drummers have this thing called the *flam*—it's one of the rudiments. And I've ripped off many Jerry Gaskill flam kinds of fills. I've told him straight up! There are quite a few of them on the Army Of Anyone record [2006's self-titled release]. Because he was a fan of that record, and I said, 'Hey Jerry, the song "Goodbye," there is this thing that I do that's totally you.' And he's like, 'No way.' It's true—us musicians, that's all we do. We pick up stuff from other people and try to make it our own. But I definitely was heavily influenced by Jerry's drumming through the years.

SHANNON LARKIN I always loved John Bonham, and the single-kick bass thing, but you've got to remember, I was in a metal band in the 80s, so the double-kick bass was all the rage. And then here is this guy coming out, and he's got a four-piece kit and killing it. So, I reconfigured my whole kit, took away a kick drum, and got a double pedal ... so I could be like Jerry Gaskill. He's tasteful—that's the main thing. He's also a perfect metronome—he's like a Phil Rudd in that aspect, in that his meter is perfect. And, live, he sits right behind the beat. They had this funky groove. They were rock, metal ... it was hard to classify them, but they had this funk beat from the way Jerry sits behind, and that's a special thing that can't be taught. Jerry has it naturally. And cymbal placement ... I can go on and on about Jerry Gaskill. He's one of my top influences as a drummer. *It was all for the song.*

JERRY GASKILL From what I understand, I think Sean Lennon was there [when Pearl Jam played *Saturday Night Live* in 1992, and Jeff Ament wore a King's X shirt], and he saw that Jeff wore the shirt. I met Sean later—my son, Joey, is a big fan of Sean Lennon. The *Friendly Fire* record is a great record. He was coming to Asbury Park, where I live, and I said, 'I'm going to go see him, because I know my son loves him.'

We were at the show, and then afterward, he did a signing thing at the merch table—at the Stone Pony in Asbury Park. A friend of mine said, 'Hey, go tell him who you are!' I said, 'I'm not going to do that. He doesn't know who I am.' She said, 'Well ... I'm going to do it!' So, she marched me right over there and said, 'Hey, Sean, this is Jerry Gaskill from King's X.' And he stopped everything he was doing and kind of freaked out! He called security over and said, 'Get this guy a chair—he's going to sit with me the rest of the time!' He made me sit next to him as he signed things for people and talked to people, and he was talking to me the whole time.

I remember a guy brought him over an acoustic guitar to sign, so he signed it, and then he took it, and started playing King's X songs on it! And he told me that King's X changed his musical life. Then he invited me onto his bus, so I got onto his bus and he bought *Faith Hope Love* digitally online, so everybody had to listen to it. We were listening, and it got to 'Six Broken Soldiers,' and he said, 'This is the most Beatles-sounding song on the record,' and I said, 'Yeah. *I liked your dad.*' [*Laughs*] And then I said, 'Hey, would you do me a favor, man? Would you call my son and say hi to him?' So, I went out to my car and got my phone, and he called my son. I ended up jamming with him that night. It was an incredible night. I think that was 2007, maybe.

Shortly after, I got to be in Bruce Springsteen's band for an entire show, at the Stone Pony, as well. I remember getting a phone call from a guy named Bob Bandiera—he was Bon Jovi's other guitar player. I'd done several gigs with him—great gigs. I got a call from him, saying, 'Hey, we've got this gig coming up with Bruce. He's doing a benefit. Do you want to do it? We're going to learn some Bruce songs, and go up there and be his band.' And I said, 'Well, yeah, I want to do it!' And then, as soon as I got off the phone, I thought, *Oh my God. What have I done? I've got to do this now!* And I learned all these Bruce songs. And I remember the whole time I'm doing this, I'm thinking, *He's going to get there that night and say, 'I'll tell you what guys—I'm just going to do this acoustic tonight, because this drummer is not cutting it.'*

And then it finally gets to the show, and he comes in—ready to do a soundcheck/rehearsal kind of thing. And I wasn't a Bruce fan at that time—I really didn't care about Bruce. But I knew Bruce was huge. So he comes in, I think we did 'Pink Cadillac,' he counts it off, we do it, and I remember thinking, *Man, this is badass. Bruce can play! All right, cool! I'm digging on this.* And before this, everybody who had played with him before said, 'Look, Bruce never talks to anybody in the band. Don't feel bad if he doesn't say anything to you. He just comes in and does his thing.' So we finish the song, and as soon as we finished it, Bruce turns around, looks at me, and goes, 'That was great, man!' And we kind of became friends. He had just done a record with Brendan O'Brien, so we started talking about Brendan, and we hung out the whole night together. It was incredible.

Then, a couple of years later, I was doing a party at Jon Bon Jovi's house, with my good friend Bob Burger and a bunch of other really great musicians. I think it was an after-summer party at Jon Bon Jovi's house in the Hamptons. An incredibly star-studded cast of people—Renée Zellweger, Matt Lauer, Billy Joel. So they sequestered us by the pool area until we had to play. We're all sitting out there talking, and then, all of a sudden, this guy comes and stumbles in through the gate, and starts walking toward us. We look at him, and we go, 'Hey … *it's Bruce!'* So, he comes up to us and says, 'Hey, where's the bar?' Then he sees me, and says, 'Hey, I really enjoyed playing with you that night, man.' The night ended with us being onstage—we were sort of the house band—and then Jon Bon Jovi comes up onstage and starts inviting people from the audience up to play with us. And we end up onstage for forty-five minutes, jamming together with Billy Joel, Jon Bon Jovi, Jimmy Buffett, Roger Waters … *and Goddamned Paul McCartney!* It was almost too good to be true, but it was true.

I remember Paul kind of sauntering to the side of the stage, getting ready to come up, and it was just like he was in *A Hard Day's Night* or something. I remember when Paul got onstage, he went up to the mic, and said, 'I thought I was on holiday.' From there, we proceeded to do a couple of Beatle tunes, among other songs. At one point, I looked into the crowd, and there was Howard Stern and his wife singing along. I think we were doing 'Take It Easy' by Eagles at the time. And then, after that, we're tearing everything down, and I saw Paul still out there. Jon had these couches and pillows—and beds, even—for everyone to be comfortable, just hanging out on his lawn. And I saw Paul still sitting out there, kind of by himself. And I thought, *I think I'm going to go talk to him!*

So I went out there, walked over to him, tapped him on the shoulder—because he wasn't looking at me, he was sitting on this big pillow—and he turns around and sees me, and goes, 'Hey man, sit down!' I sat down next to him, and we started talking for, like, fifteen, twenty minutes. And he would tell me old Beatles stories. And, at one point, we had done 'Twist & Shout' after he had left the stage, and he was out there dancing with a glass of red wine in his hand, and, as we got to the ending, for some reason, the bandleader wanted to continue on with it, and I went into the ending of the song. And Paul said to me, 'Hey, at the end of "Twist & Shout," you played it right. Those other guys didn't. You did the right thing.' And at one point, he looks at me and goes, 'You're a good drummer, man. *Keep it up.*'

25 ON THEIR OWN

A LOOK AT THE MANY SOLO AND/OR SIDE
PROJECTS OF ALL THREE KING'S X MEMBERS.

DOUG PINNICK

POUNDHOUND, *MASSIVE GROOVES* (1998)

DOUG PINNICK That was just a bunch of songs that I had written and had nothing to do with them, because King's X were writing together—it was the *Tape Head* period. I used to probably write around fifteen to twenty tunes for a new King's X record, and we would only do a few, compared to what I had. I mean, a lot of my tunes were crappy, too. And Ty wrote a lot. So I had all of these excess songs, and I said, 'I'm going to put a solo record out.' Ty had been putting stuff out, so I thought that it was OK to start doing it, too. Especially because we were on Metal Blade at the time, and Brian said, 'Hey, go for it!' And he gave me a budget, and I put those two records out—that one and *Pineappleskunk*.

I remember naming it *Massive Grooves From The Electric Church Of Psychofunkadelic Grungelism Rock Music*. I don't know, I had to put it all in there, because I thought that's the way it sounded—it was psychedelic, it was grungy, it was metal, it was soulful. It had all the elements that I liked in music, so I thought I'd name it that. I played everything on it, except the drums. I asked Jerry to play. And that was the first record I put out where I played everything with a drummer. I love the whole record. 'Red' is one of my favorites. I like 'Music,' because it's a no-brainer—just listen to the groove. It's a real simple song, and it's a lot of fun. A lot of those songs were really simple, two-part songs. I didn't spend a lot of time trying to create any landscape or make up a lot of vocal harmonies. I wanted to write these simple songs that people could rock out to. 'Stripped down' I guess is what I was going for. Shannon Larkin of Godsmack played drums on it, also.

SHANNON LARKIN The first time I met Doug, waiting in line, I immediately had a connection with him … in my young mind, anyway. The next time I met him, we exchanged numbers, and I became friends with him. At one point, he's like, 'What are you doing next month? I'm going to do a solo record—would you like to play on it?' And I'm like, '*Hell yeah!*'

He flew me to Texas, and I went into his studio he had at the time in Houston, and stayed at his house. We went out and partied and had this perfect, great time. It was more hanging out—I was probably in the studio for only a few hours and did four songs or something. But the best memory of it for me was seeing how Doug Pinnick works. To this day, I still look at him like … Robert Plant, or something. He's larger than life to me.

VARIOUS TRIBUTE ALBUM APPEARANCES (2000–PRESENT)

BOB KULICK When the opportunity arose and I was doing all these compilation CDs, the idea of using Doug worked out great—because we always needed amazing singers, and Doug was obviously one! That's what really sells the songs. There are tons and tons of guitar players and drummers, but in terms of singers, the guys that you would say, 'This guy could sing the phone book and make it sound good'—Doug Pinnick!

Of all that we did, the *We Wish You A Metal Xmas* record was amazing because of how it turned out with George [Lynch] and Doug, and his soulful vocal on that was everything that anybody could ever want. Cut to the Frank Sinatra tribute album that we did, *Sin-Atra*, with just singers—Doug sang alongside Dee Snider, Glenn Hughes, Robin Zander, and some pretty heavy hitters, yet his interpretation of 'I've Got The World On A String' is so compellingly amazing. And I really dig Glenn Hughes, Dee Snider, and all those guys. But you know what? The subtlety and the fire of this guy's voice, where he takes this stuff, it's really something special. And that's the way I feel about him as a singer. I spent some time obviously with him in the studio, hanging out. But not a tremendous amount of time.

Cut to Lemmy's seventieth birthday party—may he rest in peace—in December 2015, Matt Sorum is trying to put together the lineups and find people to participate. So I'm involved, having been Motörhead's producer on numerous projects, including 'Whiplash' [from the 2004 compilation *Metallic*

Attack: The Ultimate Tribute], the one that won the Grammy; and the theme for Triple H, the WWE wrestler ['The Game']. And Lemmy was a dear, dear friend of mine. [I went] through the list of who was attending, and it was Billy Idol, Slash, Zakk Wylde, Steve Vai, and I hooked him up with Doug. So, as fate would have it, I had the fortune of having Matt say, 'You suggested Doug—how about Doug sings with the band that you're going to be in with Steve Vai?' So, Doug was going to play bass and sing, Steve on guitar, me on guitar, and we added Lemmy's son, Paul. And that was the band that played with Matt Sorum that night—in front of Lemmy, at his birthday party at the Whisky.

SUPERSHINE, SUPERSHINE (2000)

DOUG PINNICK I remember Bruce Franklin from Trouble was always telling me, 'We need to do something together.' Finally, one day, the opportunity arose—Bruce came down to Texas, and I had my studio at the time, so we went in the studio to make *Supershine*. Bruce stayed at my house, and then Ty and Bruce mixed it, and we put it out. We're talking about putting out a second one.

POUNDHOUND, PINEAPPLESKUNK (2001)

DOUG PINNICK It's different than the first Poundhound album, because this one I had to write songs for. I thought about it a lot. I also was also taking Wellbutrin for depression. I thought I'd try some Wellbutrin to see if it helped me. And it actually made me kind of numb, and I didn't have any feelings. I couldn't find any passion to sing about. So, as a result of it, a lot of the songs on that record I feel I was looking for lyrical things to sing about. But I wasn't *feeling* a whole lot inside at the time. So it was a lot of work, finding my heart in it. I stopped taking it, and I'm back to my normal self again.

The name *Pineappleskunk*—King's X was playing in Milwaukee, I think it was, and this guy came to see us play, and we were outside after the show, smoking weed together, and he said, 'This weed is called Pineappleskunk. It comes from Jamaica.' And I was like, 'That's a cool name ... I'm going to name an album that!'

For the first two records, Metal Blade gave me a very sizable advance, and I put a big down-payment on my house, filled the whole house with new furniture, and bought all the equipment for my studio. Without those advances, I wouldn't be doing all the music that I've been doing to this day—or have my own home, finally, after all those years. Because I never made much money out of King's X to ever think about having a house and studio. I thank Brian Slagel for doing that—because he signed King's X right after we had left Atlantic, and I said, 'Hey Brian, can I put out a solo record?' And he said, 'Sure!' He gave me great promotion, too. I did a lot of work promoting those records for him.

THE MOB, *THE MOB* (2005)

DOUG PINNICK Reb Beach called me up and said, 'We want to put a record out, and we're going to call it *The Mob*.' He told me who he had with him on the record, and I go, 'Sure! It would be fun.' All I had to do was sing, and I got paid for it.

What I loved about it was, Reb made up all the melodies. He wrote all the songs, and just sung gibberish—but they were melodies. So, I sat down and went, 'It sounds like he's saying *this*'—and made up storylines and melodies that sounded like the way he said them. It was a lot of fun, and a different way for me to write music. And, also, it wasn't personal—I didn't have to write lyrics about me, like I do with King's X or my solo stuff. This is more like, it didn't matter *what* I sang about. It was just a song and it was fun.

EMOTIONAL ANIMAL (2005)

DOUG PINNICK I think that was after I saw that nobody gave a fuck about the first two records. I thought, *Maybe if I put my name on it, at least King's X fans will buy it*. The third one, I had signed to Magna Carta, and that was a whole different situation. They were completely different than Metal Blade, and it was a learning curve. I pretty much did that record in my house, and it was pretty much about what I'd been going through in my life, lyrically. Musically, it's always the same—I'm making up riffs and making them work. I can write a song a day—it's lyrics and melodies that I really feel is my weakness, and I really struggle with trying to be relatable. Music is music, to me—it's all about what you say on top of it, and how you sing it.

STRUM SUM UP (2007)

DOUG PINNICK I had gotten to a point where I was like, 'Well, I've put out all these damn records on my own—of me doing everything on them except drums. Maybe I should do a record with some musicians, get a producer, and do it in a real studio?' Hal Sparks—one of my best friends—said, 'You should come out to LA and make the record.' And he introduced me to Michael Parnin, who produced, engineered, and mixed it. I did it in his studio, and I lived with him for a while when I first moved out here to LA. I wanted to make a record that had everybody on it that gave me goose bumps when I saw them play live. So I handpicked a handful of guys that were available that I could get to. It was an awesome experience of love and respect.

I remember when I wrote all these songs for the album, I was making an updated demo of all the songs, and I felt like … you know, I'm not a very accurate guitar player—I'm more concerned about the feel. I thought, *I'll ask Wally to come over—I'll show him the parts and he can do all the songs in one day, while I'd take a week.* He played them all so perfectly—he even wanted to emulate my feel, attack, and the nuance in my playing. He captured my emotion. He has an amazing ear, so I said, 'Why don't you come to LA and make this record with me, since you know the songs?' And he said, 'But *you've* got to play guitar on it too, Doug.' So I played guitar on the right, and he played guitar on the left—when you listen to that record. It was the first time I had ever played guitar on a record in a band with another guitar player. That was a lot of fun.

I didn't want to play bass—I wanted to get Rex Brown to play bass, and he committed to it. And the day I went into the studio, he texted me and said he had been in rehab for a week, and he was sorry he couldn't do it. I thought, *What the fuck am I going to do?* So I spoke to my buddy Kolby McKinney, an old bass tech of mine and a great friend of mine. He said, 'Why don't you get Dave Henning? He's really amazing and played with Big Wreck.'

So I called Dave, and had him come over to the studio, and Michael says, 'Did you bring your bass?' And he said, 'No. I thought I was just coming over to talk.' Michael says, 'No … *we're tracking!*' So he picked up this old bass that was sitting in the corner, plugged in, and we made three songs that day, and he *smoked*—he's a badass bass player. And he said, 'Doug, do you want me to play like you, with a pick?' And I said, 'No man. You do *you*. Play with your fingers and the whole deal.' That's why the bass tone is different. And the playing—Dave is a really great, soulful finger player. His touch made that album sound fat. And it had a different vibe to it, because of that.

I really like that record a lot, because so many people played on it. Alain Johannes played lead guitar on it, and Natasha, his wife—she's deceased, may she rest in peace—sang on it. Kellii Scott from Failure—one of my favorite bands in the whole world—and Ray Luzier play drums, and Steve Stevens came in and did a lead. A bunch of friends came in to do the gang choruses.

What I really loved about that record was, they all gathered around my songs to make them exactly how I felt them. It was the opposite way from recording for me. It was my project, and I controlled every aspect. They totally understood what I was trying to do. And all are King's X fans. There was nobody saying, 'I'd like to do it *this* way. I don't like that part. Let me try this instead.' It was the most non-intimidating time I had had in a studio at that point in my life. Probably my favorite album I've ever made. I can listen to it and there's nothing I regret doing for that album.

TRES MTS., *THREE MOUNTAINS* (2011)

DOUG PINNICK Jeff Ament and I had talked about doing a project for years. And one day he called up, and said, 'Hey man, I've got a ticket. Come on up to Montana. I've got Richard Stuverud on drums—we're going to get together and make a record.' So I went up to Montana and we spent a couple of weeks, wrote eight songs, and recorded them—Jeff has a studio in his house and an engineer there. We slept at the house, hung out. Whenever we felt like we wanted to make music, we did. Whenever we got tired, we just hung out.

It was just Jeff, Richard, and me the first time. Jeff and I are both bass players, so I just brought my Strat. Tuned my guitar in drop-C, and we came up with the whole album. Jeff played in standard tuning, so it made the texture of the album very interesting. We had a great time. And then we did it a second time, and Jeff brought Mike McCready out. It was the four of us, and we wrote eight more songs. That's how the record came out. It was a lot of fun making that record. But I feel like I wasn't on top of my game, melody-wise and lyrically. I think it's one of my weakest pieces of art—when it comes to my part on the record.

We did a tour. We played on *The Tonight Show Starring Jimmy Fallon*, too, which was pretty cool. I remember that was the first time I ever toured with a rich rock star in the same band. [*Laughs*] I remember a few things—being the front man and the bass player, I always get the attention, even though I didn't realize it. With Tres Mts., as soon as we hit the stage, it was all about Mike McCready. And it kind of shocked me at first and intimidated me. And then I went, 'Well, I'm just me, so I'll just do what I do.' I remember when we played in Seattle, the review said, 'When Tres Mts. hit the stage, it was clearly Mike McCready's show … but the singer held his own.' [*Laughs*]

Also, I remember when we'd get out of our cars or limos at the venues, there would be a crowd of people that would run up to Mike and Jeff, and no one would say anything to me. Well, maybe there'd be one fan in the corner, going, 'Doug, I love King's X.' But it was like that. And the ten-star hotels. Boy oh boy, we stayed in some *nice* hotels! I'd never been in hotels like that before in my life. It was really cool to see, because I'd known those guys from the beginning and from there to now, and the changes that have happened in their lives, and how they'd become these young kids that looked up to me that I saw open for Alice In Chains, and nobody knew who they were, to one of the biggest bands in the world. It's been an honor to know them.

JEFF AMENT Making that Tres Mts. record was super fun. It was tough for us to finish that record. We started that record, then both of our bands got busy, and we just couldn't finish it. We probably lost a little bit of the original mojo that we had. But then, when we went out and played those shows, those shows were amazing. Especially with Mike coming out with us—it really fed the Hendrix-y element of that record. My original thing with that record was that I wanted to do less of a guitar record. I thought that his voice was so great that he could have made, like, an R&B record, or he could have made a Gnarls Barkley kind of a record or something. His voice is timeless, and he can sing over any kind of music. I always felt that there was a way that you could make the focal point of the song his voice and have these cool, groovy, R&B beds of music underneath it. It was my own curiosity—I was curious about making a record like that. It just didn't happen that way. There was a song on my first solo record [*Tone*, 2008] called 'Doubting Thomasina' that Doug sings on, that was sort of like my hack R&B. And I thought that was when I got the idea of, *You can make a whole record of good versions of this kind of a song, and it would be pretty interesting.*

PINNICK GALES PRIDGEN, *PINNICK GALES PRIDGEN* (2013) AND *PGP 2* (2014)

DOUG PINNICK The guys at Magna Carta called me up and said, 'Do you want to put a record out with Eric Gales and Thomas Pridgen?' And I go, '*Sure!*' I love Eric and have known him for a long time—his band toured with King's X when he was sixteen. But this project was mainly for the money, because I needed to pay my bills. So we went up to this town north of San Francisco— where the Grateful Dead did all of their albums, this studio out in the middle of nowhere. It looks like a chicken shack, but inside it's state of the art.

We went up there with our guitars, and in fifteen days, wrote an entire album—lyrics, melodies, overdubs, mixed it and everything. We did two records like that. I'll *never* do it again. To write and mix a record in fifteen days is just brutal. And to have a deadline, to know you have to get it done, is just not fun. It's like, fifteen songs in fifteen days … *are you kidding?* To me, it's almost impossible. Well, it *is* impossible, because those two records, as much as I love the band, the records could have been better. I mean, we mixed the records in two days—both records! I can't mix one song in two days.

When I listen to the PGP records, all I hear is, *Rush, rush, rush. We've got to get it done. Deadline, deadline, deadline.* So I can't enjoy it at all. It could have been so much better.

NAKED (2013)

DOUG PINNICK I had moved to LA. Back in Houston, I had gotten to the point where I was behind on all my bills. There was no money coming in—King's X was barely touring, I wasn't paying my taxes, I had no insurance. I had *nothing*. I was starting to sell guitars, and I was to the point of borrowing money from people. A friend of mine called up and said, 'When are you moving to LA?' I had been threatening to move to LA for, like, two years. And I said, 'Whenever I can get enough money to move.' And he said, 'Well, *just pick a date.*' So, I picked the date, and he said, 'I'm coming to pick you up'—him and a friend of his, in his van—'we're going to load you up and drive you to LA.'

So that's what he did. I didn't know where I was going to go, or what I was going to do. But I had to go, or I'd die in Houston. And Michael Parnin—the guy who produced *Strum Sum Up*—said, 'You can just stay at the studio for a while, to figure it out.' So I moved in and slept on the floor in a guitar tracking room, when he was tracking music in it! I had to wait until he was done to go to bed—I had a sleeping bag on the floor, and that was it. I lived there for six months or so. When I moved out, I moved into another friend's house, and rented a room.

People told me that when they first moved to LA, that it was the hardest thing that they'd ever done in their life—trying to get acclimated to how different it is here, and how expensive things are here. It's very difficult to live in LA, because everything is very expensive here. There is *nothing* free here—seriously! Not a fucking thing. I took a lot of things for granted in the Midwest. LA has its obvious bad aspects, but it's still the coolest city in the world for musicians and artists. It's not easy here, but the most opportunity is here if you're a musician. The competition is fierce, but it's exactly where I needed to be. I had that overwhelming feeling of, *This is a place where everybody is doing what I do. You're not special anymore.* I was here in the thick of it, and I needed it to wake me up.

So I was living in LA now, and I got real depressed—I felt like maybe I had made a big mistake. But there was nowhere to go—I was renting my house to tenants back in Houston, and was barely making ends meet in LA. I was constantly writing tunes, as usual—I had my Pro Tools, Superior Drummer program, and an Axe-FX for guitar. Technology had gotten to where you could make an album in your bathroom. The song 'What You Gonna Do?' tells you exactly what I was going through at that time. Plus, Jerry had his first heart attack. So everyone's future was uncertain. It was the first time I started to appreciate what I had and was a part of.

GRINDER BLUES, *GRINDER BLUES* (2014)

DOUG PINNICK This was totally the opposite of Pinnick Gales Pridgen, KXM, or my solo stuff. I met Scot Bihlman first by hanging out with Ray Luzier, at a party. I think it might have been the same party that George Lynch was at, that we talked about doing KXM with Ray. Scot said he wrote music for TV commercials and movies, and I said, 'I just moved out to LA, and I'm trying to find new ways of making money.' We talked about writing together with his brother [Jabo Bihlman], and maybe we could get some placement with some of the tunes. We stayed in contact, and I think we did actually have a small placement. I sang on a video game, also! I went out to Jabo's house in Vegas. We were just going to write some jingles.

They were telling me that they come from a blues background, and had played with Ray Charles and B.B. King, they backed up some of the biggest blues artists around. And I'm thinking, *Wow, these two white boys have got a groove feel that only brothers can create. They're really tight.* So I suggested we do a blues record, but let's do it all in drop-B. Really low-tuned, and write tunes that made us feel like we did when we first heard ZZ Top's *Tres Hombres.* '*Tres Hombres* … but *lower.*' And they said they liked that idea. So, we did it!

And the other thing about it was I wanted lyrically for it to be just old blues-type lyrics—'*My baby left me, come home.*' Nothing deep—this was going to be *fun.* I wanted to make a record where we could get up anytime, anywhere we wanted to, and just do these songs. They're that simple and they're low enough in my register where I don't have to struggle vocally. So … we did it. And, to this day, we can get up and play the whole record. It was the first time I had ever done vocals in my natural vocal range, and for touring purposes.

KXM, *KXM* (2014) AND *SCATTERBRAIN* (2017)

DOUG PINNICK KXM is me, George Lynch, and Ray Luzier. We met, I think, at the same party I met Scot Bihlman from Grinder Blues. We decided to get together and see what transpired. George rented a studio up in the mountains, called us up, and said, '*Let's go.*' George is the kind of guy that takes control—not in a bad way. He's the 'go-getter.' I think if George hadn't have initiated it, there would be no KXM—even though we all talked about doing it. And George has been the instigator ever since.

RAY LUZIER When I first met Doug, I said, 'Please let me play on a song,' and he said, 'We'll do something.' I played on a track on *Strum Sum Up.* I actually played on two or three songs, but just one of them made it. So that was my one tune, and I was like, 'I finally got on a Doug album. We'll do some more stuff.'

To make a long story short, we still have our house in Los Angeles—it's in Tarzana, up in the valley. I invited a bunch of people out to my son's first birthday party about five or six years ago. LA is the land of flakes—you invite a hundred people, fifteen show up. It's just the way it is. It's a weird place. So we invited all these people, and I started going through my Rolodex and found all my rock-star buddies, and I'm thinking, *You know what? I'm just going to invite Billy Sheehan, Dean DeLeo, Doug Pinnick, and George Lynch.* A lot of people that we invited that weren't the 'name' musician guys didn't show up, but all the rockers started showing up! It was the most bizarre thing.

The party started ending, and people started trickling out. I have this small studio in my LA house, and I'm kind of a guitar hack and a bass hack on the side—just enough to write songs. And George Lynch went in there, and he's looking at my guitars, and he's like, 'What is this weird thing here?' And I'm like, 'That's a Japanese guitar with an extra five frets.' He's playing it, and then Doug comes in, and he's like, 'What bass is that? It's a weird five-string.' And I'm like, 'It's kind of a Fieldy rip-off, because I write some really weird, detuned songs.'

He's playing that, and I'm looking around the room, and it's just us three. I'm thinking, *This would be a freaking lineup right here if we could ever make it happen.* And then, all of a sudden, George said, 'Man, we ought to do a record someday.' Literally, just as I thought that! And I'm like, 'Yeah, right. You guys are in like, seven bands a piece, and Korn never stops touring. Everyone's so busy.' He goes, 'Let's just schedule some time, see what happens, and write some stuff. Who knows?' Because it seems good on paper, but sometimes when you get together with people—and they're talented and have writing abilities—it doesn't mean that you're going to come up with good tunes. I've done it many times in the past, where you think it's a good idea and you get together with someone, and sometimes, musically you don't get along. But you get along as friends.

George was very persistent. I'll give it up—this project happened because, not that I gave up, but it would be the ultimate dream to do a full record with Doug Pinnick. Are you kidding? That would be beyond a bucket list thing. But the reality was, at that time, we had mass tours going on. Lynch Mob was out, King's X was doing shows, Doug was in like three or four recording projects. It wasn't feasible. And George kept going, 'OK, I looked at the Korn dates, you guys are off this weekend, I'm off this weekend, Doug you're off … ' He was adamant and persistent—he kept calling. And I'm like, 'All right. Let's get together this weekend.' We got together in this faraway house [Sound Mountain] in the Santa Clarita Mountains. It was beautiful, because there's nothing but horse stables. It was away from LA. I hate being in the LA atmosphere when I'm recording. And we went up on this mountain, and, man, it was the coolest thing, because we came in, and the rule of KXM is no one could write anything before—you had to come up with something right on the spot. That's how we did both records.

GEORGE LYNCH Being in KXM is the extension of the idea of me being in King's X. [*Laughs*] *What would King's X be like if I got to be the guitar player?* The only thing is, KXM is a purely improvisational band in the most genuine sense, in that our records are improvised in the studio. We don't have any preconceived song ideas. We don't have preproduction. That's our main rule, and our philosophy behind the band—we are going to create when we are in the studio. We give ourselves a very limited amount of time—which is everywhere from ten days to two weeks. We go live in the studio and woodshed, basically. You have to write a song a day at least—on the spot. And, of course, we add embellishments later, and throughout the process, but we try and keep it as pure as possible and honest as possible. I think that is inspired in part by many other bands that have inspired me throughout the decades—King's X, as well.

TY TABOR

NAOMI'S SOLAR PUMPKIN (1997) AND *MOONFLOWER LANE* (1998)

TY TABOR The title *Naomi's Solar Pumpkin* came from Jay Phebus. We were making fun of album titles, like *Gretchen Goes To Nebraska*—because it was a joke. It was the worst title someone could think of, which made us love it. It was actually just kind of a demo I was making, that I decided to release as a CD—with the idea of using that to try and get a record deal. So I got some digital recording gear and put it in my house, and made it by myself. And then decided to press it up, and it sold really well.

Metal Blade decided they wanted to do a solo album, so I took some of those songs from that album and then several other new songs and made *Moonflower Lane*. It was the first legit label album, but it had versions of some of the songs off of *Naomi* on it. So it turned out to be a nice little bonus that year—for sure.

I don't know if I have a lot of favorites on that album. It is what it is. I was younger, and the way I was writing then, my lyrics and things like that—a lot of times, things like that are embarrassing to me to look back on. It's like an old diary, that's painful to look at. 'I Do' is pretty self-explanatory. It was just where I was at, at that moment—expressing it. Because things were really good at the moment. 'Her Palace' I liked enough to re-record it years later, when I put out a live DVD [2014's *Almost Live From Alien Beans Studio*]. I've always liked that song. It's basically a song about Sam Taylor. 'The Island Sea,' I like it musically. Lyrically, I don't really care for it.

PLATYPUS, WHEN PUS COMES TO SHOVE (1998)

TY TABOR Basically, what was happening around that time was some of the members of Dream Theater were doing solo albums, and John Myung decided he'd like to do something too, while there was a break in time. He talked to Rod Morgenstein, and Rod was into it, and Derek Sherinian was already in the Dream Theater camp, and he was into it. I think they weren't sure who to get for a guitarist. And my old guitar tech, Mark Snyder, happened to be working with Dream Theater at the time, and he suggested me. So they called me one day, to see if I was interested. My first reaction was, 'I'm not sure you have the right guy, because I'm not a *muso* like that. I'm more from the heart, coming from a different angle.' But they convinced me that was exactly what they were looking for, so I said, 'OK. We'll give it a try.' Never in my wildest dreams did I realize they wanted me to be a vocalist. I thought we would be doing instrumental music—even to the point when we started writing music together, I had no idea they wanted me to do vocals until we were in the middle of the project. So it kind of turned into that. We had so much fun doing the album, by the end of it, we were like, 'Man, we really need to keep this going. That was a blast!'

That was some of the funnest stuff I've ever done. For all of us. And that's kind of what founded this band. And we're still together as Jelly Jam [minus Sherinian]. But it all started as just fun—and stayed that way for twenty years.

PLATYPUS, ICE CYCLES (2000)

TY TABOR That was also during the time I was going through all that with the breakup of my marriage. So, it was another extension of that. That whole album is about that, basically—in the same way that *Safety* was. At least for the most part. So it's a depressing album. But at the same time, it was even deeper and heavier than the first one, and we tuned down to B on a lot of songs, and made it like dirge music—some of it. It was an entirely different offering than the first one, and not even related to the first one. But at the same time, we all were extremely proud of it. There was so much work that went into it, I'm very happy with how it came out. Another album I can't listen to lyrically—but I was proud of it.

THE JELLY JAM, *THE JELLY JAM* (2002)

TY TABOR Well, Derek left the band after the second album. And, to make a long story short, I think it was because of a misunderstanding. But the truth is, I'm still friends with Derek, and all is good—I hope we'll do more music together. He's super-fun to work with, and he's a pro. But when he left, we decided, *Well, let's see if we can keep this going with the three of us. And we should probably change the name, because it's going to be different without Derek.* So that's really all the thought that went into it—we just wanted to keep it going, but not call it Platypus, because it really wasn't going to be Platypus without him. He was a huge part of Platypus.

I remember that it *rocked*. [*Laughs*] I remember that when we three came together, things sort of got even heavier. And we started solidifying into more of a focused band at that point, because Platypus was all over the place. And that was kind of the idea of Platypus—the intentional idea of Platypus. It was adventures in all directions. But then we decided to make it more focused—a one type of band kind of thing. And we've sort of been staying on that track ever since—even though we've evolved over the years, and the music has definitely changed. But we're still trying to stay focused to where it sounds like all the songs belong on the same album.

JUGHEAD, *JUGHEAD* (2002)

TY TABOR Another thing of friends calling friends and saying, 'Do you want to do an album?' I called up Derek—this is after he had left Platypus—and said, 'Let's do this.' Actually, it was Derek that called me up first about it, and I said, 'I've got some friends that would be perfect for this.' So we got a hold of Matt and Gregg Bissonette. They were into it, so we just did it.

It was a lot of fun—we were trying to do a 'Foo Fighters meets Fuel meets

The Beatles' kind of thing. The Beatles, but with a little bit heavier stuff. Lots of vocals and adventure. I was really proud of that record, too. I felt like that was a really good record. We get a lot of people who have wanted another Jughead album ever since, but as soon as we released it, the *Archie* people came down on us, and we couldn't sell the album publicly anymore. We couldn't even say the name anymore. So … we just dropped the whole thing.

SAFETY (2002)

TY TABOR *Safety* was me writing an album about the breakup of my marriage. I don't listen to it anymore … I couldn't listen to it *back then*. But it is the single work of my life that gets the most comments from people—that means the most to them. Even this week, I've had people tell me that—it never fails. I meet people that come up—sometimes crying—trying to express how much that album meant to them. So I'm glad I did it, but it was the most painful thing I ever recorded in my life. I can't listen to it. It's always somebody who has something deeply horrible they went through—that album helped them get through. For that reason, I'm very thankful I did it.

When I did the album, I was afraid to even write those kind of lyrics—they were so brutally honest. But, at the same time, I realized that my favorite music from John Lennon is the stuff that he's the most bare on. And I took that encouragement and just said, *Screw it. I'm gonna do it. People can hate it—whatever. I'm just going to do it.* And it turned out being probably the work of my life—as far as people's response and having an influence in their lives.

THE JELLY JAM, 2 (2004)

TY TABOR Every single album you can say the same thing about—we're a bunch of good friends who come together, spend a lot of time eating good food, drinking good wine … we even used to have some really nice cigars at the end of the day. It was like a retreat—a musical retreat—with friends. Every time we come together, we're just happy to be together. It's a fantastic time. It's another chapter of another retreat, and that's the album that came out of it. It was nothing but fun. I have no bad memories of any kind with any of the Jelly Jam stuff. It was always such a joy to make music with these guys. So, that one, we did our best on it, too. It's probably the one most people know and talk about of our albums. It was a lot of people's idea of our best one—until the latest. Everyone seems to think *Profit* is the best one we've ever done. It was another time capsule that's captured from three guys that really love playing together.

ROCK GARDEN (2006)

TY TABOR That's my favorite solo thing I've ever done. *Ever*. Still to this day. After delving into such depression, I just wanted to make a *rock* album. That's what I'm about. I called up an old friend I grew up with who plays drums, and said, 'Hey man, let's just me and you go into the studio and see what happens.' And that's basically what it was.

I played everything on the album except for drums, and my friend, Randy St. John, came in and played drums. It was the album I wanted to make. The first solo album I really wanted to make, that came out the way I wanted it to be. So I'm proud of that one. And it's by far my biggest-selling solo album. It's always the one people talk about—as far as rock music goes.

The song 'Ride'—which is probably the most popular song I've ever written, outside of King's X—is on that album. It's a song about motocross, which is what I was doing at the time. That's all it is—it's a song about the love of racing. 'Pretty Good' is probably the one that has the least heavy meaning to it—it's just a song about rock'n'roll.

XENUPHOBE, *1.0* (2006), *2.0* (2007), AND *DRONE* (2015)

TY TABOR This is something that Wally Farkas and I decided to do, because we're both really big fans of really freaky ambient stuff. Back in the old days, when we were touring together and he was in The Cowboys, we'd go in the back room of the bus, turn the lights off, and—very loudly—put on something like Robert Rich or really freaky stuff, and we just sit there and get into it. Everybody else thought we were insane—nobody else cared, nobody wanted to hear it. But we've always been into that stuff, and how music like that can transport you into strange places—as if you were in a movie or something.

That's what we love about it—you can really get into this stuff, and it can take you places. That's why we call it 'psychoactive music'—it's almost like taking drugs ... without taking drugs. It's like a drug trip with no drugs—making your imagination go places. And that is the idea behind it. Completely experimental, and something that we had never done before but decided to do ourselves.

THE JIBBS, 'BURNS IN THE RAIN' (2008)

TY TABOR It was raising money for some hurricane stuff that had happened in Houston [Hurricane Ike]. We actually recorded the song at my house, using solar-powered and battery-powered stuff, because there was no electricity. And the idea was to record a song like that while the power was shut down after that hurricane. Just the idea of doing it with sun power and wind power, in the middle of a desolate city that had no power for over a week—some areas of the city for over a month. Out where Wally lived, it was about three weeks before he got power. He had trees across his house, fences, and power lines. Houston was just *destroyed*. So, all my friends—because I had solar panels and green power that didn't depend on the grid—would come and hang out at my place at night. One time, Alan Doss was over there, and me and Wally, and we called up Doug, and said, 'Let's do a single.' Wally wrote the music on the spot, and we recorded it by using green power and put it up there to raise a little bit of money to raise pay for some damages.

BALANCE (2008)

TY TABOR Balance was a pretty serious undertaking. I remember it was a lot of work, and I was proud of it, too. Sonically, it's the worst-sounding thing I've probably ever done—and that's the thing that bothers me about it. I didn't master that one—I had another person master it. And that one album, sonically, I can't listen to it. But I love the songs on it. The songs, I felt like there were a lot that went into them that I was proud of at the time.

SOMETHING'S COMING (2010)

TY TABOR That was probably the closest thing to another *Rock Garden* type of album that I've done. It was me wanting to do another rock album—just write whatever was on my mind at the time. A lot of politics on that record. But I was pretty proud of that one, too. And it got the best reception of anything I've done since *Rock Garden*.

TRIP MAGNET (2010)

TY TABOR That's something that's turned out to be—without promotion, and without many people even knowing what it is—a really good-selling record. Apparently, people like to listen to it on airplanes and on long car drives. It turned out to be one of those kinds of albums. And it's still selling, believe it or not. It is right up there, equal at the top of all my sales of my other albums on CDBaby—which is nothing that I would have ever expected, seeing that it's mostly instrumental and different. But it's been a nice surprise for me—that people really love it for some reason. So I actually thought about doing another one. I've even got a whole album recorded that could be another one right now. I'm kind of holding onto it for a while.

THE JELLY JAM, *SHALL WE DESCEND* (2011)

TY TABOR I'm proud of that album. It's the least-known Jelly Jam album, because it was not released by a label, so not as many people are aware of it. But I'm very proud of that one. I felt like it was us getting even more focused, and some of it is the heaviest stuff we've ever done. It was a fun album. It was a good album, we felt. We hope that someday, people will find out about it and we will re-release it on a label, and make it part of a boxed set or something. We would like more people to know about it, because it's an album we are very proud of.

NOBODY WINS WHEN NOBODY PLAYS (2013)

TY TABOR I think some of the songs were strong; other ones, after living with it for a while, I wish I could go back and take them off the album and start over. But you live and learn.

THE JELLY JAM, *PROFIT* (2016)

TY TABOR For that one we decided to go back to a label, so people would know we had done it. So we went with Mascot on that one, and they were really very helpful in every stage. It was fun working with them on it. Especially with the artwork. Mascot are really cool people, and really tried to understand the vision and represent it, and did a really great job of doing so. And, musically, it was pretty adventurous for us.

This one wasn't necessarily the 'big rock album.' This one was like a story that went in different places, and the music needed to emotionally capture the different parts of the story and the places that it was going. So we did approach this one with a different philosophy. And I basically made all of the lyrics into the idea of the story. It's a concept album, and it's the only one I've ever done. It seems to be that people really dig the concept.

ALIEN BEANS (2018)

TY TABOR The latest album is called *Alien Beans*, and it's named after my recording studio. It's a double album, and it's my first album in many years on an actual label. I did two videos, and I just saw the charts this week, and I'm #2 on the 'Heatseekers' chart. So it's doing really well.

The idea behind it originally was to take the hardest-rocking songs from my albums that weren't released on a label and distributed. For years, I have released solo albums through Molken Music, and they weren't distributed in stores, and we didn't really push those records—they were mainly just there for the fans. So it was my manager's idea originally that it would be a good idea to put a best-of thing from that catalogue that never was released on a label, and put it on a label—so people would know about it, and then that would help the entire catalogue.

I talked to Joe O'Brien at Rat Pak about doing that, and that was the original idea—we were just going to put one or two new songs on it, as bonus tracks, and I was going to remix the old stuff and remaster it, to make it sound more modern and up to today's standards. But then I started writing a bunch of new songs, and I kept putting it on hold, saying, 'Well, we can add another new song and have three.' And then it was four … and then it was five … and then I said, 'Let's wait a while. I'm going to keep writing.' And then I made a whole new album, so it could be a double album. And it's released on vinyl, cassette, and everything—like the old days. And with great packaging. It's awesome.

The two songs that we did videos for are the two most straight-ahead rockers of the new songs. One is called 'Freight Train' and one is called 'Johnny Guitar.' I intentionally tried to make them straight-ahead and catchy—trying to do another record similar to *Rock Garden*, which was my favorite album. But I turned up the amps more and made it even more of an aggressive guitar album than *Rock Garden*—some of the tones on the new one are pretty massive.

JERRY GASKILL

COME SOMEWHERE (2004)

JERRY GASKILL I was very proud of that record. And I knew it had to be done. Ty and Doug had done solo records, and I knew I had all this music, I knew I had to make a record, and I knew it was time. I remember we were on tour, and I asked Ty if he would like to make the record with me. I had these demos I had recorded at home, and said, 'I've got this music here for you to listen to.' I remember giving it to Ty, and he went in the back lounge to listen. I sat in the front lounge of the bus, and the whole time I'm there, I'm thinking, *He's going to think it's stupid, he's going to say it was worthless. But he's going to be nice enough to say, 'I think we can do something with it.'* I was going out of my mind, man—thinking how he was going to respond to this music.

So he listens to everything I gave him, he comes back up … and he was so excited! He says, 'Man Jerry, we're going to make every second of this record great. *This is going to be great!*' It was really encouraging. We made the whole record together, just the two of us. And it was a great time. I got to play guitar, I got to sing, I got to play drums—just a great experience, to be able to get all that great music out. And the music on that record is exactly how I wrote it. And just seeing Ty play on it and being excited about the parts, and saying, 'Oh man, that's a cool part! It's badass!' was very exciting. Seeing him do some of my parts—and even having a hard time with them at times—was totally inspiring. Ty made me feel like a guitar player. It was incredible.

LOVE & SCARS (2015)

JERRY GASKILL I made that record with my friend Dan Karkos—he calls himself D.A. Karkos. We were in the middle of making it, and he said, 'Hey.

You've got to come up with a title, man.' I was driving around in my car one day, and it just hit me, *I'm going to call it King Of Hearts*. It sounded right to me. But even when I thought it … there was something that wasn't 100 percent right about it. But I didn't know what else to do.

I mentioned it to Joe O'Brien from Rat Pak Records, who was putting the record out. And he said, 'Yeah, we can call it that if you want. But I think there are other people who have used that before.' I looked up *King Of Hearts*, and I saw this one record of this rap guy—it was like a really silly kind of a rap thing to me. And it was called *King Of Hearts*. And I thought, *I cannot allow myself to be somehow associated with that*. Nothing against this person—it just didn't feel like *me*.

I was taking a shower one day, I was looking in the mirror, and all I saw were all these scars on my chest, from top to bottom. And the word 'scars' came into my mind. I thought, *Ah. We're going to have to use 'scars' in the title*. I got in the shower, and the word 'love' came to me. And I thought, *Love & Scars … that's perfect!* That's how the title came about.

On *Come Somewhere*, all the songs are exactly as I wrote them—with Ty embellishing the things he did with guitar and bass and sounds and whatever. But the songs and the structure of the songs are exactly as I wrote them—chords and everything. But on the *Love & Scars* record, I did everything with Dan. Whatever song I had, I brought to him, and he put himself into it. He would add parts, add choruses, change verses a little. Some songs were exactly as I wrote them, but it was a total collaboration—between Dan and me, as far as songwriting and everything. That's the big difference.

26 TODAY

KING'S X IN THE MODERN AGE.

JERRY GASKILL I'm not surviving on the money King's X makes. It's a very humbling thing—and it's a beautiful thing, too—but I actually have a job with a medical education company, called MedForce. It's a speaker's bureau. They set up meetings for doctors to talk about certain drugs. It's a pharmaceutical thing—working with Johnson & Johnson, and Janssen. I go to work every day—at the same place that my wife works. And it's like the most ideal possible situation—they let me come and go as I need, they provide me insurance, they give me paid vacation time, and I'm on salary. And I enjoy going there. I love the work. Without that, I'd have to really, really, really hustle and struggle. And I probably wouldn't have the things I have right now—just with the money from King's X. But I play around town a bit, and I've met some really great musicians since I've moved here. I make a little bit of money that way, too. But I'm very comfortable, man. Very comfortable living the way I live now. I don't struggle, I don't have to hustle, and I can still do whatever I have to do.

If I have to take a month off to make a record, I can take a month off, and still know that I am going to have income when that's over. So, it's kind of like an ideal situation. It's humbling to think I have a job, though. [*Laughs*] Because there's part of me that thought, *I will never have to work again.* And I moved to New Jersey from Houston, thinking, *This is going to be great! I'm going to be near New York—all kinds of things are going to open up for me.* And *nothing happened*, man. I tried and tried, and nothing was happening, and I started to freak out because I had nothing coming in. And finally, where my wife works, they said, 'Hey, do you want to come in and help us a little bit?' I said, 'Sure, I'll come in. I'll make a few extra dollars.' And I ended up staying. I've been there twelve years now, and I'm almost like one of the greatest assets to the company. [*Laughs*] That's what they tell me. It's been great. I'm very thankful.

DOUG PINNICK My personal income comes from KXM, Grinder Blues, Supershine, Tres Mts., Pinnick Gales Pridgen, guest appearances, etcetera. So, doing a side project could pay for a few months of bills, or help me catch up with the late bills. Moving to LA, I knew that was what I had to do. I sold my house three years after I moved to LA. I went there to hook up with people who wanted to do a project and make a living.

I moved out to LA about six years ago. LA and Houston are like night and day. LA is where the way of life is so driven to move forward, and do something with passion. Everybody is ready to go. Everybody out here knows that they're here to make music or do their art. That's what I love. We all realize we need each other. It's who you know in LA—totally. If your stuff is the cream of the crop, the doors always open, because there's always someone who notices and would open a small door, leading to a bigger one. And, of course, there are some really big assholes there, too. [*Laughs*]

Back in Texas, really great musicians get caught up in the domestic life. It's difficult to make music when you've got day jobs and kids. A lot of the musicians that I used to hang out with can't hang out anymore. They're taking care of families and working. You say, 'Let's jam,' and you've got to wait a week before they have a babysitter and get permission from their wife or whatever. I looked around and thought, *I'm going nowhere here, and there's no one here that has that drive anymore.* So I moved to LA. My side projects and solo stuff have been very good for my career. Plus, having a signature bass [Schecter dUg Pinnick Baron-H Bass], amp [Tech 21 dUg Pinnick Signature], and pedal [Tech 21 DP-3X dUg Pinnick Signature] keeps me busy, also.

TY TABOR Alien Beans does mastering most of the time. I did two mastering sessions yesterday, and I also do all my solo stuff out of there, and any of my side projects I work on. The Jelly Jam, half of those albums are always done at Alien Beans. So I'm always busy in there with albums and projects. Constantly.

JERRY GASKILL Basically, we make our money from touring. And a lot of it is from the merch that we sell on tour. And we get small, small ASCAP checks—

every quarter—from all the records. Whatever is being played wherever at that time, or the time distribution happens. So there is very little that comes through that. And there is no money made through royalties, because we never sold enough records to actually pay anything back, to make money off of that.

TY TABOR When it comes to making albums, I think the reality for the large majority of these people to make albums is, they assume the only money they're ever going to see off their album is whatever their album budget advance is. Because that happens to be the truth for the huge majority of all artists. You have to be selling *millions* of albums to actually be seeing money for your albums. And, if you're selling millions of albums, you don't really need the album sales anyway—you're doing way more money in merch and live shows than you are going to get for your albums. But you have to be in the big, big numbers to be able to recoup.

The way it works is … I'm not going to say these are our numbers, our numbers were at times way bigger than this, but for ease of understanding—say you get $100,000 to make an album. OK, well that's $100,000 immediately you're in debt to the label. You're not in debt in the same way as a bank loan—for instance, if you lose your deal or get dropped you don't still owe them the money. They just lose their money.

But the way they get to claim the loss of money, everything works for the benefit of the label. Because the label actually makes the money back very quickly. For instance, say we sold 100,000 albums, and we had a $100,000 advance for the album; the label has collected anywhere from $6.50 to $7.50 to $8.00 per sale. So, they have already way, way made their money back—times several times, with your 100,000 sales. But what they credit you for, first of all, they take money off the top for packaging deductions, take money off the top for the returns, so in case they overstock albums and they get returned, you get charged for everything—the printing of the albums, you get charged for whatever it costs for your product being out there. Including any ads they do—anything they do that costs anything, all gets stacked on top of that advance for what you owe for that album.

A standard deal is about 75 cents per $8.00, or whatever they collect, after the packaging deductions and all that stuff, which lowers it to less than that. Over a period of time—depending on the deal, maybe a year or a year and a half—you are supposed to get credited back any of the packaging deductions and stuff that were actually spent or were supposed to happen. But it's nothing. So, basically, at the point that the record label has sold 100,000 albums, they have pocketed a bare minimum of $650,000, but it's going to be more than that, because that's the bare minimum they're going to get. They are only crediting you back probably about $60,000 out of the $650,000 they've taken.

That's the general thing. We would still continue to have to sell a whole lot more albums—way, way more into their over-ten-times profit area—before we even get considered as recouped as even. And then, once we're even, we're still getting pennies on the dollar. So, unless you're selling millions, it's not going to amount to anything—your record sales. Your advance is your everything. We'll never see *a penny* for the first five or six King's X albums—unless they get into the millions of sales. We'll never ever see a penny for any of that.

IN 2015, METAL BLADE BEGAN REISSUING
KING'S X'S EARLY ALBUMS ON VINYL.

BRIAN SLAGEL We have a really good relationship with Warners, where we reissued a bunch of vinyl out of their catalogue. It's so weird to go back now, with vinyl being so big, and reissuing all the classic albums that came out in the late 80s and putting them out on vinyl. But we went back, and I think we put out every one of the Atlantic records of King's X on vinyl over the course of time. And we're working on CD reissues as well.

JERRY GASKILL We are planning on making a new record. We're talking about it, we're pursuing it, and, most likely, it's going to happen.

DOUG PINNICK I've got years of old tunes on a hard drive. There's never a shortage of song ideas and complete songs to make King's X songs and side projects.

IN 2016, KING'S X TOOK PART IN KISS KRUISE VI, A MUSICAL FESTIVAL ON
A CRUISE SHIP SAILING BETWEEN MIAMI AND THE CAYMAN ISLANDS.

JERRY GASKILL The Kiss Kruise was incredible. I loved it. You want to hear about my favorite part of the Kiss Kruise? Ty, Doug, and I were all hanging out with Gene Simmons. We were talking to him, and he was telling us stories, funny things—talking about religion and different things. At one point, Gene was saying something like, 'Well, if God is a God of love, then why does he allow bad things to happen? I'd like to sit down and ask him some questions.' And I said, 'Well Gene, I would venture to say, if we were talking to God, he'd probably have some really good things to say.' He looks at me, and says, 'You *are* talking to God.' [*Laughs*] It was perfect—it was so 'Gene.'

GUNTER FORD We've been working on trying to raise their profile by doing 'fly-ins' in the last few years. It's something I picked up from the band Kansas, when we did some shows with them, after Jerry's heart attack. We wanted to test going out and doing short sets. And Kansas only does weekends. It really works for them—they fly in, they do a weekend, they go home. We didn't know what Jerry ultimately could do, so we started doing these weekends. And that really allowed us to focus on the markets—Texas and the northeast—where they're really strong. And that, I think, raises the profile, because if you're playing Thursday, Friday, and Saturday, you're playing the best nights of the week. And that means there's more people there, more people to talk about it, and their audience is older, so the word-of-mouth starts to grow. And I think we put them into better venues—like small theaters—and all that helped to create a better fan experience. There seems to be more interest.

ALEXANDER FORD By and large, we end up doing a lot of breakfasts or brunches, because the time of day we get out is about noon. So, a lot of times, we're eating in Middle America or different parts of the country, so we end up in Denny's and Bob Evans a lot of times, more than anywhere else. For whatever reason, we've got probably hundreds of photos of the guys sitting down for breakfast at Denny's or Bob Evans. Whenever we wake up in the morning, it's like, flip a coin, 'Where are we going? Denny's or Bob Evans?' Or once in a while, we'll go to Cracker Barrel. Those are the 'big three' of our places to go.

Our run that we had in Europe in the summer of 2017 was a phenomenal run. Every show was pretty much sold out, and all the festivals that we played were phenomenal. And I think the best moment of the entire run in Europe was a festival in Spain that we played, called the Azkena Festival. That was absolutely insane. I've never seen that amount of people. Right before we played, Cheap Trick was playing, and the area around us—there were two main stages—and their main stage, the amount of people that were there in front of them was about three-quarters full of the max capacity. And then we played right after that, and the *entire place* was watching us. And then, after we finished, John Fogerty went on, and everybody was there to see Fogerty, but it wasn't nearly as full as it was when we were playing. It was like we happened to hit this happy window, where there was a sea of people.

I have never seen those many people screaming King's X as loud as they possibly could. It harkened back, in a way, to the Woodstock performance that they had, when the sun was setting and they hit the stage at that perfect moment. It was very reminiscent of that—the sun was kind of setting as we were playing, and the whole entire festival was watching them and going nuts. They stole the show. Without question.

Jerry made some comments about the European tour—in a joking, tongue-in-cheek way. He said, 'Guess what? I'm never doing this shit again!' And the second comment was, 'I'm not complainin', I'm just sayin''—that was his mantra for the whole trip. And, also, 'That festival shit and doing all that touring in a bus? That's a young man's game ... and I ain't fucking young.' [*Laughs*] But then, when they all came back and saw what they made from that particular tour, they were all like, *When can we go again?!*

27 LEGACY

DOUG PINNICK I've heard so much about how we've influenced people from their own mouths—musically, spiritually, humanly, in every way you can imagine. We've gotten unbelievable compliments that I think anyone would only dream of getting. It's overwhelming. It's a mind-fuck for me, though—I've been making music in some way all my life, and I don't remember the first time I sang in front of a crowd of people, so there's no gauge of understanding what people see and hear. It's like looking in a mirror and seeing your face all your life. You *have* seen it all your life—it's just your face. But the irony of it is that looking around at all these people that have said that we have influenced them or have looked up to us, or people who are alive and not dead because of something we said in a song or in an interview ... we still didn't sell any records.

I still live from month to month. And King's X, in a business sense, doesn't matter. We never sold even a tenth of the music that all the other bands sold that borrowed from us. And, again, I can't say that we originated anything, really, because we borrowed from people to become what we are. Soundgarden's *Ultramega OK* was released the same year as *Out Of The Silent Planet*, and the intro to their album and the first song ['Flower'] was eerily very similar to the intro and first song on our album ['In The New Age']. It's so weird!

I know we influenced lots of musicians because they told me all the time. But after those first two records came out, there was a definite change in the overall music scene around world. I feel like we were in the food chain. It overwhelms me when musicians tell me they were trying to imitate an aspect of King's X. And, when I hear it in a song, it makes me feel special. I'll go to a big show somewhere and hear something reminiscent of King's X, and I smile. Imitation is the highest form of flattery.

DEVIN TOWNSEND Yes. Clearly. But, I think, within a real niche group of people. But that group of people are surprisingly varied in terms of that reach. You talk to Pantera—or you talk to Metallica or any of these bands that maybe would seem unlikely to have appreciated King's X—and they are all rabidly and very clearly passionate about the band. And I think that says volumes, as well. Not only about King's X, but also about the genre in general. Like, how much saying things that mean something to you, and being decent people—fundamentally, I'm not saying that they're going out of their way to be preachy, even when they were doing sort of more religious-themed music—but the read of that is, the people that do consider them influential are successful in a lot of ways. Like, ZZ Top, and all these people that you hear talk about King's X with these revered tones, is a testament to the throw that their influence has, at least.

MICK MARS They certainly are to me. I don't really hang out with a lot of musicians, but everyone that I've talked to really likes King's X. My son is forty-six, and he loves them, too. There are a lot of people that do like them—aside from musicians.

KIP WINGER I could say that, from the day their first record came out, they heavily influenced us, and the bands around us—for many generations. Because I talk to musicians when I'm on tour, and they're always into this subject matter.

ROD MORGENSTEIN When Winger had its first album out [in 1988], and we were touring around the United States, the guys in the band were such fans of King's X. So, quite often, King's X music would be playing in the bus.

BUMBLEFOOT They totally influenced me. Throughout all those years—and even now—they're still an emotional go-to, when I'm writing. They seem to have the vocabulary for a lot of things I want to say. I will just think of some of their three-part harmonies that they're doing over certain chord changes, and just where they put the space to create a groove with the chords and everything. They have influenced so many, and I am proudly one of them.

BILLY SHEEHAN I think a lot of bands—and the whole Seattle scene—definitely were supremely influenced by the tonalities of King's X.

NUNO BETTENCOURT I don't like to assume and give credit to what they've done and what they haven't done—because I only know what they've done to me. But I would go out on a limb saying that detuned sound with those harmonies, if it didn't influence Alice In Chains, I would be surprised. It was almost like they were doing that before anybody else—that deep, down-tuned … and they were doing it darker, but with harmonies and two singers. I love Alice In Chains and what they did—and they sound nothing like King's X, per se. But I feel like from an *approach* perspective, maybe an idea went off— *maybe*—in Alice's heads. One of the first bands we toured with nationally was Alice In Chains, and they had their own pocket. But they reminded me of the approach of the darker, harmonized approach … that they *both* did.

DOUG PINNICK I got to know Alice In Chains from the beginning—even before they had a record deal. They are extremely cool guys. Layne told me my vocal style was his inspiration for the chorus of 'Rain When I Die.' And the first Pearl Jam album, my name is the first one on the thank you page. That was so awesome! Those guys are very inspiring—to me, also. I remember I was telling Jerry Cantrell how much Jerry and I used to play Alice In Chains back in the day, and he told me how much they played King's X. It was kind of fun to know that all of the bands were playing each other's music, and listening to it. I talked to Billy Corgan—I just met him at a show a while ago. He says, 'Dude, you guys were the first band to drop-D tune. When we heard that, we said, *Let's do that.*' He said that they all were listening to us back then. I was playing the shit out of *Gish* back then, and I thought those bands didn't like us.

BILLY CORGAN [Smashing Pumpkins singer, guitarist] *Really* ahead of their time. If you listen to the music that followed, they really figured things out that took many bands ten more years to figure out. King's X was always a bit of a weird thing because the influences were kind of unconventional. It's like that weird mix of heaviness, but also kind of bluesy-ness. And, obviously, Doug's singing was fantastic, but he's not like your normal 'rock singer' type of guy. The songs were kind of quirky at times—a bit of an acquired taste—but certainly super-proficient, and a great live band. And, really, probably five years too early. A band that probably, if they had come out in the mid 90s, would have enjoyed a lot more success than they did.

DOUG PINNICK Every time I ran into Layne Staley, we always got drunk. The first time I met him, they were opening for Extreme in a little teeny club that was, like, fifty people. The stage was so low that you couldn't even see the stage. After they got done playing, I sat at the bar with Layne, and we proceeded to get drunk and bond. And then, after that, they came to Houston again to play, and I saw them, hung out, and Jerry played me 'Rooster' before it was even recorded on an album, and Layne came in and said he had been clean and sober for a month. He asked me if I was proud of him. He treated me like a big brother. Such a beautiful spirit.

The next time I saw him was at Lollapalooza, and he said, 'Let's go get drunk!' We talked and drank. That's my brief life with Layne—we'd run into each other, we'd talk about really deep stuff. We talked about real life things— he talked about his drug problem and all that stuff, because he didn't want to be that way at all. And Jerry is a good friend—he would come to see us and hang out on the bus with us. Good guys. Sean [Kinney], the drummer—I remember came to see us one time in Cincinnati, and he was standing on the floor, and kept screaming 'Goldilox!' or something. He was very boisterous about us playing. So, a song ended, and he started screaming, 'Do "Goldilox"!' And I said to the kids around him, '*That's the drummer for Alice In Chains,*' and about thirty kids turned around and asked him for his autograph. He looked at me, screaming, 'FUCK YOU! FUCK YOU! FUCK YOU!' [*Laughs*]

And I loved Chris Cornell. I remember I went to see Soundgarden at Lollapalooza in Houston, and I was standing on the side of the stage, and I really didn't know him that well at the time, but he looked over and saw me over there, and walked off to the side of the stage and kissed me on the lips, and then went back out onstage and started singing! I got a friend that took pictures of the whole thing. Chris was a beautiful human being—he kissed me smack on the lips every time we would see each other. We had always talked about [possibly doing an album together].

Chris was a friend of mine. We had a really cool relationship—we loved each other. We didn't talk too much about anything in particular, but we had a mutual admiration for each other. And when we would talk, it would be really great conversations. One time, we had a conversation while they were making *Superunknown* and we were making *Dogman*, and we were laughing about how high we sang all the time, and that we didn't have anywhere to go—we couldn't go any higher. We both agreed that we're both baritones, and we didn't need to be singing that high anymore. So we both made a little pact, and we agreed to sing lower on our records. And, as a result of it, you got 'Black Hole Sun' and 'Flies And Blue Skies,' and both albums had a definite change in vocal attitude. He said, 'Let's just croon on our records,' and I said, 'Yeah! Let's do that!' I think we accomplished that.

We both had our childhood issues, so I think we related with each other. But we never talked about it personally, in depth. We were big fans of each other's voice, also. I feel like the two of us were on the same road when it came to songwriting, and we were always trying new guitar tunings. I was shocked about his death. I think about him all the time. He's my friend, and that's how I will remember him.

ALAIN JOHANNES Chris Cornell I think invited Doug up to sing. I'm trying to remember if it was Lollapalooza or something. And Chris was blown away by his voice. He said, 'That guy is a *real singer*.' Chris was a huge fan of his voice. And Doug came up and sang with Chris—with Soundgarden, it must have been. It would have been around '92, because Eleven was already touring with Soundgarden back then.

KIM THAYIL Chris spoke highly of King's X. I think I had seen a few King's X videos at that time on MTV, on *Headbangers Ball*, and Chris was like, 'I just met this guy from King's X. What a nice guy! *He's a good singer*.' I remember Chris was emphasizing the singing, and the fact that Doug was really friendly. And he took me and introduced me to him. At that time, I didn't know much about King's X—other than catching a video or two—but Chris had one of the records … or a cassette. Back then, a lot of us had cassettes—that's what worked when we were in the van, and then, later on, a tour bus. But that's my primary memory—that Chris was hyping the band to me, both as talented musicians and really friendly, amiable people.

JEFF AMENT I think if you were a band around that time and you respected musicianship and people's craft, I don't know how you could look back on that time and not say, 'Wow, King's X was really good.' There could be people that maybe it wasn't their cup of tea, but I don't know how you couldn't respect it.

They were so 'pro'—such good singers; live they were so tight and so powerful. Jerry's style as a drummer was super, super-unique. His drums were parts—it wasn't like he was just playing a backbeat. They were, like, *drum riffs*. There was so much about that band that made them unique and interesting. And all three guys were pretty critical to the originality of how they sounded. I mean, nobody sounds like them … Galactic Cowboys—who came out of that scene— sounded like them a little bit. And I think they were veteran musicians by the time that they started making records. They had all been playing a lot and, by the time that they made *Faith Hope Love*, they were crushing it musically.

DOUG PINNICK I can't forget about Pantera. So many late-night talks with Dime in his limo after a Dallas King's X show. It was some of the best times of hanging with great people who were in great bands. Also, I was in Rex's wedding procession.

REX BROWN There are tons of bands that try and copy that formula, but that just didn't do it. If you try and culminate the sound they were trying to go for, you know that they were Rush fans. As a three-piece, you know that they were Cream fans. They went through this Christian thing, and that may have been good or bad—whatever you want to call it. Maybe one guy was pushing for the Christian thing while the other guys weren't. That may have had something to do with a little bit of controversy. Which I don't really give a fuck about—it's all about the music, to me. It's a shame that they never made it.

And Doug is still the nicest, sweetest guy. Every time I see him, I kiss the son of a bitch! Because I love him. He's just one of those dudes. And I know the whole story that he's gay—it has nothing to do with that. That's just what we do—it's a Texas thing, man. If you got somebody that you're really close to, yes, you do kiss them on the cheek or mouth or whatever. It has nothing to do with your sexuality—it's just love. Doug has always been a constant in my life. Everything he does, I'm behind 100 percent. It's this never-ending story with me about King's X. It's just instilled. These guys were definitely influential about us getting out of Texas.

RITA HANEY There wasn't a time King's X came through that we didn't go see a show. Even if we had been up doing something else and we heard about it, *boom*, we'd rent a car or have somebody drive us if none of us were able to drive. But we always made the show whenever he was off the road. Darrell saw King's X *a lot* of times. I would say probably of all the bands that he'd seen, King's X is probably up in the top three that he'd seen the most. But always hanging out, smoking, telling stories, listening to tunes, and jamming together—they always did that afterward.

MIKE PORTNOY My favorite 'King's X spawn' would be the Galactic Cowboys. I was—and am—a huge Galactic Cowboys fan, and I took them out with Dream Theater in '93. To this day, I still remain good friends with the guys. But they came out right after King's X, and they came from the same manager/producer, Sam Taylor. So, they were another 'Sam Taylor band.' I immediately fell in love with their music, because they took the King's X thing and then went even heavier. They were mixing in a lot more Pantera riffs with these Beatle harmonies. So they would probably be my favorite of the bands that have been influenced by King's X, and have come in their wake.

GEORGE LYNCH Without a doubt. Absolutely. I think, in the historical rearview, that's what they'll be known for—as a band that inspired other musicians to go on to do better things.

BILLY SHEEHAN I remember when I heard the song 'Dr. Feelgood' by Mötley Crüe, I was very upset. I was like, 'Wait a minute!' I thought the intro was a total lift of King's X—which bothered me quite a bit. I have great respect for the guys in Mötley Crüe, they're nice guys, but I don't happen to be a fan of the band—no offense intended or implied. So, when I heard that, I was a little bit upset. I heard it, and thought, *Oh, great, a new King's X song ... oh, shit!* So, a lot of guys, like anything—when Van Halen came out, everybody was trying to do Van Halen.

RICHARD CHRISTY For me, personally, with my band Charred Walls Of The Damned, what I always tell Jason [Suecof]—who is our guitar player and he records our band and engineers—'We've got to get that King's X bass sound.' [*Laughs*] That's the thing I always dream of. And luckily, in Charred Walls Of The Damned, we have Steve Di Giorgio playing bass. And he's an incredible bass player. So my dream was always to blend Steve's playing with Doug's bass sound. I think on our newest album, *Creatures Watching Over The Dead*, we've finally kind of got that mix and that sound.

JERRY GASKILL It's a funny thing, because it seems as though almost every musician that's out there—whether it be in country music or rock music, everybody I meet seems to be a really big fan of King's X. It's flattering. I'm honored by it. I'm always taken aback a little. But it seems as though it's almost everybody. It seems as though, whenever we meet somebody, they're excited about King's X. Just the other night, I went and saw this band called Seether. Our old light guy is doing lights for them, and he invited me out to the show. And their drummer [John Humphrey] was one of the most inspiring drummers I've seen in a long, long time. And when I was watching him, I felt like what people say they feel like when they watch me. Which is kind of a weird thing. But that's what I felt—I could not keep my eyes off of him. We got to hang out afterward, and he's, like, the biggest King's X fan. And I'm an inspiration to him. It's mind-boggling to me, sometimes.

It's a funny thing, because I have friends that I hang out with—musicians or non-musicians—and I don't even know if they know who I am or what I do sometimes. Then, if they've had a few drinks, all of a sudden … all these King's X stories come out. [*Laughs*] It happens over and over. There is a drummer, Curt Bisquera, who is one of those drummers that nobody knows the name of, but he plays with everybody. You've probably heard him on records all over the place. But he actually called me one day, and told me he just listened to the *Dogman* record, and he was so excited. At one point, he said, 'Man, I love you so much—*I want to drink your bathwater!*' [*Laughs*] That's how people get—they almost get beside themselves at times, with excitement. Almost like they're going to fall over or something. And I don't necessarily understand, because I know what I do—I know my limits—but I'm always honored. It's always flattering.

DOUG PINNICK I just heard that there's a King's X tribute band *in India*!

TY TABOR It's kind of what keeps us going. It's the kind of thing that we've always been honored by. Because we weren't exactly setting records *selling* records—we were watching everybody around us that we've ever known get rich, pretty much … except for us. So, the one thing that allowed us to hold on and keep doing this for so long was the encouragement of everybody in the industry—from artists that we admired and looked up to, and friends of ours that expressed that we had a huge impact on them as musicians. And that kind of stuff makes you feel legitimized. Because, normally, you look at record sales to feel legitimized, I think. I know that's what we thought at first. But to have the kind of accolades and support and friendship from people in the industry at the highest level, that's been our legitimacy. That's what made us feel like, 'OK, maybe what we're doing matters,' and helped us hang in there.

RICHARD CHRISTY It's so cool that the universe worked out that those three guys met each other, came together, and made this 'musical music'—that is going to live on forever.

THE SIXTY-FOUR-THOUSAND-DOLLAR QUESTION: WHY DIDN'T KING'S X BREAK THROUGH MASSIVELY?

DOUG PINNICK I've thought about this from the beginning. I really don't know. I've come up with a hundred scenarios, and it seems like everyone has an opinion. But I look at it like this—when Coke introduces a new flavor, promotes it just about every way possible, puts millions of dollars in promotion, puts it on the shelf … and only very few buy it. They don't hate it—it just tastes a little weird. So, the company will stop selling it. Or, it ends up in a small 'ma and pa' store— for the small amount of people who are addicted to it. It's all about the taste.

Also, we always restrained ourselves from truly expressing who we really were as people back then. We had many Christian family members and friends who we didn't want to offend. They would not understand. I remember Jay's mom came to a show, and she's a sweet, beautiful, old lady. I love her. But Jay asked me not to say 'fuck' from the stage—because she was Christian and wouldn't understand. So we had to deal with things like that. Somehow, we finally later became more relaxed about everything. But back in the Sam Taylor days, especially, we came off as an uptight, pretentious band.

I remember talking to Pantera and other bands about this backstage at their shows. They couldn't understand why we wouldn't do certain things in public. It made us look hypocritical to them, at times. Jeff Ament said to me, 'Rock'n'roll was made to let go, and not be afraid to be exactly who we are.' I'm not talking about 'newsworthy' antics. Just having a drink in your hand at a club was a no-no. And God forbid anyone knowing we smoked weed. Obviously, we're not like that anymore. We let our hair down in public these days. [*Laughs*]

WALLY FARKAS Back then, they were poised to be 'the next U2'—which I think is what the UK press called them—and they're being called 'amazing' and 'wonderful' … and they're getting the electricity turned off in their house. That kind of stuff, it's like, 'What the fuck?'

BILLY CORGAN I think they were just too early. If you think about the music that was being made when they came out, there was almost nothing you could compare it to. I mean, Prong was kind of doing some similar things, and Prong—another band way ahead of its time. Prong was Pantera *before* Pantera—that sort of aggression on the low-end of the guitar.

King's X had similar sorts of things—obviously not as heavy, but kind of a similar approach. They were just ahead of their time. There was no cultural context for them to exist in. When the Smashing Pumpkins started putting out records in '91, there were *seven* alternative stations in America, and the rest were college stations. So, how many commercial alternative stations were there in 1988 or 1989? They were just too ahead of their time.

KIP WINGER Maybe they came too early. It might have been that they were just ahead of their time—that happens to a lot of artists that are ahead of their time, where they just miss it by a few years. It's unfortunate, because they deserved it more than anybody did to be extremely successful—not only on just the personal talent of each individual member, but the collective sound. And the fan base of musicians and fans reflects the idea that they should have been really huge, because there is nobody you'll ever meet going, 'Those guys suck.' *Everyone* you talk to is a King's X fan. I've never met anybody that isn't. The other key element for me was, they were a muso band, and really inspired other musicians. That was a really important point. And, back then, you needed that one song to break you through—more than you do now.

MATT PINFIELD I think it had to do with timing more than anything. They deserved to break through commercially, but one of the things that I've noticed is, if there is a band that already has some proven success, and they're more fashionable at the time, the record label will concentrate on the things that are on the lowest branch on the tree—the easiest to grab. The easiest song to get on the air. Whatever they can help muster up the charts, that's what they'll do. And that's, I think, one of the reasons. They were never quite the priority they deserved to be at the label.

Their label was probably waiting for them to bring it to a different level. And I feel they did on those early records, but I feel like they got lost in the rush of some of the other more fashionable, successful bands—with swagger, sexy lead singers. Where it worked, ultimately, for Metallica, for King's X, it didn't. But they have the same kind of thing—they weren't trying to fit into any specific genre or strain of rock'n'roll.

I feel that they really did their thing. And I think that probably has a lot to do with the reasoning, because when you do your own thing, you can go to sleep at night saying, 'Hey. This was real. This is actually *me*. I have nothing to be ashamed about or be sorry for.' And I think that's one of the things that is cool about that band. But, yes, they didn't get the push they deserved. I feel the label had other priorities, and because of the workings of labels, timing is everything.

It's whether you have a champion at the label, whether your A&R guy has been fired or your marketing manager all of a sudden is no longer on your project and went to work for a competitor, and then you're at the mercy of who's there, who didn't bring you in or wasn't there at the beginning, and you're not already a proven entity for that label. Then what happens is, a lot of times, they get lost. Which is a shame. There are so many deciding factors that are involved in the success of an artist. Let's face it—rock'n'roll, whatever is 'pop' at that moment and is making the loudest noise is what the label will attend to. All you can hope for is strides of being on the trajectory going upward. Even if it's in small steps, that's what it comes down to.

DEVIN TOWNSEND I think that maybe, had it been a few years prior … a lot of time, people say it was too early, like they were ahead of their time. Well, maybe had it been a few years prior—where people weren't as interested in piercings and neck tattoos and all that sort of shit that was happening in the early 90s— perhaps that would have been the way that they would have found success. But, again, that's why I like them. [*Laughs*] I like them because they seemed honest, decent people. And they had no competition at that time—in terms of that sort of category. I remember the Galactic Cowboys came out, and it was the same producer and a similar sort of aesthetic. And I remember listening to it, going, 'Why doesn't this do anything for me?' It was the *intention* with them. And I think that was really cool.

It's a combination of circumstance, luck, and just the way the wind blows, right? I remember talking to Doug about the Woodstock performance that they had done, and he had lamented that the way that he approached it was not the way he would have had he done it again. And there was maybe a type of idealism that I really appreciated about the band, that maybe fell on deaf ears on a cynical audience, in general. Because, as esoteric as it is and was—and as rocking as it was—it never really had sharp edges, in a sense. But because it was involved with the scene that was getting sharper and sharper right about that time—like, the amount of bands like Alice In Chains, and drugs, and Jane's Addiction, and the whole Lollapalooza thing—all those bands were really, like, personally, liabilities. And even looking back in time, you see the amount of them that are dead now … I mean, that's just what it is. King's X were nice people, and it's like you heard that in the music—and you heard that in the delivery and the intention.

JEFF AMENT I go back to the thing where they were right at the crux of music changing pretty drastically at that point. As the 80s ramped up and got toward the late 80s, it was sort of all heavy rock in excess. And, not that they were that sort of a band, but I think because they were on Megaforce, and because of the bands that they toured with, and they were playing songs in drop-C or drop-C-sharp, I think they were more 'heavy metal' and less 'punk,' and if you didn't have a little bit of that punk thing going into the 90s, it was a tough slog. Because, at that time, it was either Mariah Carey and Billy Ray Cyrus or it was … Nirvana and us. [*Laughs*] There was kind of nothing in the middle.

The bands that were big in 1989, 1990—whether it was Mötley Crüe or whatever—they had a rough go for a few years. And there are probably a bunch of other things—bands they toured with, how management presented them. The video world at that time was awful, and all of us got swept up in it. I think Pearl Jam did a pretty good job of saying, 'We're *not* going to spend $400,000 on a shitty video we have zero control over, and somebody at the record label is pulling the strings, and they're trying to take you out of your natural box and put you in this other box.' I don't remember the King's X videos, but they were kind of goofy—and they weren't really a goofy band. Their music was pretty dark, and the lyrics were pretty dark. I think maybe they got misrepresented from the video standpoint—at least in my view.

CHARLIE BENANTE I can never understand what makes one thing not sell, and then what makes a big piece of shit sell. To this day, it still boggles the mind— why people vote for somebody when they know it's a piece of shit. So, I don't know if it was a visual thing, that maybe people just heard the music and loved it, and then went to see the band—maybe it was a visual thing. Maybe there wasn't something that connected. I don't know. Because, for me, I was never brought up like that. If I loved the music, I didn't care what the band looked like. That was it—they got me.

REX BROWN Doug just said this recently in an interview—it's always been a struggle being a black man and lead vocalist in a rock band. He even said it back then. It wasn't something that crossed my mind. It doesn't matter if you're black, white, green—to me, you're a musician, number one. I didn't look at Doug any differently than anybody.

ROBERT DeLEO I think we should also touch upon … I'm sure Doug has maybe experienced this—with race. It's funny to me to think about the guy who kind of started rock'n'roll and played guitar was Chuck Berry. He was a black man. There's not many black dudes who play guitar now. And a black guy leading a band, that plays rock'n'roll … I don't know if the public really gets their head around that. It's such a simple thing to get your head around, because with Chuck Berry, that's where it all originated from. And to have someone like Doug fronting that band and singing, *it's perfect*. It's musically perfect.

MICK MARS You want me to be really honest? They didn't have the right management. That's my opinion. I know they could have been pushed harder and promoted more, in-your-face more, done a lot more stuff. If I was their manager, those guys would be *exhausted*—doing early morning TV stuff. Like, we did *Regis*. I'd have them on morning shows, I'd have them on wherever I could put them on—late-night talk shows. I would have pushed the hell right out of those guys. If I was their manager, this is how I'd think. I don't think their manager did enough for them. And I don't know him, and I don't want to talk bad about him. But in my own feeling, I felt that he could have done more for them.

JON ZAZULA .Sometimes, the world isn't made for an iPhone. That detuning was very strange. Doug's spiritual voice was very strange. The Beatle harmonies were so good that you wanted to hate them—if you were trying to be The Beatles and you were a musician all your life! They were in their own world. There's nothing like them. *Still today*.

MARSHA ZAZULA When you think back, once we left Atlantic, that label laid down on them. They kind of got put them in that 'catch 22'—no good label support. And, if you don't have good label support, you don't have tour support, and you can't get into the upper echelon as easily as some other bands whose labels were throwing trillions of dollars at them.

EDDIE TRUNK I don't think they fit any categories, and I don't think people knew what to do with them. They were critically loved, but the public didn't really know what to make of them. They didn't know what category they fell into. Radio didn't know what to make of them. Radio couldn't quite figure out what sort of niche they filled—were they a hard rock band? I mean, the image of the band was completely different to what was going on then. Even the production of the records, if you think about it—back then, records were very big-sounding. There were these huge gang choruses and these huge riffs and things that really screamed out at you, and these huge guitar solos and pretty boy singers. And King's X had *none* of that. They were the opposite of that. In all ways. I think it was so different that nobody really knew what to do with it, and it fell between the cracks for a lot of people.

JAY PHEBUS The one thing that really aggravated me was how they were so staunch in the beginning, to separate themselves from being labeled as prog-rock, or the whole glam scene. And I was like, 'Look at the pictures of you guys when Mötley Crüe and everybody else was out in the day. *There's no difference!* But you try to separate yourself from it, when you look like the same style.'

Now, obviously the music is different, but you can look at the photos back then—with all the spiked hairdos and everything. They looked just like everything that was coming out of LA in the mid-to-late 80s. But then ... they were the 'grandfathers of grunge.' They were grunge *before* Soundgarden, Pearl Jam, Stone Temple Pilots, Live, and all the rest of them came out. They were drop-D tuning, and did that back in the late 80s.

Then, all of a sudden, in '92 or so, Pearl Jam hits the scene, and that's what's happening. We went through that whole transformation—appearance-wise, they changed, and musically, as well, because after the fourth record, Sam was gone. The record with Brendan O'Brien, *Dogman*, was sonically, stylistically ... everything had changed. And a lot of it was intentional—they were trying to separate themselves from the past with Sam Taylor. That was a huge change. That, by the way, was their 'chance'—with Brendan. Because, at that time, there wasn't a better position King's X could have put themselves in, because they were on Atlantic Records, they were with ICM Booking Agency, and we just signed with Rush's manager, Ray Danniels. There were no better moves to be made—we were with one of the biggest record companies, we were with one of the biggest booking agencies, and with one of the most successful managers.

And, then, you have a band with the talent of King's X. You go, 'How on earth can this recipe fail?' And they managed to do it! Because the converse thing is, you have people going, 'Why isn't King's X bigger than U2?' I hear it all the time. And I go, 'Poor management decisions.' And then it got to the point where Ray finally said, 'I can't do for you guys what you need done.' It was a big step up from what Sam and Ty were doing previously ... but Van Halen fell into his lap. Van Halen's previous manager [Ed Leffler] had died, and Ray Danniels was a brother-in-law of Alex Van Halen. And that's also the time when Extreme got picked up by Ray. So, at one time, Ray had Extreme, King's X, and Rush. Then Van Halen fell into his lap, and that's how Gary Cherone did the one record with Van Halen [*Van Halen III*, 1998]. But when that all happened, he wasn't planning on taking on Van Halen.

DOUG VAN PELT I was at South By Southwest, sometime around 2006, 2007, and I asked Doug that same question, and he gave me five reasons why he thinks King's X never broke. I can't remember all five ... but most of them involve Sam Taylor! But one was, Sam never let Doug be Doug. He never let Doug be in the forefront. Doug is very much charismatic, and he is very opposing as a figure—he's very handsome, he's a great front man. And, from a visual standpoint—he always had great haircuts and dressed like a rock star. He should have been out front.

NUNO BETTENCOURT It's one of those things where it took me a minute to realize that the only difference between them having massive success and what happened with them was a generational thing. I felt like it was the right album at the wrong time. If *Faith Hope Love* comes out in the late 70s, maybe early 80s, even maybe early 2000s ... I felt when they came out, it was almost like people didn't know how to wrap their heads around it. Neither did radio. But, to me, that stuff is some of the most timeless stuff I've ever heard. Honest to God. I think *Faith Hope Love* is one of the greatest albums.

BRIAN SLAGEL In my opinion, it's about the marathon, and not the sprint. And we have a lot of artists like that, too, on Metal Blade—Fates Warning, Cannibal Corpse, Gwar—that never had one gold record themselves, but when you look at the course of their history, they sold a ton of records, and they're still able to go out there and play. A lot of those bands from the late 80s/early 90s that are one-hit wonders, they don't exist anymore. They might have one big record, but the thread of what King's X has done is still viable, and that we're still talking about them *now* shows you that what they did and what they're still doing is pretty special.

ANDY SUMMERS [The Police guitarist] A few years ago, I discovered them, and God, this is a great band! They've got an incredible feel. They've got the best kind of bluesy rock—they've got so much feel. They rock and they really swing, as well. Great voice, the guitar player's great. I don't know why they're not huge, that band. I guess they've done OK. But I ended up buying all of their albums. There was a period where I was so into it—some of these tracks like 'Lost In Germany' were wonderful. Fantastic riffs, and very talented. I think they're easily one of the best rock trios anywhere. I don't think they've been equaled. They should be much more famous than they are. Tremendous players. Complexity in their riffing. They took that kind of rock and do it better than anyone—if not the best.

BILLY SHEEHAN I'm glad you're doing the book, too, because it's really a crime of omission that more people don't know King's X.

HOW DOES THE MUSIC OF KING'S X HOLD UP TODAY?

CHARLIE BENANTE Any record that King's X will come out with, there would be songs on there that make you just … *happy*. I think it's timeless. I really do. I don't think it sounds dated. It sounds as genuine to me nowadays as it did when it came out. And I really do believe that. But I think the 80s stuff holds up way better than the other stuff does.

JOHN MYUNG It has the timeless quality where, you put the record on, and, to me, it resonates really well. King's X is one of those bands that have influenced so many bands and so many people. I see them as one of the important cornerstones of rock music—in terms of how they related to musicians and being there as an influence. As something that was of value to them on the creative level.

RICHARD CHRISTY It holds up as good as The Beatles' music holds up. It's really amazing songs, great songwriting, beautiful harmonies. It's timeless. That's why The Beatles are still as popular as they were back then—because the music is great. And it will never age. King's X music will never age. People will never get tired of beautiful harmony vocals and great songs. And the production was way ahead of its time. When I heard *Gretchen* in the 80s, it was way ahead of its time. And, to me, it doesn't sound dated at all. I think their music is eternal. It doesn't matter that they didn't have that really big radio hit, because the people that like them are going to like them forever—because their music is timeless. For me, it brings back great memories when I hear them. Even to this day, I love introducing my friends that don't know about King's X to King's X, because I know people are going to love them, because it's great music and great songs. *It's eternal.*

MIKE PORTNOY It's timeless. Any band that is going to tap into classic elements like they do, is going to create timeless music. Beatles music is timeless. And I think you can say the same thing for King's X music, because they come from the same world. They're not following trends; they're not trying to tap into something that's popular at the time; they make music that is real music from the heart, with all three of them singing in harmony, and great songs that are catchy and memorable. If you follow The Beatles' book of songwriting and album making, you can't go wrong—you're going to make music that is going to be around forever.

BILLY SHEEHAN My wife is from Italy. We've been together twelve years, married ten years. When I first got together with her, a lot of music that I knew of, she didn't know. And she's a big fan of a lot of music, so I said, 'I've got to play you something. *Check this out.*' I put on 'Goldilox,' and it blew her mind. This was maybe almost twenty years after the fact, and it goes to show you, people who haven't heard that, when they hear it now, it's brand new.

To most of the population of planet earth, King's X is a brand new band, because they have not heard them. It can be discouraging for a lot of bands to be out there for ten or twenty years, and in their minds, they think, *Well, everybody's heard it and everybody's passed on it.* No, no, no—nobody's heard it. A small microscopic portion of the people of the world have heard it, and if more people heard it, it would blow their minds. And I thought the proof of it was when my wife heard that song, she went crazy. And then we started singing it together all the time! She's got a pretty good voice, so, when I play guitar, we'd sing 'Goldilox,' and do the harmonies.

That's the proof of it—I can take somebody off the street right now and say, 'Hold on a second. Let me play you something. What do you think?' 'Holy cow! *Who is that?*' Because they've never heard it before. And I think it's a good point to make—that it's new to most people in the world who have not heard it. So there's always hope that someday it gets on a movie soundtrack or something like that, and the whole world goes, 'How did I miss this?' And the revelation will come. It would be good to see somebody cover 'Goldilox'—I think that [could be] a smash hit. I've got an extensive iTunes collection—almost two terabytes—and I've got all kinds of stuff from all different eras. There's a lot of times I'll hear a song and I go, *Man, this could have been a huge smash.*

GUNTER FORD There are probably three or four King's X songs like that, and 'Goldilox' is certainly one of them. There was a kid that won *American Idol*, David Cook, who was going around playing 'Dogman' live. Sure, if Taylor

Swift covered 'Goldilox,' or somebody like that, who has a huge audience ... it is a smash song. *No doubt*. Their audience singing it is almost a smash, because the audience is good—every night, it's a fantastic thing. Something like that, we've tried it, we've put the feelers out—and we're still doing that, all the time. But that's one of those 'timing and luck' things. If maybe someone who's an artist who grew up with the music of King's X gets big and suddenly decides they love the band and wants to cover them—it's going to have to happen that the artist or a producer discovers it, and thinks, *Oh yeah ... let's cover this*.

GEORGE LYNCH That's the beauty of them—I think they're historically significant, and they do hold up over time. And many other great bands that I put them in the same league with—Cream, Led Zeppelin, Jimi Hendrix, The Yardbirds, and bands that I admire from the late 60s and early 70s, and onward, that have stood the test of time and their music has maintained its integrity over the decades—I feel the same way about King's X.

EDDIE TRUNK I don't think the music of King's X sounds dated in any way. I think it's still very relevant. I think, in a lot of ways, it was ahead of its time. And I think that there's still a lot of people that love the band. Even though they never got that huge fan base that they should have gotten and that crossover they should have gotten, the base they do have is incredibly passionate about the band. In America, they're a club-level act, but they're a *good* club-level act—they're a good draw. The fans they have, they still have that same passion for them.

JOHN CORABI I can still listen to that whole *Best Of King's X* record, and nothing on it sounds dated. I think that's an important thing—lyrically, their lyrics stand up. They're deeper than just ... I don't mean this as an insult, but when you listen to a song like 'Talk Dirty To Me' or 'Girls Girls Girls,' it's kind of time-specific. And I don't think King's X has anything like that.

REX BROWN It's *timeless*, And that's what all good music should be. Any of those records, there is hardly a fluff on any record they've put out, where I go, 'Nah, I can't listen to that,' or 'That's a filler track.' Because there's not. There are not bands like that anymore. There are not bands where you can listen to a whole record all the way through. And that's not the case these days—kids just want to hear two or three songs off Spotify, and there you go. Which is a problem with the state of our whole industry. But what I'm saying is, those records are as timeless as Neil Young's *Harvest* or The Beatles' *Abbey Road* or anything like that in my playlist. Abso-fucking-lutely. They're *that* worthy of praise. Or, in my book of what I think great records are. In that time, they were so far ahead of the curve. Those guys were *it*. They just didn't make it. And it sucked. We were hoping so bad that they would get that plug. But we listened to the music, and talked on the phone—this was before texting, you know—so we've always been in contact with them. Pantera were there when they started, and we were fans through and through.

RAY LUZIER I think they still hold up great. Sometimes, my preshow ritual when I warm up and hitting the drum pad, I'll throw on *Dogman*. And it's funny—I'll put it on, and some guy from our road crew will come in and go, 'Who's that?' And it just breaks my heart, because they never heard of them ... or some of them heard of them, but never really gave them a shot. And I'm still turning people on to them today. It's insane. If there were a million more people like you and me who turn people on to them, maybe they would have gotten more of a fair shot, and as many as Kiss! [*Laughs*]

JEFF AMENT It holds up great. I have twenty or thirty records that I revisit. You find yourself going, 'I really need to hear *Gretchen* today. It's a *Gretchen* kind of a day.' And I think *Out Of The Silent Planet* is the same. I think, because I heard *Gretchen* first, *Out Of The Silent Planet* is always second place, three quarters of *Faith Hope Love*, and the self-titled record—those are the next ones. *Gretchen*, to me—from top to bottom—is a smash record. Great songs, so original. And some of it, subconsciously, was probably that whatever internal conversations they were having about their backgrounds of their religion and all that stuff, I think that stuff was probably hitting me subconsciously and I didn't know it. Because I was feeling the same exact thing.

ROBERT DeLEO I think it was ahead of its time. When you realistically think about what they've done, it was pretty landmark. Things like drop-D ... it's funny, because everybody thinks that drop-D tuning came from the grunge era. But we learned that from Brian May in Queen, and Jeff Lynne in The Move. The

Move was tuning drop-D, and all this music from the 70s was this drop-D thing. I don't know where those guys personally got it from. But they were doing it and making it a thing before it got recognized as a label. So I think, in a way, they were kind of the pioneers of something happening. To me, that was heavy songs with a great Beatles influence, with a lot of soul to it. And to me, that's a great incarnation of great rock'n'roll right there.

MICK MARS It sounds as fresh as the day I first heard them.

JON ZAZULA What makes it so wonderful is that it's absolutely real. There's nothing contrived about King's X. Nothing. It's what it is, it's what you get—a magical night. You can sit there and watch Jerry play drums all night if you want, and then come back another night and watch somebody else in the band if you want, and it will be great.

MARSHA ZAZULA It was my proudest signing to Megaforce. I can say that. Still to this day.

KIP WINGER It's totally timeless. It will be revered in five hundred years. It's very interesting that the internet is going to encapsulate a lot of this stuff. I think a lot of it will go away. But theirs won't go away. I think that it's stood the test of time. I haven't seen them lately, and I don't know what kind of audience comes to their shows, but I would count on betting that it's half under-thirty people that goes to see them, because new generations are probably rediscovering that music … or just *now* discovering it. And it's every bit as current right now as it was when it came out.

DEVIN TOWNSEND I think a lot of that has to do with the fact that the production isn't dated. I mean, dated in the sense that maybe the fidelity of it isn't as broad as things can be now, but because it was idiosyncratic, it still sounds like them—three guys singing and three instruments.

MATT PINFIELD I love it still. I think it's great. I pulled out *Faith Hope Love* about six months ago. I just started hearing one of the songs in my head, and I pulled it out and listened to the entire record. Of course, it's on my iPod, so it's not like I can 'pull it out.' [*Laughs*] But I do think it holds up. I almost feel like the thing that is interesting about King's X is it doesn't sound like it's from any particular time. It's as valid today as it was then. And even then, it wasn't fashionable. I think it absolutely holds up, because it was its own entity. They've always had a following that is 'cult status,' but the people that do love them are in 100 percent. And I think that's really important. That shows the signs of a really important band who create passion among their fans who listen.

WALLY FARKAS [It's like] The Stooges or The MC5, or even pop stuff, like Big Star—they never got their due at the time. But because of their legacy, I think their legend will only grow. It's not like they're going to be forgotten in ten years or twenty years. It's going to be stronger.

LEA PISACANE Rush was on the label here, and Rush's fans are old, but they bring their kids, and they turn their kids on to Rush. That's so great for a band, because that gives the band new life, and they'll never die. So we need King's X fans to bring their kids to their shows. I saw them the other night on Long Island … and I didn't see any kids there! We need that to have them be alive forever, because they deserve to be.

NUNO BETTENCOURT I still turn people on to those albums—today. Recently. When I'm on tour with other bands, I'm like, 'You're kidding me—you never heard them?' I put it on, and it sounds like I'm playing something that should be out now. And if it was out now, I think it would do amazing. So that's how you know good albums, because you don't play it and go, 'It didn't age very well.' *Not at all.*

ROD MORGENSTEIN I think their music is going to be around for ages. There's something really special about the music—it has class, it's this incredibly tight package of sound that is made by just three guys. I think their audience will follow them until the end of the earth.

BILLY SHEEHAN Doug lives in LA now, too, so I get to see him a lot more than I used to. I played on Jerry Gaskill's record recently—what a great collection of songs, too! Very Beatles-esque and adventurous. And I've heard a lot of Ty's stuff, too. See, those three guys together, as King's X, the components make sense now—when you see all three sensibilities put together. *Really great*. And I hope they continue on to do more. And, maybe someday, the world will wake up.

JERRY GASKILL Whenever I make a record, perform, or put music out there, I believe in it. And I feel like that's the greatest thing I'm doing, and the greatest thing I can do. And I want to feel that way. And I like to think that the music also can represent that—that it also has that 'timeless' element to it. But it's hard for me to say or know those things. I can only go by what other people say to me. And other people do say those things to me.

I remember one time, we were doing this acoustic show in Houston, at what was called the Summit. Now it's Lakewood Church. It was a star-studded cast of people performing—it was for KLOL, the radio station there. I forget what it was for—maybe a benefit. But I met Earl Slick that night, Heart, John Waite … and I remember standing on the side of the stage with Roger Glover of Deep Purple, watching some band—I don't remember who it was.

But Roger Glover turns to me, and goes, 'I've got to tell you. There's only a few bands that have come along, and have had *that thing* about them. The Beatles, the Stones, Deep Purple … *and you guys*.' That's the only stuff I can judge by. It's what people say to me. So, hopefully, we can put out a new record, and maybe it can translate to the public. Who knows? If not, we still have the whole catalogue that translates to the people that it does translate to.

DOUG PINNICK There was a time when I thought we were fooling ourselves, like in the children's book, *The Emperor's New Clothes*. Probably from the first record, I never thought they sounded good sonically—until we got to *Dogman*. *Gretchen* sounded really clean and clear—but had no balls, I thought. But about ten years ago, I started seeing a lot of young kids coming to see King's X, and all of a sudden, I'm meeting lots of twentysomethings here in LA who are just getting turned on to King's X. We have a huge catalogue for them to dissect—and they are. They don't know the timeline, so it's all the same. And that's really great—it's timeless. If you pull out a King's X record now and put it on those little JBL Bluetooth speakers, it rocks just as hard as everything else. Which is cool. I realize that it does hold up when a fifteen-year-old comes up to me and says, '*Dude*, "Goldilox" is the best song ever written,' and that's, like, twenty-five years later. That makes me realize we did something cool that has affected people. Our music has held up. I don't know why. I don't know how. *I'm glad it did.*

TY TABOR The only thing I know is, every night we walk out and there's a house full of people, singing every word—from the youngest of kids to people older than us.

JERRY GASKILL I always feel that King's X has a very unique story to tell. It's unlike any other story out there. We seem to have this thing that seems to inspire other musicians, and, at the same time, it's never really translated to the general public. And a lot of the people who have been inspired, somehow, figured how to translate everything to the general public! They became huge.

It's a unique story. I'm glad it's going to be told.

Becoming Elektra: The Incredible True Story Of Jac Holzman's Visionary Record Label Mick Houghton

Shredders! The Oral History Of Speed Guitar (And More) Greg Prato

Fearless: The Making Of Post-Rock Jeanette Leech

I Scare Myself Dan Hicks

Staying Alive: The Disco Inferno Of The Bee Gees Simon Spence

Earthbound: David Bowie and The Man Who Fell To Earth Susan Compo

Shadows Across The Moon: Outlaws, Freaks, Shamans And The Making Of Ibiza Clubland Helen Donlon

The Yacht Rock Book: The Oral History Of The Soft, Smooth Sounds Of The 70s And 80s Greg Prato

What's Big And Purple And Lives In The Ocean? The Moby Grape Story Cam Cobb

Swans: Sacrifice And Transcendence: The Oral History Nick Soulsby

Small Victories: The True Story Of Faith No More Adrian Harte

OTHER BOOKS BY GREG PRATO

Music

A Devil On One Shoulder And An Angel On The Other: The Story Of Shannon Hoon And Blind Melon

Touched By Magic: The Tommy Bolin Story

Grunge Is Dead: The Oral History Of Seattle Rock Music

No Schlock … Just Rock! (A Journalistic Journey: 2003–2008)

MTV Ruled The World: The Early Years Of Music Video

The Eric Carr Story

Too High To Die: Meet The Meat Puppets

The Faith No More & Mr. Bungle Companion

Overlooked/Underappreciated: 354 Recordings That Demand Your Attention

Over The Electric Grapevine: Insight Into Primus And The World Of Les Claypool

Punk! Hardcore! Reggae! PMA! Bad Brains!

Iron Maiden: '80 '81

Survival Of The Fittest: Heavy Metal In The 1990s

Scott Weiland: Memories Of A Rock Star

German Metal Machine: Scorpions In The 70s

The Other Side Of Rainbow

Shredders!: The Oral History Of Speed Guitar (And More)

The Yacht Rock Book: The Oral History Of The Soft, Smooth Sounds Of The 60s, 70s, And 80s

100 Things Pearl Jam Fans Should Know & Do Before They Die

The 100 Greatest Rock Bassists

Long Live Queen: Rock Royalty Discuss Freddie, Brian, John & Roger

Sports

Sack Exchange: The Definitive Oral History Of The 1980s New York Jets

Dynasty: The Oral History Of The New York Islanders, 1972–1984

Just Out Of Reach: The 1980s New York Yankees

The Seventh Year Stretch: New York Mets, 1977–1983

PICTURE CREDITS

Unless otherwise noted, the photographs in this book are from the band's archives. King's X and Greg Prato Steven J. Messina; Doug in fedora, snapshots from an early tour (x4) Kevin Mourning; Doug Ritz, Jerry Cat Club, the Megaforce crew, Poughkeepsie (x2) Frank White Photography; Ty Fender Elite, Doug and Jerry 1992 Steven J. Messina; Woodstock '94 Henry Diltz/Getty Images; Ty Millbrook Sound Frank White Photography; live 2008 (x2) Steven J. Messina; Goldilox Greg Prato; Jerry bashing the beat Frank White Photography; live 2017 (x2), meeting fans Steven J. Messina.